CARL VON CLAUSEWITZ

Historical and Political
Writings

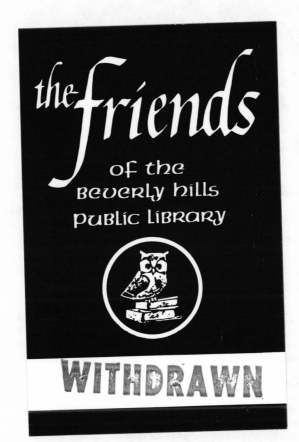

A NOTE TO A LIBRARIAN

In the note, written in 1820, Clausewitz requests five books. The first two are on England: "1. Schmalz über England 2. Vinke dito —," i.e., Theodor Anton Schmalz, *Staatsverfassung Grossbritanniens* (Halle, 1806), and Ludwig von Vincke, *Darstellung der innern Verwaltung Grossbritanniens,* (Berlin, 1816). The third, "Herders Zerstreute Blätter," is a volume of Herder's essays and his collection of Greek lyrics and epigrams. The fourth, "Schillers Gedichte," is an edition of Friedrich Schiller's poetry. The last work, "Religion für das Herz, auserlesene Stellen aus geistvollen Schriften unseres Zeitalters," refers to an anthology of thoughts on religion, whose full title read "Religion for the Heart, or Testaments of Faith, Love and Hope, selected from the Spiritual Literature of Our Age." The place and date of publication, "Stuttg[art], 1802," are added at right in the librarian's hand. (Collection of Peter Paret)

C ARL VON C LAUSEWITZ

HISTORICAL AND POLITICAL WRITINGS

Edited and Translated by

PETER PARET *and* DANIEL MORAN

PRINCETON UNIVERSITY PRESS

PRINCETON, NEW JERSEY

Copyright © 1992 by Princeton University Press

Published by Princeton University Press, 41 William Street,
Princeton, New Jersey 08540
In the United Kingdom: Princeton University Press, Oxford

Library of Congress Cataloging-in-Publication Data

Clausewitz, Carl von, 1780–1831.
[Selections. English. 1992]
Historical and political writings / Carl von Clausewitz; edited
and translated by Peter Paret and Daniel Moran.
p. cm.
"Contains selections from Clausewitz's historical writings and the
majority of his essays and notes on political topics"—Preface.
Includes index.
ISBN 0-691-03192-4
1. Europe—History—18th century. 2. Europe—Politics and
government—1789–1900. I. Paret, Peter. II. Moran, Daniel.
III. Title.
D286.C552513   1992   940.2'53—dc20   91-478

This book has been composed in Linotron Electra and Melior

Princeton University Press books are printed on acid-free paper,
and meet the guidelines for permanence and durability of the
Committee on Production Guidelines for Book Longevity of the
Council on Library Resources

Printed in the United States of America by Princeton University Press,
Princeton, New Jersey

1 3 5 7 9 10 8 6 4 2

IN MEMORY OF

Felix Gilbert

CONTENTS

List of Maps   ix

Preface   xi

Acknowledgments   xv

List of Abbreviations   xvii

List of Sources   xviii

PART ONE
Historical Writings

Introduction   3

1   "Some Comments on the War of the Spanish Succession after
    Reading the Letters of Madame de Maintenon to the Princess
    des Ursins" (1826 or later)   15

2   "Observations on the Wars of the Austrian Succession"
    (early 1820s)   19

3   From *Observations on Prussia in Her Great Catastrophe*
    (1823–1825)   30

4   "On the Life and Character of Scharnhorst" (1817)   85

5   From *The Campaign of 1812 in Russia* (1823–1825)   110

6   From "Strategic Critique of the Campaign of 1814 in France"
    (early 1820s)   205

PART TWO
Political Writings

Introduction   223

7   Notes on History and Politics (1803–1807)   237

8   "The Germans and the French" (1807)   250

9   Notes on History and Politics (1807–1809)   263

10 Letter to Fichte (1809)   279

11 From the "Political Declaration" (1812)   285

CONTENTS

12 On the German Federal Army (1818)   304

13 "Our Military Institutions" (1819)   313

14 "On the Political Advantages and Disadvantages of the Prussian
    Landwehr" (1819)   329

15 "Agitation" (early 1820s)   335

16 "Europe since the Polish Partitions" (1831)   369

17 "On the Basic Question of Germany's Existence" (1831)   377

    Index   385

MAP 1   *The Campaign of 1812 in Russia* Vilna to Smolensk   121

MAP 2   *The Campaign of 1812 in Russia* Smolensk to Moscow   138

MAP 3   *The Campaign of 1812 in Russia* The battle of Borodino   150

MAP 4   *The Campaign of 1812 in Russia* Vilna to Riga (Vicinity of
         Tauroggen)   183

MAP 5   *The Campaign of 1814 in France*   210

MAPS 1, 2, and 4 are details from the "Operationskarte für den Feldzug von 1812 in Russland" that accompanied the first two editions of Clausewitz's *Hinterlassene Werke*. Map 3 is reproduced from Dmitrii Buturlin, *Atlas des plans, légendes et tableaux d'organisation de l'histoire militaire de la campagne de Russie en 1812* (Paris, 1824). Map 5 is reproduced from A.J.F. Fain, *Manuscrit de mil huit cent quatorze* (Paris, 1823).

This volume contains selections from Clausewitz's historical writings and the majority of his essays and notes on political topics, excluding memoranda he wrote in an official capacity. One selection, from the "Political Declaration" of 1812, comes close to having an official character. Clausewitz drafted it with the help of others at a critical point in Prussian history to justify the political views of the radical military reformers, including men who held positions of authority in the state, and to oppose the impending alliance with France. The "Declaration" therefore expresses the position of a faction, but many of its passages bear such a pronounced personal note that its inclusion here seems justified.

The texts are grouped into two categories—"Historical Writings" and "Political Writings." Here, too, no precise dividing line can be drawn. Clausewitz developed his political ideas in part out of intensive historical study, and his political reasoning proceeds in conjunction with historical argumentation, drawing at every point on historical references, examples, and analogies. History performs a similarly creative role in Clausewitz's development of military theory. Nevertheless, in nearly every case it is not difficult to determine whether his primary concern is to understand the past or to express opinions about the present or future. The fusion of history and politics is perhaps most complete in his early "Notes," and in the essay "Agitation." We have placed these in the category of "Political Writings" because it is apparent that they were primarily stimulated by a desire to understand contemporary conditions—the increasing diplomatic isolation of Prussia and the threat posed to the balance of power by Napoleonic France in the first case, the demands for political change in Germany that followed the defeat of France in the second.

The editors have divided their task; Peter Paret was responsible for the historical writings, Daniel Moran for the writings on politics. The translations are a joint effort. English versions of extended passages from several of the historical writings and most of the political works are contained in Peter Paret's monograph, *Clausewitz and the State* (rev. ed., Princeton, 1985), but to the knowledge of the editors, only one of the works in this volume, *The Campaign of 1812 in Russia*, has ever been translated into English in its entirety; it appeared in London in 1843 and was last reprinted in 1977. That translation was based on the German text in the seventh volume of Clausewitz's posthumous works, which varied considerably from the original manuscript. The present translation is based on Clausewitz's original version. Similarly, the first section of the essay "On the Life and Character of Scharnhorst" is based on Clausewitz's manuscript rather than on the text that Ranke published in somewhat altered form in 1832. In both cases, passages omitted by the original editor are printed within curly brackets. A few illustrative examples of editorial substitutions intended to moderate Clausewitz's language have also been reproduced in the footnotes.

The translation of the German of Clausewitz's time into modern English presents problems with which anyone who has attempted a similar task will be familiar. The educated language of the *Goethezeit* was elegant and specific, characteristics that are difficult to reconcile in English with an equally characteristic proclivity for passive constructions and the use of abstract nouns as the subjects of transitive verbs. Clausewitz exhibited both tendencies to some extent, and over the years they have contributed to his undeserved reputation among foreign readers for abstruseness and complexity. His stylistic peculiarities are of course related to the substance of his thought. That he should have preferred, on occasion, to speak of individuals as being possessed by ideas rather than as possessing them, or to present events as the objects rather than as the agents of historical forces, is not surprising in someone whose intellectual horizons were defined by the methods and attitudes of German idealism and historicism. But these tendencies should not be overstated. Clausewitz had little use for abstractions or for theories divorced from personal and historical experience. What finally stands out even in the most intricate Clausewitzian sentence (and a few occur in almost everything he wrote) is the concrete reference, the piling up of evidence, the specificity of its point.

The search for an English equivalent to Clausewitz's prose demonstrates once again the pertinence of Walter Benjamin's observation that all translation is, in the end, interpretation. The translators have tried to preserve or at least reflect those elements of Clausewitz's style that are most distinctive of his way of thinking: his preference for dialectical modes of argument; his sometimes extreme efforts to present the reader with all relevant considerations in the same breath; his occasionally labored parallelisms, which were a stylistic corollary of his desire for objectivity. But there has been no hesitation in settling for less than literal equivalence, when to do otherwise would have resulted in preciousness or evasiveness. Nor has it seemed advisable to translate the same words in the same way in every instance. Expressions like *moralische Grössen* and *innere Bewegungen* admit a wide range of meanings, and Clausewitz put no stock in rigid or artificially systematic terminology. Language always took second place to thought.

Clausewitz frequently emphasized words or phrases. His emphases have been preserved as italics in the translations; phrases in parentheses are also his. Numbered footnotes, and emendations in square brackets, are supplied by the editors; footnotes marked with an asterisk are in the original. Clausewitz rarely mentions the first names of individuals, or the dates of the events he discusses. These are included in the index.

ACKNOWLEDGMENTS

The editors gratefully acknowledge the support their work received from the Hoover Institution on War, Revolution and Peace of Stanford University, and from the Institute for Advanced Study in Princeton.

For information on issues of fact and interpretation they are indebted to the late Werner Hahlweg of the Westfälische Wilhelms-Universität, Münster; Joachim Niemeyer of the Militärgeschichtliche Museum, Rastatt; Diethelm Prowe of Carleton College; and Gunther E. Rothenberg of Purdue University. Princeton University Library kindly permitted the reproduction of the map of the battle of Borodino from Dmitrii Buturlin's *Atlas des plans, légendes et tableaux d'organisation de l'histoire militaire de la campagne de Russie en 1812* (Paris, 1824); and the editors of *Central European History* graciously allowed the inclusion, in the introduction to the Political Writings, of material that first appeared in that journal in somewhat different form.

The editors also want to thank the members of the staff of Princeton University Press who saw the book into print, most especially our editors Joanna Hitchcock and Alice Calaprice, and the designer Laury Egan.

In the course of preparing the manuscript for publication, the editors repeatedly discussed issues of translation and of interpretation with Felix Gilbert, whose responses never failed to illuminate and expand on the issues raised. Felix Gilbert died in February 1991. With our gratitude and affection this book is dedicated to his memory.

ACKNOWLEDGMENTS

The following short titles are used throughout:

On War	Carl von Clausewitz, *On War*, ed. and trans. Michael Howard and Peter Paret, rev. ed. (Princeton, 1984)
Paret, *Clausewitz and the State*	Peter Paret, *Clausewitz and the State*, rev. ed. (Princeton, 1985)
Pertz-Delbrück, *Gneisenau*	G. H. Pertz and H. Delbrück, *Das Leben des Feldmarschalls Grafen Neithardt von Gneisenau*, 5 vols. (Berlin, 1864–80)
Politische Schriften und Briefe	Carl von Clausewitz, *Politische Schriften und Briefe*, ed. Hans Rothfels (Munich, 1922)
Rothfels, *Politik und Krieg*	Hans Rothfels, *Carl von Clausewitz: Politik und Krieg* (Berlin, 1920; reprinted Bonn, 1980)
Schriften	Carl von Clausewitz, *Schriften–Aufsätze–Studien–Briefe*, ed. Werner Hahlweg, 2 vols. in 3 (Göttingen, 1966–90)
Schwartz, *Leben*	Karl Schwartz, *Leben des Generals Carl von Clausewitz und der Frau Marie von Clausewitz geb. Gräfin von Brühl*, 2 vols. (Berlin, 1878)
Verstreute kleine Schriften	Carl von Clausewitz, *Verstreute kleine Schriften*, ed. Werner Hahlweg (Osnabrück, 1979)
Werke	*Hinterlassene Werke des Generals Carl von Clausewitz über Krieg und Kriegführung*, 10 vols. (Berlin, 1832–37)

Historical Writings

In Clausewitz's thought, history and theory were closely linked. They did not, however, interact on a level plane. Clausewitz believed that a valid theory of such social phenomena as politics or war could be developed only by taking account of the past as well as the present. Without the instrument of history, theory should not be constructed. On the other hand, he did not believe that a theoretical understanding of government and of armed conflict, although desirable, was essential for their historical reconstruction and analysis. Long sections in his historical works reveal neither theoretical arguments nor foundations. Theory might assist but did not direct Clausewitz's historical interpretations. History not only tested and validated his theories, it gave rise to some of them.

One reason for Clausewitz's elevated view of the importance of history may at first seem paradoxical: his conviction that theory must remain as close to reality as it was possible for an abstraction to be. In a comment on one of his theoretical studies that preceded *On War*, he noted that its

> scientific character consists in an attempt to investigate the phenomena of war and to indicate the links between these phenomena and the nature of their component parts. No logical conclusion has been avoided; but whenever the thread became too thin I have preferred to break it off and go back to the relevant phenomena of experience. Just as some plants bear fruit only if they don't shoot up too high, so in the practical arts the leaves and flowers of theory must be pruned and the plant kept close to its proper soil—experience.[1]

Put differently, Clausewitz's theoretical writings on war were based on the experience of war—his own experience and that of his generation, but also on another form of experience that only history can transmit. By opening up the past for us, history added to the fund of knowledge that we can acquire directly and also made possible universal concepts and generalizations across time. To enable history to do this, the historian must be as objective or—as Clausewitz would have said—as scientific or philosophical as possible.[2] In fact, the two latter qualities encompassed more than objectivity. They also represented the search for the essential quality of the phenomenon studied—violence in the case of war—and the consequential tracing of this quality in

---

[1] "Author's Preface," *On War*, 61.
[2] "Wissenschaftlich" or "philosophisch"—terms that Clausewitz often used interchangeably.

its changing forms through all parts of the subject. The theoretical reflection of this dynamic reality should focus on its basic structure rather than seek completeness.

Clausewitz's comment on the scientific character of his theories, as just quoted, opens with the combative assertion that the "scientific approach does not consist solely, or even mainly, in a complete system and a comprehensive doctrine."[3] Even as a young man, in his first attacks on the convoluted military theories of the late Enlightenment, he argued that a closed system of laws, principles, and prescriptions could be achieved only at the expense of reality and of history, which represented past reality. History in the service of a philosophic worldview as Hegel encapsulated it, for instance, would not serve Clausewitz's purpose.

Clausewitz's demand for objective, analytic, nonteleological history gained further strength from the affinity between this ideal and the character of his theories. The purpose of his theoretical writings was not to teach a specific doctrine that would lead to successful strategies and increase operational effectiveness, but rather to contribute to an understanding of war as an apparently permanent element of human experience. By enabling the theorist to join past and present, objective history might make possible generalized insights into the timeless reality of war. Consequently historical study became a major component in Clausewitz's pursuit of theory.

Social scientists today might find little to disagree with in this position, although few would base their hypotheses and arguments as firmly on historical interpretations as Clausewitz did. But the reciprocal relationship between the effort to understand the uniqueness of the past and the effort to generalize and conceptualize is so pervasive in his writings that the reader soon comes to feel that more is at work than the belief that history must nourish and control theory. Clausewitz's writings reflect the mind of an author who is fascinated by the specific and unique as much as he is by the general. The study and writing of history, it might be said, responded directly to his need to understand and indirectly by sharing in the development of theory. In consequence, his historical work assumed many different forms once it progressed beyond the school exercises that he wrote as a young officer, exercises that were not important in themselves but that accustomed him to think historically. On War and his other theoretical writings are filled with references to the past, discussions of past events, and even more or less self-contained historical essays that analyze a development over time. An example is chapter 3B of Book VIII of On War, which traces the interdependence of military, political, and social forms from antiquity to the nineteenth century.

Clausewitz also wrote a large number of separate historical studies. In

[3] On War, 61.

4

some of these the theoretical motive was important, perhaps even dominant, even if he did not always communicate this to the reader. He believed he could not draw theoretical conclusions from the available accounts until he himself had worked through and reinterpreted the material. Several of these studies were brief; a few were very long and demanded years of effort. The histories of the campaign of 1796 in Italy and of the war of 1799 in Switzerland and Italy fill three volumes in the posthumous collected edition of his works. Both were written in the second half of the 1820s, at a time when Clausewitz had decided to revise the manuscript of On War so as to strengthen the treatment of two concepts that he had come to regard as major themes of the work: the political nature of war, and the distinction between absolute and limited war. Other works are marked by a strong personal element. The author reports and interprets events that he himself had witnessed or in which he had taken part, conditions that he had experienced, individuals he had known. Still other writings, which treat war only marginally or not at all, have a political motive. The past is drawn on to illuminate domestic politics and foreign affairs of Clausewitz's own day. Finally, some of his historical studies lack either a personal, a political, or a theoretical note; the sole motivation behind them appears to be the author's fascination with the past.[4]

Clausewitz's ambition to see the past truthfully and objectively did not mean that he excised all personal opinions from his texts. On the contrary, the author is ever present, as observer, commentator, even judge—especially when he writes about conditions or events he himself had witnessed. In the chapter "Critical Analysis" of On War, Clausewitz distinguishes between "the critical approach and the plain narrative of a historical event," and further identifies three paths that the critical approach might take: "The discovery and interpretation of equivocal facts . . . ; the tracing of effects back to their causes . . . ; [and] the investigation and evaluation of means employed. This last is criticism proper, involving praise and censure."[5] In his previously cited essay on Clausewitz, Hans Delbrück argued that despite his "eminently historical bent" and his "extraordinarily rare faculty of absolutely objective perception," Clausewitz had chosen the last of these paths. "By vocation and intent Clausewitz was a military critic and solely a military critic."[6] This seems to confuse criticism with an analytic interpretation that goes beyond plain historical narrative, and judges Clausewitz's writings from a historicist

---

[4] For general discussions of Clausewitz's historical writings, see Hans Delbrück, "General von Clausewitz," in Historische and politische Aufsätze (Berlin, 1887); Rothfels, Politik und Krieg; Rothfels's introduction and notes to Politische Schriften und Briefe, which discuss a number of historical texts; and Paret, Clausewitz and the State, 78–89, 327–55.

[5] On War, 156.

[6] Delbrück, Aufsätze, 218.

position of impossible purity. But undoubtedly Clausewitz was prepared to make sharp judgments, even if he always sought to understand the conditions obtaining at the time. Several of his works could not be published immediately after his death because they would have given offense to the court and to senior personages in the government and the army. Other manuscripts that were included in the first posthumous edition of his collected works or that appeared separately had their language toned down. Recently it has been recognized that editorial emendations and substitutions were far more frequent than had been supposed. Two motives are apparent from the changes: the replacement of unusual words and phrases to make the text stylistically more conventional; and the reduction or even elimination of the author's criticism of personalities and of Prussian institutions and policies.

The restored texts not only reveal Clausewitz's individuality with greater precision, they also offer additional evidence for his political views, which in the sixteen years he was to live after Napoleon's downfall placed him among those groups in Prussia that favored a constitution, responsible ministerial government, equality of legal rights, and a degree of political participation of the upper classes. To the conservatives that regained full control of the government and army after 1815, he was a man of doubtful political reliability who had never renounced the radical reformism of his earlier years. When the prospect arose of his being made ambassador at the court of St. James, his conservative critics succeeded in reversing the appointment, because, as the British envoy reported to his government, in Berlin "there is not that confidence in his being wholly free from revolutionary views."[7] These views did not shape Clausewitz's historical interpretations, but occasionally they enriched them with a grace note.

His urge to explore past reality was strengthened by the succession of events that began with the fall of the Bastille a few days after his ninth birthday. Four years later, as an ensign in a Prussian infantry regiment, he first fought against the armies of the new republic, and until his thirty-fifth year, when he served as chief of staff of a Prussian corps in the campaign that ended with the battle of Waterloo, his existence was largely determined by the French Revolution and its political and military consequences. In particularly intense form his career reflected a more general experience. The French Revolution was the central political and social fact of Clausewitz's generation. Its material and intellectual forces changed the political map of Europe, accel-

---

[7] Clausewitz's prospects for a diplomatic career between 1818 and 1820, and the reasons for their eventual failure, are reconstructed from archival sources in Peter Paret, "Bemerkungen zu dem Versuch von Clausewitz, zum Gesandten in London Ernannt zu Werden," *Jahrbuch für die Geschichte Mittel- und Ostdeutschlands* 26 (1977): 161–72; Harald Müller adds further details in "Die Karlsbader Beschlüsse und Clausewitz," *Jahrbuch für Geschichte* 36 (1988): 7–25. The episode is summarized in Paret, *Clausewitz and the State*, x, 319–23.

erated the opening up of society, and beyond these pressures and dislocations affected large areas of European thought. New possibilities emerged, but at the cost of old certainties. If this was at first especially marked in philosophy and political theory, it soon spread to the study of history—understanding the Revolution and its causes became an urgent necessity. In a more general sense, the fact that the Revolution had occurred at all altered people's ideas about the past as such, changed the character of historical inquiry and interpretation, and especially in Germany helped raise historical scholarship to a position of cultural dominance that it was to retain for several generations.

Among the great variety of reactions to the Revolution, Clausewitz's response stands out for its nonpartisan, complex realism. From the time when he began to set down his ideas on the history and present condition of Europe as a young officer of twenty-three, he seems to have been convinced that the Revolution had been inevitable, that the administrative system of the French monarchy and its economic and social institutions were so inefficient and inequitable that a violent correction had to come.[8] His view of a society regaining its balance and progressing toward its full potential of power was accompanied but not clouded by a strong distaste for revolutionary rhetoric and mob rule. On the other hand, his recognition of the need for change and his sympathy for the claims of at least the educated and commercial elements of the Third Estate did not weaken his sense of the danger that a reformed, rejuvenated France posed to Europe. He never doubted that war alone could bring French expansion to a halt.[9] This way of looking at the Revolution as it blended into the Napoleonic empire, which emphasized the inevitable interaction and conflict of interests and energies instead of making moral judgments, was closely linked to attitudes that were to characterize his historical writings: a sense of impermanence in human affairs, disbelief in progress, denial that the social and political status quo reflected a God-given order, and rejection of any teleological force in history.

Revolutions demonstrate the reality of great and sudden change. In an unusually direct manner, the events of his youth and early maturity confronted Clausewitz with the need to explain the changes that were taking place, and offered him the choice between two different views of history. In the beginning the French Revolution presented itself to Clausewitz largely in military terms. It coincided with revolutionary innovations in military organization, tactics, and operations, first implemented on a large scale by the Republican armies, and until the Napoleonic empire collapsed it was more urgent for Clausewitz to understand these innovations and turn them against

---

[8] References to the French Revolution abound in his writings. The most important analysis of its causes occurs in the essay "Agitation," pp. 338–45, below.

[9] For a characteristic statement of this view, see his note of 1803 beginning "Whether the Franks are like the Romans?" p. 239, below.

the French than to fit the Revolution into the larger processes of European history. On a deeper level, he took for granted that, like the Revolution, the revolution in war could be accurately interpreted only if the conditions preceding it were also taken into account. To many of the more reflective soldiers of his day this posed no particular difficulty. Jomini expressed a widely held belief when he claimed that Napoleon, the heir of the Revolution, had discovered permanently valid principles of war, and that earlier wars were merely stages in a long, continuous development leading to the Napoleonic pattern of large armies launched on campaigns of deep penetration, aimed at destroying the opponent's forces and occupying his capital. According to this view, the most gifted commanders of the past, Frederick the Great for example, acted whenever possible according to strategic principles that subsequently were fully implemented by Napoleon in a military environment that had changed little between the 1740s and 1815.

Clausewitz never questioned the links—ranging from the central element of all wars, organized mass violence, to the use of similar or even identical weapons—that joined warfare before and after the Revolution. But he also insisted on important discontinuities. The military institutions of the ancien régime, he wrote in an essay on the life of his teacher, Scharnhorst, "had collapsed in the wars of the French Revolution; its forms and means were no longer appropriate to the changed times and new political conditions."[10] The earlier period should not be dismissed as merely preparatory to the present, and the present was misinterpreted if it was regarded merely as the fulfillment of past strivings. This fundamental difference aside, individual human beings should not be regarded as interchangeable. Clausewitz noted the uniqueness of the creative personality—a historical force that in his theories reappeared as the concept of genius—each acting in conditions that could never be duplicated. Frederick the Great and Napoleon not only governed and waged war in dissimilar environments, they also differed in character and personal circumstances. That Napoleon reigned not by inheritance but as a newcomer who needed to establish his dynasty and demonstrate the permanence of his rule might have compelled him to take greater risks than a hereditary monarch was likely to accept. The norms of war that some writers thought they had discovered were not only dependent on the circumstances of the times, they were derived from the unique situation and interests of one individual, which might not recur under altered conditions or in different personalities. Napoleon's mass armies and all-embracing strategic goals were made possible by new conditions and also expressed a highly personal conception of war. In the same way, the society, economy, and politics of the ancien régime had been conducive to, and had justified, limited operations.[11]

[10] "On the Life and Character of Scharnhorst," p. 102, below.
[11] Clausewitz's view of this issue is discussed more extensively in Peter Paret, "Continuity and

In his differentiated view of the past and in his efforts to interpret each period according to its own measure, Clausewitz reveals certain affinities with Ranke and other scholars of the Restoration era who were introducing a new outlook to the study and writing of history. This marked a departure from nearly every historian he had read in his youth. Between his arrival in Berlin in 1801 and the outbreak of war in 1806, he made excerpts of Schiller's *Revolt of the Netherlands* and of Johannes von Müller's *History of the Swiss Confederacy*, which he read with sufficient care to recognize that a passage was paraphrased from Machiavelli. Notes from those years refer to Machiavelli's *Discourses* and *Art of War*. Among other historical works he read before 1806 were books and essays by Montesquieu, Robertson, Ancillon, and Gentz. Justus Möser's *History of Osnabrück*, themes of which reappear in an essay Clausewitz wrote in 1807, he had perhaps already encountered in the 1790s, and he had begun the intensive exploration of Frederick the Great's *History of My Times* and *History of the Seven Years' War*, which resulted in important studies in the 1820s. The number of specifically military historians cited or referred to in his early writings is even greater.[12]

We can guess which aspects in the works of these writers were most interesting or appealing to him. Machiavelli's frank recognition of the primacy of political and military power might have had a liberating impact on his thought. He must have valued Montesquieu's skepticism, specificity, and recognition of the importance of irrational factors; years later Clausewitz singled out his work as a model for his own theoretical efforts. In the same way, he valued Möser's belief in the individuality of historical epochs and his replacement of the Enlightenment's concept of progress with the more earthbound, less abstract sense of historical evolution. He might have learned above all from Schiller, the author most frequently cited or referred to in his early manuscripts and correspondence, that a historian need not express himself in convoluted, academic-bureaucratic German, but could develop ideas and narrate events in vigorous, carefully structured prose. But particular influences are difficult to trace. Perhaps Frederick's irony and easy use of antithesis helped inspire similar characteristics of Clausewitz's prose, but he encountered such elements in other authors as well. Far easier to recognize are the important differences that distinguished Clausewitz even in his youth from writers who could stimulate, nourish, but not fully satisfy his intense wish to reach back and understand the past.

Above all, his historical writings are free of any teleological message. Much as he admired Schiller, he could not write history in order to celebrate

Discontinuity in Some Interpretations of Tocqueville and Clausewitz," *Journal of the History of Ideas* 49 (1988): 161–69.

[12] On Clausewitz's early reading, see Paret, *Clausewitz and the State*, 78–97.

the idea of freedom or, indeed, the workings of any abstraction supposedly revealed through the realities of the past. In the same way, the patriotic, idealistic purposes of Müller's *History of the Swiss* could never have served as a model for him—neither in its purpose nor in its style—although this did not prevent him from studying Müller's works and learning from them. Schiller and Müller were born in the 1750s; their elevation of moral absolutes as the dramatic goals of social, political, and military events was an essential part of their struggle against narrowly rationalistic and judgmental tendencies of Enlightenment historiography. But even some scholars who were Clausewitz's exact contemporaries and who published their most important and influential works during the last decade of Clausewitz's life differed sharply from him in the concerns they carried to the study of history. Friedrich Christoph Schlosser saw himself as an educator of liberal Germany, and regarded his histories as means of strengthening ethical values and building moral character. Heinrich Luden and Friedrich von Raumer both idealized the German Middle Ages, and Raumer in particular helped turn the Hohenstauffen emperors into heroic figures for the Germans of the Restoration, symbols of a past empire that held out the promise of renewed German unity in the future. They used history for purposes external to it. Clausewitz studied and wrote history to gain greater understanding of the past, and—by means of the contribution history could make to theory—of the past, present, and future phenomenon of war.

One author, Scharnhorst, whom Clausewitz not only read with the greatest care but who also strongly influenced his scholarship was not primarily a historian. Like Schiller and Müller, Scharnhorst was born in the 1750s, but he was never entrapped in the moralizing assumptions of late-Enlightenment historiography, nor did he seek to rise above them by writing history as a drama of ethical grandeur and conflict. In his voluminous theoretical and technical works on military institutions and war, the interpretation of the past is only one among several fields of study. He was nevertheless convinced that the study of history should be at the center of any advanced study of war, and the historical passages in his writings are anything but mere background or decoration. Historical examples fill his theoretical treatises and manuals and illustrate how the techniques under discussion functioned in reality. In *On War* Clausewitz praises Scharnhorst's use of historical material even in manuals meant to be carried on campaign in the officer's saddlebag—examples drawn from earlier wars whose analysis helped to bridge the ever-present, dangerous gap between theory and practice—and his own extensive use of historical examples owes much to Scharnhorst.[13] The expert, sober manner in which Scharnhorst outlined these circumscribed episodes of military his-

---

[13] "On Historical Examples," *On War*, 170.

tory carried over to his more extended historical studies, whose subject was no longer the formation of combat patrols or the effectiveness of land mines but strategy and national policy. Particularly interesting in this group is a long essay of 1797 on the reasons for the French successes in the revolutionary wars, which Scharnhorst wrote as an analytic introduction to a history of these wars. The essay is an original and farsighted effort to appraise the more important components of the French effort, from the Republic's geographic position and its unified political and military command to ideology and psychological factors. That the author was a serving officer who had fought the French for years in the army of an absolutist state did not prevent him from emphasizing the importance of political and popular energies that were generated in a society more open than his own.[14]

Scharnhorst's thorough knowledge of military engineering, siege warfare, and the design and employment of firearms is often reflected in his historical works. Clausewitz's campaign histories contain little of this. They focus mainly on the relationship between government policy and military action, the psychology and ability of the commanders, and on the construction of often highly detailed analytic narratives of strategic decisions and their operational implementation. They are also more openly speculative and seek illustrations and comparisons across a wide spectrum of the European past. The writings of teacher and pupil nevertheless show a number of related traits. Some psychological and social affinities may have helped Clausewitz incorporate parts of Scharnhorst's historical style, and perhaps made the process of adoption possible in the first place. Like his teacher, he valued the specific. If he could never quite attain Scharnhorst's profound realism, he always strove for it, and both men held nonpartisan, utilitarian views of the political and military forces whose histories they interpreted. Clausewitz developed even his abstractions in a remarkably concrete manner, surrounding them with examples and analogies drawn from the sciences and everyday experience; he liked to characterize states, armies, and the processes of conflict in terms borrowed from physics and mechanics.[15] Perhaps he adopted

[14] On Scharnhorst's writings, see Rudolf Stadelmann, *Schicksal und geistige Welt* (Wiesbaden, 1952); and the chapter "Scharnhorst's Mediation Between Old and New," in Paret, *Clausewitz and the State*, 56–77.

[15] One of the most striking examples of this approach is the concept of friction, which Clausewitz describes in part in the following words: "The military machine—the army and everything related to it—is basically very simple and therefore seems easy to manage. But we should bear in mind that none of its components is one piece, each part is composed of individuals, everyone of whom retains his potential for friction. . . . A battalion is made up of individuals, the least important of whom may chance to delay things or somehow make them go wrong. . . . This tremendous friction, which cannot, as in mechanics, be reduced to a few points, is everywhere in contact with chance, and brings about effects that cannot be measured, just because they are

this device from Enlightenment authors. And yet to imagine large institutions and their component parts as machines, levers, ratchets, or counterweights, subject to the pull of gravity and the retarding force of friction, might have contributed to the evenhanded, practical note that runs through his historical interpretations—an interest in understanding how things really work that was further strengthened by a social fact: like Scharnhorst, Clausewitz did not belong by birth to the traditional or even to the recently ennobled elites among whom he spent his life. Scharnhorst was an outsider, Clausewitz's background was only marginally more privileged. Each had made his own way, and each thought about society and his place in it in highly pragmatic, unideological terms.

Clausewitz's writings are marked by the struggle for an objective interpretation of the past, a quality he thought essential for its own sake as well as for enabling history to create theory. But what historian did not seek or claim objectivity, which in any case is an ideal of many meanings? In his *History of the Thirty Years' War* Schiller tried to be evenhanded, and, according to Johannes von Müller, he succeeded. This did not prevent him from glorifying Gustavus Adolphus as the inspired champion of religious freedom while condemning Catholic obscurantism and political ambition. Clausewitz's objectivity was more encompassing, and his rejection of myths in favor of more mundane realities perplexed many of his early readers. His evaluation of Frederick the Great became famous for its sober recognition of the king's superior qualities and its total lack of adulation. When one of his first, long manuscripts, "Gustavus Adolphus's Campaigns of 1630–32," was at last published in 1837, the editor felt compelled to note that "Clausewitz's characterization of the king [did not] sufficiently emphasize that the war was a matter of conscience for him, and that his true greatness had another basis than military ambition."[16] Perhaps ultimately Clausewitz's historical objectivity derived from his matter-of-fact belief that the urge for power and expansion was inherent in most political and social entities. Even if the scholar favored one side over the other, his recognition that the opponent also functioned according to his nature and interests served as a brake on partisanship. Clausewitz's refusal to judge the past by the standards or concerns of the present did the rest. Indeed, as his political essays demonstrate, he was far more critical of his own time than of any period of the past, and the evenhandedness that generally marks his historical writings is unusual not only in comparison with the historical literature of his day, but perhaps even more so in comparison with the historical literature of the following generation.

largely due to chance." "Friction in War," *On War*, 119–20. An early version of this statement is found in *The Campaign of 1812 in Russia*, pp. 165–66, below.

[16] "Gustav Adolphs Feldzüge von 1630–1632," *Werke*, 9: v.

Ranke published his first books toward the end of Clausewitz's life. Clausewitz was familiar with at least some of them. He read *The History of the Serbian Revolution* shortly after it was published at the beginning of 1829, but we do not know his opinion of the work.[17] In his own historical writings, Clausewitz approaches his younger contemporary in his rejection of abstract and teleological elements in history, in his emphasis on the unique, and in his respect for the separateness and particularity of each epoch. Even their views of the state and of the European community of states reveal certain similarities, grounded in their understanding of political and military power. But Clausewitz does not follow Ranke in combining a sense of the uniqueness of each age with a belief in God's immanence in historical forces, nor was he inspired by visions of large structures and patterns of history, akin to the unity and division of the Latin and Germanic peoples that for Ranke defined the European experience since the rise of Christianity and the decline of the universal empire of Rome. Equally, perhaps even more significant, Clausewitz's historical writings show no sign of the methodological revolution initiated by Ranke and by a few older scholars whose work influenced or paralleled Ranke's: Savigny, Karl Ritter, Niebuhr—once again almost exactly Clausewitz's contemporaries. Nothing in Clausewitz's treatment of his material points to the new, more systematic comparative analysis of documents, accounts, and traditions that these men developed to reveal the genuine facts of the past and gain a firmer sense of the dynamic of events. He possessed only the most limited recognition of the importance of archival research and of the systematic exploitation of the available material, and seems on the whole to have been prepared to accept published texts as faithful to the original manuscripts. His sources were other historical accounts, as well as published memoirs, reports, and correspondence. His sparse references suggest that he based his works on a small number of sources, which he read critically and compared to one another. He put himself in the position of the writer, as he always tried to put himself in the position of the people that he and others wrote about. His treatment of Napoleon's memoirs in his history of the Italian campaign of 1796 is a good example: he uses the memoirs to help him understand events and compares the events with Napoleon's account to evaluate the memoirs, always conscious of the personality, exceptional ability, and the political and private motives of their author.

Taken together, these practices suggest a writer who in historiographical terms is a transitional figure: a rigorous thinker who has left past preconceptions behind but has not acquired the new methodological tools that are being developed; an amateur scholar, not an academic, untouched by the na-

---

[17] Clausewitz to Gneisenau, July 8, 1829, in *Schriften*, 2, part 1, 549.

scent professionalism of the discipline of history. We may regard him as a precursor of German historicism whose work has not yet acquired scientific character. But as always when we are faced with a scholar who rises above the average, what is most interesting and valuable about his work transcends methodological and historiographical categories.

ONE

"Some Comments on the War of the Spanish Succession after Reading the Letters of Madame de Maintenon to the Princess des Ursins" (1826 or later)

Clausewitz wrote these comments in or after 1826, the year of publication of the edition of Mme de Maintenon's correspondence that he must have used.[1] *The notes exemplify his manner in maturity of working with historical sources and of thinking about the past. He is interested in differences in conditions and attitudes between former times and his own, differences he tries to understand by putting himself in the position of the people he writes about. On the other hand, his frequent observations on strategic factors almost always link past and present—for instance, he comments that the best route by which to invade France is still from the northeast, as it was in the age of Louis XIV. The notes also demonstrate the dialectical form in which he liked to develop his interpretations. The opening paragraph begins with a statement emphasizing the serious dangers facing France between 1706 and 1711. This is immediately followed by the observation that France was not as weak as is usually assumed. The paragraph ends with the assertion that not weakness but the superior talents of the allied commanders caused France to lose the war. In subsequent paragraphs, however, nothing is said about Marlborough and Prince Eugene—both of whom are frequently mentioned by Mme de Maintenon—but a great deal about the personalities of the French commanders and the limited scope of their authority, which in turn help explain the success of Marlborough and Eugene.*

The comments end with an extended gloss on a passage of one of the letters, which expressed approval that Louis XIV did not directly involve himself in the conduct of military operations. Mme de Maintenon's statement, Clausewitz believes, reflected a general attitude toward kingship and war, which in part is explained by the limited character of war at the beginning of the eighteenth century. Perhaps it was no accident that this passage caught his attention: at the time he wrote, in the second half of the 1820s, he was refining his analysis of the nature of limited and unlimited war, making the distinction

---

[1] *Lettres inédites de Mme de Maintenon et de la Princesse des Ursins*, 4 vols. (Paris, 1826). An earlier edition of selections (*Lettres inédites de la Princesse des Ursins a M. le Maréchal de Villeroi, suivies de sa correspondance avec Madame de Maintenon* [Paris, 1806]) does not include Mme de Maintenon's letter of April 28, 1708, which Clausewitz discusses.

15

between the two forms the basis of his entire theoretical work. We cannot say whether Clausewitz knew that Mme de Maintenon's letters to the Princess des Ursins, first lady-in-waiting to the queen of Spain, had a pronounced official character; but it was obvious to him that Mme de Maintenon expressed not so much her own views as ideas widely held at court, which makes her letters significant beyond their account of personalities and events. The refusal of Louis XIV to lead his armies thus becomes a key to the understanding of his times.

We see from these letters:

1. In what perplexities, distress, and anxiety France found herself between 1706 and 1711. A few successful campaigns might threaten her very existence! To be sure, people always talk of a Europe united against Louis XIV. But this Europe consisted merely of Austria, parts of the Holy Roman Empire, the Dutch, Great Britain, and intermittently Savoy. Ranged in opposition were France, the greater part of Spain, and the insurgent Hungarians, against whom Austria was waging war. If we consider how badly located were the armies that England, Holland, and Savoy could use against France, how inconsequential were the armed forces of the Holy Roman Empire, and that Austria was compelled to divert part of her army to Hungary, we will scarcely claim that their political superiority over France was very great, and that the cause of their eventual success lay in this superiority. No! Success was brought about by the two great and enterprising commanders of the alliance.

2. That of all perplexities, the need for money was the greatest, which demonstrates how completely war was dependent on money at that time.

3. That although favor and caprice had far less influence on the appointment of senior commanders than is usually assumed, secondary considerations did often play too large a part, which significantly damaged the king's cause. In 1708 the duke of Burgundy was sent to Flanders because opinion in the army strongly favored the presence of a prince of royal blood. Vendôme's authority was reduced, soon disputes arose between him and the prince, and matters grew even worse when Berwick arrived in Flanders with units of the army from Germany and became the prince's councilor. Now the army had three commanders in chief. According to these letters, the battle of Oudenaarde, usually regarded as the work of the duke of Burgundy, seems to have been opposed by him: Vendôme alone made the decision.

The failure of this campaign kept Vendôme from serving in the following years, and he did not regain command until 1710 in Spain. In 1709 Villars, who until then had been successful in Germany, was made commander in chief in the main theater of war, Flanders. A bold, gay, somewhat reckless personality, he was regarded as the best of the senior commanders, or at least

16

the luckiest. However, the king seems to have felt uneasy, and the sixty-five-year-old Boufflers, who had restored his reputation the previous year by his defense of Lille, and since then had gained considerable trust and made himself seem important through his honest zeal in carrying out administrative assignments, was sent to the army in Flanders. It was said that this was a precaution in case Marshal Villars met with some accident; but presumably the careful and conscientious Boufflers was sent to assist him. This is how the matter appears when the letters allow us to look backstage, while before the footlights the drama of the aged veteran hurrying to serve under a young marshal is presented as an act of enthusiastic patriotism, designed to inflame the spirit of the entire army.

As is known, Villars actually was wounded in the battle of Malplaquet, and Boufflers made himself very useful to the army when he took command of the retreat. But surely it had been hoped that his usefulness would consist in preventing a battle of Malplaquet from being fought at all.

Unless the duke of Orleans (the later regent) is numbered among generals of the first rank, the French lacked sufficient commanders of this quality for all their major armies. They fought in four theaters of war: Flanders, Germany (that is, the upper Rhine), Italy or Savoy, and Spain; but they had only three commanders of more or less equally high quality: Villars, Vendôme, and Berwick.

4. We learn from these letters that the French court was always much more concerned about Flanders than about the other theaters of war. This is only to be expected, because despite the many fortresses in Flanders the area is so much nearer the capital, which could also be regarded as the core of the monarchy. At the same time, the concern of the court points to the policies that the allies should have pursued.

If one operates in conjunction with England and Holland, the line of advance from Brussels to Paris is far superior to an advance from Strasbourg. For one thing it is much shorter, besides it runs through rich, level, populated areas, with few warlike inhabitants; and finally (and this is the main point) the line is not flanked by the mass of French territory as would be the case with an advance from Mainz, and even more so with an advance from Strasbourg. Immediately to its right is the sea, and on its left—since the invading force would cross the French frontier in a southwesterly direction—only as much enemy territory as is gradually left behind during the advance. By contrast, an advance from Strasbourg to Paris has all of southern France, or rather five sixths of the whole of France, on its left. This consideration is even more important today than it was in the past when extraordinary means of defense [for instance, guerrilla operations] were less common.

5. We see that the operation against Toulon did alarm the court, because the loss of this city would have meant a significant reduction of the state's

resources. But we also find that it was not difficult or costly to protect the city. An offensive in Provence is the poorest measure one can take against France. In those days, of course, people still feared an insurrection in the Cevennes, which might have been coordinated with such an attack.

6. As already noted, Villars emerges in these letters as a bold, somewhat reckless commander; Vendôme as lazy, cynical, but enterprising; Berwick as thoughtful and cautious.

7. On April 29, 1708, Madame de Maintenon writes to the Princess des Ursins: "No, Madame, the king will not go to Flanders, for the same reason that the king of Spain will not place himself at the head of his armies. Their affairs are not in sufficiently bad shape to warrant desperate actions, nor sufficiently favorable to allow them to do something that is worthy of their greatness."

Elsewhere she praises the king of Spain for not having joined the army, "because he would not have been able to do anything brilliant."

We should not be misled by the fact that these are the words of a woman, moreover a woman, as Madame de Maintenon says of herself and as is evident, who has no talent whatever for matters of state and for war. She merely voices the opinions of her environment, but this environment is made up precisely of the individuals whose opinions and points of view matter to us: the king, the senior commanders, princes, ministers, etc. If we take Madame de Maintenon's statement as the considered opinion of these men, it becomes highly significant. That a ruler who is not also a great man may quietly hold the view she expresses should surprise no one familiar with human weaknesses. But that such a point of view is openly stated, in a sense preached as a political principle, is most remarkable! It is explained by the fact that in the conditions of the French state at the time, war—even a very serious and dangerous war—appears to be a matter of secondary importance, not worthy of the king's personal involvement, unless the war, like some luxurious object, can be used to glorify the monarch's person and his reign. Certainly people had learned from European history that war could come to dominate a state, that a state could be drawn into the whirlpool of war and be threatened with extinction. But the size of the French monarchy was so disproportionate to the limited nature of war in the early eighteenth century that no one could think extinction was a possibility for France. The limited intensity of war gave rise to the opinion that for France war was a secondary matter, and in turn this point of view influenced the character of the war.*

---

* On July 22, 1675, after Louis XIV had left the army in the Netherlands, Turenne wrote to Louvois: "I am pleased with the king's decision to leave the army. This is no longer the time for His Majesty to remain, and it seems to me that nothing can be more prudent than his decision to leave after having demonstrated so much resolve during the time he was here."

TWO

"Observations on the Wars of the Austrian Succession" (early 1820s)

Aside from the Napoleonic Wars, the wars of Frederick the Great are the military episodes most often discussed and cited in Clausewitz's writings. Together they make up over three quarters of the references to military history in On War. The young Clausewitz was undoubtedly brought up on the triumphs, hardships, and legends of the Frederician campaigns, and after he returned, a fifteen-year-old lieutenant, from the War of the First Coalition, he began to study them seriously and continued to occupy himself with the subject for the rest of his life. In the early 1820s he decided to set down his ideas in comprehensive chronological form. The manuscript was printed in the tenth volume of his posthumous works under the title, "The Campaigns of Frederick the Great from 1741 to 1762." It is not a true history but rather, as the subtitles of the two main parts indicate, Bemerkungen—remarks, observations, comments, some no more than one or two sentences long, set apart by § signs. The text that follows is of the first main part, "Observations on the Wars of the Austrian Succession."

At the time of writing, Clausewitz notes, relatively little had been published on the first two Silesian wars, from 1740 to 1742 and 1744 to 1745, in contrast to the Seven Years' War, on which the literature was already extensive. The first part mentions only one source, Frederick the Great's Histoire de mon temps. *To this should be added Jacob de Cogniazo's* Geständnisse eines österreichischen Veteranen, *which contains material on the early period, but is not referred to until the second part, and probably Ludwig Müller's* Kurzgefasste Beschreibung der drey schlesischen Kriege, *a work Clausewitz must have known because he was Müller's student in Berlin from 1801 to 1804. A few articles as well as references in memoirs and other larger works complete the narrow historiographical base available to him.*

"In no war was strategy as saturated with politics as in this one." With this comment in §3 of the "Observations," Clausewitz does not mean to suggest that other wars were to any lesser degree instruments of policy, but that in the Wars of the Austrian Succession policy and political considerations determined strategy and even the movement of subordinate units to an unusual extent. The wars, which began in December 1740 when Frederick exploited the political uncertainties following the death of the Holy Roman Emperor,

Charles VI, by occupying Silesia, were an alternating sequence of fighting and negotiating between powers, some of whom changed sides more than once. Throughout the conflict, the victories the Prussians gained were more important psychologically and politically than in their direct military impact. At last two victories over the Austrians in the summer and fall of 1745, combined with the defeat of Austria's ally, Saxony, led to the Peace of Dresden, which left Frederick in undisturbed possession of Silesia for the next eleven years. The wars marked an important phase in the development of the Frederician and post-Frederician army and in the growth in power of the Prussian state—the traditions and environment in which Clausewitz spent his early life. They also differed significantly from the wars of the Napoleonic era. Repeatedly, Clausewitz interprets a course of action that his own generation might find flawed or incomprehensible by referring to the conditions of the times and to attitudes and assumptions then current. The "Observations" are a step in a lengthy comparative process. Similar studies of the Napoleonic era, for instance his critique of the campaign of 1814, also included in this volume, gradually led Clausewitz to comprehensive interpretations of the character of war in both periods and eventually also to his theory of the dual nature of war.

In the first paragraphs of the "Observations," Clausewitz discusses his subject from the perspective of war, not of diplomacy, although political factors are always in evidence and occasionally become preeminent. His comments follow an approximate chronology of events. He opens with a specific operational phenomenon that might be regarded as of secondary significance but which is linked to fundamental issues of war and society of the times: surprising the opposing army when it is dispersed in quarters. Several encounters of this kind occurred in the war because reconnaissance was poor, especially on the Prussian side. In part, these tactical surprises were a consequence of the social conditions of an age when the rank and file consisted primarily of mercenaries and of men pressed to serve. The organization of the troops, their march formations, and to some extent even their tactical deployment were influenced by the need to prevent desertion. Scouting and patrolling were therefore best left to the minority of men whose loyalty could be trusted and who knew how to act on their own. In the Wars of the Austrian Succession these requirements were met by the Austrian light troops, most coming from the so-called military frontier at the southern edge of Hungary. A brief paragraph in the "Observations" refers to these units, which were one of the institutional forces that gradually transformed the armies of the ancien régime into the more flexible mass armies of industrializing Europe.

The treatment of specifically military topics is accompanied in the "Observations" by a section on the political and strategic fragmentation of the war, and above all by an essay on the manner in which Frederick's political concerns determined his operations, a discussion that takes up over half of the entire work. The predominantly military focus broadens to encompass policy and diplomacy in an analysis that Hans Rothfels judged to be exemplary in its "energetic bringing together of military and political factors."[1] *Its unusual character is perhaps best appreciated when the "Observations" are compared with studies of eighteenth-century wars by Clausewitz's contemporaries. A similar integration of diplomatic, strategic, and operational analyses is found only in the works of Frederick the Great; the accounts by other participants or academic historians concentrate either on diplomacy or on the fighting. But even in military history as it is written today a comparably comprehensive approach would be very rare.*

Few readers who are not military specialists will want to follow the operational movements in detail. What matters far more is to gain an impression of the way in which Clausewitz clarifies the political and strategic reasons for operational decisions, and in turn analyzes their political and strategic consequences. The result is a remarkable case study that brings out the essentials of limited war in the eighteenth century.

---

1. *Surprising the Enemy in His Bivouacs*

(1741) In its opening the campaign of 1741 is very strange. With about 39,000 men on two roads over Zuckermantel and over Johannisberg, Field Marshal Neipperg breaks into the Prussian bivouacs, which extend along the mountains toward Troppau. Frederick the Great is with the upper Silesian corps at Jägerndorf; in the little time available he can assemble only thirteen battalions. His forces at Frankenstein, Neisse, Brieg, and Jägerndorf are separated from one another. Neipperg advances on Neisse, raises the Prussian siege of the town, and continues toward Brieg. The king hurries back, is already too late to cross the Neisse River by Sorgau, marches down river, and crosses near Michelau. He has now been joined by the forces from Neisse and Brieg and intends to march to Ohlau to cover his wagons and heavy equipment when he encounters the Austrian bivouacs near Mollwitz. In the true sense of the term, Neipperg had surprised the king in his quarters, and had cut off his direct line of retreat so that the king was forced to fight with his front reversed. Had Neipperg won the battle, it would have been the most brilliant campaign imaginable. The king wins the battle, but he does not exploit his victory. Instead of assaulting Neipperg once more at Neisse, to which he has withdrawn, Frederick is satisfied with reoccupying Brieg.

[1] *Politische Schriften und Briefe*, 244.

2. Defense of Large Rivers

(1744) The defense of the Rhine by Marshal Coigny and General Seckendorf against Prince Charles of Lorraine in 1744 deserves closer analysis, although it led only to average results. One would probably find that the defense might have achieved much.

3. The Political Nature of Wars at the Time

The Austrians succeed in crossing the Rhine—and do nothing, although they are the superior force. Noailles reinforces the French considerably, and the Austrians, in any case called back by Frederick's new offensive, withdraw across the Rhine and move to Bohemia. The French remain on the Rhine, lay siege to Freiburg with 70,000 men, and detach only a small number to General Seckendorf. In short, the campaign is very much in tune with the times.

In no war was strategy as saturated with politics as in this one. Except for Austria, none of the powers had interests that called for an all-out effort, and the dispersed location of the belligerents led to a variety of plans and operational choices unequalled in any other war. The Austrians faced the French in Italy, on the upper Rhine, in Flanders, but also in Bohemia and Austria proper. One year men fought in Bohemia, the next on the Danube, then along the Rhine. In Flanders the French faced the Dutch and the British but could also turn against Hanover.

4. Leaving Garrisons in Unimportant Towns

When Frederick the Great quits Tabor and Budweis in October 1744, he leaves the towns garrisoned, in part because he doesn't want to give up the few hundred ill and wounded soldiers who remain there. This [sort of] measure, which scarcely seems justified and nevertheless occurs often, is characteristic of the time. And in general, this campaign in Bohemia consists of many insignificant steps, if we exclude the rapid conquest of Prague with its garrison of 12,000 men.

5. Characteristic Deployment of Forces

(1745) Frederick the Great's position in Bohemia before the battle of Soor is curious. In his camp near Chlumetz and later between Jaromirs and Smirschitz he faces the Elbe, and his supply lines and lines of retreat over Trautenau to Schweidnitz as well as over Braunau to Glatz lie nearly in front of him. The prince of Lorraine between Königgrätz and Jaromirs also has his supply line in front of his left wing in Pardubitz and Deutsch-Brodt. The County of Glatz is occupied by Prussian troops under Fouqué, who engages the light troops of the Austrians with good success. The Austrians have far more light troops than the king, who is forced to fight for each transport as it arrives from Schweidnitz every five days. This situation lasts 4½ months. To cover his supply lines the king also detached forces to Glatz and to upper Silesia, so that the army of 65,000 men with which he had entered Bohemia was reduced to no more than 18,000 in the camp at Studenz and in the battle of Soor, while the prince of Lorraine had 40,000 men.

6. Character of the First Four Battles

(1741–1745) Basically all four battles of the first Silesian wars—Mollwitz, Czaslau, Hohenfriedberg, and Soor—are true encounter battles, defensive actions that occur by chance, in which at the last moment Frederick the Great goes on the attack. The exception may be Hohenfriedberg, a battle that he more or less foresaw and wanted to fight. In the others, the enemy appeared close at hand, it would have been dangerous to retreat—in any case the political situation made a victory desirable—and so he went ahead in God's name. As a result he gained no advantage from these battles other than the prisoners he took and the trophies he won. In much the same way, the Austrians weren't really interested in fighting a battle. They did not advance with the firm intention of seeking out the opposing army and attacking it. They did not hunger for a victory. They advanced because their government had ordered them to attempt something. And in every case they wanted to maneuver the enemy back toward his own borders and gain some territory rather than to win a genuine victory. They fought merely because a battle wasn't diametrically opposed to their purpose, and because the king advanced so rapidly that they couldn't easily avoid him.

7. Frederick the Great's Plans of Campaign in the First Silesian Wars

The strategic plans of Frederick the Great in his first four campaigns link up very simply with his political plans. In 1741 he wanted to occupy Silesia, then defend it, and nothing more. He even signed a secret agreement mediated by the British, according to which the defense of Neisse was only for show. But the king realized that he was not yet able to gain a satisfactory peace. Consequently he could not do without his allies; new prospects of conquering a part of Bohemia appeared; if he could not retain these territories they might always serve in a trade for the firm possession of Silesia. In the campaign of 1742 he consequently decided to help in the relief of M. de

Ségur's army, enclosed in Linz, and to make a diversion through Moravia against the Austrian border, which simultaneously would give him control of Moravia. But far from employing all the troops available to him, he used only 15,000 men. The rest were to remain in Silesia and Bohemia. He secured an additional force of 15,000 Saxons and a French contingent of some 10,000 for this project, which obviously was nothing more than a diversion. Still, if the Austrian army had appeared and an opportunity had arisen to fight it, Frederick would not have refused it. But he never thought of a major offensive against Vienna. It could never be in Frederick's interest to reduce the Austrians severely, and then see the French play the master. His *Histoire de mon temps* is explicit on this point.

In this fashion he fulfilled his obligations under the alliance, frightened the Austrians, did not lose the important Silesian territories he had already gained, had a chance of conquering Moravia, and risked very little. Brünn could not be occupied because the Saxons were unwilling to expend their forces on this task. The Austrians under the prince of Lorraine were approaching, the French were already ordered to withdraw, and the Saxons were about to leave as well; early in April, therefore, he withdrew from Znaim to Chrudim in Bohemia, where he still retained a good part of Bohemia and soon afterwards won the battle of Czaslau and with it peace.

In 1744 Frederick the Great renewed the war because the Austrians were beginning to acquire a dangerous superiority, and because he was fully convinced by the international situation that Austria, Saxony, and Great Britain were intent on depriving him of Silesia. The Peace of Breslau did not yet sufficiently guarantee him possession of the province. Frederick the Great needed to demonstrate his power and his readiness to use it once more to make this possession secure. His plan was to invade Bohemia, occupy Prague, which would give him a new hostage, and help the French on the Rhine with a diversion that would draw away part of the Austrian army. After occupying Prague he meant to stay on the defensive, and it was only out of consideration for the French and to give greater force to the second part of his plan, the diversion, that he pushed as far forward as Budweis and Tabor, and increased the threat against Austria. This offensive thrust quickly succumbed to its inherent weaknesses. The king, everywhere encircled by Austrian light troops, is cut off from Prague and Silesia. The main Austrian army under the prince of Lorraine approaches, and the king, who had not reached his most advanced position until the end of September, retreats again on October 8. His aim now is to consume the food supplies of the area through which he is withdrawing; he therefore takes four whole weeks to move from Tabor to Kolin. The prince of Lorraine follows him and constricts him on both flanks as much as he can. After Frederick the Great crosses the Elbe on November 9, he gains another fourteen days by drawing up behind the river, which he uses to protect his front, while the garrisoned towns of Kolin and Pardubitz secure his flanks. The army bivouacs until the end of November, when the Austrians cross the Elbe in the center of the king's position, and he decides to move into winter quarters in Silesia and to give up Prague again.

In this campaign Frederick the Great shows no great desire for battle. The prince of Lorraine, whom the Saxons have joined, is stronger than he; the enemy's light troops have interfered with the supply of his army, which is now much weakened by illness. Under these circumstances Frederick the Great does not think it advisable to risk everything for the acquisition of half of Bohemia. He is content with having satisfied his obligation under the alliance and with having retained Silesia. He feels stronger in Silesia, and decides in the coming campaign to await the enemy there in order to defeat him.

In short, the occupation of Bohemia in 1744, like the occupation of Moravia in 1742, must be seen as a mere diversion. The possibility of retaining the conquest fades into the background.

We have so little information on this war that we cannot say whether Frederick the Great could and should have attacked the prince of Lorraine. To be sure, a victory that enabled Frederick to take winter quarters in Bohemia would have been very beneficial to him. He could then have shown the Austrians how much they needed to fear him and that they might well lose a second province if they insisted on continuing to recover the first. All of this would have been conducive to bringing about the kind of peace he wanted. But an ordinary victory would hardly have led to this result. The prince of Lorraine would have withdrawn a few days' march, and for the king to take up winter quarters in Bohemia would always have been risky. We can therefore fully understand the king's plan in terms of a style of warfare that, while far from timid and showing great determination in moments of danger, was generally cautious and knew how to conserve its limited resources.

In the campaign of 1745 against the Austrian army in Bohemia, Frederick the Great decided to remain on the defensive. It was in this spirit that he fought the brilliant battle of Hohenfriedberg at the foot of the mountains, and then followed the Austrians only to the Elbe, where he halted to exhaust the resources of the immediate area, live at the expense of his enemies, and keep the opposing army from moving into winter quarters. He fought the battle of Soor in part because the Austrians gained a measure of surprise over him, and he could not easily withdraw, in part to retain his political and psychological ascendancy. His victories were meant to bring him not only territory but also renewed respect. As he himself says, it was only for the sake of honor that he remained on the battlefield for five days; then he slowly withdrew to Silesia.

In the winter campaign of 1745 in Saxony the king wants to counter the Austrian and Saxon intention to advance on Berlin and the Mark Brandenburg. He positions an army under the prince of Anhalt at Halle, and with another army based in Silesia decides to attack them in the flank as they advance through Lusatia. He merely wants to block their offensive, but, to be sure, in such a way that a new victory would give him new advantages. With the Silesian army he surprises the bivouac of the prince of Lorraine near Görlitz; in the engagement of Katholisch-Hennersdorf he takes a few thousand prisoners, and compels the prince to retreat to Bohemia with a loss of 5,000 men. These successes may be regarded as the equivalent of a moderate victory. Perhaps Frederick the Great might have achieved more had he acted with greater boldness, but he did not want to abandon caution. Half a victory sufficed; to reach for a greater triumph meant exposing oneself to greater risks, and that did not fit into his plans.

After gaining these important advantages he renews his peace proposals, without raising his demands in the least; they are rejected. The prince of Anhalt advances on the Saxon army, which is assembling at Leipzig under Rutowski. The Saxons withdraw toward Dresden, followed by the prince, who is reinforced from Meissen by a corps of the king's army under General Lehwald. On December 15 he attacks the Austrians at Kesselsdorf. He defeats them completely, and the prince of Lorraine, who only two days earlier had arrived at Dresden from Leutmeritz and quartered his troops in the city, must withdraw to Bohemia. On the day of the battle, Frederick the Great reaches Meissen.

It is curious that both men, the king and the prince of Lorraine, permitted their subordinate commanders to fight a battle of such importance before they had joined them and without knowing whether they were confronted by the combined forces of the enemy.

Even this splendid victory, which places the king in control of all of Saxony, does not cause him to raise his conditions for peace. As before, what matters to him is to secure his possession of Silesia.

This degree of military success and of political moderation at last lead to his goal. Without further delay, in December, the Peace of Dresden is concluded, which again confirms him in the possession of Silesia.

In all these cases Frederick would certainly have terrified the Austrian government and induced it to accept his conditions at an earlier date if he had attacked the main Austrian army with his combined force, defeated it, and then advanced on Vienna. That he would have been able to do this in 1742, as well as in 1744 and 1745, is more certain than most things are in war. But the following considerations, *derived from the conditions of the time*, must be weighed against it.

1. To supply the army in the manner that has become usual since the French Revolution, which to be sure was already possible at the time, nevertheless went against accepted practice. It would have been regarded as completely despoiling the country, and would have led to powerful reactions in people's emotions and opinions. Nor would it have been all that easy to live off the land because the army's organization and administration were not designed for such practices. In Frederick's mind the problem of supply would therefore have seemed a great impediment to an advance on Vienna. In 1744 it already proved difficult enough for him to bring his flour and bread transports as far as Budweis.

2. A more aggressive war would more strongly have affected the instruments with which it was conducted, that is, the army and the treasury. If the king lost perhaps 20,000 men in a single campaign like that of 1742, 1744, or 1745, using far greater energy would have led to the loss of twice that many. We may assume that the loss of one soldier would cost the state around one hundred taler—if we include artillery and cavalry—because his entire equipment was lost with him. For that reason alone a more aggressive campaign would cost a few million more. If we add the long-distance transport of ammunition and supplies, costs increase by perhaps another million. We can therefore appreciate that someone with only a few million remaining in his treasury would put a high priority on preserving them. Of course the king might have raised part of the additional sums through forced contributions; but if they had been as substantial as they needed to be they would have created a new obstacle to peace and new motivation for hatred and resistance.

The value that Frederick the Great placed on manpower may be appreciated from his practice of forcing the prisoners he took to serve in the Prussian army. In his *Histoire* he prides himself on sparing Prussia these additional recruits. Someone who is that economical with money and men will always first calculate the cost of the effort required, and he soon arrives at a line that he regards as the limit of the possible, which may not be crossed regardless of the potential results.

3. After Frederick the Great had conquered Silesia almost without firing a shot, his positive purpose had been achieved. From then on the only thing that mattered to him was the retention of his conquest. He now found himself on the defensive. An offensive would have made sense to him only if he had to fear that he might waste favorable opportunities and later have to bear a heavier burden in less advantageous times. In two respects this was indeed the case. One was the general situation in which everyone who does not exert the fullest possible effort finds himself: the danger that his opponent eventually goes to extremes and outdoes him. Had the Austrians decided to make the kind of effort that, as we have learned since those days, is possible, they would easily have regained Silesia. But that was not to be feared, because no

one at the time thought of such a thing. Just as Frederick the Great calculated with taler and recruits, so did the Austrian government.

The second consideration was the possibility that Frederick the Great's allies would gradually leave him in the lurch. Basically, if he wished to retain Silesia whatever the consequences, no one had a motive as strong as his for fighting the Austrians. It might therefore be expected that unless Austria were defeated, forced to satisfy all demands, and made incapable of taking revenge, the others would gradually leave the alliance. Prussia would stand alone and would be defeated. But there was still a way out of this dilemma: the way of politics. At the time Prussia was undoubtedly Austria's most dangerous enemy. If she used the period of Austrian feebleness not to crush the state but, by intentionally holding back, to help the state recover, she would have put Austria in her debt, and that debt could be repaid with the surrender of Silesia. With this single province Austria could assure the possession of all others. This is what happened, and Frederick preferred this solution to an all-out decision by arms. That he succeeded, despite the heavy price to Austria of losing a province like Silesia, and despite the envy of the other princes involved in the settlement, was owing to the political situation. Of all of Austria's opponents, only Prussia and France mattered. If the others left the alliance it meant little; they were too insignificant. It would of course have been a natural move for the Austrians to satisfy France by ceding her a few towns in the Austrian Netherlands. Such a transfer would not have diminished Austria, nor increased France, by much. On the other hand, the transfer of a province like Silesia not only weakened Austria, it made a neighboring state into a true rival. But Maria Theresa believed that in the future she could regain Silesia more easily than she could towns from France. She also hoped to recover Lorraine, while in France the party of Marshal Belle-Isle advocated a weakening of Austria, and so Frederick the Great was able to outsmart old Fleury and bring his Silesia into a safe harbor.

8. Protection of Provinces Some Distance from the Theater of Operations

In these two wars, the king never failed to cover upper Silesia with a separate corps. Without this measure the Hungarian light troops would always have been in control of half of Silesia.

9. Austrian Superiority in Light Troops

One further interesting feature of these two wars is the Austrian superiority in light troops, which disrupted the Prussian lines of communication to a

degree rarely seen in the history of war. In 1744 Frederick the Great in Budweis and Tabor was without news from Silesia for four weeks. In 1745 he was
compelled to send the entire regiment of Ziethen's hussars to Jägerndorf to
bring Margrave Charles the order to withdraw, and other such episodes were
frequent.

THREE

From *Observations on Prussia in Her Great Catastrophe* (1823–1825)

In the 1820s Clausewitz planned to write a history of Prussia from 1805 to 1807, the period in which its policy of armed neutrality collapsed, the state drifted into war with France, its main armies were defeated in October 1806, and continued resistance was brought to an end in the battle of Friedland on June 14, 1807. To study these years of decline and disaster, at a time when the monarchy had regained its former power and more, argues an unusual degree of critical detachment from one's environment. Clausewitz was drawn to the subject in part by his dissatisfaction with the political developments in Restoration Prussia and by his awareness of continued or renewed weaknesses in the state's civil and military institutions. Perhaps he also wished to reconstruct conditions and events that he himself had experienced. Nor may it be without relevance that Prussia's catastrophe—which at the time deeply troubled him—did make possible the period of exceptional activity and hope that followed, the years of reform, which for Clausewitz personally proved to be the most profoundly satisfying time of his life. The significance of these personal considerations may be confirmed by the fact that he carried out only the first half of his original plan, discussing the background of the campaign of 1806 and the campaign itself, in the course of which he was taken prisoner. He did not extend his manuscript to the fighting in 1807, which he observed only from afar, interned in France.

Although the exact date is unknown, the manuscript was written between 1823 and 1825. An added comment on Savary's memoirs indicates that Clausewitz checked it again and made some changes in 1825 or later. It is apparent that he was selective in his use of the very extensive literature on the subject that had been published by the early 1820s; one source that he used but does not cite are his own articles on the October campaign, which he wrote almost immediately afterwards and which were published early in 1807. These "Historical Letters on the Significant Military Events of October 1806" remain an unusually well-informed and balanced account, but in them Clausewitz showed himself more charitable to the leadership and performance of the Prussian armies than he was to be two decades later. The Observations on Prussia were far too critical, and their tone was far too personal, to allow inclusion in his posthumous works, which came out in the 1830s, when—so their author would have thought—little had improved since the time he had written. Instead the manuscript was deposited in the archives of the Prussian general staff, where it was made available to a number of scholars until it was finally published in 1888, fifty-six years after its author's death. Marginal comments and inconsistencies in the text indicate that the printed version was based on a manuscript that awaited a final revision. The author refers to himself in the first person singular, the third person singular, and also in the first person plural. Dates, ages of individuals, and similar factual details are not always accurate and seem to be set down as the author recalled them. Once or twice a discussion of a particular issue is promised, but then is missing later on. The text that follows represents the first three chapters, which discuss Prussian institutions and society before the war, the leading personalities, and the "causes of and preparations for the war." The fourth and last chapter, a frequently very technical overview of the campaign, is omitted.

The Observations on Prussia differ from most of Clausewitz's historical writings by their author's direct knowledge of the times and people he is writing about, as well as by his approach to them, which is conclusive rather than explorative. Usually Clausewitz wrote about the past in order to gain a better understanding of it. Here he had no need to marshal the evidence and develop interpretations to learn what had ruined the state. A comparison of the Observations on Prussia with letters he wrote in 1807 and 1808 shows that he had long ago made up his mind on that point. Instead, the work expresses firm convictions, often in very strong terms. It is subjective, not objective; at most, Clausewitz restrains himself here and there in order to be more persuasive to the reader, although he must have known that he would not be able to publish a work so openly critical of the state during his lifetime.

A similar degree of personal engagement and partiality is present in only one other historical manuscript that Clausewitz wrote, his essay on Scharnhorst. On this and on other grounds the two works belong together. The Observations on Prussia explain what had gone wrong since Frederick had driven Prussia to the edge of being a major power. "On the Life and Character of Scharnhorst," although written earlier, celebrates one of the men who tried to put things right. Clausewitz's cutting, often derisive analysis of Prussia's decline is matched in emotional intensity by his admiration of the leader of the military reform movement, and by his bitterness over the ease with which Prussian conservatives diminished or forgot Scharnhorst's achievements after his death of wounds in 1813.

Clausewitz's depiction of the state before 1806, its institutions, and its leading personalities is neither all-embracing nor unfailingly accurate. At times he engages in hyperbole. It is unlikely that the muskets of the Prussian army were the worst in Europe, or that every rope or nail in the Berlin armory was rotten. But the point he wants to make—that the army placed more em-

phasis on appearance than on substance—is certainly correct, as are his strictures on the rationality and efficiency of the institutions of government.

Most striking, and frequently quoted, are his characterizations of the king, other members of the royal family, and senior officials and soldiers. The descriptions of General Rüchel, Prince Louis Ferdinand, or of the two cabinet councilors Lombard and Beyme, Bismarck's maternal grandfather, combine psychological and stylistic brilliance with a profound understanding of the environment in which these men worked and lived. In these miniatures Clausewitz appears less the scholar than a very attentive and knowledgeable contemporary. In the final analysis the greatest value of the Observations on Prussia *is not as history but as historical source. Only some memoirs and collections of correspondence give us a comparable sense of the atmosphere of the times; but here the atmosphere, and the author's recollections of his youth, which have not lost in emotional intensity, are combined with a firm analysis of a system of government that the country had outgrown.*

Prussia in the Year 1806

CHAPTER 1. A GLANCE AT THE SPIRIT OF
THE ARMY AND THE ADMINISTRATION

All unprejudiced observers of Prussia as it was before and during 1806 have concluded that the state was wrecked by its institutions.

A vain, immoderate faith in these institutions made it possible to overlook the fact that their vitality was gone. The machine could still be heard clattering along, so no one asked if it was still doing its job.

The spirit of order and economy of Frederick William I,* the creative vigor of Frederick the Great, had long since disappeared from these institutions, which *these men* above all had established in the state. Life had gone out of these forms, and the government had eyes only for appearances.

The General Directory, which under Frederick William I constituted a true ministry with which he worked in person, had been well suited to provide his administration with the necessary unity. Now it was a dead institution, an object of ridicule, seldom if ever honored by the presence of a minister.

Ministries organized by provinces still survived from the old, simpler administration of the small state. Since the days of Frederick William I, new

---

* Basically, Frederick William III was as devoted to order and economy as his great-grandfather had been, but without his energy and his enthusiasm for them.

needs had caused a number of departmental ministries to spring up among them like weeds, more, indeed, than are thought necessary in states without provincial ministries, e.g., Ministries of Mines, Forests, the Post, etc. But no one wanted to heed these warnings of nature, and the old order remained intact.

It was in the nature of these provincial ministries that they called forth conflicting interests and attitudes. Each was administered for itself alone, without any association apart from routine correspondence, and without any unified leadership or common purpose. When conflicts arose, each minister felt duty-bound to defend the particular interests of his province, which he often confused with his own interests and those of his position.

During the eleven-year reign of Frederick William II, when seventy to eighty million taler were spent from the treasury and thirty million more were borrowed, people took comfort in the belief that this was a natural outcome of the campaigns on the Rhine and in Poland and of other mobilizations of the army; no one suspected that bad management was involved. And indeed it would have been hard to say who, apart from the king himself, might have had this thought: the minister of Brandenburg, or of Silesia, or the minister for indirect taxes?

On ascending the throne Frederick William III named Count Schulenburg-Kehnert controller general of finances. But this new office was attached to an older one, the Superior Audit Chamber, and was merely its extension, so it could not possibly lead to anything other than petty interference without substantial achievement.

The new code of laws, which first saw the light of day under Frederick William II, was considered beyond improvement, because it was the first and only one in Europe to be organized systematically. Being convinced of its excellence, people could only think of making it more complete by adding new laws rather than reviewing it continually, and preparing a thorough revision. It was deemed sufficient for an independent law commission to function simply as a committee of experts. No one recognized that this commission required the leadership of an outstanding mind, someone capable of being the nation's lawgiver, and so the committee churned out statutes like factory goods made to order. Every incidental need brought forth a new law.

To an even greater extent than the bureaucracy and the legal system, however, Prussia's military institutions had declined into empty formality. All strength had gone out of those exhausted muscles. We shall have to discuss this more fully later on.

The government itself, that is, the direction of the machinery of state, was a so-called cabinet government.[1] It originated mainly with Frederick the

---

[1] "Cabinet government" [*Kabinetts-Regierung*] refers to government from the private cabinet

Great. His father had still worked directly with his ministers, but Frederick the Great had little contact with them, since, being an autocrat in the fullest sense of the word, he scarcely wanted their counsel. Usually he informed them of his decision in writing. But the decision was his own and expressed in a few words; for this purpose he had no need of advice—a mere clerk sufficed. Consequently there was no mention of cabinet councilors during his reign.

Under a strong and enterprising prince, cabinet government is unquestionably the strongest, most efficient, and most vigorous form of administration. For that reason, and because it had appealed to Frederick the Great, it was supposed that the form itself was sufficient to secure all these advantages.

But the state had almost doubled in size, the variety and complexity of social conditions and needs had greatly increased, and not everyone could rule like Frederick the Great. His successors, Frederick William II and Frederick William III, believed that if they decided all matters large and small themselves, by means of cabinet orders in the manner of their great predecessor, they personally governed the state with strength and justice. Here, too, the form was mistaken for substance.

Frederick William III, from youth distinguished by serious and firm principles, had too little trust in his own abilities and the abilities of others, was too full of that cold, Nordic sense of doubt that undermines the spirit of enterprise, opposes enthusiasm, and inhibits every kind of creativity. His invincible tendency to doubt everything points his accurate intelligence and powers of observation narrowly toward human weaknesses and imperfections, which he soon perceives and which intensify his lack of trust almost into a contempt of mankind. For a personality such as the king's, cabinet government is the least desirable. The ministers are not trusted, without power, without real responsibility; they cannot dare to come forward with a significant new idea or a comprehensive plan; they merely try to keep things limping along in the accustomed way and hold on to their offices. The three cabinet councilors, for the interior, foreign affairs, and military affairs (the so-called expediting general adjutant), are not suited to take the place of ministers; they lack the necessary power, prestige, and confidence. They are half secretaries, half advisors to the king but certainly not the recognized representatives and leaders of the bureaucracy, which must be led.

---

of the king, and in this context conveys almost the opposite sense from that of "ministerial government," with which it would normally be synonymous in English. It is this distinction that concerns Clausewitz here. Prussian "cabinet councilors" were not administrators or executive officers, but personal advisors and secretaries to the king. They served alongside a mixed system of provincial and departmental ministers who were responsible for carrying out the king's wishes, which may or may not have been informed by the advice of his cabinet councilors. A collective executive comprising these various individuals did not exist.

Despite the best intentions, their influence is never uniform because it has no basis in law. At times they decide despotically, without full knowledge of the issue at stake; at other times they act as if they were merely mechanical spokesmen for the king; and by the same token the ministers, for their part, are alternately too proud and too humble toward them. The cabinet councilors are even less well placed than the ministers to advance significant ideas, since they must immediately entrust their implementation to others. The worst aspect of cabinet government is that it makes it as easy for the prince to do nothing as the prime ministerial system does, but without possessing the advantages of the latter form. To a greater or lesser extent, a prime minister takes the place of the prince, and can do as well or as badly as the prince himself; but at least the government will never lack a chief in whose hands everything is united, and who can guide the helm as circumstances demand.

To be sure, a cabinet government keeps the prince very busy, and at first glance the claim that it leads to idleness seems paradoxical; but what great things can this external, superficial activity achieve if there is no creative genius at work and if the prince is not a true autocrat?

A prince working in concert with his ministers must make himself felt, because it is not a matter of simply saying Yes or No, as it is in his cabinet, but rather of leading a group of men, often with conflicting opinions, toward a common goal. To do this he must be decisive and clear in his own mind, he must focus on the main issue, he must be firm in his convictions, and be prepared for objections. Such are the natural requirements for this type of government, and whenever a prince possesses them to any extent the system will stimulate and concentrate them and raise him to a higher level of activity and independence. It is very different in a royal cabinet, where all activity dissolves into questions, answers, and isolated decisions. The decisions could emanate just as easily from the councilor as from the prince himself, who, if he is inclined by lack of energy or self-confidence to leave these matters to others, will soon cease to rule. He will become a kind of supervisor of the government, but will not run it himself; he will work much with his councilors, and appear industrious; he will sign his name often, and appear effective; and yet he may well be doing little or nothing. Frederick William III is distinguished by a quick, practical mind, great acuity, and also by a strong sense of seriousness and duty. It is hard to imagine that such a king, surrounded by a well-chosen circle of ministers, should not have achieved independence, a clear understanding of his state's position, and of the means available to guard against approaching danger, or to meet it with dignity. But for a cabinet government the king had the worst possible quality: lack of confidence in his own abilities, which soon led to a fruitless negativism in both domestic and foreign affairs. Prussia's outdated cabinet regime thus contributed its full share to the state's decline into a morass of meaningless red tape, and to the complete vitiation of her excellent king's nobler qualities.

Only in one respect did this cabinet government display a consistent over-all sense of direction, namely, in a certain liberalism. To the minds of the various councilors who succeeded each other in the area of internal affairs, the chief responsibility of their office seemed to be the promotion of freedom and enlightenment, in the sense in which the words were understood at that time. They saw themselves as popular tribunes of a sort, placed beside the throne to keep a tight rein on the aristocratic sentiments of the noble minis-ters and to enable the government to act in accord with the spirit of the age. This role was not difficult for them since, on the one hand, they did not belong to great families themselves and so were free of inborn aristocratic sympathies; rather, they expected that democratization and enlightenment would bring only advantages and nothing detrimental. On the other hand, they believed that to swim with the current was the best way to escape from its pressures. That is how they hoped to weather the storm that had been rising in Paris since 1789.

It is, of course, rather unusual—though not unknown in history—that an absolute king who rules a country subject to feudal institutions is influenced by democratic tendencies; the Prussian government in particular had dis-played this characteristic since the days of the Great Elector. Here more than anywhere commoners of modest birth, and foreigners without property or connections in the country, were called to become the king's closest advisors and ministers; and it cannot be denied that this condition greatly weakened the dominance of the native nobility, which always develops in a feudal so-ciety, and that it prevented the nobility from consolidating its power later on. But this liberalism of the Prussian crown, whether it be regarded as logical or illogical, was in fact only a superficial gilding, a courtly gesture toward the spirit of the times, confined to unimportant matters. The essential institu-tions of the state were not changed, nor was anything done to prepare them for future reform; at bottom, this democratic posturing produced nothing ex-cept a petty pride and determination on the part of the middle classes, partic-ularly the middle-class bureaucrats, not to concede the nobility even an inch of official status above themselves.

I have already said that the army, more than any other institution, had succumbed to the lassitude of tradition and detail. It is difficult to know where to begin to describe the pervasive rottenness of this structure. Since the days of the Great Elector, Prussia had devoted herself preeminently to the craft of arms and had played a military role out of proportion to her size and strength. This could only have been brought about by highly unusual mili-tary institutions. The most important of these, which survives to the present day, is the obligation of the subject, stronger than in other countries, to perform military service. In the past it took the form of the canton system. The Prussian canton regulations were based on the principle of compulsory military service. To be sure, the universality of this duty was limited by a great many legal exceptions and exemptions, and by as many more extralegal ones, stemming from custom and abuse. But for those days the concept represented a source of unusual strength, and since the Silesian wars Prussia was rightly considered the European state with the best military institutions. The unusually large force of native subjects was augmented by a program of foreign recruitment pushed to extremes. Weapons, equipment, pay, and uniforms were attended to with the greatest diligence, a spirit of pedantic order and firm discipline ruled the whole, and thus it became possible for this second-class power not only to raise itself to first-class status in military affairs, but to be preeminent in them until the wars of the Revolution.

During the Middle Ages it was in the nature of things that military power rested in the hands of the nobility and aristocracy; in later centuries it became the property of the princes, based on their new systems of finance and administration; more recently it has come to express the total strength of the nation. We can see at a glance that in the first two periods the armed forces were subject to entirely different limitations and requirements than in the last. Under Frederick the Great the Prussian army was a typical princely force, raised to the highest level of excellence. Today it seems perfectly natural that such a force would inevitably be defeated by the energies released in a *revolutionary war*. But it is also true that in 1792 the Prussian army no longer was what it had been under Frederick the Great. Its generals and commanding officers had not grown gray in arms, but old and soft in peace; military experience had mostly faded, Frederick's spirit no longer coursed through the whole; the old budget was retained unchanged despite rising prices in all areas, and the army's equipment declined into useless decrepitude. In the Berlin armory the artillery equipment was stored with such care that every last rope and nail was at hand; but ropes and nails were equally useless. The soldier's weapon was kept scrupulously clean, barrels were painstakingly polished with the ramrod, stocks varnished every year; but the muskets were the worst in Europe. The soldier was never in arrears in pay and clothing; but the pay was not sufficient to satisfy his hunger, the clothes did not cover his nakedness. Of course, it calls for great skill to push a military establishment far above the level ordinarily appropriate to the resources of the state, and to keep it at that level of strength and preparedness during a half-century of peace. Mere adherence to precisely fixed budgets, endless penny-pinching and cheese-paring will not do.

It takes a good mechanic to judge the efficiency of a complex machine while it is at rest. It is not enough to check that all parts are there; the condition of each must be tested. And what machine equals a military force in

37

the complexity of its construction? The spirit that watched over the Prussian army was not suited to prevent its slow, unnoticed decay.

King Frederick William II busied himself with the army because it was the traditional thing to do, but took no personal interest in it. Frederick William III was a young man, did not know war, and had not yet turned his attention to the institutions of other states, because his education had failed to develop his spirit of independence and curiosity. Naturally he lacked self-confidence. In his cabinet, all matters pertaining to the army were in the charge of a military councilor, called the expediting general adjutant, since all reports, proposals, orders, and so forth passed through his hands. It is true that the so-called Superior War Council, which was responsible for all equipment and supplies, included several very senior figures (the duke of Brunswick as its chief, and Field Marshal von Möllendorff as its vice-president), but these were only courtesy appointments and without substance. The War Council also included a minister, the so-called minister of war; but in 1806 he headed only one department, the quartermaster branch, and not the whole service. Thus, although the War Council appeared to act as if it were a true ministry, its real position was that of an office responsible to the expediting general adjutant. Moreover, it consisted only of worn-out old men, who in youth were distinguished from their comrades by the ability to read and write, and in maturity by their decrepitude. Nothing could be expected from such an organization except pedantic routine.

The expediting general adjutant was usually chosen from that group of officers who were not only familiar with the ways and details of the service, but also possessed skill with the pen, a knowledge of French, and a little social sophistication and polish. Significant practical experience, a broad view of affairs, talent, and originality could not come into it, since men of that kind rarely possessed the other qualifications. Thus the very character of the men appointed to this position insured that nothing substantial, innovative, or stimulating could be expected of them. The character of their position compounded the problem. They exercised continuous influence over the military machine, but it was entirely negative, like that of a pendulum on a clock. A great deal of power is necessary to bring about important changes, because innovations always give offense and meet resistance; but the general adjutants possessed no power at all.

They would have had to win the king's complete confidence for their plans and then carry them through on his authority. But in such matters the king regarded the professional experts as his natural advisors, that is, the very men against whom his power was to be used, men so completely caught up in the spirit of routine that they were bound to resist change. Besides, it takes more than ordinary ambition, as the French say, to embark on difficult undertakings. As a rule this ambition is roused only by the prospect of success and the satisfaction that comes with it. Projects that mean nothing but added responsibility, whose success brings neither honor nor glory and whose failure means dismissal, certainly will not call forth acumen, ingenuity, and zeal. Under a monarch who on principle trusted the judgment of other men rather than his own, this factor more than any other made cabinet government an obstacle to substantial, fundamental innovations. Everything was tied up in endless red tape, and the insistent observance of external forms caused people to lose sight of what really mattered.

Here, then, was the main source of the decay. Had the minister of war been given appropriate authority, had a little effort been made to find an outstanding man for this post, he might well have won the king's confidence and convinced him that his aims were right. Genuine responsibility on the one hand and security of place on the other would have allowed him to strengthen the monarch's will. The sickness would have been discovered, and with it the cure. It would have become apparent that the furlough system, although indispensable at the time, contained a highly destructive germ: an invincible love of peace, which needed to be counteracted in some way. As it was, every man in the army except subalterns lost half his income when war was declared,[2] with no expectation of gaining anything in return. It would have become apparent that the prevailing system of foreign recruitment worked well in a successful war but was not suited to defending the Thermopylae Pass against the Persians. It would have become apparent that a state contemplating a war to the finish needed great stores of weapons to make up great losses, and that for an army of 230,000 men a factory turning out no more than ten thousand muskets annually was as good as no factory at all. And, knowing that the old guns were useless, one would not have spread the acquisition of new ones over a period of thirty years at a time when one could not count on thirty days of peace.

I cannot expand on all the faults of our military organization in those last years, faults that arose in part because the system no longer suited the changed times but, having been moved off its foundation, was full of cracks and gaps, in part because the system itself was rusted and decayed. I must be content merely to mention the faults, and will summarize them here once more:

The senior commanders were without spirit; the higher ranks down to staff captain as a group were old and decrepit. Many of the soldiers were also too old. A military day-laborer who has already borne the cares of life for forty or fifty years (it required twenty-five to thirty years of service before one could

---

[2] Clausewitz refers to the financial losses suffered by "owners of companies," officers of the rank of captain and above, who in peacetime benefited from surpluses of the company budget; and also to losses by the native rank and file, who, unlike foreigners in the ranks, were furloughed for much of the year during peacetime and earned money in civilian occupations.

be declared exempt) brings only exhausted powers of mind and body to the field. His equipment was the worst in Europe; the artillery, excepting the gun barrels themselves, was no better. The soldier's food and clothing were beneath contempt, his field equipment was designed for a former type of war, consequently too cumbersome for modern needs. The spirit of the army was unwarlike to the highest degree, its training was merely one-sided, mired in Prussian conceits, without interest in events elsewhere, unappreciative of the latest developments in war. Maneuvers were inappropriate, in their endless, sterile imitation of the old and obsolete. Add to this a rare arrogance, which lulled to sleep even natural uneasiness and misgivings.

Even after scrupulously searching his conscience the author can delete nothing from this description. He grew up in the Prussian army. His father was an officer in the Seven Years' War, filled with the prejudices of his class. In his parents' house he saw almost no one but officers, and not the best educated and most versatile at that. In his twelfth year he became a soldier himself and served in the campaigns against France in 1793 and 1794; throughout the first part of his career, until 1800, he was suckled on no other opinions than those prevailing in the service: that the Prussian army and its methods were of surpassing excellence. In short, from the beginning, *national* feeling and even *caste* sentiment were as pronounced and firmly rooted in the author as the lessons of life can make them. Further, the author must say that he always fared better in the Prussian army than he deserved. Under these circumstances his judgment should surely not be suspected of deriving from prejudice, discontent, bitterness, etc. The author was a Prussian officer in every sense of the word, and if he soon came to think differently about Prussia's military institutions than most of his comrades, this was simply the result of reflection. Despite his natural partiality toward his fatherland and his class, a great many things seemed imperfect to him. Later, from 1806 on, his acquaintance with people who had seen more of the world opened the author's eyes still further to the weakness of his country's military system. Even so, he has retained a great fondness for it; but the greater and more deeply rooted this fondness was, the more he felt himself driven to uncover its weaknesses without reservation, the more he recognized the need for a revivifying, creative spirit, for a strong hand to renovate the building before it collapsed. In his youth the author saw war, without understanding it, to be sure, but still he retained an overall impression of it. How then would it have been possible, with a little reflection, not to realize that the autumn maneuvers in Potsdam and Berlin were totally unlike the war we had fought? It was especially painful for the author to recognize that these mock battles, arranged long in advance, thoroughly discussed and prescribed in every detail, were carried out by the most distinguished men of the army—men like Möllendorff and Rüchel—with an all-absorbing seriousness and intensity that bordered on weakness.

The author mentions this to show how his doubts were aroused, his faith shaken, and how the spirit of independent judgment awakened in him.

Accordingly the reader may decide how much trust to place in that judgment.

Our observations on the army have taken us far from the Prussian state as a whole; we must return to it briefly in order not to be misunderstood.

The decay of which we have spoken was primarily a decay of the machinery of government, not of social conditions as such. The people undoubtedly felt a sense of well-being in their daily lives. Trade and science flourished, a mild, liberal government allowed considerable freedom to the individual, and the nation progressed steadily toward greater prosperity.

If progress was not as rapid as would have been possible under a more enlightened social system, this shortcoming was hardly felt: only a few recognized it. Under the circumstances serious discontent could scarcely exist in Prussia, and in fact if one excludes the Polish provinces it was not to be found. The bleak seriousness of the north German temperament might often complain of hard times, and quibbling political theorists might scoff at existing institutions; but the prevailing attachment of the people to the state, and even more to the ruling house, was nevertheless unmistakable. If Prussia could have continued to vegetate in peace, her defects would never have been noticed.

If, however, a great society is not merely to live quietly by itself, but act as a state in the international arena, two factors that mean little in ordinary peaceful existence must be given great weight.

The first is the effectiveness of the machinery of government, by which the masses become as one. The second is the spirit of the people, which gives life and strength to that unity.

As we have already shown in some detail, the machinery of government was desiccated, decrepit, and entirely unsuited to the times and the needs of the moment; inevitably the spirit of the people became alienated from great issues and unaccustomed to great exertion. A conventional monarchy, in which the citizen's political energy is not awakened by participation in public affairs, needs a war from time to time; or at least the government must adopt a martial attitude, move forcefully, conduct itself honorably and effectively, must be feared, respected, and relied upon by its allies. Only thus can the citizen's pride and self-esteem be flattered. Neither of these means was available to the Prussian people. The campaigns of 1778, 1787, 1792, 1793, and 1794, on the Rhine and in Poland, were not of a kind to make the army, and with it the people, warlike. They only weakened the citizen's confidence in the arms of their ruler and gave free reign to the fault-finding of the political philosophers. Prussian policy after the Peace of Basel was the exact opposite of what it should have been if one wished to prepare the people for a vigorous struggle: eyes always averted from danger, constant praise for peace and neutrality. Given the character and institutions of the army, nothing more was needed to make both army and people fainthearted and pacific.

If one now asks what effect a different system of government might have had, and whether it might have helped avert the catastrophe that befell Prussia in 1806, I would reply as follows:

Major changes in the laws and the organization of government could hardly be expected in such a brief and critical period. In fact, great changes would have risked creating dissatisfaction at home, which could not have been resolved in time, and which would have proved dangerous when the support of all segments and classes of the population was essential.

But had the king chosen a number of trained, experienced, and energetic men for his ministers, to consult them on the affairs of the state and the dangers confronting it, it would have been seen that these dangers could not be met by lackadaisically contemplating the outside world and sauntering along quietly at home. Measures would have been taken to prepare the army for modern war and for the conflict that was approaching, and to base the army and the conduct of the war not on a few tons of gold in the treasury, but on the resources of the entire nation. Preparations would have been made for extraordinary expedients and exertions; the spirit of the people would have been guided in this direction; men of character and resolution would have been placed in the most important administrative posts; in short, every effort would have been made to show the world a new Sparta. In foreign affairs, the government would have recognized the necessity of making common cause with other powers to restrain France, or—if one preferred the dangerous strategy of delaying a decision to the last moment—of finding in the nation's inner strength the courage to act with dignity, to speak firmly and honestly. It would not have been reduced to deceiving itself and the people with worthless sophistry, and it would not have lost the respect of the courts of Europe and public opinion everywhere. In the end, whatever the outcome of the *unavoidable* struggle might have been, we would have *existed with honor, or succumbed with honor.*

CHAPTER 2. CHARACTERIZATIONS OF THE LEADING PERSONALITIES

The last years of the Seven Years' War, when nothing seemed to go quite right for him anymore, had to some extent transformed DUKE KARL OF BRUNSWICK from a hero to a shrewd, clever man of the world. He was intelligent, well educated, and experienced in war, but had no trace of boldness and could not rise proudly above adversity. His adroitness would have made him the ideal man to steer successfully around difficult obstacles, had he not lacked the courage to grasp the helm. As it was, his reputation collapsed and, like others, he became absorbed by petty intrigues and still pettier military exercises.

It was said that Frederick William III was not fond of the duke; but given the king's frank desire to do the right thing and the duke's reputation as a general and statesman, this would not have prevented the duke from rising to head the entire state if he had only possessed the necessary ambition, or rather courage. He was the most distinguished figure in the Prussian army, its most senior field marshal, well informed about European affairs, familiar at every court, renowned as a wise administrator of his own small state, related to the Prussian ruling house by birth and marriage—indeed, both the nephew and protégé of Frederick the Great. His principality was surrounded by Prussian territory—what better claims to the first role in the state could there have been than those that were combined so exceptionally in the person and position of this man? Of course, it might be supposed that precisely the superabundance of his claims kept him from the highest office, since a young king might fear that little would be left for himself if he turned the reins over to such a man. But that Frederick William harbored no very great envy is shown by the role later played by Prince Hardenberg; nor was the duke of Brunswick the man to inspire these misgivings. I am convinced that it would have been within the duke's power to become Frederick William's first minister, up to a point even against the young king's wishes, for he lacked neither the cleverness nor the adroitness needed to do so. What he did lack was the necessary courage. He was far too intelligent to ignore the difficulties that were rising up on all sides. He did not feel equal to them, and rather than arrogantly pretend to be capable of anything and dwell on the failings of those who were overwhelmed by events—as unintelligent and narrow-minded people did, and still do—he may well have thanked God that he was not called upon to be more active than he was.

The failure of his campaign in France in 1792 and his inconclusive campaign the following year further reduced his self-confidence; he was neither inclined to grasp the helm nor even to put himself forward in the councils of government.

Because he was not deeply involved in the state's principal affairs, the innate shrewdness of his character gradually turned to pettiness. He assumed the manners and habits of an obliging courtier to the point of caricature. His facile manner in small things and excessive pliability deprived him of mastery over men and circumstances, so that under the prevailing conditions he could no longer lead the army successfully. As a soldier he still would have

43

been well suited to the task. He had kept up to date more than anyone else in the Prussian army and understood the new ways of warfare well enough to adopt them himself. Much practice in the leadership of troops, experience of war, personal courage, a lively mind, calmness in the face of danger—these were qualities that, combined with his natural adroitness, would ordinarily have made him an excellent leader. But the command of an entire army requires self-confidence and complete authority; the former he denied himself, the latter he was unable to wrest from other men.

In 1806 the king placed him in charge of operations, but in name only. Not only did the king accompany the army himself, which is always a hindrance for a commanding general, but he was joined by Field Marshal Möllendorff, General Zastrow, and Colonel Phull, all men who [at the time] were not in his entourage, but only now were called to it. The king thus showed that he felt he needed their advice. The duke was not the man to overshadow these superfluous notables. Prince Hohenlohe was given command of half the army—under the supreme command of the duke, to be sure, but obviously because it seemed impossible to satisfy his ambition with anything less. This unusual division of the army into two forces within a single theater of operations was itself a major calamity, which could only erode an already weak chain of command and endanger the army's unity of action. The error was grave enough but made even worse by the restless spirit and undisciplined mind of Colonel Massenbach, who took to the field as Prince Hohenlohe's quartermaster general.

General Rüchel, long a firm enemy of the duke, commanded a small third army; and in view of his status he was also inclined to assume a degree of independence.

In short, the duke of Brunswick assumed supreme command without being at the peak of reputation and authority. His determination was paralyzed by endless concessions and compromised by disunity; what remained was rendered ineffective by people questioning his orders.

Having allowed his spirit to be overwhelmed by these circumstances, he was fortunate enough, despite mistakes and confusion of every kind, to arrive on the battlefield of Auerstädt at the head of a force of 50,000 men, facing a French corps of 25,000. His seasoned military mind might now have acted undisturbed in its own element; but soon after the battle began he was shot through the eyes, the wound ending his life in a manner that was as painful as it was tragic.

FIELD MARSHAL MÖLLENDORFF. On the surface he had not, like the duke of Brunswick, adopted an ingratiating, courtly manner, but rather a solemn, martial demeanor, which went well with his tall, strong figure and the dignity that comes from eighty years of undiminished vigor. His whole appearance was imposing and inspired confidence. In reality he was not one whit less a courtier than the duke; and being very much the duke's inferior in intelligence, knowledge, and experience, his actions and opinions counted for nothing in the government.

As a field-grade officer in the guards during the Seven Years' War he had distinguished himself, mainly, it seems, by great courage and raw determination. With these warlike qualities and somewhat rough manners, he emerged from the war a true son of Mars. But thirty-one years of peace, from 1763 to 1794, when he was given command of the army on the Rhine, together with a completely uneducated mind, had gradually sapped his powers, and years of court life had undermined his natural strength of character.

He commanded an army only once, during the campaign of 1794, which he waged according to the same scientific principles of mountain warfare that had been in fashion for some time, and that he later repeatedly criticized—a sure sign that he allowed himself to be led by others and was not equal to his task.

And so this man, by nature well suited for war, who might have won much glory in a time of great events, sank to the level of a serviceable bit player in military pageants.

GENERAL RÜCHEL. An ebullient mind without intellectual discipline; a character as vehement as nitric acid; a most superficial education pieced together from phrases and bits of ideas; ambition that would have blazed forth like fire had it not evaporated in vanity; bold and confident—and at the same time exceptionally brave in the face of the enemy, an open personality capable of some enthusiasm—these were his characteristics, which went together well with a small, compact, lively figure, curly, prematurely white hair, a high forehead, flashing eyes, a commanding tone, decisive bearing, and some martial posturing.

Frederick the Great found this determined and fiery young officer promising and singled him out during the last years of his life. This pushed young Rüchel forward. Frederick the Great was his every third word. The spirit that the old king raised to dominance after the Seven Years' War and personally infused into the army in Potsdam—a certain sternness and precision, which occasionally picks on an insignificant detail to show that nothing is being overlooked, a certain thunder-and-lightning military rhetoric—all this was exaggerated almost to the point of caricature in Rüchel. He was not without superficial learning, read whatever worthwhile books were published, had himself appointed head of the cadet corps, and joined a learned military society founded by Scharnhorst; his writings were full of imagination and energetic rhetoric. But he lacked the capacity for solid, orderly thought to such an extent that his writings were nearly always absurd. Nor had he seriously followed the changes in the art of war; he was convinced that, with courage and determination, Prussian troops employing Frederician tactics could over-

45

run everything that had emerged from the unsoldierly French Revolution. But of course he understood Frederician tactics to be nothing more than those qualities cultivated in drills, reviews, and autumn maneuvers, if inspired—and this was unquestionably the main point—by fierce determination. General Rüchel might have been termed a concentrated acid of pure Prussianism. As inspector of the guards and governor of Potsdam, he liked to make himself seem as important as possible; but, even if he meddled from time to time in matters of war and peace, he did not seek a truly significant position. Having been singled out as a young man by Frederick the Great, he was commonly regarded as the old king's evangelist and was rapidly promoted. In the Rhine campaigns, at an unusually early age, he now and then was given an independent command, in which he distinguished himself through youthful energy and enterprise. Had he possessed a more straightforward character, he could have made a useful general; he would never have been suited for a senior position, for supreme command in war.

GENERAL VON ZASTROW. He had served as the king's expediting general adjutant for many years and was considered exceptionally shrewd, prudent, and knowledgeable, which was why the king did not want to do without his counsel.

He was indeed shrewd and prudent to a high degree, but far from intelligent, and his knowledge was limited to what he had picked up from incidental reading and in his bureaucratic career, that is, commonplace ideas based on commonplace experiences; he had no knowledge of foreign developments. His personality was considered neither pleasant nor direct.

COLONEL VON KLEIST. The future Field Marshal Kleist von Nollendorf was at that time the king's expediting general adjutant, and so in a sense secretary of state for war. He was a sensitive, very upright man whose views extended somewhat beyond the petty confines of service pedantry, and possessed an excellent civilian education and great personal dignity. Neither his understanding nor his knowledge was comprehensive, and his practical experience rose only slightly above the average.

In short, he was just competent to fill his post conscientiously and to the best of his ability, but without accomplishing much of anything. This was not enough for a time like 1806. Consequently, he saw everything collapse without any inkling that he himself might be partly to blame, and without the least idea, before the catastrophe was complete, of how matters might be improved somewhat. An acquaintance of the author learned that a royal order granting an officer's request to marry reached Silesia from Stettin. At the time, the king stopped briefly in Stettin while hurrying to East Prussia, to assemble whatever forces remained for further resistance, and must have been occupied with other things. But the essence of our administration in those days was always to do the old things in the old way, to be precise and punctual; while beyond the accustomed rounds a complete vacuum reigned.

PRINCE HOHENLOHE.   He has become even better known for the capitulation of Prenzlau than for the defeat at Jena; but it would be a great mistake to conclude that he lacked courage or a sense of honor.

Prince Hohenlohe was a very amiable, bright, and enterprising man whose most outstanding quality was ambition. Unfortunately, this was supported only by enthusiasm and natural courage, not by outstanding intelligence. He had read diligently, but without achieving any intellectual independence. Moreover, he was almost seventy years old,[3] and his natural virtues, though not yet extinguished, were somewhat diminished. In the Rhine campaign he had commanded with distinction, in part because as a prince he had achieved high rank relatively young, in part because his personality was well suited to war.

But his education had been confined to the parade ground, and to a man of limited understanding this could only result in a conviction that battalions smartly advancing in line and firing volleys by sections would defeat all comers.

The notorious Massenbach had already served under him as a general staff officer on the Rhine; they had kept in touch ever since, and in 1806 Massenbach became his chief of staff, dragging him down into a whirlpool of confused ideas and feelings.

Hohenlohe was suited to carry out the orders of others. But Massenbach persuaded him that they were the two chief supports of the monarchy and ought to play leading roles, and inflamed his ambition until he was unwilling to cooperate with others. Hohenlohe was just the man to fight his way out of Prenzlau; but Massenbach overwhelmed him with his confused theories, and ensnared him in his own intellectual bankruptcy.

That he should have been beaten at Jena was surely not surprising. Even the best general would have fared no better: he had 33,000 men and faced Bonaparte at the head of 60,000. But that he capitulated at Prenzlau was due only to his seventy years, which had left him unequal to such cares and exertions, and, as we have said, to the intellectual bankruptcy of the man on whom he depended far too much.[4]

PRINCE LOUIS OF PRUSSIA.   He was the Prussian Alcibiades. A somewhat disorderly life had prevented him from maturing fully. As though he were the first-born son of Mars, he possessed huge gifts of courage, daring, determination; but as lords of the manor, proud of their wealth, usually neglect

---

[3] In 1806 Hohenlohe was actually in his sixty-first year.

[4] Hohenlohe surrendered the fortress of Prenzlau to a smaller French force without firing a shot, in part because Massenbach encouraged him to accept a false French claim that he was outnumbered and surrounded.

other matters, he too had not done enough to educate and develop his mind seriously. The French called him *un crâne* [a skull]. If they meant by this that he was empty- and hot-headed, they misjudged him badly. His courage was not a brutal indifference toward life but true longing for greatness—genuine heroism. He loved life and enjoyed it only too much, but at the same time *danger* was a *necessity* for him. It had accompanied him since childhood. If he could not find danger in war, he searched for it on the hunt, in raging streams, on wild horses, etc. He was extremely clever, with refined manners, full of wit, widely read, talented in many fields, among them music, for on the piano he might rank as a virtuoso.

He was some thirty years old, tall, slim, and well built, with fine, noble features, a high forehead, slightly curved nose, small blue eyes with a bold look to them, a ruddy complexion, and curly blond hair. His dignified bearing, firm stride, and a way of carrying his head and chest suggested just that measure of pride and confidence that was appropriate to a prince and an audacious soldier.

Unbridled enjoyment of life had prematurely aged his fine features, but they showed no trace of coarse sensuality. His expression was not that of a well-born libertine, as one might have supposed; too many great ideas stirred in him, and the inner need for greatness and glory shone in his face.

With such exceptional qualities, and belonging to the highest circles, he would inevitably have become a great commander had he matured in the course of a long war, or had a more serious, less playful temperament enabled him in peacetime to study thoroughly and reflect on the major issues of the day. Unlike most of the men we must describe here, the prince had not remained ignorant of recent military and administrative innovations; he did not cling blindly to the conviction that the Prussian realm must inevitably rise above all others, and that nothing could withstand Prussian tactics. He was genuinely interested in contemporary events; new ideas and developments attracted him and raced through his head. He scoffed at the pettiness and pedantry that pretended to greatness, and sought the company of the best minds in every field; but—he could not give an hour to serious, calm, constructive thought, and as a result never had substantial ideas of his own, never any firm conviction that would lead to action. The company of outstanding intellects did him more harm than good, because he skimmed their ideas off the surface and nourished his mind on them, without ever producing an idea of his own. His overweening courage gave him a false sense of security. His conception of war was therefore no clearer than his conception of anything else. The methods of modern war remained foreign to him; and at Saalfeld, when the moment for action had come, he could think of nothing better than the drill he had learned on the parade grounds of Berlin, Potsdam, and Magdeburg. As might be expected, he overestimated what *his own* courage could achieve and asked for the impossible. He fell victim to the iron force of circumstances because he tried to resist not with his head, but only with his heart. He met death because he clung to the battlefield like Talbot to his shield—and that is the last, irrefutable proof of his just claim to fame and greatness.[5]

In the revolutionary wars Prince Louis, although barely twenty years old, was already a general and had fought with distinction at the head of a brigade. If he did not accomplish more at that time it was only because of the cautious system, à la Daun and Lacy,[6] by which the war was waged and the Philistine manner in which everything else was managed. If one had understood how to exploit the unusual abilities of this young lion, the state would even then have profited greatly, the three years that the war lasted would have laid a sound foundation for the prince's future.

Young and handsome, a general and prince, nephew of Frederick the Great, distinguished by audacity and courage and a high-spirited enjoyment of life, he was soon idolized by the soldiers and the younger officers—but the old, cautious generals in their long waistcoats shook their heads doubtfully over such a young gentleman, and judged that, until his exuberant gifts were properly subordinated to the rules and garrison routine of the service, they were of no use. In quarters in Frankfurt the prince tried to escape the military pedantry in which they had tried to ensnare him and found an outlet for his energies at the gambling table and in the pleasures of society.

After the war he served as lieutenant general with his regiment in Magdeburg, without any other command or responsibilities. By rights he was entitled to the post of an inspector of infantry, and he could usefully have headed a cavalry inspectorate because he was one of the most daring horsemen in the kingdom. But that would have contradicted the spirit in which the army was run. A somewhat dissolute and thoughtless young prince could not be trusted with anything, not even the *indirect* responsibility an inspector general bears toward the regiments in his inspection. In time of war, of course, he had been entrusted with a brigade, that is, with the lives of thousands of men; but that was understood to mean little more than that he faithfully transmitted his commander's orders to the lower echelons. To make him into

[5] At the battle of Saalfeld, which preceded Jena and Auerstädt by four days, Louis led the Prussian advance guard, about 8,000 men, against a French force several times as large. The battle ended with a gallant but futile charge in which the prince was killed. The Talbot to whom Clausewitz refers is John Talbot, Earl of Shrewsbury, the chief English commander during the last phase of the Hundred Years' War. Talbot's rashness led to a major English defeat at Patay (1429).

[6] Field Marshals Count Leopold von Daun and Count Franz Moritz von Lacy were, respectively, commander and chief of staff of the main Austrian army during much of the Seven Years' War. In its aftermath they led the reform of Austria's armed forces in line with Prussian principles of disciplined fire and close-order drill.

a cavalry commander would have been even more unusual; in short, the Prussian monarchy could find no way to use or occupy such an excellent young prince.

So he continued his gay life, made heavy debts, wasted his energies on nothing but pleasure, did not always keep the best company; but he did not succumb to these forces, kept his head above water, and in spirit remained in nobler regions, always attracted to the great affairs of the state and the fatherland, always longing for glory and honor. Around the turn of the century, when France began to let the other powers feel the weight of her superiority, there were some even in Prussia who recognized that the part Prussia had been playing since the Peace of Basel was neither very honorable nor particularly clever or prudent. This view grew stronger every year and reached its peak in 1805, when Austria declared war on France. Of course, a variety of opinions existed even then; Prince Louis was among those who believed resistance to France was unavoidable and should begin sooner rather than later. His sense of honor as a Prussian prince and nephew of Frederick the Great, his impetuous courage, even his recklessness, inevitably pushed him in this direction.

Calmer, more serious and reflective men held the same opinion, and some for better reasons than he, but that did not prevent them from joining him on this issue, and in a sense he became the head of the party that regarded war with France as essential.

This conviction reached fever pitch in 1805, when the French contemptuously violated Prussian territory in Franconia during their advance on Austria. Prince Louis eagerly embraced the cause, but characteristically without any specific plan of action, and in the end he only made himself a nuisance to the government. The king, in any case, did not especially care for him. His wild way of life was repugnant to the king's seriousness. He suspected the prince of an equally boundless ambition, which naturally will always cause a monarch some concern, and his brilliant qualities appeared insufficiently solid to the king's skeptical mind. The main result of the convergence of views among the most distinguished minds in the capital was a small explosion, insignificant in itself, which nevertheless was unprecedented in Prussian history. It was generally believed that the state's timid policies were entirely the fault of the foreign minister, Haugwitz, and the cabinet councilors Beyme and Lombard. Prince Louis and his political allies therefore decided to persuade the king, by means of a political memoir, to dismiss these men and declare war on France. As always in such a case, they probably counted on their signatures carrying more weight than their arguments in moving the king to change his minister and his policy, if either can be called that. The memoir was written by the famous historian Johannes von Müller, who was well known to Prince Louis, and signed by the king's brothers, Prince Heinrich and Prince Wilhelm; his brother-in-law, the prince of Orange; Prince Louis and his brother, Prince August; General Rüchel (who, incidentally, was not in Berlin but had already joined the army); General Count Schmettau; Minister Baron vom Stein; and the two colonels Phull and Scharnhorst.[7] As could have been foreseen, the king took great exception to this step, dressed down some of the signatories severely, immediately ordered the princes to the army, and left the memoir unanswered. This incident was not made to improve the king's opinion of Prince Louis. The prince joined the army and took command of the vanguard of the forces advancing from Silesia under Prince Hohenlohe.

LIEUTENANT GENERAL COUNT VON SCHMETTAU. He had made a name for himself with an excellent topographical work, the map of Mecklenburg, and even more with a very frank critical history of the campaign of 1778, which, however, incurred the displeasure of Frederick II. This caused him to leave the service. Thereafter he lived in Berlin as a wealthy man and close associate of Frederick's brother, Prince Ferdinand, whose adjutant he had been for many years. Since he was only about sixty years old, which in those days could be regarded as a young age for a Prussian general, and possessed great strength and good health, he eventually grew tired of dignified retirement, as most people would, and asked to return to active service. He was appointed lieutenant general and at the battle of Auerstädt commanded a division, at the head of which he was fatally wounded. He had a somewhat old-fashioned education, and, if as a great critic he had once been a little in advance of the ideas and conventions of his time, he had never changed his views and was now overtaken by the new age, an age he preferred not to notice too closely. But he was a straightforward and resolute man, a calm, firm, decisive personality, who would still have made an excellent soldier.

LIEUTENANT GENERAL VON GEUSAU. He was chief of the General Staff and of the Corps of Engineers, the general inspector of fortifications, and the current head of the Superior War Council. An ancient at seventy, we mention him only because of the position he occupied but failed to fill. He was a small, fat, lively man, an industrious and conscientious worker, not without mental agility, and well schooled in the old ways; but he was completely incapable of a large or creative idea, overwhelmed by paperwork, and stubborn and irascible.

The General Staff was divided into three sections, responsible for three theaters of war: the eastern theater, Prussia; the central theater, Silesia and Poland; and the western theater, Westphalia. The sections were headed by three colonels, Phull, Massenbach, and Scharnhorst, as lieutenant quartermasters general. The business of these three sections consisted in the training

---

[7] Contrary to Clausewitz's belief, Scharnhorst did not sign the document.

and education of the officers assigned to them, the study of their respective theaters of war, and the development of operational concepts appropriate to them. This last function was entirely illusory, since no concepts were developed or adopted. Each of the three colonels went about his task in his own way. Phull developed a feeble and one-sided system of supply depot radii, within which operations were supposed to take place. Massenbach put great weight on the so-called higher theory of terrain, that is, an amalgam of tactics, strategy, and geology—precisely the same miserable material on which the campaigns of 1793–94 were based. Scharnhorst had his officers study the history of earlier campaigns conducted in the area.

Old Geusau took little notice of all this staff work. Although superficially on good terms with the three colonels, he did not trust them and considered all of them hostile to his authority. His effectiveness as chief of the General Staff was therefore nil.

As chief of the Corps of Engineers and inspector of fortifications, Geusau performed the usual administrative tasks, but took none of the exceptional measures that the times and circumstances demanded. The senior engineer officers and the fortress commanders were as decrepit as most of their fortresses. Magdeburg and Stettin were hardly considered fortifications at all, since they were partly in ruins and, according to conventional wisdom, too large to be defended; the Silesian fortresses were not armed until the summer of 1806, and Erfurt was entirely ignored. Subsequent events are proof enough of how poorly this department was provided for. A conscientious but mediocre administration might have kept things limping along as usual in peacetime; but it could not meet the exceptional challenges of the coming catastrophe.

It was his position as head of the Superior War Council that occupied General Geusau the most. He had to mobilize and demobilize the army four or five times—that is, place it on a war footing, then return it to a peacetime footing—and there was no end to calculating, reviewing, and criticizing! This mountain of paper swallowed up the last traces of intelligence of the quartermaster general and de facto minister of war.

As has been mentioned, the three colonels—Phull, Massenbach, and Scharnhorst—were the heads of the General Staff. All were men in their forties,[8] that is, in full possession of their mature powers. All three were distinguished from the rest of the officer corps by virtue of their education, and even more by their intellectual originality. All three were highly regarded, but each had his own school and faction, as suited his individual ideas and attitudes. Outwardly they were on fairly good terms and did not actually hate each other or harbor petty jealousies against one another. But one could not

[8] Scharnhorst was already fifty.

have found three men more dissimilar in their ideas, education, character, and outlook anywhere in the kingdom. It followed that they could not pursue a common course, and could not hold together.

Phull and Massenbach were Württembergers, that is, compatriots, and sufficiently intimate to address each other in the familiar second person singular; they had been friends off and on since the revolutionary wars. Scharnhorst of course was Hanoverian, brought into the Prussian service only a few years earlier by the duke of Brunswick, at first in the artillery, and only since 1804 on the General Staff. Phull was considered a genius, somewhat crotchety and inflexible but of great strength of character. Massenbach liked to shine as a brilliant military scientist, and since the revolutionary wars had made his reputation by pushing himself forward with a tireless and unsolicited production of books, articles, and memoranda. Scharnhorst was well known as a theoretical writer but otherwise still very much the outsider. Those who had not been his students at the military academy in Berlin thought of him more as a knowledgeable but plodding pedant than as an outstanding soldier. Phull and Scharnhorst strongly favored war with France, while Massenbach was just as strongly in favor of a French alliance.

We depict these three men with the characteristics that were attributed to them by the public and the government at the time, in order to indicate the positions in which they found themselves, keeping in mind that public opinion proved false in all three cases. Since Scharnhorst and Phull will be discussed again in more important contexts, we postpone a detailed description of them at this time.[9]

It is true, of course, that in the campaign of 1806 Scharnhorst served as quartermaster general of the duke of Brunswick, and thus of the entire army. Nevertheless he remained so much the outsider that, apart from the duke himself, no one high or low at the congresslike headquarters of the army had the kind of confidence in him that his task demanded. His influence must therefore be considered as limited and unimportant. We confine ourselves to a more detailed consideration of Colonel Massenbach, who played out his part in this campaign, making himself much talked about in the process.

MASSENBACH was short and stocky, with full, round features; a shiny bald head with a high, imposing brow; small brown eyes, wide open and very fiery; and a fresh, ruddy complexion—at first sight the very picture of the enthusiast, ruled by sentiment and imagination. Such people never lack a receptive, creative intelligence, which is enough to make a brilliant impression; but they are wanting in tact, judgment, and fundamentally sound ideas. That, too, was the case with Massenbach.

[9] A reference to the planned second part of this manuscript, on the campaign of 1807, which Clausewitz failed to write. He did, however, write a separate essay on Scharnhorst (see below), and discusses Phull extensively in *The Campaign of 1812 in Russia* (see below).

The trouble with people of this type is that an inner unrest drives them to attempt great things, which go beyond their intellectual capacity. They want to carry others along, and when people do not follow them and their project eventually fails because they have not been able to think it through, they turn mean. They lose the kindness and nobility with which they first ingratiated themselves, hate as passionately as they once loved, and without realizing it betray truth, loyalty, and faith. In a crisis an enthusiast will always lack consistency and steadfastness, or calmness and self-possession; these qualities depend upon a prescient intelligence, or a zeal so strong as to transcend the intellect altogether.* Colonel Massenbach's entire career bears this out. During the revolutionary wars, although already in his thirties, he was filled with a youthful, touching enthusiasm for the duke of Brunswick, for Prussia (which after all was not his homeland), for the cause of the German princes, and for the cause of Germany. With the Peace of Basel he immediately changed his mind. For a time he played the Machiavellian, finding Prussian glory in a sudden alliance with the state she had just fought, *against* the states she had left in the lurch. It did not take long for Bonaparte's career to kindle a new enthusiasm in him, and now he could conceive of nothing wiser or more glorious for Prussia than to place her fate entirely in the hands of this hero and become a satrapy of his empire. One cannot call that good-natured, nor even intelligent. In his private affairs, too, he did not always display the selfless feelings that the enthusiast likes to claim for himself. Already in 1797 he petitioned the crown for the gift of an estate in the newly acquired Polish Territories and, having received it, submitted a request for a second estate, which he himself admitted was immodest. Later, having been brought down by his own mistakes, with his career and good name in ruins, he became more spiteful and venomous, at which point his memoirs appeared. These revealed that he had always been in the habit of making notes about everything on the spot, including the most confidential conversations with people to whom he owed the greatest consideration and who had plainly stipulated that no one should ever know what passed between them. This revealed a great coarseness of feeling, which seems all the worse for having emerged early in life, during his years of greatest success.

He had served well in the brief campaign of 1787 against the Dutch rebels, receiving a wound in the hand. During the revolutionary wars he was a major and became quartermaster general of Hohenlohe's corps. He again distinguished himself by hard work, fire, and zeal and by an uncommonly scien-

---

* What I have said here about enthusiasts pertains only to that group of men to whom the epithet is commonly applied. No slight is intended toward enthusiasm as such, in the sense of a specific, heightened commitment in the heart of the feeling individual; still less should the enthusiast be confused with the quiet, self-absorbed visionary, who is in every respect precisely his opposite.

tific approach to warfare—which, however, already displayed an unfortunate tendency to give too much weight to terrain and geographic considerations and to spatial relationships in general, while completely losing sight of the army itself, as well as of battle and its consequences. Nevertheless, everything he wrote about the revolutionary wars was well thought-out, more instructive than the events themselves, and still more so than the Prussian tactics modeled on Saldern's system.[10] During the war he often urged this or that course on the duke of Brunswick, who found him sympathetic and treated him with distinction; Massenbach would have dearly liked to infect the duke with his enthusiasm. But that canny, experienced man, old beyond his years, could not be easily moved. After the war Massenbach bent all his efforts toward influencing matters that were not his official responsibility. In itself this was certainly not blameworthy; on the contrary, it is a sure sign of Philistinism when everyone does only what he is paid to do. But Massenbach's projects were often impractical and not infrequently presumptuous in form and substance. Political memoranda without number rained down on the duke of Brunswick and the royal entourage, full of ingenious ideas— generally directed against Austria and Russia and in favor of France—but they never quite meshed with reality. His restless nature drove him to this sort of thing day and night. In military matters his chief interest and preoccupation was the reorganization of the General Staff. This actually occurred in 1803, although one of Massenbach's favorite ideas was rejected, according to which the quartermaster general and his three lieutenants would constitute a committee, virtually a ministry, reporting directly to the king not only on important military matters, but on the state's political affairs as well.

With the opening of the campaign of 1806 Massenbach became quartermaster general to Prince Hohenlohe. Even during this brief campaign he could not resist the impulse to drag others into his conceptual orbit, which substantially added to the indecision and confusion of an already peculiar command.

As far as his official duties were concerned, Massenbach proved less capable and useful than one might have expected. His constant eccentricity had destroyed the capacity for calm reflection and caution essential in a soldier, and his mental confusion and intellectual weakness manifested themselves in surprising ways.

GENERAL OF INFANTRY VON KLEIST. Sadly, he has become known for the surrender of Magdeburg, but he deserved a better fate than that.

As a young man he had served with distinction in the Seven Years' War, and was covered with wounds. During the revolutionary wars he was never-

---

[10] Friedrich Christoph von Saldern was one of Frederick the Great's inspectors general. He raised military drill to new levels of speed and complexity.

theless among the youngest and most vigorous of our generals, and his brigade was therefore usually employed on independent operations. He had a
quick and not uneducated mind and was a tough, capable soldier, admirably
calm in battle; but he was also a smooth man of the world, with strong political inclinations. After twelve years of peace, by now high in his seventies,[11]
he had grown weak and infirm, and the political and social side of his character had gained the upper hand. He thought it was merely politically astute
to surrender Magdeburg—and a garrison commander without brains or
heart, with a foolish, physically weak lieutenant general at his side,[12] was not
likely to change his mind. Added to this, when the king passed through
Magdeburg during the retreat, he did not attempt to encourage and fortify
Kleist but rather let drop a few words about compassion and moderation,
which did not fall upon barren ground. The truth about his decision is to be
found neither in cowardice nor in betrayal.

That this veteran had been appointed governor of Magdeburg, and remained in this position in 1806, should be blamed on no one. Although old
and infirm, he still gave the impression of an energetic soldier and a level-
headed general; by the standards of the time his career had been brilliant. It
was therefore natural to expect at least as much from him as military honor
and decorum required. But that the king's general adjutant, Colonel Kleist,
should have had his brother-in-law [Colonel du Trossel] appointed commandant of the most important Prussian fortress, simply because it was a decent
post in which to await retirement and despite the fact that during the revolutionary wars a military tribunal had sentenced the man to fortress arrest for
being deficient in his duties—that, certainly, is indicative of the lax administration that characterized the army and the state in those years. General
Kleist was a small man, stooped and battered, but with martial, and at the
same time very distinguished, features. He was one of the most striking figures in the army of that period.

LIEUTENANT GENERAL COUNT WARTENSLEBEN. He was the most senior of
the nineteen generals assembled in Magdeburg, whose combined age came
to some thirteen hundred years. Under favorable circumstances he might
well have fought bravely, he might even have shown more initiative than the
others; but not in times of crisis, when the state was collapsing on all sides
and a clear head or a stout heart was needed to face the threat of being buried
in the ruins.

[11] Kleist, born in January 1736, was seventy-one when the war began.
[12] Clausewitz refers to Lieutenant General von Wartensleben, who is discussed immediately
below—an example of the unevenness of the manuscript that a revision would have corrected.
Wartensleben was the ranking general of the forces stationed in Magdeburg, and with the governor and the commandant of the fortress occupied one of the three senior positions in the town.
For his part in surrendering Magdeburg, he was sentenced to imprisonment for life.

GENERAL VON GRAWERT.   He might have become the Prussian Lacy, given the right opportunity. His outstanding qualities were a cold, calculating, prudent mind, great calmness and composure, and much firmness of purpose; but he lacked warmth, imagination, or initiative, and as a result his virtues could only have negative effects. He was an expert in the theory of terrain, having been intensely occupied with its study for years, and it is no surprise that he should have become a leading apostle of the new school of tactics that had developed since the middle of the eighteenth century, in which the army was married, so to speak, to the ground. The battalion defends the hill; the hill defends the battalion. The advanced study of terrain, at that time highly developed in the Prussian army, lent this school a scientific air, which made it seem more intellectual. A great many intelligent men were taken in, to the point where questions of geometrical and spatial relationships became predominant, and one only talked of positions, approaches, flanks, rears, and lines of communication, but never of the strength of the military forces that were fighting.

The campaign of 1792 was not conducted in this manner because it was an offensive undertaking and because at bottom Frederick William II rather than the duke of Brunswick actually commanded the army. Colonel Grawert, the oldest officer on the General Staff and de facto quartermaster general (a position nominally held by Major General Pfau), was prevented from showing his abilities to full advantage—but he may have been the chief cause of the duke's failure to risk an attack at Valmy, since he firmly advised against it.

The campaigns of 1793 and 1794, on the other hand, in which Prussia wished to remain decorously unengaged, were all the better suited to his talents by virtue of the army's position, which spread across the Vosges Mountains. The defensive outpost-and-cordon system was pushed to the limit in both campaigns. That the Prussian forces did not suffer more heavily for employing such a system was the fault of the poor quality of the armies that opposed them.

Grawert did not become quartermaster general of the army—presumably because the general adjutants feared he might become too influential and get in their way. Consequently he was merely the *chef* of an infantry regiment in 1806, even though he had now risen to lieutenant general. At Jena he commanded a division, which fought in the central engagement of the entire battle, the action around Vierzehnheiligen. There he showed that he understood as little as Prince Hohenlohe about employing troops and leading them in battle. Deploy your line, advance by echelons, volley by alternate sections—that was the end of it.

In 1812 Napoleon requested Grawert as the commander of the Prussian contingent of the *Grande Armée*, because he was known as a long-time advocate of a Prussian alliance with France. General Scharnhorst, who still had influence at that time, feared that he would give in too much to the French and arranged that General Yorck be made second in command. Grawert became ill during the campaign, and command of the contingent fell into Yorck's hands.

COUNT HAUGWITZ.   A short man in his forties, with pleasant features and agreeable manners that expressed superficiality, irresponsibility, falseness; but these blended so perfectly with the man's calm, gentlemanly behavior that there was nothing comic about him. Such was Count Haugwitz's demeanor; and that was also his personality.

As a wealthy young count he had acquired a better than ordinary education and a good deal of polish by means of study and travel. A passing interest in Pietistic devotion gave him a certain reputation for goodness, which such people do not find difficult to maintain. In Italy he came to know the grand duke of Tuscany, and that was the reason why, in 1792, when the grand duke became emperor of Germany [as Francis II], Haugwitz was made Prussia's ambassador to Vienna. He insisted on serving without pay, thus demonstrating with one stroke his recklessness and his hypocrisy, for he was more a spendthrift than a stoic and not rich enough to carry off such generosity. Correspondingly, he allowed himself to be compensated for this sacrificial gesture by gifts of estates in Poland, just as he sought recompense for the sacrifices demanded by piety in a way of life that was far from decent.

Frederick William II summoned him to court in 1793. His pleasing manners, calm sophistication, and easy way of managing affairs soon won him the king's esteem. Count Herzberg had quit the court dissatisfied, Count Finckenstein was an old man who in any case had not played a leading role for some time, and Count Alvensleben was even less significant. It was therefore Haugwitz whom the king appointed in Herzberg's place as minister of foreign affairs. * He soon became the king's confidant, and from then on directed the state's foreign affairs. Some claim that he opposed the Peace of Basel and favored Prussian adherence to the Second Coalition in 1799. But this posture was at best superficial, perhaps adopted only *pour la bonne façon*; at least those who make the claim still owe us proof that the Prussian government included men of sufficient weight to overrule Count Haugwitz in a matter that was preeminently his responsibility. Prussian policy between the Peace of Basel and the catastrophe of 1806 is marked by weakness, timidity, thoughtlessness, and on many occasions an undignified agility, all of which are qualities deeply rooted in Haugwitz's character. If he really not only saw the danger with which France threatened Europe, but also feared it, it is just

---

* Count Schulenburg-Kehnert had succeeded Herzberg briefly, but had given up the portfolio.

another proof of his foolhardiness that he should have let matters drift as they did. If Count Haugwitz encountered any obstacles at all in his political career, they probably arose from the characters of the two princes he served. Count Haugwitz would have been just the man to surrender completely to France, and make Prussia a French satrapy; but this was altogether contrary to the natures of Frederick William II and Frederick William III. Count Haugwitz was a close friend of the Countess Lichtenau, from whose hand he received the Order of the Black Eagle. It was therefore imagined, with good reason, that Frederick William III would dismiss him at once.[13] But the king may have felt that Count Haugwitz's subtlety and malleability were well suited to someone in his position; and the old General Köckritz, whom he had especially charmed, may also have supported him.

In 1804 Haugwitz turned over the portfolio of foreign affairs to Baron Hardenberg, apparently because other governments distrusted him too much; but as a cabinet minister he remained in close touch with political affairs, and in consequence the king chose him in 1805 to convey to the French emperor the joint convention concluded by Prussia and Russia at Potsdam on November 3. His behavior on this occasion crowned his career. We will have more to say about it in our comments on Lombard's memoirs.

CABINET COUNCILOR LOMBARD. He was a member of the Huguenot colony in Berlin and of low birth. His father had been a wig maker, and he married the daughter of a regimental surgeon. As is well known, in the old Prussian army men of this calling began their careers as company surgeons and barbers. This caused Lombard one day to make fun of his wife, who was somewhat more sensitive about matters of family background than he, by asking her: "Quel vers préférez-vous, ma chère? 'L'hirondelle d'une aile rapide frise la surface des eaux' ou '. . . rase la surface des eaux?' Le premier me rappelle mon père, et le second le tien."[14] I relate this anecdote because it helps to characterize the man.

He showed himself an able young student at the *Collège français,* and during the last years of Frederick the Great's reign succeeded in being appointed one of the king's assistant secretaries. From there he made his way as a *bel esprit,* by virtue of an attractive appearance and pleasing manners; after Frederick's death he won the favor of the Countess Lichtenau, through whom he found his way to the office of cabinet councilor for foreign affairs before he had reached his thirtieth year. He himself said that it was difficult for him to hold onto his place when Frederick William III came to the throne, but he

[13] Wilhelmine Enke, Countess von Lichtenau, was Frederick William II's long-time confidante and, for a time, mistress. Her character and propensity for intrigue were offensive to his more austere son.

[14] "Which verse do you prefer, my dear: 'The swallow, with beating wings, curls across the water,' or '. . . shaves across the water?' The first reminds me of my father, the second of yours."

managed it by firmly tying himself to Count Haugwitz. His education tended more to arts and letters than to a thorough knowledge of history, and yet only the latter would have provided the necessary basis for the qualities needed to make a statesman.

A comprehensive knowledge of the various states and their relations, a broad and practical view of public affairs, a clear understanding of war and diplomacy, a familiarity with the great figures on the world's stage, confidence in one's conviction, firm resolve—was the young man supposed to acquire these at the Gymnasium? Or perhaps in the drawing room of Countess Lichtenau? To be sure, the cabinet councilor for foreign affairs was far less important than his colleague responsible for internal affairs, because the minister for foreign affairs dealt personally with the king on the more important matters. In a formalistic sense the duties of a councilor in that department were really not much different from those of a secretary, a kind of position for which Lombard's talents might well have been sufficient. But if we consider what it means for a man to be placed between the king and his ministry, to have the right and the constant opportunity to participate in discussions, we would scarcely conclude that such a man would remain without influence, whether he opposes the minister or plays along with him note for note. And if the councilor influences the spirit of the cabinet, we must ask about the spirit of the councilor.

Lombard was not ambitious or enterprising, but rather a soft, flaccid, sickly, blasé man, whose outstanding qualities were mental facility and *esprit* of the French sort. He was astute enough to recognize the ascendancy of French power in all matters, and limited enough to believe resistance impossible. Submission to France suited someone with his weak constitution, and limited understanding and inner resources, as much as it suited a mind nourished on French conversation and French wit; and his memoirs leave no doubt that at heart he favored the interests of France. Nor was he sufficiently careful or circumspect to disguise this inclination; those who knew him soon divined his true feelings from the cold, emotionless sarcasm with which he responded to other people's passionate hatred of France. For this reason public opinion condemned him more than any of his colleagues. Animosity toward him reached such a pitch that when he stopped in Stettin during his flight to East Prussia a mob gathered, and sent up such a hew and cry that the queen, who happened to be present, was induced to order his arrest. He was, of course, quickly released at the king's order, and in Königsberg soon afterwards he resigned his office.

He returned to Berlin and in 1808 wrote a small book entitled *Matériaux pour servir à l'histoire des années 1805, 6, et 7, dédiés aux Prussiens par un ancien compatriote.* In it he attempted to justify the policies of the Prussian cabinet and, more generally, to defend the Prussian state, which at the time was generally reviled in the press.

He emigrated to Italy that same year, where he soon died.

CABINET COUNCILOR BEYME. In 1799, when he was chosen to be cabinet councilor for internal affairs, he was thirty-four years old and an appeals court judge. Distinguished by a sound knowledge of the law and the capacity for hard work, he was also regarded as a markedly honest and upright man. These qualities could have meant a good deal in an obscure judge, but whether they were sufficiently brilliant to *distinguish* the man when he be-came councilor to the king was obviously another question. The quotation may be a little unusual here, but it may still be appropriate to say, *"Tel brille au second, qui s'éclipse au premier."*[15] At court and in affairs of state rectitude has its risks, and if honesty is to be a mark of distinction it must be incorporated into a higher understanding. As his colleague Lombard observed, Beyme brought a certain judicial stiffness of mind to his post, which, however, he soon lost. That may also have been the case with his rectitude and unusual honesty, because although Beyme always remained an entirely honorable man, he usually sailed with the wind, making common cause with good men and bad, often behaving in a tactically clever way; he never proved himself better or stood taller than the passing moment demanded. He was a good jurist, but without administrative experience. It was common for cabinet councilors to be chosen from the ranks of the court of appeals, and they generally obtained their bureaucratic education by gradually mastering the business of their departments. This was certainly a very bad system, since it took a long time for a councilor to learn his job, and even then he would only grasp it in a highly pragmatic, one-sided way. So it was with Beyme, who for that matter was smart enough to learn the ropes quickly. Like Mencken before him it did not take him long to become an important figure in the cabinet. He followed in his predecessor's footsteps by seeking to promote himself while promoting liberalism in government.

He did not have the political convictions needed to improve or reform the machinery of state, and in routine administrative matters put himself completely in Count Schulenburg's hands. Nor was he able to find his own way politically, and was therefore always of one mind with Count Haugwitz and with his colleague Lombard, who exerted some influence over him in any case. It could not have been otherwise in the career and position of such a man, unless he had the most outstanding intellectual abilities. These Beyme did not possess; he was simply a good worker. But he might well have shown somewhat greater energy and strength of character had his situation been different, and had he known how to take advantage of it. In times of deepest

[15] "He shines in the second row, who is eclipsed in the first," from Voltaire's *Henriade*.

crisis he always displayed greater composure than others, and after the Peace of Tilsit he proved to be a strong proponent of rebirth and reform, which was rare for an officeholder of the old system. The talent that served him best was his ability to persuade the king of his exceptional personal loyalty, which he was said to achieve by means of altogether unusual flattery, Frederick William III not being susceptible to the ordinary kind. Yet the king's good will, which he retained to the end, was not strong enough to save him from being torn loose from his post three times. He remained a cabinet councilor until 1807; but when Baron vom Stein was called to Königsberg to become prime minister, the posts of cabinet councilors were abolished, and Beyme, whose influence Stein seemed to fear, had to go. Stein was mistaken, because Beyme was perfectly capable of entertaining new ideas, and without overweening ambition; he would have gladly subjugated himself and would have supported Stein strongly. But Stein is a passionate man and held fast to his hatred of the old cabinet.

By the time Stein had to leave Prussian service in 1809, however, his opinion had changed and he proposed Beyme as minister of justice, with the title of high chancellor.

Beyme had to step down again in 1810 when Baron Hardenberg was made chancellor of state, because Hardenberg, who had fought some tough battles with him earlier, made Beyme's departure a condition of accepting the new office. After several appointments as provincial governor during the Wars of Liberation, Beyme, thanks to *great effort*, returned to the ministry in 1816 as head of the justice department for the Rhine provinces. Prince Hardenberg generously allowed himself to be talked into creating this post especially for Beyme. But he did not enjoy the position for long. In 1818 he was persuaded to join Humboldt, who then shared the Ministry of the Interior with Schuckmann, and Boyen, the minister of war, in opposing the projected reorganization of the government. When Humboldt and Boyen resigned the following year, Beyme did not take this step and had to swallow the humiliation of receiving his dismissal by messenger.

His constant following the lead of others is enough to show that neither his opinions nor his strength of character amounted to much. He married twice for money, obtained large gifts from the king, bought property cheaply, and after his last humiliating dismissal did not refuse a substantial pension, having previously exchanged his first pension for an endowment. With God's help he had become a rich man, who lacked nothing save a patent of nobility, which he obtained in 1816. At the very least, all this demonstrates a certain weakness of principles.

Nor was Beyme's appearance likely to make a very favorable impression. Large, bulging black eyes were his only distinctive feature, and these contrasted strangely with his small, plump, spindly legged physique. But even the eyes suggested a craving for princely favor. His speech was no more noble than his appearance, nor was his way of expressing himself particularly distinguished, although he had a talent for orderly, coherent exposition, with which before his final dismissal he shone in meetings of the council of state.

CHAPTER 3. BACKGROUND AND PREPARATIONS
FOR THE WAR

Under Frederick the Great, Prussia had begun to assume a place among the *major powers*, although her size and population were barely a quarter as large as that of the others. Frederick's fame as a general, the wisdom and economy of his administration, and the strength and skill of his army were the tools with which he operated. Nevertheless, shrewd and skillful policies were required to maintain this artificially elevated position. The Great Elector had also ruled with such means, and one may well say that Prussia owes her greatness to their cunning. But fishing in troubled waters is a dangerous business, which must be combined with great strength and firmness of purpose; for unless others fear us they will never allow themselves to be outwitted with impunity.

Prussia's psychological ascendancy gradually disappeared after Frederick's death, until in the end nothing was left but the prestige of an army that excelled in all military virtues. What, one may ask, could have taken the place of Prussia's crafty and shifting policies, which could only be employed by talented and enterprising rulers, in order to retain Prussia's new power and transform her artificial position into a relatively natural one? Only great economy and austerity in the state's administration, combined with unremitting care of its military institutions and a frank, honest, but strong posture toward other powers, always demonstrating that the state did not fear the danger in whose shadow it had grown.

With ten million inhabitants, and provided such a posture was maintained internally and externally, Prussia was already too large not to emerge from the powers of the second class, and it became easier to maintain her position in the first rank once fear and jealousy were diverted by the great new danger arising in the west.

Frederick William II was a genial man and a gallant prince, to whom a frank and open policy came naturally. But his advisors and cabinet councilors were unable to rise to the occasion, a policy of this nature being generally difficult for such a group to implement. Strength and cunning disappeared, as did consistency and unity. In 1787 we boldly marched against Holland, to bring the Dutch rebels to reason, and succeeded. In 1790 we secretly favored the same rebels against Austria; in 1792 we wished to suppress the French rebels, as the Dutch had been suppressed in 1787. Frederick William undertook this last campaign as a matter of chivalry. But his cabinet and the duke of Brunswick were already thinking in more political terms and left the required courage and enterprising spirit at home. Frederick William did not take charge himself, he could not manage without the others, and left his army in 1793, troubled in his own mind by the role he was playing. A war conducted in such timid fashion could not feed itself; the whole burden fell on Prussia's finances, which were soon exhausted. The king naturally did not know where to turn, and from then on the kind of politics that thought *only* of safety and momentary advantage gained the upper hand. The energy needed for deceit and cunning, for consequential dishonesty, was lacking. Prussia concluded the Peace of Basel, left her former allies in the lurch, now and then fawned on the French but lacked the courage to make common cause with them. The king's sense of honor and the honor of the men who joined him in this flawed policy took refuge behind the bulwark of armed neutrality, intended to protect northern Germany, and the only deception the cabinet could manage consisted in deceiving the king and the people with this bugaboo. The harder the blows suffered by the Austrian and imperial armies, the greater the tendency to believe in the wisdom of the chosen course of action. At the same time the state gained important territories in Poland and Germany, the domestic economy improved, and every humiliation inflicted on Austrian arms seemed to increase the glory of Prussia's, which had remained intact. That was the view taken in Prussia, and to some extent even by unthinking people elsewhere, and the French did everything in their power to praise the wisdom of Prussia's policy. But, needless to say, the respect other governments had for Prussia and their trust in her declined steadily, and all men whose minds and hearts were caught up in the great conflict with France were deeply wounded or embittered by Prussia's behavior. Of course the Prussian cabinet could not deceive itself completely about the dangers that faced Europe and threatened the state. But it shied away from probing the wound too deeply or facing its own actions squarely—in part because people at the top believed that, should the worst happen, Prussia would now be better able to defend herself because of her territorial acquisitions, in part because they thought things do not always turn out as badly as one fears. In short, to avoid being drawn into dangerous activity, one avoided thinking too much about the facts and left well enough alone. Thus passed the last years of Frederick William II's reign, and the first years of his successor's. In 1799 England, Russia, and Austria called on Prussia to join the new coalition. The duke of Brunswick and Minister von Haugwitz spoke for war; but the imminence of the danger, the failures of the past, and the tremendous exertions that war required spoke against it. The king vacillated; his two advisors, far from urging him on, may have spoken as they did simply for the sake of public opinion. Timidity prevailed, and the old system survived.

And so 1805 approached. That this kind of leadership in stormy times did not constitute a careful guardianship of the state's highest interests is self-evident. Though it did not appear so on the surface, the reputation of the state, its safety, strength, and honor, were squandered. Like a loafer who consumes but earns nothing, the government vegetated and gambled on a lucky card in the lottery of fate. The policy would deserve quite a different name if the long-lasting restraint on Prussia's energies had been a true conserving of strength for the decisive moment.

Neither the Peace of Campo Formio, nor that of Lunéville, nor even that of Pressburg, had reduced Austria to the point where she could not be expected to fight once more before succumbing altogether. Despite her losses, Austria remained an empire of more than twenty million inhabitants. Russia was intact, England grew stronger every day. It was to be expected, therefore, that Prussia could still find the right moment when her strength might tip the balance.

If this had been the intention, great measures carried out in secret would have been necessary to prepare for the role: not an expansion of the army, for which there were no funds, but weeding out older officers and even the overaged, worn-out plowboys among the rank and file; stockpiling of the vast number of weapons that every war requires and that was not yet available; arming the fortresses near the theater of war, and appointing better commandants; a detailed study of the probable theater of operations, and so forth. I will not mention innovations within the armed forces themselves, for at that time only a few men in the Prussian army recognized the weakness of existing methods. But the Prussian cabinet could only dimly grasp the part the state would have to play in the next ten years and left things as they were. Baron Hardenberg was still without settled convictions and firm resolve, and also without full authority. Count Haugwitz was a man without a conscience. He had turned the portfolio of foreign affairs over to Baron Hardenberg in 1804 because Russia and her allies could no longer trust him; but he remained the soul of Prussian policy, if one can credit it with having a soul. Count Haugwitz was considered a fervent partisan of French interests, and many believed he had sold himself to them. A French spy, the Chevalier Méhée de la Touche, even published a book in which he claims to have received large sums from the French government, which he employed for that purpose. Presumably this is all hot air; the only thing needed to induce Count Haugwitz to favor the French was his own limited and misguided understanding, which saw the danger but not the means to meet it. He considered it foolish for Prussia to continue at all costs to play the part of a great power, and certainly not a misfortune if circumstances would gradually turn her into a

French client state. His aim was to guide Prussia toward that end, without great convulsions that might endanger the state or himself. All the means at his disposal—deceitful, insidious, and equivocal expedients—he devoted to this end. Haugwitz's assistant, Cabinet Councilor Lombard, was as careless as his minister was unscrupulous, and unrestrained by formal responsibility. The duke of Brunswick excelled himself in caution. The king, still lacking experience, confidence, and self-reliance, left the final decision to others. He was too acute and intelligent not to recognize the shortcomings of the whole military establishment or not to suspect how unequal it was to the power of France, grown strong in its victories. But he also saw the difficulty of a complete change of course, and no one of those around him was capable of giving the advice and example needed for the effort.

So Prussia once more decided to remain neutral, and in 1805 did not join the third coalition against France; or rather, neutrality was adopted because no decision could be reached.

Two events revealed to France the contempt in which Prussia was now held. Austria, Russia, and England prepared and concluded their third coalition without even bothering to inform Berlin for fear of being betrayed to the French. Furthermore, once the allies had mobilized their forces the Russian army advanced to the Prussian border, and the czar, in a brief note delivered to Berlin by General Wintzingerode, demanded free passage through Silesia for his troops. He wished to draw Prussia into the conflict, as Austria wanted to carry Bavaria along. The czar did not intend to offend or discredit the king with these two humiliating actions—they had been close friends for some years. Rather, he believed he would be doing the king a favor by sparing him the need to make an independent choice and sweeping him along with the current. But this revealed his contempt of the Prussian government too openly, and the clumsy maneuver could only misfire. Prussia showed herself determined to resist the Russian passage by force of arms, and the Russians gave up the idea.

To avoid at all costs putting the French in a similar position, Councilor Beyme again proposed the idea that Prussia's Franconian provinces be declared neutral, that is, not subject to Prussian sovereignty, and that both sides be granted free passage through them. The only thing in favor of this disgraceful suggestion was that a similar arrangement had in fact existed since 1795. At that time, however, Prussia had drawn a cordon of neutrality around all states in northern Germany, not only around her own territory, so free passage through Franconia might be regarded as merely a small compensation [to the other powers]. Under present circumstances such a declaration, freely made, would have been not merely an admission of weakness, but of cowardice in the face of France. Baron Hardenberg opposed the proposal and represented to the king that it was impossible to make such a major concession in the absence of a request from one of the warring powers. The idea was therefore dropped.

While the government was occupied in concentrating forces to defend the eastern frontier and was secretly worrying about the security of the southern territories, word arrived that the French under Bernadotte, without having asked permission, were marching through Franconia. The immediate answer to this step was simply a strong protest by Hardenberg to the French embassy, and prompt permission for the Russians to pass through Silesia; but it had the further effect of again bringing Prussia into close contact with the allied courts. The czar came to Berlin personally to persuade the king to join the coalition, and in November a convention was signed at Potsdam in which the king declared that unless peace could be restored on the basis of the most recent treaties he would join the alliance against France. Prussia, sword in hand, would make one last attempt to persuade Bonaparte to keep the peace. Count Haugwitz was to present this ultimatum to the French emperor. On the one hand, his choice reflected the same indecision that had brought Prussia to her present state: it was hoped that the firm language of the ultimatum would displease the emperor less coming from this messenger. On the other hand, Count Haugwitz seems to have done the utmost to be chosen by the government for this mission. He was determined at all costs to use this last opportunity to perform one final service for Prussia by bringing the two powers together. The convention had been concluded on November 3; on the 14th Haugwitz departed. He foresaw that a decisive battle would soon take place between the French and Austrian armies in Moravia and did not doubt that the French would win. He hoped the blow would fall before he reached Vienna, and under pretext of illness traveled so slowly that he did not reach the city until November 26, that is, [until] he had been on the road for fourteen days. Even so, he arrived too soon and was forced to meet with the French minister Talleyrand before the battle was fought. This was unfortunate because Haugwitz had based his plan mainly on the fact of an Austrian defeat, which would have excused him at home for acting against his instructions. Count Haugwitz took the risk of completely concealing the purpose of his mission, and instead began an unimportant discussion of the military situation in Hanover. *

* According to Savary's memoirs [Anne-Jean-Marie-Savary, duc de Rovigo, *Extrait des mémoires de M. le duc de Rovigo, concernant le catastrophe de M. le duc d'Enghien* (Paris, 1823)], Haugwitz arrived in Brünn as early as December 1, before the battle [of Austerlitz]; but he was not allowed to see Napoleon and was sent back to Vienna instead, because the emperor also wished to avoid a break with Prussia and expected that a victory would change the minister's language, while a defeat would not make it any worse. The crucial question here is whether Count Haugwitz really did not speak to the emperor in Brünn on this occasion, and consequently whether he had to go to Brünn twice.

Because it would be more than daring—it would be insolent—to disguise a mission of this kind, one can hardly avoid the suspicion that Count Haugwitz frankly informed the French minister of his real mission and, in the same breath, that he personally disapproved of it. The battle of Austerlitz was fought on December 2. Count Haugwitz followed the emperor Napoleon to Brünn, had several audiences with him, and then, in Vienna on December 15, concluded the famous agreement by which Prussia guaranteed the French the terms of the not-yet-concluded Peace of Pressburg, ceded Ansbach, Neufchatel, and Cleve with Wesel, and in return accepted Hanover, which meant acknowledging that France had won Hanover by right of conquest [and could now dispose of it].

Count Haugwitz did not dare send this treaty to Berlin by courier, because he feared he would be disavowed. He decided to be the messenger himself, left on December 17 and, not greatly hurrying, arrived in Berlin on the 25th.

Considering that Bonaparte must have known of the czar's presence in Berlin and of the convention of November 3, and that he could therefore easily have guessed the real motive of Count Haugwitz's appearance in Vienna, it can scarcely be believed that he allowed Haugwitz to persuade him that the count's mission was to conclude an alliance with him.

It was not yet in Bonaparte's interest to break with Prussia, because that would have disturbed the negotiations for the Treaty of Pressburg, and he would be better prepared to face her six months later. It is therefore understandable that he should have done nothing to betray his knowledge of Prussia's true intentions to the Prussian cabinet. But it is hard to believe that Bonaparte's personal conduct toward Count Haugwitz was equally lacking in candor, or that he played the *bonhomme*. Presumably, Count Haugwitz frankly confessed his true mission while explaining that he had undertaken it only to forestall such a mad gesture, that the emperor's magnificent victory had given him the best means to do so, and that he would again make himself master of affairs in Berlin and prevent such foolishness in the future, if His Majesty were to make this possible by granting him good terms. This attitude of the Prussian minister only made it easier for Bonaparte to put off and deceive the Prussian government. Considering the matter in this light, we must again be astonished at Count Haugwitz's audacity; or rather, we recognize it as a sign of a weak government, unaccustomed to clarity, firmness, and discipline, with whose views an irresponsible character like Count Haugwitz might well play fast and loose. At first his conduct naturally caused a great outcry in Berlin, since he had been sent to deliver a declaration of war and returned with an alliance. No one had imagined that an emissary might pursue a completely contrary policy on his own, in effect forcing his government to return to a position that it had decided, after long deliberation and not without considerable distress, to abandon. No one believed that in our day the sort of Machiavellianism that was being demanded of the Prussian government could be feasible or salutary. No one thought so little of international law as to violate it against England in the manner proposed here. But the indignation of weak men always succumbs to the maneuvers of cold cunning and resolute depravity.

Baron Hardenberg was outraged, but Count Haugwitz won over the cabinet, at least to the point where it accepted the agreement, subject to a modification intended to neutralize its most poisonous element, the *betrayal of England*. The exchange of territory was to be concluded only after a general peace had been signed, that is, after England had agreed to it; until then Prussian troops would occupy Hanover. Under these circumstances Baron Hardenberg felt obliged to give up the portfolio for foreign affairs and returned it to Count Haugwitz, retaining only the ministry for Magdeburg, Halberstadt, etc. Count Haugwitz was at least punished to the extent that he was ordered to convey these modifications to Paris. Bonaparte did not reply at once, keeping Prussia in the belief that her amendments would be accepted, and waited until the Prussian army had been demobilized. Then, in mid-February of 1806, he bluntly declared not only that the exchange of provinces would occur immediately, but also that Prussia would have to close her harbors to the British. On February 15 Count Haugwitz signed a new agreement in Paris to that effect.

The Prussian government, placed in a thoroughly untenable position by Count Haugwitz, without allies and unprepared for war, gave in once more.

The czar may well have shaken his head doubtfully at Prussia's behavior. But he had just experienced what it meant to face Bonaparte sword in hand and was probably not displeased that, having concluded a hasty peace, Austria would ask no further favors of him. He seems to have been satisfied to sit out this hand; he did not reproach the Prussian cabinet for its extraordinary conduct, but rather declared himself ready to come to its aid at any time should this prove necessary.

The king of England protested the occupation of Hanover in a manifesto dated April 20 and on June 11 declared war on Prussia. By then Prussia had already inspired a second declaration of war. The king of Sweden, Gustavus IV, had wished to make common cause with England and Russia against France, and had been given the command of their combined forces in Hanover. He still occupied the Duchy of Lauenburg, and was only too pleased to play the knight errant opposite the king of Prussia. He declared himself obligated by his alliance with England to protect the small territory from Prussian occupation, though the king of England, far from welcoming this, advised against it. In the event the king withdrew his army to Swedish Pomerania, while leaving a garrison of 500 in Lauenburg, declaring that he would view their expulsion as a breach of the peace.

69

After our forces drove off this detachment in April, Sweden formally declared war, and Prussia was forced to move a corps under Count Kalckreuth up to the Peene River.

Matters remained in this belligerent state until August, when Prussia once more mobilized against France and therefore had to give in to Sweden; peace was restored through an exchange of conciliatory letters between the monarchs.

During these hostile moves by England and Sweden, which resulted directly from the Vienna agreement, Prussia's relations with France ripened to maturity, and, as fruits do, suddenly changed color in the process.

The new convention that Count Haugwitz had concluded with the French government was dated February 15. Fourteen days later, on March 2, after changes in the English cabinet resulting from Pitt's death opened the possibility of peace with that country, Bonaparte declared at a meeting of the state council that he would always be ready to conclude peace with England, based on the Treaty of Amiens. In the first exchange of notes between the two governments, England demanded Russia's participation in the negotiations, while France declared the independence of the Ottoman Empire to be a preliminary condition.

This political sheet lightning from France already signaled the storm gathering over Prussia. France had not offered to compensate England for Hanover; one could only conclude that she intended to give it back. Furthermore, it would have been no more than fair for France to insist on Prussia's participation in the negotiations, because France was the sole reason why Prussia and England were at war. But far from demanding Prussian representation, the French never thought to mention it.

At the beginning of June, M. de Talleyrand frankly declared to Lord Yarmouth, Fox's negotiator, that Hanover would never become a bone of contention. At this point the Prussian government began to have doubts about its relations with France; it felt vaguely anxious and recognized that the state's honor would again be put to the test.

As brief as the period had been since Count Haugwitz had signed *his* Vienna agreement, this latest affront—whether more of an insult or a betrayal is hard to say—was only the most recent of many serious infringements of Prussia's interests:

1. The establishment of the Confederation of the Rhine, immediately following the Treaty of Pressburg, without being mentioned during the negotiations, so that neither Austria nor Prussia knew about it.
2. The intrigues that France promoted to undermine the establishment of a north German confederation by Prussia, although France herself

had proposed this as a counterpart to the Confederation of the Rhine.

3. The offer of Fulda to the elector of Hesse if he joined the Confederation—Hesse being one of the main members of the proposed northern confederation, and Fulda the property of the brother-in-law of the Prussian king, the prince of Orange, whose just claims were nevertheless ignored.

4. The seizure of the abbeys of Essen and Verden by the grand duke of Berg,[16] though they had never belonged to Cleves.

5. The occupation of Wesel by France herself, though Prussia had ceded it only in favor of the grand duke of Berg.

These various violations of Prussian interests—Bonaparte's steadily more threatening advance into Germany; the prospect of losing Hanover in a manner even more disgraceful than the way in which it had been acquired, and then to become the laughing stock of Europe—combined with the last reports of Marquis Lucchesini, who, despite his wife's fondness for Paris, finally decided to open the eyes of his government and declare frankly that nothing could be expected from Bonaparte but war and a hard peace, filled the cup to overflowing, and led to a decision by the Prussian government that must be described as an act of desperation. This decision derived more from the king's personal sense of honor, and that of Minister Hardenberg, who had been brought back into the deliberations, both of whom felt matters had finally gone too far, than from any change of heart by Count Haugwitz and Cabinet Councilor Lombard—although in the end they both feigned acquiescence out of fear that further resistance would arouse suspicion that they favored France too much.

The orbit of Prussia's political interests had gradually been drawn so tight that mind and heart had become one and at last judgment could derive from feelings alone. A passage in the Prussian manifesto expresses this clearly:

Les intentions de Napoléon n'étaient plus douteuses. Il voulait porter la guerre en Prusse, ou metter cette monarchie à jamais hors d'état de prendre les armes, en la conduisant d'humiliation en humiliation, jusqu'à un point de dégradation politique et d'affaiblissement, où privée de ses boulevards elle n'aurait d'autre parti à prendre que de se soumettre à la volunté de son redoutable voisin.[17]

[16] Joachim Murat, Napoleon's brother-in-law.

[17] "Napoleon's intentions were no longer in doubt. He wished to make war on Prussia, or to render that monarchy forever incapable of going to war, by heaping humiliations upon her to the point of political degradation and enfeeblement, so that, deprived of her defenses, she would have no choice but to submit to the demands of her powerful neighbor."

Since the French still had an army of 80–100,000 men in southern Germany while another was gathering on the lower Rhine, the Prussian court recognized that the ill will of the French emperor would soon descend on it like a thunderclap. It therefore decided at the beginning of August to return the army to a war footing and concentrate it in Saxony.

Prussia was forced to mobilize again at the very moment Russia and England were negotiating a separate peace in Paris. It was a real stroke of luck for Prussia that the two powers could not reach agreement with France. The czar refused to ratify the pact that Oubril, his emissary in Paris, had too hastily concluded. This treaty had a peculiarly clumsy genesis. Oubril, whose instructions basically were directed toward the achievement of a comprehensive treaty, learned shortly after his arrival in Paris of the establishment of the Confederation of the Rhine, whose charter was signed on July 12. Rather than be warned off by this and seek new instructions from his government, Oubril regarded the confederation as a direct threat to Austria, which he believed he could forestall by concluding a definitive peace with France, whose central provision was that the French troops should immediately leave Germany. How Oubril could have imagined that such a proviso would have placed even a diplomatic obstacle in the way of war with Austria or Prussia is hard to understand. The measure was no better conceived than that of children who try to catch a bird by putting salt on its tail.

English negotiations in Paris were likewise approaching a fruitless end, which was hastened by the death of the famous Fox.

By September Prussia could again contemplate the prospect that, at least in the long run, she would not have to fight France alone.

Relations with Sweden, as was said earlier, had already been mended in August, when Prussia yielded in the matter of Lauenburg. It was also easy to dispense with hostilities toward England, since, after the death of Fox, Grey had left the opposition and entered the cabinet; he was less eager for peace with France than his predecessor had been. Nevertheless, an agreement with England on subsidies and assistance was reached only later, a few days before the battle of Auerstädt.[18]

Russia was still more or less an ally, and in September Colonel Krusemark was sent to St. Petersburg to confer about the auxiliaries Russia was planning to send.

An alliance was concluded with Saxony, which increased Prussia's forces by 20,000 men; negotiations were also opened with Hesse, whose elector did not want to show his hand too early.

And so the strands leading to Prussia's catastrophe came together.

We have merely outlined Prussia's political situation between the Peace of

---

[18] Negotiations with Great Britain actually began in the late fall of 1806, and an agreement was signed in January 1807.

Basel and 1806, because it is already discussed more fully in the second chapter of this work, which is primarily devoted to that subject. A small book published by Cabinet Councilor Lombard in 1808 to justify his actions, as well as the policies of Count Haugwitz and the Prussian government, has provided the guiding thread for our remarks.[19] It has seemed worthwhile to recall its perspective again, since it is important that posterity come to understand the Prussian cabinet's point of view. But of course we also accept the proverb *audiatur et altera pars*,[20] and hence have believed it necessary to present the public with opposing views of Prussia's situation.

No matter how difficult the political role of a state that finds itself in the ranks of far stronger nations, and regardless of how difficult the condition of Europe since the French Revolution advanced on its destructive course with a hitherto unheard-of degree of state power, we are convinced that Prussia's desperate position in 1806 was due entirely to her own poor policies. Even the most effective policies might not have prevented her collapse, but defeat would have been accompanied with more honor, respect, and sympathy, which together with the greater expenditure of her energies would have prepared a better basis for future resurgence.

We will now turn our attention to the political mood of the Prussian people, since a great deal has been said about it, and then consider the preparations for war.

In pure monarchies the people only concern themselves with public affairs when they sense an immediate connection between larger events and their own welfare—for instance, when the state is at war, or when the wounds inflicted by another state still bleed. This was the case in Prussia in 1809, when all hearts prayed for an Austrian victory, and in 1812, when hatred against France far outweighed the insignificant public interest in the honor of the Prussian auxiliary corps on the Duna. We are speaking here of real public concern, not the crackpot opinions of coffeehouse newspaper readers. The war of 1792 had attracted reasonably broad but divided public interest. People were for or against the war, depending on whether the French Revolution offended their habitual views and feelings or stimulated speculative ideas, plans, and hopes. The former was certainly the stronger impulse among the mass of the people, the latter applied mainly to the educated middle classes. Opposition to the war grew as military success lent unexpected splendor to the French cause, and simultaneously undermined confidence in the old ways. But when the government and the upper classes grew weary of a war that seemed increasingly impolitic and irrelevant to Prussia's main interests and began to prepare for the Peace of Basel, public interest in the war and its objectives faded away, except among a few men here and there

---

[19] Lombard's memoirs. See p. 54, above.
[20] "Let the other side be heard," a legal proverb.

who could see a little farther ahead. Popular concern was reduced to nothing more than a desire for peace, and when this was satisfied at Basel it disappeared altogether. At that time the public was still far from viewing France as everyone's enemy. Only the Prussian government sensed this, but it neither spoke out, nor did it encourage other voices that might have done so, because the immediate fear of war and financial distress obscured the more distant danger. Nor did the government wish to undermine public confidence in its so-called neutrality system. Until 1805 the people remained without any real sense of participation in European affairs. The victories of France and its territorial growth since the Peace of Lunéville seemed to have been fully matched by Prussia's own gains, because our understanding, like our eyes, always finds nearby objects more imposing than those farther away.

Nevertheless, interest in politics grew more intense and widespread among the upper classes as the growth of the French universal monarchy became more evident, and Austria in 1805 received a blow that threatened her collapse. Three parties emerged, two of which sought the same goal. The first admired French institutions, French glory and brilliance, and would have considered it a good thing for Europe to be placed under the tutelage of France. *Thus, no war with France!* The second party had the same objective, but only because it dreaded nothing so much as seeing the prevailing peace and tranquility disturbed, and because it feared to risk the strength of the Prussian state on a dangerous and unpromising course of action. *Thus, again, no war with France!* The third party saw France's progress in Europe as leading toward a universal monarchy that threatened Prussia's existence. Therefore, *war with France!*

Slowly people came to realize that Prussian policy was not the dignified neutrality that one might have imagined it to be from the newspapers, and here and there feelings of national honor stirred. Those for whom this became the dominant consideration strengthened the third party—they were primarily younger officers, and a few exceptional people among the older generation, most of whom, however, belonged to the second party. This is how things stood among the upper classes in 1805. Now came the illegal march of the French corps through Prussian Franconia. It outraged everyone whose patriotism was not utterly asleep and strengthened the third party, particularly in the army. Indeed, no one who had not been rendered insensitive to every national interest by a perverse admiration for the French monarchy, or who was so deeply mired in Philistine anxiety that he dared not open his eyes, could have failed to take offense.

We can therefore say that by 1806 the war party had been greatly strengthened among the educated classes, but that the mass of the people, the workers and peasants, were still not truly aware of what was going on. There were few traces of interest in the French or their institutions among these people. Love of peace is endemic to the north of Germany, because the strong, cool north German mind always seeks a sound basis for action; it cannot be brought to a high pitch of enthusiasm by a mere hint of the truth. The government had done nothing whatever to show the people the danger facing Prussia and Europe and hid as best it could the insults it had to endure from France. So the people remained uninvolved, but there is no question that it would have been easy to awaken their patriotism. The war itself provided the first impetus but did not last long enough for national feeling to take hold before disaster struck. It takes longer for an idea to penetrate the minds of ten million men than that of a single individual.

But this description also suggests how forgivable it is if the Prussian population did not respond to the events of 1806 with the indignation and hostility that might be thought natural and appropriate in a noble people; and why, on the other hand, the younger members of the nobility, most of whom served in the army, were driven to almost arrogant expressions of national pride, and pride in their own caste and their arms. It would be narrow and erroneous to suppose that such behavior was confined to a few units. But it is also clear that public sentiment could have influenced the cabinet's decision in 1806 only to the extent that the government felt it necessary not to allow the public's pride to collapse completely, and not to fall into public disrepute itself. But this concern with the power of public opinion had nothing in common with acting in a certain way out of fear of popular violence. Anyone who lived in Berlin in 1806 can only find such a suggestion ridiculous, although Cabinet Councilor Lombard hints at it in his book, in order to provide a stronger motivation for the decision to go to war.

The actual preparations for war were limited to mobilizing the army, arming the fortresses that were immediately at risk, concentrating the army, and assigning the various commands.

The Prussian state had always taken great pride *precisely in this*: that it needed no lengthy preparations for war but was always armed, so that only one order had to be given to bring the army to a full state of readiness four to six weeks later. This state of readiness was the triumph of Frederick the Great. But it was tailored to his time, to his opponent—*Austria*—and to his theater of operations—*Silesia*. The ability to appear on the battlefield at any moment with 100,000 men, Frederick the Great believed, was all that was necessary to keep Austria at bay. The Austrian empire seemed to him like a Polish magnate of enormous wealth but of equally great needs that cause him much incidental expense, so that, entangled in debts and mortgages by bad management, he is never the master of his own fortune. A small man of lesser means but greater prudence and industry, and with hard cash, can often lay down the law to a rich and elegant gentleman. Under Frederick the Great, Prussia was such a small man. Against Austria we had to rely above

75

all on our own resources; but against other, *more distant powers,* political alliances were essential to maintain the balance. With 100,000 men always at the ready, Frederick the Great commanded the respect of Austria and through her the rest of Europe. In Prussia since then the word *mobilization* had been the spark that would touch off the mine, and no one thought that anything more needed to be done.

The French Revolution had lent a new character to European politics and to war, which Frederick the Great had not anticipated, as on the eve of changes we seldom can predict the direction matters will take.

Through the power and energy of its principles and the enthusiasm that it inspired in the French people, the Revolution had thrown the whole weight of the nation and its strengths into a balance that had formerly weighed only small standing armies and limited state revenues. Despising the petty interests and concerns of the European cabinets, France wanted to rule the continent and above all extend her own territory to what she considered her natural frontiers.

French military might strode defiantly across the land, contemptuous of the political calculus with which other governments anxiously weighed enmities and alliances, weakening the force of war and binding the raw element of conflict in diplomatic bonds. To their own and everyone else's surprise, the French learned that a state's natural power and a great simple cause were far stronger than the artificial structure of international relations by which other states were ruled.[21]

Such a fundamental transformation was least of all expected at a time when many believed that highly developed state finances and standing armies had led to a level of civilization at which the strength of the people was completely excluded from public affairs. Everything was reduced to a few strands—treasury, credit, army—which the cabinet held in its hands. So great a transformation was imaginable least of all in Prussia, where it was believed the strands were woven more tightly than anywhere else. Nor could anyone have predicted that the great events set in motion in 1792 would be understood at once, or that they would immediately lead to changes in attitudes. But in the fourteen years that separate 1806 from 1792 it might well have been concluded that we were facing a struggle against an entire people, a struggle for life or death.

Even if the German governments did not yet know how to oppose the Franch nation with their own peoples, as they did in 1813, we might still have reasonably expected something more from them than the simple act of mobilization.

[21] Compare the discussion of the wars of the French Revolution and Napoleon in *On War,* 591–93.

The Prussian army was approximately 200,000 men strong; it could be anticipated that barely 150,000 would serve in the field. Such a force would certainly not insure victory, and if it had been sufficient then [it would have been so] only against the force with which France would attack us at the outbreak of the war. There could be no doubt that another French army would soon reach the theater of operations, nor that considerable Prussian losses would have to be replaced in the first few weeks.

In the preceding forty-five years the Prussian army had conducted only a few campaigns, and even in these only parts of the army were engaged. The principle of promoting exclusively by seniority had filled the higher positions with worn-out old men. In peacetime they might just manage to keep going, but to rely on them in war, a war of life or death, against young, vigorous commanders, was more than audacious.

Prussia's relations with the other powers were the result of her previous policies, and the pace at which these could be brought over to her side could not easily be accelerated. But the small principalities scattered among the Prussian territories formed a natural political unit with Prussia and could and should have been stirred to the same extraordinary exertions as Prussia made.

The elector and dukes of Saxony, the elector of Hesse, the duke of Brunswick, the princes of the two Mecklenburgs, Anhalt, Schwarzburg, Lippe, etc., collectively could have raised a force of 60–70,000 men. Instead, only 18,000 Saxons were in the field in October 1806. But in battle much can be decided by 10,000 men, not to mention 50,000.

Because there was little prospect of success at the outset of the campaign and of holding on in Saxony until the Russians arrived, the war should have been envisioned as extending to the Vistula and all preparations worked out accordingly.

These preparations should have included the following extraordinary measures:

1. The creation of a substantial cash reserve, whether by borrowing or through war taxes.
2. A domestic levy of 100,000 men in August when the decision to go to war was made, to form reserve battalions.
3. The formation of a proportionate number of field batteries, using bronze guns taken from the fortresses, which could be replaced by iron guns.
4. Purchase of several hundred thousand muskets in Austria or England.
5. The removal of all military supplies from open stores to fortresses.
6. The establishment of bridgeheads on the Elbe, Oder, and Vistula Rivers.

77

7. The pensioning off of over-aged generals, senior officers, and company commanders; the promotion of some younger men to senior positions; and the assignment of commands to younger, ambitious men.
8. Lastly, the adoption of friendly but firm policies to influence the smaller states.

Not even one of these eight measures, which ordinary common sense contemplating the prevailing danger would have demanded, was undertaken because everyone was accustomed to think only of—the process of mobilization.

The following summary provides a general idea, allowing for some small errors, of the nominal strength of the Prussian army in August 1806.

INFANTRY

1. 58 infantry regiments, of 2 battalions of 5 companies each; each company consisting of 172 men, exclusive of officers and musicians	
Total musketeers	99,760 men
2. Joined to these 29 grenadier battalions, of 4 companies of the same strength	
Total grenadiers	19,952
3. 24 fusilier battalions, of 4 companies of the same strength	
Total fusiliers	16,512
4. One regiment of *Jäger*, composed of 3 battalions of 600 men	
Total *Jäger*	1,800
5. 5 guards battalions of 4 companies	3,400
Total Infantry	141,464 men

CAVALRY

1. 12 cuirassier regiments of 5 squadrons, each squadron consisting of 132 horse, thus 60 squadrons	7,920 horse
2. 14 dragoon regiments, 12 composed of 5 squadrons, 2 of 10 squadrons each; each squadron consisting of 132 horse, thus 80 dragoon squadrons	10,560

3. 15 uhlan squadrons of 162 horse each, totaling   2,430
4. 9½ hussar regiments, composed of 10
   squadrons of 162 horse each, thus 95
   hussar squadrons   15,390

     Total cavalry, in 250 squadrons   36,300 horse

ARTILLERY

4 regiments of foot artillery, composed
of _____ companies of _____ men each; 10
companies of mounted artillery, of _____men
   Total artillery   8,000 men

    Total field forces   185,764 men

GARRISON TROOPS

58 reserve battalions of 500 men   29,000 men
58 invalid companies of 50 men   2,900

   Total garrison troops   31,900 men

   Total strength of the army   217,664 men

This sum can be considered as roughly 200,000 men, since of course not all these formations were up to established strength, and what with one thing and another a shortage of one-twelfth can probably be taken for granted.[22]

Of these 200,000 one would normally have expected at least 150,000 to be in the theater of operations, if one deducts 50,000 men of second-line troops and field units necessary to man a few fortresses. But the actual total was not so favorable.

For reasons difficult to grasp, the forces in East Prussia were not immediately mobilized and consequently not available in the theater of operations in Saxony. Some people believed this was done to save men and money, on the assumption that these troops were meant to join up with the Russian auxiliary forces, and that until then one could save the additional expense of having them on a field footing. Related to this idea was another—that it was

---

[22] Clausewitz's figures agree on the whole with the mobilization totals for 1805 and 1806 published in subsequent general staff histories.

essential to hold an army in reserve. This completely confused concept haunts some minds even now. As much as tactical reserves are a good thing, the idea of a strategic reserve of battle-ready forces is nonsense. The reason is that battles decide the course of the war, and, while tactical reserves are used to affect the decision, strategic reserves are only used after it has been reached. What would one say of a coachman who unhitched half his horses at the edge of a pit in the road, to hold them in reserve in case the others get tired? The belief in the benefits of a strategic reserve, which still appears quite often, must have seemed very plausible to people at the time, so it is understandable that the supreme command thought it both practical and economical to leave the East Prussian troops peacefully in their quarters for the time being. Their nominal establishment amounted to 21,000 men. Ten thousand men were also left behind in the Duchy of Warsaw for a reason that, though more usual, was no better. Warsaw was not considered politically reliable, and one did not want to strip it entirely of troops. Of course it would have been worth the trouble to prevent a revolutionary uprising in Warsaw by maintaining a strong garrison there, *provided one possessed ample forces overall*. But under circumstances like those of David setting out to fight Goliath, the only *possibility* of success lay in the most determined concentration of all forces against the main enemy. If the French were defeated in Franconia, the Poles would have remained quiet for the time being; if the French were victorious, the detachments left in Poland would have had to be brought up anyway.

In Silesia, too, six infantry battalions remained behind because the garrison troops were regarded as too weak to hold the fortresses. Since the Silesian fortresses were in no way threatened as long as the fighting was limited to Saxony, and since in case of a retreat a corps could have been detached to Silesia, these 4,000 men could and should also have taken the field against the enemy.

From the full establishment of 186,000 combat troops, we must therefore subtract:

Those remaining in East Prussia	21,424
Those remaining in Silesia	4,300
Those remaining in south Prussia	10,320
Those attached to artillery	2,000
	38,044

Therefore only 148,000 remained available for the major operations.

Of these, however, 11,700 were stationed in Westphalia, some to garrison the fortresses at Hamel and Minden, others as a small observation corps under General Le Coq, which left only 136,000 men available in the Saxon theater of operations.

Yet at the end of September our army in Thuringia amounted to barely 110,000 men, 26,000 fewer than the establishment called for. This is not surprising if one considers that under the existing system of forced recruitment and the high rate of desertion associated with it, units could seldom be kept up to strength, still less so now that foreign recruitment had ceased to exist. The last domestic levy had been raised in the spring; many invalids, with which the army swarmed, had to be left behind during the mobilization; rapid marches, to which the troops were unaccustomed, increased illness to some extent; and finally, the regiments were not used to the harsh conditions of wartime, and many men continued to be detailed to perform trivial tasks instead of being available for combat. Under these circumstances a shortfall of 25–26,000 men, that is, about one-fifth of established strength, is not exceptional, and the Prussian government should have foreseen it and taken steps to compensate for it.

Thus, of Prussia's famous battle-ready force of 220,000 men, only half were actually present and ready for the most decisive conflict in which they would ever have to fight.

The political preparations for the war were no better. Because the government feared war more than anything, it could not bring itself to give up the last hope for peace. This sort of shrinking from danger, by grasping at the last glimmer of hope, no matter how improbable, is among the clearest and most common ways in which weakness reveals itself. Nothing is more disastrous than a refusal to face unavoidable danger squarely. But, to be sure, if princes are to know when a danger is truly unavoidable, they must turn their backs on toadies who tell them only what they want to hear, rely on their own common sense, and consult those men whose hearts are in the right place.

Even in August and September the government still believed it was possible to avoid war, that is, it was hoped that some grounds for compromise with Bonaparte could be found; therefore it did not wish to become involved with England and Russia too deeply or too soon. The final decision was postponed until General Knobelsdorff's first report arrived from Paris, a delay that makes it clear that this sorry emissary was not sent to Paris simply to mislead the French; rather, his personality was supposed to ease matters at the last moment. What a wretched expedient! His report did not arrive until September 17. Had one not waited for it, the alliance with England could have been concluded in London in September, rather than in East Prussia in November.[23] Instead of doing everything possible to gain help from England, above all to receive weapons and money quickly, the government waited for Lord

[23] See note 18, above.

Morpeth to reach army headquarters in Weimar; and since he only arrived on October 12, two days before the battles of Jena and Auerstädt, a treaty naturally could not be concluded before the battles were fought. Even so, Marquis Lucchesini's explanation that the negotiations depended on the outcome of the battle remains remarkable. One would ordinarily have expected such an explanation from Lord Morpeth; but while England's policy and the whole attitude of her government was too firm, strong, and majestic to shy away from any possible change of fortune, Prussia had grown so flabby that when misfortune struck she could not cling to a stronger ally in order to continue to resist. In short, Prussia gained nothing from England's support in the campaign of 1806.

Relations with Russia were no better. Colonel Krusemark could have been sent to St. Petersburg at the end of August, because the czar's position was already known; but he did not leave until September 18, the day after General Knobelsdorff's report arrived. He was supposed to undertake the negotiations necessary to the dispatch of an auxiliary army. But the results show that Prussia did not press for immediate assistance because the Russian army, although only 50,000 strong, was ready at the frontier, prepared to march, and could have been on the Oder by mid-November, which would have made an enormous difference. In view of the czar's friendly and obliging attitude, political difficulties or delays were not to be expected. That the Russian army did not cross the frontier until November was certainly caused by the same mistaken attitude of the Prussian government that allowed the troops in East and South Prussia to remain in their quarters. As late as the end of October the Prussian government still concluded an elaborate convention in Grodno respecting the provisioning of Russia's auxiliary army. In such mechanistic formalities effective help for the campaign of 1806 was allowed to dissipate.

The choice of the man sent to St. Petersburg further proves that the mission was not deemed very important but was simply intended to arrange the implementation of earlier agreements. Colonel von Krusemark was Field Marshal Möllendorff's adjutant, or rather merely his distinguished errand-boy, a man of refined manners, but completely ignorant, without conspicuous natural talents of any kind, who had never previously been employed in any political capacity except for a few insignificant diplomatic missions. Since his position and personal stature did not lend him any real weight, it was easy to realize that he was not sent to accomplish anything out of the ordinary. At the time it was said that he was supposed to discuss the plan of operations with the Russians; but that subject would have been more alien to him than any other, and in any case the time had not come for such discussions because the Russian army was still almost seven hundred miles to the east of the Prussian.

With difficulty, an agreement with Saxony had been concluded, according to which 18,000 men, roughly half her armed forces, were to join the Prussian army. This arrangement was settled so late that the Saxon troops were the last to move into position, causing several days' delay. The two Mecklenburgs, Anhalt, Schwarzburg, Lippe, the Saxon duchies, and the duke of Brunswick had generously been allowed to remain neutral, as if such a large army had been accumulated that 10,000 or 20,000 men were of no account. Only the duke of Weimar sent a *Jäger* battalion.

The elector of Hesse twisted and turned just as Prussia had. He wanted to await a Prussian victory before declaring himself; in case of defeat, the sacred rights of neutrality would keep him safe, like a rock in a raging sea. That his weak character was immediately punished by the most degrading catastrophe was only fair and right; it would have been outrageous for such a policy to be crowned with success. But that the Prussian cabinet allowed the Hessian court to pursue this policy was equally weak: our troops crossed Hessian territory on the way from Westphalia to Thuringia, which should have been enough to leave the elector no choice, and the addition of 15,000 Hessians was not to be despised.

That is how it happened that, instead of 50,000 allies, the army Prussia concentrated against the French in Thuringia had no more than 18,000 Saxons.

Were it not for these mistakes by the government and the military leadership, Prussia, without exceptional effort, simply by making use of existing forces, might have opposed the enemy with 200,000 men, instead of the 130,000 actually there. If, despite the resulting superiority, the first battles were nevertheless lost, they would not have been lost in the same manner, they would not have been total defeats.

In Paris, too, Prussia's interests were poorly represented. Lucchesini, having finally sounded the alarm, had to be recalled. General Knobelsdorff was sent in his place because the French were known to like him; they favored him because he was the son-in-law of the Dutch ambassador to Constantinople, Count Dedem, and at the time of his mission to Constantinople had been altogether captivated by French interests, and also because he was a weak diplomat.

Feeble, too, were the evasions Knobelsdorff practiced while in Paris before he was instructed to deliver our court's ultimatum. Throughout the month of September he pretended that Prussia's preparations for war were the result of insinuations made to the king by those who hated and envied France, from whom the deluded monarch would soon turn away. This language immediately betrays the influence of Count Haugwitz, on whose instructions Knobelsdorff acted. Shamelessness of this sort must at least be accompanied by great acumen if it is not to seem repulsive and absurd.

On October 1 General Knobelsdorff was finally forced to change his tone and present the Prussian ultimatum to the French ministry.

By this ultimatum, Prussia insisted on the following preliminary conditions before demobilizing:

1. That all French troops without exception withdraw immediately beyond the Rhine.
2. That no further obstacles be placed in the way of a northern confederation.
3. That Wesel be separated from France and ceded to the Grand Duchy of Berg.
4. That the three abbeys illegally occupied by the Grand Duchy of Berg be reoccupied by Prussian troops.

An answer to the king's headquarters was peremptorily demanded by October 8.

Although this ultimatum did not even address the main issues at stake and the French could have satisfied its demands without Prussia's position being improved in the least, to deliver it in Paris six days after Bonaparte had left to join the French army was tactless and clumsy. If Prussia still sought a way out through last-minute negotiations, they could only have been carried on at imperial headquarters, and it would have been far less presumptuous to use a decided tone there, rather than to Talleyrand in Paris, just as it is far less discourteous to insult someone to his face than to do so through his servant. But the language chosen was not appropriate in any case. The emperor Napoleon could have been told of all matters that concerned the king of Prussia in a form that was altogether passive and impersonal, without betraying Prussia's dignity or determination in any way. Prussia's diplomatic language would have remained on the defensive, just as her political system was defensive. One would not have exposed oneself to ridicule based on the double contrast between Prussia's peremptory tone and the long-standing meekness of her policy, between the most recent language adopted by General Knobelsdorff on the one hand, and the inadequacy of her political and military power on the other.

But the Prussian government was composed of contradictory elements, and two things are always lacking in such cases: unity and harmonious movement. One always flops back and forth from one extreme to the other.

To have expected any answer but war to such an ultimatum, and therefore to delay military operations for another fourteen days, was more the result of weakness, of clinging to a last hope, even if it appeared to be quixotic generosity.

FOUR

"On the Life and Character of Scharnhorst" (1817)

The man who exerted the greatest influence on the development of Clausewitz's historical and theoretical thought was Gerhard von Scharnhorst, who became his teacher at the Berlin military academy in 1801 when Clausewitz was twenty-one and from then on took a close interest in the young officer's progress. After the defeats of 1806 and 1807, Scharnhorst was appointed chairman of a commission established to reorganize the army. When Clausewitz returned from internment in France the following fall, he joined Scharnhorst's staff and was given increasingly important assignments in formulating and carrying out the military and political reform program. In the spring of 1812 Napoleon compelled Prussia to mobilize an auxiliary corps as part of the force about to invade Russia; Scharnhorst remained in the army but did nothing to dissuade Clausewitz from resigning his commission and joining the Russians. The two men were reunited at the beginning of the following year as Prussia was shifting from the French to the Russian alliance. In March Scharnhorst was appointed quartermaster general, in effect chief of staff of the Prussian forces mobilized against Napoleon, and Clausewitz served on his staff until Scharnhorst was fatally wounded in the battle of Grossgörschen.

Scharnhorst's death symbolized the end of the reform era and the failure of some of the reformers' most cherished plans, just as six years earlier the appointment to high office of this atypical soldier, neither a native nor of noble birth, indicated the extent of the defeat and how great, for the moment, was the army's loss of confidence in the traditional system. Since then conservatism had rallied, and Clausewitz's sense of loss at the death of his teacher and friend was intensified by his belief that too many of the men who now ruled ignored or maliciously misinterpreted Scharnhorst's achievements.

The official obituary, at the time believed to be by Gneisenau but almost certainly written in collaboration with Clausewitz, contains a paragraph that suggests resentment of the opposition and injustice Scharnhorst had encountered: "What he meant to the state, to the people, and to Germany as a whole may be recognized by a few or by many, but it would be disgraceful if anyone remained indifferent to this sad event." The censor wanted to replace this bitter sentence with a brief, positive statement: "Scharnhorst's merits are univer-

sally understood and acknowledged," and Gneisenau had to protest to Hardenberg, the Prussian chancellor, before the text could be printed unchanged.[1]

After the collapse of the Napoleonic empire, the defense of Scharnhorst's memory became linked in Clausewitz's mind with the need to defend the spirit and achievements of the reform movement, which were now increasingly under threat. In 1817 a friend with connections in London suggested he write an essay on Scharnhorst for publication in a British journal, and he grasped the opportunity. He wrote a sketch of Scharnhorst's life in which he sought to take account of British unfamiliarity with German conditions by such phrases as "the famous Baron vom Stein," and by introducing summaries of complex developments. The result was a somewhat awkward, uneven manuscript that still required extensive revisions. In a letter to Gneisenau requesting additional information, especially on Scharnhorst's secret diplomatic missions to St. Petersburg and Vienna in 1811, he nevertheless expressed the hope that he possessed sufficient tact "neither to mystify and displease the British public with German originality, nor to antagonize the so-called impartial readers (that is, those with a cold heart) with odelike flights of praise, nor to displease others with boldly dismissive judgments or even by simply stating the naked truth and compromising people."[2] *In his response, Gneisenau voiced doubts that an article on Scharnhorst would interest the British public, tactfully referring to the United Kingdom's current unstable political situation, which preoccupied everyone, and Clausewitz put the essay aside for the time being, without ever correcting or completing it.*[3] *As the forces of political reaction gathered strength, even the essay's relatively muted criticisms of Prussian policies before and during 1806 and its outspoken support for the reforms would have made publication in Germany problematic, at least for an author who was a serving officer.*

On the last page of the manuscript he sent to Gneisenau, Clausewitz noted that "for German publications it would be appropriate to add a brief survey of [Scharnhorst's] literary achievements and a characterization of his personality. But I believe that for British publications neither would be appropriate."[4] *It is not known whether at that time he had already drafted the sketch of Scharnhorst's personality that forms the second, much superior and polished*

---

[1] The obituary was followed by a sketch of Scharnhorst's life, whose style and choice of words suggest that it, too, was a collaboration of Clausewitz and Gneisenau. Its similarities with parts of Clausewitz's later essay on Scharnhorst are striking; indeed, in a letter of April 28, 1817, to Gneisenau (*Schriften*, 2, part 1: 260–66) Clausewitz noted the resemblance. The piece was signed "S," which stands for the name of a member of Gneisenau's staff who seems to have served as the official author. The texts of the obituary and the biographical sketch are in Pertz-Delbrück, *Gneisenau*, 3: 32–37.

[2] Clausewitz to Gneisenau, March 18, 1817, *Schriften*, 2, part 1: 255–60.

[3] Gneisenau to Clausewitz, April 7, 1817, Pertz-Delbrück, *Gneisenau*, 3: 203–4.

[4] The note is printed in Werner Hahlweg's reconstruction of the original text of the first part of the essay, in *Schriften*, 2, part 1: 288n.

part of his study when it was published in 1832, the year after his death, in the first volume of Ranke's Historisch-politische Zeitschrift.

Possibly the manuscript was called to Ranke's attention by Christian von Bernstorff, the Prussian foreign minister and sponsor of the new journal. Bernstorff had been close to Clausewitz and knew that his wife and friends were preparing Clausewitz's works on the history and theory of war for publication. An article by Clausewitz in the Historisch-politische Zeitschrift *might benefit this edition, the first three volumes of which appeared in the same year that the journal was launched.⁵ But however Ranke came to know of the manuscript, it fit nicely into his program of publishing studies of recent history, "particularly of the French Revolution and its aftermath, analyses of Prussian and German affairs, and historical accounts from any period that contributed to a true understanding of politics." Not only was it an interesting historical document, it usefully recalled to its readers a heroic period in which, so Ranke thought, the Prussian state had been set on the path of peaceful progress and intelligent preservation, as opposed to "actual liberalism" on the one hand and "reactionary attempts to retain the past" on the other.⁶*

Nevertheless Ranke took advantage of the privilege of self-censorship that had been granted to the Zeitschrift. *Near the beginning of the essay he deleted a paragraph that criticizes Prussia's military leadership, institutions, and practices in 1806. The paragraph is included in our text. Several pages later a discussion of public opinion during the reform era, positing a party favoring association with France and another that waited for the opportunity to renew the war, lost its concluding sentence: "Which of these two opinions more closely reflected the feelings of the common people may remain undecided here; but in the upper and middle levels of society the former party [i.e., favoring the French alliance] was visibly the stronger." Finally Ranke excised four passages, nine lines in all, from a letter by Scharnhorst to Clausewitz, one of several letters he printed as an appendix to the essay. Again the cuts were meant to minimize reports of sharp conflicts among the leadership and to smooth over or eliminate criticisms of prominent individuals.⁷ Ranke also made a host of small stylistic changes to smooth transitions, fill gaps, and clarify the text of Clausewitz's unrevised draft.⁸*

For his sources Clausewitz drew on printed material and on some letters,

---

⁵ In a postscript to the essay, Ranke wrote that "we believe we have acted according to the wishes of the deceased if this memorial to his dear friend and teacher, though incomplete, is given precedence over his other writings intended for publication." *Historisch-politische Zeitschrift* 1 (1832): 213.

⁶ See the discussion of Ranke's prospectus for the *Zeitschrift* in Lawrence J. Baack, *Christian Bernstorff and Prussia* (New Brunswick, N.J., 1980), 304.

⁷ The letters are not part of the essay. They were added by Clausewitz's widow and are not included in this edition.

⁸ As noted in the Preface, Ranke's deletions are enclosed in curly brackets.

*but he based himself mainly on his personal knowledge of Scharnhorst. A fur-
ther reworking would have corrected a few errors of detail—Scharnhorst was
born in 1755, not 1756, and was promoted to the rank of full colonel in 1804,
not 1806—and might also have achieved a closer integration of the two parts
of the essay. Presumably without realizing it himself, Clausewitz wrote the
"Portrait of Scharnhorst" in an emotional, dense style that contrasted with his
customary even and circumstantial manner. But the author's personal involvement is apparent even in the earlier, unrevised sections on Scharnhorst's
life. Clausewitz admires and is deeply attached to the man he writes about;
his approval of Scharnhorst's social and political environment, on the other
hand, is qualified and ambivalent. The essay is not only a work of contemporary history, it is also the account and reflections of a sometime eyewitness
and constant partisan, who demonstratively takes the side of reform and confronts the reader with the formulations and rhetoric of a cause that has gone
out of fashion. Two timeless themes help shape the interpretation of Scharnhorst and his specific historical situation: the encounter between an honorable,
dedicated and courageous individual with the common run of men; and the
psychological configuration and experiences that made it possible for a fundamentally uncompromising personality to become politically effective. Later
scholars have not followed Clausewitz's hero worship, but have found nothing
significant to alter in his interpretation of Scharnhorst. In his essay he established a model that has retained its interpretive power.*

*The second part of the essay, however, goes beyond a considered, carefully
executed character analysis. It contains in miniature an account of the revolution in war that accompanied the French Revolution and of the efforts of
theorists to understand the new combination of seemingly unlimited military
energy with expansive political power emanating from France. In Clausewitz's
view it was Scharnhorst who first reached a practical understanding of this
phenomenon, and the writer's admiration for Scharnhorst's achievement is as
apparent as his desire to emulate it. Detached from the figure of Scharnhorst,
the argument of this part of the essay echoes through the pages of* On War,
*finally to reappear in expanded form in chapter 3B of Book VIII, in which
history and theory achieve their ultimate synthesis in Clausewitz's work.*

I. Account of Scharnhorst's Life
and Circumstances

On June 28, 1813, Gerhard David von Scharnhorst, lieutenant general in
the Prussian army, died in Prague of a wound he had received on May 2 at
the battle of Grossgörschen.

His sterling, effective service, in close proximity to the throne and at the center of a state that by the force of circumstances of those days had itself become almost the center of the European state system, gives him an important place in the annals of that politically tumultuous age.

He was born at Bordenau, a small hereditary leasehold in Hanover, on November 12, 1756,[9] received his early education at the military academy founded by Count Wilhelm von Bückeburg at Wilhelmsstein, and was quickly singled out by that great man for special attention. He began his military career in the Hanoverian army, first in the cavalry but soon as a gunner, and served with the allied armies in Flanders and Holland during the campaigns of 1793–95.

An intensely active mind, supported by exceptional energy, he wrote a manual for officers during the campaign of 1793—a work that in Germany is still regarded as a classic of its kind. He was one of those rare individuals in whom theoretical knowledge and scholarly ambition are combined,[10] and in the next campaign showed himself to be an outstanding officer in combat. As gunnery captain he served as principal staff officer to the Hanoverian general von Hammerstein when the latter defended Menin in 1794 and fought his way out with the garrison. Such rare exploits in the history of war redound to the glory of all who took part; here the major credit belongs to the Hammerstein—an honorable soldier highly respected in Germany and England—and after him to his assistant, Scharnhorst. The best account and clearest evidence of what we mean to say is contained in the following report by General Hammerstein to General Wallmoden, who commanded the Hanoverian contingent, and should not be forgotten in the chronicle of these times:

CONCLUSION OF THE REPORT BY GENERAL HAMMERSTEIN TO GENERAL WALLMODEN ON THE RETREAT FROM MENIN

Above all others, I am duty-bound to mention Captain Scharnhorst. Throughout his service at Menin, during both the shelling and the final breakout, he demonstrated ability and talent, together with incomparable courage, unflagging enthusiasm, and admirable self-possession. The success of my plan to fight our way out of the town I owe to him alone. In every action he was the first, and the last. I cannot possibly

---

[9] Clausewitz mistakes the year; Scharnhorst was born in 1755. Ranke introduced two additional errors: Scharnhorst is said to be born on November 10, in Hämelsee.

[10] Ranke added three words he believed Clausewitz had left out: "combined *with practical skill*."

describe in detail how useful this exemplary officer was to me, or how deserving of recognition.

I must therefore most respectfully entreat Your Excellency to mention all the above-named officers in Your Excellency's report to His Majesty [the king of England]. Were it possible I would ask special rewards for all of them, for they are truly deserving. But I most earnestly beg a favor from His Majesty for Captain Scharnhorst; for if ever any man received a reward for extraordinary service, he has now earned it in the highest degree.

Ecklo, May 3, 1794

R. von Hammerstein

After the war Scharnhorst rose to the rank of lieutenant colonel in the Hanoverian service and occupied himself with numerous writings on military subjects. In 1801, at the urging of Duke Karl of Brunswick, who was to be killed at the battle of Auerstädt, he transferred from the Hanoverian to the Prussian service and on the pressing recommendation of the duke was appointed lieutenant colonel in the Prussian artillery. He brought with him a reputation as an erudite soldier, especially in the science of gunnery, but as is often the case encountered much envy and resistance from his fellow officers. It prevented him from being as useful to the artillery as his knowledge and energy would otherwise have permitted and was the reason he preferred a position on the general staff, to which he was posted in 1804 as lieutenant quartermaster general.

Between 1802 and 1806 Scharnhorst devoted himself primarily to the education of infantry and cavalry officers. He expanded the curriculum these men had received in Berlin—taught by a single teacher since the days of Frederick the Great—and created a true military academy, with himself as director. He taught the part of the art of war that until then had been virtually ignored in our books and lecture halls: war as it actually is. It was here that the new methods of waging war introduced by the French Revolution and brought to fruition by Napoleon were first expounded in Prussia—innovations that were still little known in the army because they had not yet been fully developed during the campaigns of 1792–94, and in consequence had exerted no influence on Prussian ways of fighting.

The educational institution that he created still exists in the Prussian army.[11]

His exceptional merit was soon recognized and led the king to raise him to the nobility in 1805 and to promote him to colonel in 1806.

[11] Ranke added, "and has trained most of Prussia's general staff officers."

In 1806 Scharnhorst was among those who regarded war with France as necessary. As chief of staff to the duke of Brunswick he helped devise the operational plan that called for the army to advance through the Thuringian forest and surprise the French in their quarters in Franconia.

{Scharnhorst's opponents have held him responsible both for the unhappy outcome of the campaign and for the lost war. But we should consider that he was subordinate to many others—some of ancient Prussian lineage, others with service extending back to the days of Frederick the Great, qualities that together with the brilliance of showy talents influenced the opinion of the government and of the people far more than did the newcomer, with his very unprepossessing appearance. He was far from having the kind of authority normally attributed to a chief of staff in Great Britain or France, because his commanding general, the duke of Brunswick, scarcely possessed it himself. Prussia's main error lay in not acting quickly and energetically and in not mobilizing all resources. The plan of campaign was sacrificed to the indecisiveness that has been widely imputed to the duke of Brunswick in his later years, and which is in any case the natural consequence of a system of command in which eight or ten advisors make operational decisions. Finally, it is not particularly remarkable that 150,000 Prussians and Saxons should have been defeated by 200,000 battle-tested Frenchmen commanded by Bonaparte. If we weigh all these circumstances, we will see that it is quite unnecessary to reach for other arguments to disprove such idle accusations. We leave it to posterity to judge whether it was wise for Prussia to go to war against France in 1806, or whether war might in fact have been avoided. We only claim that it is honorable for a soldier to have shown himself at all times an eager enemy of oppression.}

In the battle of Auerstädt Scharnhorst was slightly wounded in his left side, which did not prevent him from remaining with the army.

During the retreat the army was divided into three corps. The first, 20,000 men under General Kalckreuth, had taken no part in the battle of Auerstädt. Near Magdeburg it joined a second corps that Prince Hohenlohe had collected from the remnants of his force beaten at Jena. The third corps, under Lieutenant General von Blücher, formed their rear guard. Scharnhorst had lost his commanding general in the battle of Auerstädt and his position in the reorganized defeated armies, because General Kalckreuth's, and later Prince Hohenlohe's, chief of staff was Colonel von Massenbach (author of the well-known memoirs).[12] He therefore attached himself to Lieutenant General von Blücher, who was already known in the army as an energetic and able soldier. As senior staff officer, Scharnhorst guided the movements

---

[12] *Memoiren zur Geschichte des preußischen Staats unter den Regierungen Friedrich Wilhelms II. und Friedrich Wilhelms III.* (Amsterdam, 1809).

of this rear guard, which remained two days' march behind the main army because Blücher could not bring himself to seek salvation in forced marches, which would have dispersed the troops and left them unfit for battle.

This rear guard was later joined by the corps under the duke of Weimar, the original vanguard of the Prussian forces, which had thrust through the Thuringian forest into Franconia while the French were advancing over Hof, and therefore had not taken part in the battle.

It was mainly the events of this retreat and the rapid capitulation of the Prussian fortresses that destroyed the reputation of the Prussian army. The collapse was the consequence of the moral ascendancy that the French army had gained throughout Europe at this time, and of the long peace that had made Prussia and Saxony too soft for a war to the death.

Blücher's retreat to Lübeck and the engagements he fought along the way, {some with good success,} are undoubtedly still the most commendable events of this period and preserved his good name at a time of general disintegration, when so many military reputations were ruined.

What Colonel Scharnhorst was for General Blücher and the manner in which he acquitted himself as a soldier during these difficult days are once again indicated in the verbatim report his commander addressed to the king of Prussia:

CONCLUSION OF GENERAL VON BLÜCHER'S REPORT
ON HIS RETREAT

I feel it is my first duty to recommend to Your Majesty's particular favor Colonel von Scharnhorst, who merits it in every respect. The success of my arduous retreat was largely due to his unflagging energy, firm resolve, and perceptive counsel, such that I gladly acknowledge that without his vigorous assistance I would hardly have accomplished even half of what the corps did in fact achieve.

[Signed] Blücher.

Scharnhorst was taken prisoner in Lübeck with the rest of Blücher's staff but was freed after capitulation, in an exchange of prisoners arranged by General Blücher. He sailed for East Prussia, where the king appointed him quartermaster general of the army, under the command of Lieutenant General von l'Estocq.

There the reputation of Prussian arms recovered somewhat, so far as the weakness of the army and the short duration of the winter campaign allowed. Factions arise easily at the headquarters of a losing army, and Scharnhorst was among those who were always prepared for the honorable and heedless self-sacrifice and use of one's last energies that the small Prussian army was to demonstrate at the battle of Eylau.

Because Scharnhorst had once more proved himself worthy of the king's trust, he was promoted to general after the Peace of Tilsit, and because the army had to be completely re-created he was placed at the head of the Reorganization Commission.

Scharnhorst's influence on the great events of 1813–14 in Prussia can be traced back to this period, in which all his efforts were aimed at giving strength and cohesion to Prussia's military institutions and implanting the army of 40,000 men that Prussia was allowed by the Treaty of Tilsit with seeds of rapid growth that would flourish if external pressures should relax. His main goals in the reorganization of the army were

1. Weapons, equipment, and an organization consonant with the new methods of warfare.
2. To improve the individuals making up the army, and to raise their morale and dedication; consequently the abolition of foreign recruitment, steps toward universal service and the abolition of corporal punishment, and the establishment of good military schools.
3. An appropriate system of promotion to supplement promotion by seniority alone, and the careful selection of the commanders of larger units. [13]
4. New training methods appropriate to modern warfare.

Because in Prussia the monarch always pays particular attention to military affairs and is personally involved in them and because the king agreed with Scharnhorst's proposals, their realization naturally became that much easier. Nevertheless, as always in times of great change, there were many controversies, which gave Scharnhorst the opportunity to demonstrate the firmness and moderation of his opinions and the firmness and strength of character that make him a great figure in the political sphere. [14]

All unprejudiced observers will attest to the healthy development of the Prussian army under his counsel. Freed from the many abuses of a long period of peace, the army stepped forward rejuvenated, with a fresh spirit, and

[13] Ranke expanded this paragraph considerably: "A careful selection of officers to command the larger formations. Seniority, which until then had held excessive sway in the Prussian army and provided its leaders, was reduced in scope and was linked with a principle that for the moment was most salutary: preferment should go to those who had served in the last war up to the end, or who had in some way distinguished themselves. In fact, the majority of those who were later to become Prussia's best commanders were brought forward under Scharnhorst's administration."

[14] Ranke eliminated the political reference: "the opportunity to display a fairness of judgment and firmness of character that marked him as a great man."

even in peacetime gained new self-confidence. The same change is demonstrated on that first memorable day of the battle of Grossgörschen, when amid the barrenness of an unsuccessful battle the glory of Prussian courage brought forth new and vigorous green shoots. {If the first part of the task was perfectly solved, the second proved more difficult—to prepare the ground for the army's sudden, rapid expansion.}

The French not only enforced strict compliance with the Treaty of Tilsit, they also raised a thousand difficulties before vacating the occupied provinces, and by constant threats held Prussia in rigorous subjugation. This, combined with the sorry experience of the war itself, fostered the growth of a large party of despairing and fainthearted people, to whom anything like resistance—indeed, any measure displeasing to the French—meant a betrayal of the country. Finally, the strongest impediment to any exceptional measure was the country's total exhaustion.

In 1808 the king had placed Scharnhorst at the head of the War Department, without giving him the title minister of war. The famous Baron vom Stein was first minister at that time, and the close cooperation of these two excellent men facilitated the early steps of Prussia's internal revival. The administration reorganized by Stein brought order and economy to the state's finances, and the political development of society took an important step forward, which infused new life and confidence in the citizen. Stein's successors continued to work along the lines he had laid down, as far as their altered circumstances permitted, and they supported Scharnhorst whenever they could. He never lost sight of his objectives, which he pursued in a spirit of wise economy and admirable political astuteness by cutting through the old, bumbling spirit of routine and rejecting the opposition of so-called experts, focusing only on essentials. In a few short years, and without noticeable resources or support, Scharnhorst created the arms and equipment for a force three times larger than the Prussian army at the time. He restored the fortresses and introduced a system to the army under which every three months a new group of recruits could be called up, trained, and given leave. Thus the country acquired a large number of half-trained soldiers, who could come to the colors at the first call to arms. Even more important was his promotion of the concept of a universal *Landwehr* on the Austrian model.[15] Although this scheme could not yet be implemented, it was nevertheless of decisive importance that it slowly matured in the minds of men and gained

[15] Austria established a conscript national militia, or *Landwehr*, in June 1808 as part of a general effort to reform the army following its defeat in 1805. Although similar in structure to the Prussian force created in 1813, the Austrian effort was more important as a political precedent, with which Scharnhorst tried to disarm his critics, than as a military model. On the Prussian *Landwehr* and the controversy it inspired, see "Our Military Institutions" and "On the Political Advantages and Disadvantages of the Prussian *Landwehr*," below.

broad currency—that the belief in the possible usefulness of this salutary institution began to spread.

At that time the political climate in Prussia was what it would have been anywhere under similar circumstances. To the extent that the calm north German character permitted, two parties had formed: one believed that France could not be toppled from preeminence and that the only road to salvation lay through close alliance with her; the other counted on new wars, on popular resistance, on any unforeseen event, and feared nothing so much as an alliance that would tie Prussia's hands at the critical moment or, worse, that would cause Prussia to forestall such a moment rather than hasten it. {Which of these two opinions more closely reflected the feelings of the common people may remain unresolved here; but in the upper and middle levels of society the former party was visibly the stronger.}

After Stein was dismissed in 1809, in consequence of the famous letter,[16] the ministry maintained a discreet silence. If a few of its members believed that escape from the prison in which they found themselves was neither immoral nor impossible, none felt obliged in this particular situation to say so out loud. Scharnhorst, however, had dedicated himself to preparing for just such deliverance, and he could not help but feel that among the weapons he was trying to place in the hands of his monarch a spirit of resistance, giving rise to some stirring of indignation at Prussia's present subservience, was precisely the noblest and most effective of means. Consequently he became the representative of this spirit and this party at court, to the extent that the relentless mistrust of others toward these ideas made his advocacy necessary. Although Scharnhorst's tact, calm, and profound reticence allowed him to avoid attracting the attention and suspicion of the French for some time, his position and his political opinions were too well known in Prussia for the anti-French party not to turn to him. In time he became their spokesman, forming a salutary connection between them and the king.

The foregoing general outline contains the entire history of the so-called League of Virtue, to the extent that it actually existed in Prussia at that time.

The first step toward forming a league or association seems to have been taken in 1808 in Königsberg, when the court was still there, under the very eyes of the king, and was anything but secret. A group of scholars, officers, and others formed a so-called ethical and scientific club, and submitted their bylaws and membership list to the king. They appear to have had no great political aim nor any very distinct goal. A few members may have hoped to introduce some political ideas into the club, which would someday bring

---

[16] A letter from Stein to a colleague had revealed Stein's complicity in plans for an insurrection against France. Its contents were betrayed to the French and provided a pretext for his dismissal, at Napoleon's insistence, in November 1808.

forth good results. But these efforts died by themselves, and the society as a whole accomplished nothing for good or ill. In those parts of Prussia and Germany still occupied by the French, however, a kind of coalition arose, mainly among former officers, officials, and students whose aim was to raise the whole population against the French. A real organization, with a clear leadership, statutes and structure, never developed, at least as far as could be determined in Prussia at the time. Later on Scharnhorst was regarded as the head of this loose association, which came to call itself and was known, God knows how, as the League of Virtue. If the notion of a formally organized league seems false and inflated, Scharnhorst's supposed relationship to it is even more exaggerated. Some of the Prussian members of this coalition did approach him, because they regarded him as the leader of the anti-French party and acquainted him with their plans in the hope of establishing contact with the throne through him. They succeeded to some extent. Scharnhorst brought the affiliation to the attention of the king, believing that the sentiments and good intentions of this group deserved respect, that certain providential events might someday render it useful, and that, in any event, it seemed prudent to keep an eye on it. The king agreed, and so became acquainted for the first time with the ideas that Scharnhorst's opponents had been portraying as dangerous to the country and, to some extent, as a partisan scheme directed against the throne itself. These views and, even more, jealousy and resentment of Scharnhorst's high position, inspired frequent denunciations at that time, which, since access to the throne is open to everyone in Prussia, always quickly found their way to the ears of the king, but naturally could not prevail against the truth.

Scharnhorst retained his position and effectiveness until 1810, when financial problems forced a change in the ministry. The present chancellor, Prince Hardenberg, who headed the new administration, undertook to pay off the indemnity still owed to France. Although a Hanoverian by birth and anti-French by reputation, his personal resourcefulness, moderation, and flexibility were well suited to the task of maintaining relations with France on a bearable plane, without forfeiting the confidence of the other powers. Scharnhorst had helped bring about Hardenberg's rise and remained in close touch with him, but nevertheless felt the time had come to withdraw somewhat from the stage, if only to forestall a French demand that he be removed altogether—a prospect that became more likely every day and would have robbed him of such influence as he retained by resigning voluntarily. He therefore gave up his post as head of the War Department, while remaining in the service, with effective authority over the army's equipment and supplies, matters in which the new officials were ordered to seek his advice.

In 1811 the buildup of atmospheric pressure in Germany and especially in Prussia that would find release in the terrible storms of the following year could already be felt. We are in no position to say what plans, attitudes, or inclinations may have existed in the cabinets in Vienna, St. Petersburg, and Berlin at that time. It is certain, however, that among those few men in Berlin who nurtured a secret hope of resistance against France, Scharnhorst was the only one to try to bring it about. In the summer of that year he made a clandestine trip to St. Petersburg, and in the fall another to Vienna.

Both journeys were so secret that even now only a few in Prussia know they took place, and their true purpose remains a mystery. Probably Scharnhorst wanted to investigate conditions at both courts for himself, to see if there was a realistic basis for renewed resistance, and to avoid presenting the king and the chancellor with a plan based on false assumptions. The results seem to have neither fulfilled all his hopes nor to have destroyed them totally, since it was not until the spring of 1812 that Prussia was finally driven to the hard step of seeking an alliance with France.

In February 1812, before the proposed treaty was accepted in Paris, a French column under Davout suddenly marched from Magdeburg toward Berlin, without the slightest notice of this move having been given to the court. This caused general alarm {in the Prussian government} because it seemed as though the French were delaying the treaty in order to pick off Prussia like an outpost and open the campaign of 1812 with this *coup de main*, which, it was later learned, had been proposed by Talleyrand.

It is difficult and perhaps unnecessary to determine just what Prussia might have accomplished had resistance been forced upon her in this way. If we are to understand her conduct, it is enough to note that, without sacrificing the surface calm that comes naturally to the king, the cabinet took the necessary military steps to find a way out of this trap with a guerrilla's courage, resolution, and skill.

Saxony had quartered the part of its army that was to serve with the French on the border of lower Lusatia. Scharnhorst suggested that, if the expected courier from Paris did not arrive in time, the 10,000 Prussians stationed near Potsdam and Berlin should either make their way through the Saxons to Silesia or withdraw to East Prussia by way of the still-unoccupied city of Frankfurt on the Oder.

At this critical moment the courier arrived with the signed treaty, which settled the question of whether Prussia would become a desperate opponent of France or, like Austria, a reluctant ally.

The French had requested General Grawert as commander of the auxiliary corps, but because Grawert suffered from ill health and the frailties of old age the cabinet decided as a precaution to appoint General Yorck second commanding general.

After that, Scharnhorst retired to Silesia and took no further part in events until the Russian army appeared on the Silesian frontier.

Once the king had moved to Breslau he recalled Scharnhorst, who now had the great satisfaction in these changed circumstances to give vent to his long-suppressed desires and to use his talent and energy as a spur to speed the Prussian cabinet toward new objectives. First he hastened the conclusion of a treaty with Russia, by convincing the king to send him to Kalisch, where Czar Alexander received him as an old friend to his cause.

The vast mobilization by which Prussia hoped to raise itself into a leading position in the coming war—the construction of the great edifice that had been secretly prepared—was not the work of a few weeks, for it had been impossible to do anything about equipping the *Landwehr*, which would eventually double Prussia's strength.

But it could be foreseen that Bonaparte would appear in Saxony with a new army within six to eight weeks. Half of Prussia's regular army had entered Russia with the *Grande Armée*; whatever had survived was still in far-off East Prussia and had to be reorganized. Part of the other half was scattered throughout West Prussia and Pomerania, leaving only some 12–15,000 men in Silesia. Within a few weeks these troops were turned into a vigorous, in every respect outstanding army of 30,000 men under Blücher's command, while in East Prussia General Yorck was increasing his corps to 20,000 men and General Bülow was creating a similar one in Pomerania. By April, Prussia had built up the 30,000 troops remaining after the Russian campaign into a force of 70–80,000 men, with which to support an ally weakened by the long, arduous campaign of the previous year. If one considers that Russian strength did not exceed 70–80,000 men at that time, the significance of this prompt assistance from Prussia becomes clear. And, although the battles of Grossgörschen and Bautzen showed that the allies were not strong enough to defeat the new French army, they nevertheless broke the tide of French resurgence and brought about an armistice that gave Austria time to arm and allowed Prussia to raise the *Landwehr*. Scharnhorst, whom during this period the king promoted to lieutenant general, was made chief of staff of the Silesian army, which entered Saxony. Because he enjoyed the confidence of the king, Czar Alexander, old Blücher, and nearly all the Russian commanders, it was Scharnhorst above all who maintained the harmony and unity of allied operations, which might so easily have been lost for lack of a true supreme commander. He also organized and equipped the *Landwehr*, his prestige allowing him to overcome the many obstacles with which new institutions must always contend.

At the battle of Grossgörschen, in which Blücher generously placed himself under General Wittgenstein's command, Scharnhorst was equally modest in confining himself to the role of quartermaster general of a subordinate corps. At seven o'clock in the evening, in the murderous fight between Grossgörschen and Kleingörschen, he was struck in the leg by a musket bullet. He had to leave the battlefield and was taken to Zittau in upper Lusatia. As he did not consider his wound dangerous, he soon left for Vienna, in order to employ the time in which he would be useless in the field to further the cause there. On the way his wound became worse, so that he had to turn back, and allowed himself to be taken to Prague. There his condition became critical, and on June 28 he died, an event that was deeply felt in Prussia, even during the great excitement of those days, and caused a painful sensation even in a foreign city like Prague.

His intimate friend and loyal assistant in his efforts, General Gneisenau, took his place in Prussia and completed the magnificent structure that he had begun.

––––––––––––

If it is always difficult to measure precisely the influence of a statesman {who is not a ruler,} it is the more so in a case like that of General Scharnhorst, whose achievements were combined with personal modesty and reserve and {who lacked the distinction, outward appearance, and public ceremonial that make up the resonance of fame.

For the contemporary observer it is impossible to document his share in great affairs and demonstrate his role to the world.} But any fair-minded observer of Prussia during her six-year crisis will agree that this remarkable man may be regarded as the core and fulcrum of political resistance, as the seed and the vitally creative force for spreading the ideals and attitudes of citizenship.

The rebirth of the Prussian army, the bringing together of the various classes of society, the creation of the *Landwehr*, the tenacious resistance to the defeatism of the times and the mistrust of parties—all these are anchors that this able pilot tossed into the threatening seas, anchors that enabled the royal vessel to defy the storms breaking around it.

II. Portrait of Scharnhorst

His Mind

Scharnhorst had a calm, not particularly agile, but keen and penetrating mind. Once focused on a subject he always produced apt and forceful ideas, but unlike more buoyant personalities never toyed with dazzling and flowery fantasies. His mind lacked neither sensitivity, delicacy, nor quickness, but only the kind of restlessness that flits from subject to subject. He kept his thoughts, like his feelings, to himself. His comprehension was rapid and he caught the least detail, but one could not tell this by looking at him. It was only natural that his intelligence was linked not to imaginative brilliance but rather to an exceptional clarity of conception.

Such a mind brought noble ideas quietly to fruition but was not like a resplendent tree in bloom. Scharnhorst resembled plants whose bounty forms the staff of life but flower inconspicuously, while the eloquent and witty among us may be compared to flowering bulbs whose sole product is a delightful if often stupefying scent. I am not speaking of poets, of course—they are true creators—but rather of those coy spirits whose only business it is to take up and embellish whatever has already been done, whatever already exists, whether it is true or false.

Men of this type were his exact opposite, and are here mentioned to serve as backdrop, against which his true qualities stand out more clearly. As in this account, so in life he was always opposed to them, and the result was that in the eyes of the world his true worth paled beside their superficial glitter.

Two characteristics marked Scharnhorst's thought, and above all lent his life the significance that it now possesses for us.

The first was his absolute independence of judgment, unconstrained by any authority, be it that of a great name, of age, or of precedent.

The other was his great preference and respect for the power of historical evidence in all matters that occupied him.

A penetrating intellect that is not joined to a powerful imagination will favor theoretical constructs and speculative thought only so far as they coincide with reason and with the appearances of this world. At the point where imagination leads the brilliant systematizer beyond specifics, Scharnhorst would quietly turn back and direct his energies toward reconciling ideas and reality, carefully fusing the two by theoretical or by historical analysis, as the particular issue demanded.

Only a mind of this type is suited to public life in general and to war in particular. In war mere imagination has no creative power at all, while the truth that emerges from the congruence of reality and analysis is indispensable.

These two qualities—intellectual independence and respect for historical evidence—gave Scharnhorst's ideas in teaching and in action the degree of originality and practicality necessary for great success. His intense examination of life as it really is also helps explain why, when he wanted to persuade others, he employed his free-ranging intelligence to link the power of historical evidence with the psychological power exerted by authoritative individuals. He labored to compare his own ideas with the opinions and actions of distinguished historical figures and would often discover a congruence that was new to most people. He knew the power that famous names exert on the mass. His practical and clear mind, which was always attentive to men's attitudes and conditions, sought to convince others by whatever means would encounter the least resistance. As far as possible, he steered clear of eddies of stubbornness and prejudice that might disturb the steady progress of his work. Whenever he could he advanced his views along customary channels, convinced that once they had surrounded and penetrated the great mass, their natural strength would undermine and collapse the rocks of even the most hardened preconceptions. Like a skilled engineer, he erected a dam against people's opinions in those areas where they felt inhibited only a little or not at all, and so imperceptibly turned the flow of their convictions against their own prejudices.

Some reformers who verge on charlatanism or use their genius like a club flatter themselves that their ideas are wholly new and unprecedented. Scharnhorst instead tried to reassure people that everything he planned was basically nothing new, only slightly modified and rationalized.

It is odd that Scharnhorst expressed himself in a decidedly awkward manner. Wit, vitality, imagination, and a pyrotechnic display of speculative ideas lend brilliance and eloquence to speech, and it is not surprising that when these qualities are lacking the manner of speaking should also remain simple and plain. But Scharnhorst's speech was actually clumsy, as though he found it difficult to communicate his ideas. A long-winded, vague, and halting speaker was the first impression, and in ordinary social intercourse, when people often speak only to hear themselves, there was no opportunity to correct this judgment. And yet Scharnhorst was an excellent teacher, as even those who only half understood him admitted, and a very precise writer. In fact, his awkwardness was merely verbal not conceptual, or at least it affected his concepts only insofar as they were vehicles of exposition. He was well aware of this shortcoming. When he spoke of important matters he would repeat himself, employing different expressions, so that one statement might make up for anything left vague in the other. He did not shrink from this seeming prolixity, and in the end never failed to make his point with the utmost clarity. His long-windedness, the product of clumsy speech, was more apparent than real and quite different from confused thinking, which drags in irrelevant concepts and gives undue weight to small things, and therefore had an entirely different effect. The time lost through repetition and awkward turns of phrase is repaid a hundredfold if one is left with a substantial idea. Diffuseness was therefore never in evidence in his written work, for he kept correcting and revising his text until his exceptionally precise mind was entirely satisfied and not one word seemed out of place. But it is not surprising that this awkwardness in speaking, made worse by his slow Hanoverian dialect, always misled public opinion about him. Elegant society, not excepting some able and intelligent men, considered him a dry scholar and pedant; the army took him for an indecisive, impractical, unmilitary scribbler. Never was a judgment so mistaken—exactly the opposite qualities distinguished him. Far from being a pedant, he placed little value on the raw material of knowledge and paid attention only to the intellectual and spiritual values that can develop from it. Nor could anyone be more practical and active in his entire being. This showed unmistakably in his judgment and selection of men for important assignments: native intelligence, common sense, even crude, natural instinct counted for more with him than any amount of learning that had not yet proved its relevance and usefulness. How admirable and inspired is this preference for natural ability in a man who devoted his entire life to studying and comprehending the facts of his profession.

Scharnhorst's career is noteworthy in part because of the influence his writings had on military science in Germany; in part because the reform of the Prussian army and military organization after the catastrophe of 1806 was initiated by him; and finally, because of the influence his statesmanship and political views exerted at a time of greatest crisis for Prussia and Germany.

We do not mean to describe these accomplishments, because we are concerned with his character, not his career. But we must devote a few words to his role as author and teacher.

The perceptive reader can readily distinguish even Scharnhorst's earliest and to all appearances not outstanding works—his manual of military science and his monthly journal—from the common sort of compilation produced by less talented authors. The officers' manual that followed became a classic because of its soundness and practicality. But his mind was fully revealed in ideas—for the most part unpublished—that he developed in his lectures and in conversation.

The old military system had collapsed in the wars of the French Revolution; its forms and means were no longer appropriate to the changed times and new political conditions. Everyone felt this, and the French sword made it clear. As usually happens, opinions outstripped fact, and faith in the old system was undermined even more than reality justified. The revolutionary methods of the French had attacked the traditional ways of warfare like acid; they had freed the terrible element of war from its ancient diplomatic and economic bonds. Now war stepped forth in all its raw violence, dragging along an immense accumulation of power; and nothing met the eye but ruins of the traditional art of war on the one hand, and incredible successes on the other. But no new military science emerged—no new path to wisdom, no constructive understanding of how these new forces could be used. War was returned to the people, who to some extent had been separated from it by the professional standing armies; war cast off its shackles and crossed the bounds of what had once seemed possible. But this was all that could be grasped from the flow of events. It remained to be seen what sort of structure could be erected on this larger, stronger foundation.

Such times are a boon to system builders. Even while Bonaparte was transforming war in the field, a succession of the most diverse theories appeared one after the other, each claiming to be the germ of a general science of war.

Bülow considered envelopment the key to victory in battle, and from this principle developed a geometrical system, to which—as all charlatans are want to do—he ultimately gave a veneer of mathematical elegance.

A host of others, headed by Mathieu Dumas, discovered that the fundamental principle lay in the possession of the higher ground. By way of numerous half-truths and doubtful conclusions this led to a highly picturesque system of geological analogies. The neighbors of the clouds, the highest mountain peaks, rule the lands below them, while rivers become the couriers of their might. The art of war seems to arise geologically from the bowels of the earth, its feet barely grazing the loftiest mountain chains; with a few deeply hidden scientific laws it rules magically over the infinite mass of events that make up the lumbering course of war.

General Jomini, finally, emphasizes the concentration of power at a single point and deduces from this a geometric *system of internal lines* directly opposed to that of Bülow.

We ought not be surprised that these fanciful or one-sided systems should have emerged and even found acceptance at a time when war itself, so to speak, stood at the lectern and every day offered practical instruction to its students. The spirit of speculation is quickly aroused by real events, but to understand them takes time. Men are overstimulated, do not wait for developments to run their course, and will not study them from every side.

It was to Scharnhorst's great credit that he was not in the least influenced by these pretentious theories, which at that time were overwhelming everyone who did not unthinkingly cling to the past.

He recognized both the unchanging elements in the present age and the inadequacy of old methods, but he wanted the new to emerge from the old, and he wanted to arrive quickly and with as little fanfare as possible at a new, appropriate method.

Scharnhorst discussed the major elements of war in his lectures in the same way that he had discussed its minor elements in his manual for officers. Thoroughly and with common sense he examined earlier and more recent events and drew from them the rules and principles that constitute the essence of modern war. He did this at a time when hardly anyone in Prussia questioned the infallibility of traditional institutions and methods as they were derived from Tempelhoff's writings and handed down in the annual reviews and autumn maneuvers. And if we saw the Prussian army operate a few short years later in a manner appropriate to contemporary conditions, we can say that this was largely Scharnhorst's work. With a few sensible explanations he persuaded the king to accept the basic principles on which the army's new *organization, training,* and *tactics* were built, while his lectures and private conversations disseminated his ideas throughout the army itself.

That Scharnhorst, unlike so many system builders who pride themselves on their science, refused to base his theories on his first impression of current events says much about the solidity of his ideas and the deliberateness with which he developed and made them his own. At that time Bonaparte's campaigns were known only through newspaper accounts—for that reason Scharnhorst did not solely or even principally choose the most recent wars as subjects of study, but rather the history of war in general, especially the campaigns since the 1740s, from the Silesian wars on. By painstakingly assembling the specific details of certain episodes, especially those in which he himself had taken part, he sought to re-create the events for his listeners and readers. Like a judge in a court of law, he exhaustively questioned each historical source, his practiced judgment suggesting rather than imposing the correct conclusions, which he allowed common sense to draw for itself. And since he proceeded from a broad base of actual events, both he and his listeners seemed to arrive together at the same basic principles—not by rejecting the old system as such, but through the calm, objective apprehension of the salient characteristics of different times and circumstances.

We cannot describe his views on war in greater detail, nor even touch on those principles that seemed to him inherent in all elements of war, great or small. But we must once more emphasize two aspects of his thinking. The first is that in broad outline his principles were in accord with the development of warfare since the turn of the century—although, taken in detail, Scharnhorst's ideas showed far more subtlety, cleverness, and cunning than the massive, somewhat crude offensive system favored by French commanders. Second, Scharnhorst's analytic spirit stimulated objectivity and common sense and defended them against the presumptuousness of sham brilliance and sterile pedantry. He encouraged men to think for themselves, and the salutary effects of this genuine awakening of the mind will surely be felt for years to come. His influence will continue to oppose artificial and learned theorizing by encouraging a certain naturalness of thought, which defeats empty phraseology and brings the false conflict between theory and practice to an end. In his own lifetime, however, his unpretentious manner could not attract the notice necessary to win over the public. Men love to attire their minds, like their bodies, in shiny fashions; when they must acquire ideas from someone else they prefer those that they believe are *attractive* and suit them. A mind decked out in a brilliant system will seem far more splendid than one clothed in the plain truth. Consequently the unprepossessing views of this wise teacher were almost ignored by what is called public opinion, which preferred the foolishness of French and German system builders. Even intelligent men often thought of Scharnhorst as a conventional compiler rather than as a creative genius.

If a glorious death had not cut short an even more glorious life, Scharnhorst's great achievements in the theory of war would have emerged fully in his writings and would have become apparent to all. The last part of his revised work on artillery would have sufficed by itself. In this volume he originally intended to describe the use of artillery in the field—mainly, as was his custom, by means of examples. Because on the modern battlefield artillery is so closely integrated with the other two arms, and because it plays such a large role in every type of combat, he was led to the study of battle in general—and since this was his favorite subject, he proceeded with real pleasure and gave full rein to his genius. He had already gathered most of the material, which can probably still be found among his papers. But it would be difficult to put these quarried stones together without the architect himself, because his ideas were so original and his approach so different from that of other men. Even if all the components were available, it is to be feared that the soul, the creative form, would still be missed.

His Heart

Scharnhorst was a spirited, very sensitive, even a truly *gentle* person. His strong feelings did not handicap him in public life only because he was aware of them, and because of the surface imperturbability that he assumed.

Deep in his heart he was *just, honorable,* and *incorruptible;* every action, public or private, testified to his *forbearance, tolerance, equanimity,* and *amiability;* his intimate companions felt his *childlike sympathy, openness, indulgence,* and *good humor.* How could anyone who had felt the stirrings of such a heart, even in passing, not feel his own heart deeply touched in return?

His perceptions remained fresh and youthful; in his leisure hours he liked to read again the books that had moved him in his youth, and he never found it difficult to enter warmly into the ideas and feelings of the young people around him.

On this point I appeal to the judgment of women, whose more delicate sensibility is better suited to expose and comprehend our feelings.

His Character

Scharnhorst's ambition to work on issues of broad significance combined with the nobility of his heart to create principles of strict and unyielding civic virtue. They dominated and controlled every trait of his character, among which daring, prudence, firmness, tirelessness, self-possession, cunning, and reserve were the most prominent.

He hated men who served only for money, kept his distance from men who sought distinction and honors above all, and scorned those who without higher ambition simply followed routine. But men who *sacrificed* themselves for a noble goal immediately earned his affection and respect, whatever other qualities they might possess. Love of accomplishment for its own sake, without regard for the money or honor it might bring, he thought the hallmark of a person. In his own life he bore witness to this by his extreme modesty, in relations with others by the political choices and appointments he made, which were guided primarily by this principle. Yet the practicality of his mind kept him from being led astray by his idealism. Very few individuals were entirely to his taste—those who with a clear and vigorous intelligence had not lost *all* powerful emotions—and to have sought out only these few would have been a delusion. Therefore he also brought forward men of more conventional ambition, recognizing that the service of the state would benefit from the exertions to which such men are driven.

As a soldier, he valued nothing more highly than courage in war. Even if one takes bravery for granted as a commonplace virtue among armies and peoples, it is always possible to rise above the norm, and it is characteristic of Scharnhorst's practicality and nobility that such a distinction counted for more in his eyes than anything else—because it is not easy to achieve, but is the best and most useful quality in war.

The noble, grandiose, quiet ambition that drove him expressed the daring nature of his character and gave rise to the great ideas with which he achieved so much.

A stranger in the country and the army, without family, connections, even without friends or acquaintances, without talent for life at court and in society, and yet to become advisor to a monarch to whom he was personally an utter stranger and on whose complete confidence he could not count during his first years, and from this position to undertake to reform the entire army; and, at a time when the country was defeated and oppressed and everyone thought only of submission, to prepare secretly the means for gigantic resistance—that, indeed, might be called boldness in times of peace. He would have shown the same boldness on the battlefield, for he had already demonstrated it in his subordinate role during the breakout at Menin.

His boldness was accompanied by the greatest prudence—how could his plans have succeeded otherwise? Only luck can make up for lack of prudence, and in his difficult position Scharnhorst owed nothing whatever to luck.

This firmness of purpose and strength of will, without which nothing significant is accomplished in public life, seemed to stem more from Scharnhorst's intelligence than from a stubborn, dominating nature. They were well hidden, indeed quite undetectable in his everyday manner, which allowed him to confront an opponent with them when the latter was already worn down—an advantage that he must have cherished. His greatest peculiarities of mind and character were the tirelessness with which he pursued his plans and the endless expedients to which he would resort. In matters that were dear to him he was utterly fearless and thick-skinned, and nothing—whether dogged opposition, anger, or suspicion—could dissuade him.

What is perhaps most difficult to convey is how Scharnhorst could be so sensitive and subtle in his perceptions, so vital and quick to understand, and yet so calm and self-contained, even at moments when excitement would have seemed entirely appropriate. Constant self-control had made coolness and equanimity second nature to him, as indolence is to a glutton; his rare outbursts of temper were therefore reserved for those against whom he had a long-standing grievance, or for ideas and conditions against which he had spoken repeatedly. It is unlikely that they were ever directed against anyone at first meeting.

A character trait whose precise limits were not discernible to coarse men, and whose extent malicious people liked to exaggerate, was a kind of harmless cunning. The conviction that most people can be floated off the sandbank of their prejudices only by imperceptible levers, and the study of war, in which it is vital to hide one's intentions, had given his character this turn, which was encouraged by his intelligence and made necessary by his gentle, sensitive nature. But just as good-natured men have a sense of humor that doesn't become malicious, so Scharnhorst's cunning never became treacherous. Those with whom he dealt could always find out where they stood, as long as they were prepared to break through the first shell of conventional forms. His external awkwardness made real *deception* impossible for him, and he was by nature incapable of it in any case. He was never known to insinuate himself into the circle of his opponents, or to cultivate them under false pretenses—indeed, he was less well equipped to do this than was necessary for a statesman in his position. To flatter people's pride or to indulge their follies were impossibilities for him; at most he could be expected to show patience and restraint. In 1813 he would have liked nothing so much as to mislead the French about himself and his plans, but he could not bring himself to approach them or their supporters. And as little as the French knew about him, taking him for an impractical scholar, one thing they knew perfectly well: he hated them mightily.*

It was in war that Scharnhorst gave the freest rein to his capacity for cunning. His whole system was charged by it. He also employed it as a states-

---

* In a memorandum describing the most prominent figures in Prussia, taken from Lefebvre, the secretary of the French legation, Scharnhorst was identified as "a learned man, Hanoverian by birth, formerly a professor at Göttingen, who hates the French government."

man, on the one hand in the schemes he devised to circumvent the foreign power that opposed Prussia's interests with sword in hand, on the other to loosen the fetters of prejudice and habit that were strangling Prussia's spirit at that time.

The contrast he drew between cunning and dishonesty was most apparent whenever Scharnhorst talked about the campaigns of Duke Ferdinand of Brunswick, which he had studied with particular care. He liked to point out the cleverness of this commander, but afterwards expressed his disgust, half in jest, half in earnest, over the personal dishonesty of which the duke was accused.

An impenetrable reserve, impervious to the heat of passion and the temptations of ambition, supported Scharnhorst's cunning and gave it the scope and power necessary to influence events affecting the whole nation. But as his cunning was simply a feature of his intellect, applied only to great and virtuous endeavors, his personal relations lacked any trace of suspicious aloofness in his character, which was in fact ruled by just the opposite quality: the innocent openness of a child.

Scharnhorst as Soldier

Most people mistook Scharnhorst's simplicity and forbearance for indecision and lack of nerve, and so it is not surprising that they denied him the cardinal virtues of a soldier and assumed that he was simply a learned officer who would inevitably cut a poor figure in battle. Even men who had attended his lectures, and were in no doubt about the clarity of his mind, the breadth of his views, and the strength of his character, missed his lack of martial bearing, which is given greater importance in the peacetime Prussian army than it deserves. Nothing would have been more natural than to consider Scharnhorst's war record; one would have been led to a wholly different opinion by the judgment expressed long before 1806 by an old soldier like Hammerstein, and still more, in the years after our defeat, by the views of Blücher, that past master of the sword. But for reasons that defy understanding, mankind prefers to rely on transient personal impressions rather than on historical facts, and so Scharnhorst's life remained unexamined. The notion that he was a better man in the council chamber than in the field survived until his death, and to this day his most eager defenders still think they are displaying their acuteness and impartiality if they accept this distinction.

Our conviction is quite the opposite. We can only think it unjust and exaggerated to impute the highest value to the externals of military bearing— a certain decisiveness and self-assurance, which, to be sure, the soldier is apt to develop. When these qualities are joined by others that are even more superficial—daring horsemanship, an imposing figure in the saddle or afoot, an imperious way of speaking, and so forth—and when these trivia imperceptibly influence the judgment even of intelligent people, then we must wonder at how credulous men become when they let down their guard. We need only review the roll of great commanders whose character is known to us to realize that, whether by accident or not, the majority were not distinguished by a martial bearing. A man's nature is not always expressed by his outward appearance, and where this analogy does apply it often requires a sharp eye to detect it. On the other hand, men without character often find it easy to put on a mask and thrive—and even if the mask turns into caricature it does not on that account lose its effectiveness.

When I imagine Scharnhorst in 1794 during the defense of Menin and the breakout of the garrison, with his daring advice to Hammerstein and his courage and resolution in the struggle, compelling that old soldier to the noble admission that his success was mainly Scharnhorst's doing; when I recall him at the battle of Auerstädt, remaining in the field despite his wound and helping the left wing stand fast longer and better than the rest of the army, although it suffered the sharpest attack; when I picture him in the pervasive confusion that followed the battle, joining Blücher simply because Blücher is able and brave; when I imagine the two of them and their men, with three French corps on their heels, fighting their way to Lübeck, where only accident prevents their escape by sea; when I recall Blücher's report to the king, praising Scharnhorst's resoluteness and firmness; when I then recall Scharnhorst in the campaign of 1807, using all his persuasive power to lead the Prussian army to Eylau on February 8, reinforcing the left wing of the Russians, where the fighting was most fierce, because he believed that in a battle for their country's survival Prussians ought take part, that they should be in the front ranks and not in the rear—when I think of all this, I can only conclude that on the field of battle this was an officer whose equal is rarely seen. If I also recall his individuality, his daring, his caution and imperturbability, his composure in moments of crisis, his practicality, cunning, and secretiveness, all bound together by an exceptional theoretical and operational understanding of war, then I do not see how he could have been anything other than a great commander.

What Scharnhorst told me about the conduct of the war in 1813 and what I saw of him on the battlefield of Grossgörschen have only confirmed this opinion. Had he attained command of a great army, just as he had succeeded in becoming the head of the Prussian military establishment, I do not for a moment doubt that he would have impressed the world as greatly in the one career as he did in the other.

FIVE

From *The Campaign of 1812 in Russia* (1823–1825)

The Campaign of 1812 in Russia *pieces together three chapters and other short sections that Clausewitz composed at different times, probably beginning in 1814 and ending in 1823 or soon afterwards.*[1] *Originally, as his widow suggests in her preface to the work's first edition, Clausewitz may have intended two different treatments of the war in Russia—one would have been an impersonal strategic and operational narrative of the campaign, the other a strongly autobiographical account. Possibly the first served as a preliminary study for the second, but the remaining evidence is contradictory. Between 1823 and 1825 he nevertheless combined these disparate parts into a single, consecutive manuscript, which remained unpublished until 1990. A later and now lost revision of this compilation, almost certainly by an editor, not by the author, seems to have served as the basis for the first published version in the seventh volume of his posthumous works in 1835. The heavily edited text omits large segments of the manuscript of 1823–25, among them its brief second chapter, and differs as well in many details, softening Clausewitz's descriptions of individuals and making other changes, which resulted in a text that has been described as "occasionally feeble, at times almost flattened out."*[2] *The present translation is of the first chapter and four-fifths of the third chapter of the unedited manuscript of 1823–25. The brief second chapter of Clausewitz's original manuscript, which was not printed in 1835 and duplicates material in the third chapter, is not included; nor is the long technical record of the campaign that was mislabeled "Chapter 2" in the 1835 edition, a narrative that is occasionally reduced to tabular form and reproduces the operational material contained in the other two chapters.*[3] *An appropriate alternative title of the work as it appears here might be: "The Campaign of 1812 in Russia as Clausewitz Experienced and Observed It."*

In a footnote to an early episode of the war, Clausewitz comments that *"here as elsewhere in this account of the campaign, the author has not assem-*

---

[1] On the history of the manuscript, see Marie von Clausewitz, "Vorrede," in *Werke*, 7: v–vi; and Werner Hahlweg's comments in *Schriften*, 2, part 2: 726–28.

[2] Hahlweg's comment in *Schriften*, 2, part 2: 727.

[3] For simplicity's sake the two selections have been labeled Parts I and II in the translation. As noted in the Preface, passages omitted by the original editor are enclosed in curly brackets.

bled detailed information about dates, locations, and numbers of troops. Whoever seeks such historical data in these recollections will be disappointed. It is rather the author's intention to add some color to the picture that posterity has of these events by describing the impressions they made on him at the time and the reflections to which they gave rise."[4] The data that he does provide are often somewhat inaccurate. He checked his manuscript against early histories of the war by Russian, French, and German authors, which themselves often disagreed; but in general The Campaign of 1812 has the immediacy of an account by a participant who at the time was rarely able to establish exact figures and at a later date was above all concerned to understand the intentions of the opposing political and military leaders and the logic of the operations in the field, which often escaped from their control. Here and there the text repeats or paraphrases passages of letters that he wrote at the time to his wife or to former associates in the Prussian reform movement. But there are also some observations that prefigure and even closely parallel theoretical passages in On War.[5]

In his histories of campaigns and wars Clausewitz rarely gives much space to particular battles, preferring to discuss the larger forces of which battle was a result and that generally determined its outcome. The Campaign of 1812 nevertheless includes an extensive discussion of the battle of Borodino. It is valuable not only as an eyewitness account, but perhaps even more so for illustrating the workings of a mind that constantly moves back and forth between small details and the largest conceptualizations. If Clausewitz does not often embark on descriptions of battles, his analyses of political and strategic issues, here as in his other writings, are always linked to very practical discussions of tactical and administrative details. He notes the many small ammunition carts in the Russian army, which affect the space occupied by a regiment, the difficulties cavalry encounters in charging an infantry square, even the quality of Russian army biscuits—"very bad . . . [but] not unhealthy."

Clausewitz's personal situation in Russia both favored and hindered his role as observer and analyst. He arrived at the czar's headquarters in the second half of May, a month before the first French units crossed the Niemen, and was appointed a lieutenant colonel on the general staff. It soon became apparent that as a foreigner who did not speak Russian he would be limited to a marginal role. He did not wish to remain with the imperial headquarters, which was rapidly becoming the political rather than the military center of Russian resistance, and for the next six months served on a number of smaller

---

[4] See p. 129n, below.

[5] See, for example, the paragraph beginning "But the main thing is always the difficulty of execution . . . ," (p. 165, below) which paraphrases the first discussion of the concept of friction in On War, 119–21 (pp. 11–12n, above).

staffs, here too essentially as a supernumerary, reduced, as he wrote to his wife, "to a complete zero."[6] *His isolation is reflected in the manuscript.*

It opens with his arrival in Vilna, where he was one among a number of foreign, mainly German, officers seeking service with the Russians, and with an evaluation of the strategic situation, interspersed with brief characterizations of Russian and foreign officers whom he came to know or of whom he heard. Compared with his portraits of leading personalities in his account of Prussia before the war of 1806, the analysis is thin. The descriptions often reveal great insight, but rarely is a person grasped in the round, and the author is too much the outsider to weave the rich network of relations and bonds between individuals and their environment that distinguishes his Observations on Prussia. An exception is his expansive discussion of Karl August von Phull, whom he had known in Berlin before 1806 and who now served as a senior military advisor to the czar. It was one of the two useful, even important contributions Clausewitz was able to make to the success of the campaign that he joined the opposition to Phull's scheme of having the main Russian army retire to a so-called fortified camp at Drissa between the roads to Moscow and St. Petersburg, and that subsequently he persuaded Phull, who had lost the czar's confidence, to leave the army.

Clausewitz's second and more dramatic contribution came at the end of the campaign, when he helped persuade General Yorck, in command of the Prussian auxiliary corps serving with the French, to detach his force from the remnants of the Grande Armée, *although this step was not authorized by the Prussian government. Within weeks the corps' neutrality turned into open support of the Russians, and Prussia's change of alliances had become an irreversible process. The sequence of events leading to the Convention of Tauroggen, which was naturally enough condemned as treason by the French, and which proved to be anathema to most Prussian conservatives because it placed the judgment of an officer above that of his king, is carefully described and its necessity and impact are analyzed. Clausewitz must have wished to put his version of the negotiations on record. But he neither emphasizes nor minimizes his own share in the decision; his main concern is to interpret Yorck's character and his behavior, which at a climactic point he likens to that of Schiller's Wallenstein.*[7]

That a senior officer who had served in the Prussian army since the reign of Frederick the Great changed sides without orders to do so was an act of free will that could not have been predicted. Many other initiatives and independent decisions of an operational or tactical nature were taken by men on both

[6] See p. 194, below.

[7] The Convention is placed in the larger context of the Prussian reform movement in Peter Paret, *Yorck and the Era of Prussian Reform* (Princeton, 1966). Its influence on Clausewitz's subsequent career is discussed in Paret, *Clausewitz and the State*, 232–33.

sides. Some succeeded, others failed; in sum, they may have roughly canceled each other out, but they occurred in a context that increasingly favored the Russian defenders. Clausewitz places great weight on these individual decisions, but he also emphasizes a degree of inevitability in the campaign, once the invasion itself had been decided upon. Although he believes Napoleon was overconfident and often careless, he defends him against the criticism that he should not have based his strategy on the capture of Moscow. Once he had begun the invasion it was the only policy that held out a chance of success, even if the Russians were bound to win once they refused to give up after Moscow had fallen. Clausewitz's interpretation is very different from Tolstoy's depiction of the war as an inevitable ebb and flow to Moscow and back again to Paris, a process in which everything happens as it must, subject to a law of necessity against which the reason and actions of men are helpless. Nevertheless, the views of the participant in the war and of the novelist who took the war as his subject are not totally opposed. In War and Peace *Clausewitz appears briefly as a typical German staff officer, a figure of derision who labors under the delusion that his calculations can control events. The Campaign of 1812, on the contrary, makes it apparent that its author recognizes and acknowledges the sliver of truth in Tolstoy's universalist, mystic vision. There is such a thing as inevitability, but in historical processes, Clausewitz believes, it tends toward high probability; he does not regard it as the only determining force in this or in any war.*

Part I

ARRIVAL IN VILNA—THE PLAN OF CAMPAIGN— THE CAMP AT DRISSA

The alliance between France and Prussia against Russia was concluded in February 1812. Those in Prussia who still felt the courage to resist and refused to acknowledge the necessity of such a union might properly be called the Scharnhorst party, since apart from him and his close friends there was hardly anyone in Berlin who did not regard this point of view as near lunacy. In the rest of the monarchy as well, only a few scattered traces of this attitude might have been found.

Once the alliance was a certainty, Scharnhorst left the inner circle of government and went to Silesia, where as inspector of the fortresses he retained a degree of influence. He did so to escape both the scrutiny of the French and the distasteful obligation of working in concert with them, without entirely giving up his place in the Prussian service. Under the circumstances this half-measure was most appropriate. He could still prevent a good deal of harm, namely too much compliance with the French, particularly with respect to the occupation of the Prussian fortresses. At the same time, he kept his foot in the stirrup, ready to mount again when the time came. He was a foreigner with neither property nor position in Prussia; he had always remained something of a stranger to the king, and even more to the leading men in the capital and the state; and the value of his activities over the past years was still widely questioned at the time. Had he quit the service altogether it is doubtful that he would have been recalled in 1813.

Major Boyen, his close friend, who had reported to the king on personnel matters in the army, resigned and on his departure received the rank of colonel and a small sum of money. His intention was to go to Russia.

Colonel Gneisenau, who at that time held the position of state councilor, left the service with the same intention.

Several others who belonged to the warmest supporters of Scharnhorst and of his political views, but who played no significant role in the state, did likewise; among them the author.

The king granted everyone's request to leave the service {but only more or less unwillingly. Earlier he had several times told Scharnhorst that if things should come to this pass he would not prevent anyone from leaving.}

In April the author, provided with some letters of recommendation, went to Vilna, at that time the headquarters of the emperor Alexander and General Barclay, commander of the First Army of the West.

On his arrival in Vilna he encountered several Prussian officers. Among the most important were Gneisenau and Count Chasot, who had traveled together by way of Vienna. Gneisenau, however, had already resolved to go on to England. Although he had been warmly received by the emperor, he had nevertheless recognized that, all things considered, Russia did not offer him much opportunity for a suitable military assignment. He did not speak Russian and so could not hold an independent command. He was already too senior in years and rank to accept a subordinate position on the staff of some general or in a corps, as the author and the other officers did; he could have participated in the campaign only as part of the emperor's entourage. What that involved, or rather did not involve, he saw only too clearly, and he felt that nothing appropriate to his abilities would come of it. Imperial headquarters was already overrun with distinguished idlers. To have made oneself noticed and useful in such a crowd would have required the dexterity of an accomplished intriguer and a thorough command of French. Colonel Gneisenau was deficient in both. He was accordingly averse to seeking a position in Russia and hoped that in England, where on an earlier occasion he had been well received by the prince regent, he might do much more for the good cause.

While in Vilna, Gneisenau soon became convinced that the Russian preparations were insufficient for the magnitude of the emergency, and rightly fearing the worst believed that the only hope for the allies lay in the difficulty the whole enterprise presented to the French. But it was still essential to do everything possible to persuade England, Sweden, and the German states to create a diversion in the rear of the French invasion. This view strengthened his determination to proceed to England, and he soon left.

The Russian forces on the western frontier consisted of the First and Second Armies of the West and a reserve army. The first was about 90,000 strong, the second 50,000, the third 30,000—in all about 170,000 men, to whom 10,000 cossacks may be added.

The First Army of the West, under the command of General Barclay, who was also minister of war, stood along the Niemen; the second, commanded by Prince Bagration, was in southern Lithuania; while the reserve, under General Tormassov, was in Volhynia.

The second line, which ran along the Dnieper and Dwina Rivers, consisted of garrison troops and recruits, about 30,000 men.

The emperor wished to assume supreme personal command over the entire force. He had never seen action in the field, much less commanded troops, but for several years had studied the art of war in St. Petersburg under the guidance of Lieutenant General von Phull.

Phull had held the rank of colonel on the Prussian general staff. In 1806, after the battle of Auerstädt, he left the Prussian for the Russian service, in which he had since risen to the rank of lieutenant general, without ever holding a field command.

In Prussia Phull passed for a man of genius. In 1806 he, Massenbach, and Scharnhorst had been the senior officers on the Prussian general staff. Each had his own very particular qualities. Scharnhorst's were the only ones to prove useful in practice, while Phull's qualities were perhaps the most unusual but very difficult to characterize. He was a man of much intelligence and cultivation, but wholly ignorant of real life. From his earliest days he had led such a secluded intellectual existence that he knew nothing of day-to-day realities. Julius Caesar and Frederick the Great were his favorite authors and heroes. He had occupied himself almost exclusively in fruitlessly reflecting on their military ideas, without the slightest historical perspective. The developments of modern war passed him by {touching him only with the feeble, wretched opinions that he heard from one of the parties}.[8] In this way he had constructed a dreary, one-sided theory of war, which could bear neither philosophical investigation nor historical comparison. If his knowledge lacked almost all historical perspective and his life almost any contact with

---

[8] The party in question was the traditionalists in the debate over the nature of modern war.

the external world, it was on the other hand also natural that he should be the enemy of the commonplace, of superficiality, falsehood, and weakness. It was primarily the bitter irony with which he assailed these failings of the majority that caused him to appear brilliant, deep, and forceful. His isolated, self-centered nature made him a complete eccentric, but because his outward manner was in no way peculiar he did not give that impression.

Despite all this, Phull's straightforward nature and fundamental decency, his abhorrence of falsehood and meanness, and his instinctive recognition of true greatness would have made him a distinguished man and a good soldier, if only his mind, so estranged from the external world, had not become confused whenever real events impressed themselves upon it. The author has never known a man who so easily lost his head, who while thinking only of great matters was so easily overwhelmed by the smallest aspect of the real world. This was the natural consequence of a withdrawn, autodidactic way of life. Sensitive and pliable though he was, he had taught himself to affect a breadth of vision and a decisiveness that went against his nature, and, isolated as he was, he had failed to grow into this assumed character by means of dealing with real problems and real people. Before 1812 his career had never forced him to do so. During the wars of the Revolution he had generally played a subordinate role, and it was only after the end of hostilities that he acquired importance as quartermaster general to Field Marshal Möllendorff. During the years of peace he served on the general staff, where, like most staff officers in peacetime, he occupied himself with illusory mental exercises that came to nothing.

In 1806 he was the general staff officer assigned to the king {or, so to speak, his quartermaster general}; but as the king was not actually in command, Phull, too, had no real duties. After the catastrophe he suddenly unleashed his irony on the feebleness and wretchedness that he saw everywhere. He laughed at the rout of our armies like someone gone half mad, and instead of stepping forward to fill the mental and psychological vacuum left by defeat and making himself useful, as Scharnhorst did, by weaving together new threads with whatever sound remnants remained of the lacerated fabric of the state, Phull gave up everything for lost and entered the Russian service.

That was the first time he showed that he did not feel able to deal with difficult situations. His transfer, too, he arranged awkwardly, by seeking and accepting a position in St. Petersburg while employed there on a mission for the Prussian government.

Had the emperor Alexander been a sound judge of character,[9] he would surely have had little confidence in a man who gave up a failing cause so quickly and did it in such a clumsy manner.

---

[9] 1835 edition: "a better judge of character."

At Field Marshal Möllendorff's headquarters at Hochheim in 1795, Phull had declared: "I don't trouble myself about anything; it is all going to the devil anyway." During his flight in 1806 he remarked, after scornfully raising his hat: "Farewell Prussian monarchy!" In November of 1812, at St. Petersburg, after the French had already begun their retreat, he said to the author: "Believe me, no good can come of this business." In short, he always remained true to himself.

The author has dwelt at length on this man's character because, as we shall see later on, much depended on him, and because then and subsequently an even greater influence over events was attributed to him than his personal peculiarities would ever have permitted him to achieve.

But if we have judged his intellect and understanding not altogether favorably, we must say in all fairness that one could not imagine a better heart or a more disinterested character than he displayed on every occasion.

{It was Phull, then, who had given the emperor Alexander lessons in the art of waging war. If the teacher's understanding of war was simplistic and inadequate, one can imagine that he generated few creative ideas in his pupil, who could hardly have been helped and strengthened by such lessons unless he possessed an innate gift for the subject, which was not the case with the emperor.

The emperor felt that he was still a novice in this alien world and therefore took his teacher with him to the battlefield, to question him the way Socrates questioned his guardian spirit.}

Impractical as Phull was, he never thought of learning Russian during the six years he had been in the country, nor, which is even more striking, of meeting the leading figures in the government or of familiarizing himself with the structure of the state and the army.

Under the circumstances, the emperor felt that Phull could only be considered an abstract genius who could not be appointed to a specific position. He was therefore merely the emperor's friend and advisor, and, pro forma, his general adjutant. Already in St. Petersburg he had prepared a campaign plan for the emperor, which he brought with him to Vilna, where some preliminary steps were taken to execute it.

The other principal figures in the emperor's entourage were:

PRINCE VOLKONSKY. He was senior general adjutant to the emperor and administrative chief of the general staff. As such he might have considered himself the de facto chief of staff as soon as the emperor assumed command. He did not do so, however, and in the end took virtually no part in the campaign. He was a good-natured man, a true friend and servant of the emperor {but very limited and insignificant}.

LIEUTENANT GENERAL ARAKCHEEV, a Russian in every sense of the word, with great energy and cunning. He was chief of the artillery, and the emperor had great confidence in him; but the duties of supreme commander were quite foreign to him, and his involvement in the campaign was no greater than Volkonsky's.

GENERAL ARMFELD, the well-known Swedish soldier, always passed for a great schemer; the conduct of war on a large scale was foreign to him as well, and he sought no active role in it, contenting himself, like Phull, with the title of general adjutant, but was inclined to become involved in intrigues.

GENERAL BENNIGSEN. He was one of the most senior generals in the Russian army but at this time had not received a command, probably because his poor performance in 1807 had not been forgotten.[10] Supposedly he was present at Vilna purely as a matter of courtesy; his estates lay nearby, and as a general adjutant to the emperor he could not well remain absent. Nevertheless, he must have hoped to be given a command.

Others at headquarters, among them several lieutenant generals—including Count Schuvalov, Count Osarovsky, and others—were even less significant and had no influence whatever.

We see from this how little the emperor had done to prepare himself for assuming supreme command. He seems never to have thought the intention through clearly, nor to have formally expressed it. Because the two armies were still divided and Barclay had some modest control over the Second Army by virtue of being minister of war, the concept of a unified high command actually rested only in him and in his staff. This included as chief of staff Lieutenant General Labanov, as quartermaster general General Muchin, an intendant general, and so forth. {Although the first two had no understanding of the tasks entrusted to them,} all these individuals were already seen carrying out their duties; General Barclay issued orders daily, received reports and briefings, etc. No such regular organization attended the emperor. For the most part he commanded through Barclay, sometimes through Volkonsky, once in a while even through Phull.

When the emperor and Phull arrived in Vilna, Phull found himself completely isolated, a stranger among Russians who looked on him with envy, distrust, and jealousy. He did not know the language, did not know the men and institutions of the government and the army; he had no position, no authority, no adjutant, no staff; he received neither reports nor messages, was not in communication with Barclay or anyone else at headquarters; he did not even speak with them. What he knew of the strength and condition of the army he heard from the emperor; he did not have a single accurate statistical table nor any of the other documents that need to be constantly studied in preparation for a campaign. In his memoranda he was often at a loss

---

[10] Bennigsen had been commander in chief of the Russian army when it was defeated at the battle of Friedland.

for the names of the commanders he wished to discuss and had to help himself out by describing the positions they occupied.

In such circumstances it would have been incredible folly to assume command in a campaign that could be expected to be as difficult as that of 1812. The Russian army was at most 180,000 strong, while the enemy, at the lowest estimate, had 350,000 men, and Bonaparte was their leader.

Phull should either have dissuaded the emperor from the idea of supreme command altogether, or he should have assisted in organizing that command differently. He did neither, proceeding instead like the proverbial sleepwalker who strides along house roofs regardless of danger, until he is awakened and falls to the ground.

At the very moment when the Russian forces on the frontier numbered no more than a 160,000 men, it was claimed that Alexander had 600,000 men in his pay—and this assertion, which at the time the author took for a sarcastic exaggeration, although he heard it from the intendant general, Kankrin, turned out to be the plain truth.

The Russian forces actually on hand were distributed roughly as follows:

On the Polish and Prussian frontiers	180,000 men
Depots and new levies on the Dwina and Dnieper	30,000
In Finland	20,000
In Moldavia	60,000
On the eastern frontiers	30,000
Depots and new levies in the interior	50,000
Garrison troops	50,000
Total	420,000 men

The cossacks are not included here. If we add this great swarm (whose true strength in the west did not exceed 10,000 men at the start of the campaign, and never exceeded 20,000), and count as well the army of officers' orderlies and other supernumeraries, and if we consider how many convenient fictions were treated as semi-official truths in the Russian army and how great the difference must therefore have been between the numbers on the payroll and those actually in the field, then we understand that if the number of effectives was 420,000, the number being paid could well reach 600,000.

During an entire year of preparing for war with France the size of the army had not been significantly increased, which demonstrates Russia's inability to do much more. We can assume that, at the outbreak of the war, perhaps 80,000 men joined those already in the depots, which provided the reserves that reinforced the army on the Dnieper and Dwina and later at Smolensk and Kaluga, and which—not counting the militia—could not have been more than 100,000 men.

The results of these calculations suggest:

First, that the Russian army's nominal strength amounted to 600,000 men, a figure that presumably could not have been increased without excessive strain on the country.

Second, that in 1812 no more than 400,000 regular troops were actually present.

Third, that of these only 180,000 could be deployed against the French at the onset of the war.

Such a dissipation of force occurs at all times; we need only remind ourselves that in 1806 Prussia paid 250,000 men, but at the beginning of the war could concentrate only 100,000 against the French in Thuringia. Even if we can work out better arrangements than those of Prussia in 1806 or Russia in 1812, it is still useful to recall these earlier results, if only to avoid overestimating our enemy.

As it was, the Russian preparations were somewhat delayed, and peace with Turkey should have been concluded several months earlier. Two months later Russia could have put an additional 150,000 men in the field, almost doubling her available force.

Consequently, the emperor and Phull were correct in finding that, because the army would not be strong enough on the frontier, real resistance could only begin later, and further in the interior. Phull therefore proposed to draw the operations well back into Russia in order to move nearer to reinforcements and gain time, while weakening the enemy (who would be compelled to detach forces as he advanced) and gaining the space necessary for a strategic attack on his flank and rear. This plan appealed to the emperor all the more because it reminded him of Wellington's Portuguese campaign in 1811.

If we consider this idea in the abstract we might believe that it actually reflects the entire Russian campaign of 1812. But this is not the case. Proportion counts for a great deal in war. A plan that promises great success over 450 miles can prove illusory over 150. One cannot even say that Phull provided the small model according to which the campaign was later conducted on a colossal scale. Rather, as we shall see, the campaign developed according to its own logic, and Phull's idea has even less claim to be regarded as its guide because in its own terms it was incorrect. And yet his plan was the accidental cause of the turn the campaign did in fact take.

Phull's plan called for the withdrawal of the First Army of the West to a fortified camp, for which he chose a site along the middle Dwina, where supplies were to be stockpiled and the first reinforcements sent. If the enemy followed, he would be attacked in the flank and rear by Bagration, commanding the Second Army of the West. Tormassov was to remain on the defensive against the Austrians in Volhynia.

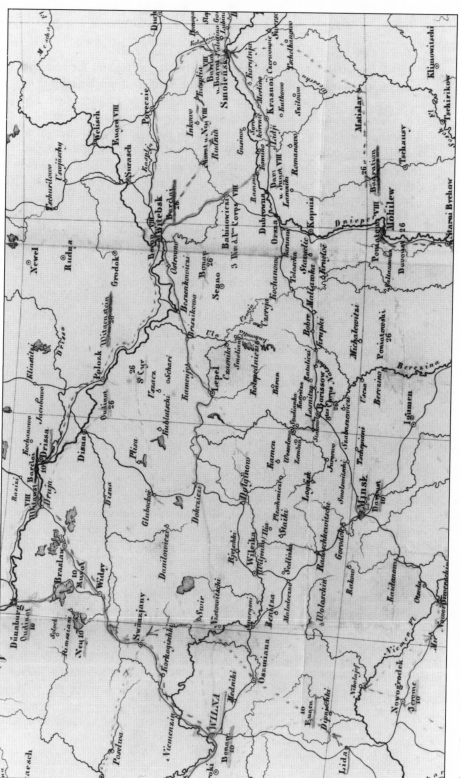

MAP 1. Vilna to Smolensk. Reproduced from the "Operationskarte für den Feldzug von 1812 in Russland," in Clausewitz, *Hinterlassene Werke*, 7 (Berlin, 1835).

What were the effective principles behind this scheme?

1. *Moving close to one's reinforcements.* The site selected for the rearward concentration lay some ninety miles from the frontier. It was hoped that by retreating the First Army would increase its strength to 130,000 men. But the reinforcements that had reached the area were fewer than expected—as the author heard, barely 10,000 men—which brought the total strength to about 100,000 men. In other words, the retreat was not far enough to increase the army's strength significantly. However, this flaw of the plan should not be considered a flaw in the idea itself. The emperor may have deceived himself about the numbers, and for Phull to have done so would have been even more excusable.

2. The weakening of the advance is never substantial over such a short distance if the enemy is not delayed by fortresses, and should in this case have been discounted almost completely.*

3. *Bagration's attack on the enemy's flank and rear* is not in itself an effective principle, because if his army were to fight in the enemy's *rear*, it could not fight on his *front*. The French would only have had to oppose Bagration with an equal force to restore the situation and would have gained the additional advantage of now being placed *between* our armies, each of which could be attacked with superior force.

Strategic flanking maneuvers are an operational principle in their own right when the enemy's lines of communication are long and extend through hostile territory from which occasional raids may threaten them. Efforts to protect the lines of communication significantly reduce the main army. This was the case in 1812 when the French had reached Moscow but controlled the provinces on their left and right only as far as the Dnieper and Dwina.

Such flanking operations are also effective when the enemy army has reached the limits of its possible advance, so that it can no longer exploit a victory over the forces facing it—in which case we can reduce these forces without risk. Finally, they are effective when the main decision has already been reached and all that remains is to harass the enemy's retreat, as in Tshitsagov's advance on Bonaparte's rear in 1812.

In all other cases nothing is accomplished simply by turning a flank. On the contrary, because this measure *leads to greater and more decisive results,* it necessarily involves greater risk. That is to say, it requires more strength than a frontal defensive and is therefore unsuited to the weaker party. Phull had grasped none of this—and indeed no one at that time had yet learned to

---

* In reality French losses proved very heavy, because the vast concentration of troops, inadequate supplies, and a week of heavy rain cost the French an incredible number of men in the first two weeks of the campaign. But that could not have been predicted.

think clearly about these matters—and instead based his judgments mainly on instinct.

4. *The fortified camp.* That in a strong position a few may resist many is well known. It is essential, however, that such a position have its rear free, as at Torres Vedras, or at least that it be firmly linked to a nearby fortress, like the camp at Bunzelwitz in the Seven Years' War, so the defenders cannot be easily starved out.[11]

The position chosen for the Russian camp was near Drissa, on the Dwina River. In St. Petersburg, Phull had persuaded the emperor to send his adjutant, Colonel von Wolzogen, a talented and knowledgeable officer who had left the Prussian service for Russia before 1806, to find an appropriate site. We do not know what his precise instructions were; but in an area nearly devoid of useful military positions, Wolzogen could find no other site than a small wooded area near Drissa, partly protected by morasses, with sufficient space for a camp with its back to the Dwina. Its advantages were: that the river here forms a concave semicircle about 2½ miles across; the camp's front extended across this distance in a slight arc, beginning and ending on the river, which runs between sandy banks about fifty feet high. A number of smaller streams, of which the largest is the Drissa, flow into the Dwina from the right bank above and below the camp, affording good positions from which to oppose an enemy who crossed the river to attack the camp from the rear.

General Phull ordered that the flat curve formed by the front of the camp be fortified with three rows of open and closed works, while seven bridges across the Dwina were to provide an easy avenue of retreat. No works were prepared on the other side of the river. Since in this area the Dwina is an insignificant stream, fairly broad but shallow enough to be easily forded, it can be seen at a glance that the tactical strength of this position was not great; on the contrary, it consisted entirely of the earthworks.

The strategic situation was even less reassuring because Drissa lies between the roads that lead from Vilna to St. Petersburg and Moscow, rather than on either one of them.

The shortest route from Vilna to St. Petersburg runs through Druga on the Dwina, then through Sebezh and Pskov; the shortest to Moscow passes through Vitebsk. Drissa lies eighteen miles from the first and one hundred from the second.

The indefinite character of this position was particularly disliked at Vilna; no one there knew what to make of it. The author asked General Phull which

[11] The lines of Torres Vedras were a defensive position that backed onto the sea. Its defense in the fall of 1811 was the turning point of the Peninsular War. Bunzelwitz was a fortified camp that Frederick the Great's army occupied undisturbed for six weeks while virtually surrounded by enemy forces.

line of retreat he contemplated, toward Moscow or toward St. Petersburg. Phull replied that this would depend on circumstances, a sure sign of confusion and irresolution on his part, because a decision of such significance could not be made on the spur of the moment.

Because the rear of the Drissa camp was covered only by the river, on the other side of which were no fortifications, nor even a defensible village—only a row of wooden sheds full of bags of flour—and because the river itself was no obstacle, an army encamped there would constantly have to worry about its supplies, which were protected neither by earthworks nor, in the near vicinity, by favorable terrain.

In short, the stronghold at Drissa remained merely an idea, an *abstraction*, because none of its essential features actually existed. A *gently curved front on level ground*, surrounded by woods eight hundred paces away, with both flanks against a fordable river, is in fact a miserable battlefield. Furthermore, any position that does not lie on a direct line of retreat but is torn out of the operational system and left to itself, without the sea or a fortress or even a proper town for a base (Drissa is a wooden village, and lay not behind the camp but on one side), such a position has no strategic value whatever.

We cannot, however, lay the blame for these defects on Lieutenant Colonel Wolzogen. General Phull had chosen the general area, and in that part of Lithuania one must thank God for a clearing large enough to hold a sizable army.

The strength of this position could therefore hardly be thought of as raising the strength of the Russian army. At bottom the scheme was merely a play of Phull's imagination, without substance, and consequently it vanished at once on contact with the real world. The only good that came of it was that it led the army to retreat for the time being as far as the Dwina.

We find in Phull's plan itself no principle capable of increasing the army's power of resistance, nor any compensation for the disadvantages it incurred by deviating from the simplest form of resistance and retreat.

The leading individuals at the headquarters in Vilna, including Generals Barclay, Bennigsen, and Armfeld, could not reconcile themselves to this plan and did their best to shake the emperor's confidence in it, and in Phull. A kind of intrigue developed by which the emperor was to be persuaded to accept battle in the neighborhood of Vilna. Presumably it was imagined that the French would cross the border on a front as wide as the one the Russians were deployed to defend, that is, from Samogitia to Volhynia, in which case one might hope that overwhelming force would not be brought to bear on Vilna. Without such a calculation—which to be sure was absurd—the idea of accepting battle in this area was quite incomprehensible.

Already in Vilna, then, controversy and disagreements arose, which certainly shook the emperor's confidence in Phull's plan.

At this point Colonel Wolzogen arrived in Vilna after serving briefly as chief of staff to the corps under General Essen. He was fluent in Russian and better acquainted than General Phull with the key figures at headquarters. He decided to seek a place on General Barclay's staff, with a view to building a bridge between him and General Phull. He induced Phull to ask the emperor for an officer to act as his staff assistant. The choice fell on the author, who was ordered to Drissa, to see how far the earthworks had progressed, and to identify suitable campsites for the march there.

The author left on June 23, accompanied by a Russian guide. On his arrival in Drissa, the officer in charge would have liked nothing so much as to treat him as a spy, because his only identification was an order written in French by General Phull, who was not regarded as holding any sort of authority in the army. But the author succeeded in allaying the officer's mistrust and received permission to inspect the camp.

This incident confirmed what the author had already feared—that General Phull would suffer nothing but humiliation in his ambiguous position, while causing the most dangerous sorts of confusion.

The author found the camp's defensive works laid out according to a system devised by General Phull himself. The outer circle comprised a line of embrasures for light infantry; fifty or a hundred paces back of this was a line of alternately open and closed earthworks, the former intended for artillery and the latter for the infantry battalions assigned to protect it. Some five or six hundred paces behind this defensive ring lay a second, shorter semicircle of closed works which was envisioned as a reserve position to cover the retreat. Behind that line, in the center of the position, was a somewhat higher earth wall, a kind of redoubt.

Although this system of fortification was obviously too artificial—the number of works too large and the whole design too impractical—its defense by a sizable force, particularly one with the known valor of the Russians, promised serious resistance. Indeed, one can confidently assert that if the French had tried to take this camp from the front they would have exhausted themselves without reaching their objective.

The earthworks were well designed but the ground was sandy, and because no one had thought to strengthen the position by means of palisades, felled trees, traps, etc., much was still to be desired in this respect. The author convinced the staff officer in charge to consider such additional measures, and to prepare them at once.

Of the seven bridges to the rear, not one had been put up, and as the officer responsible lacked practical knowledge of such matters, he confessed his embarrassment to the author, in particular that he did not know how to make use of the unequal sizes of pontoons with which he had been supplied. The author described some of the expedients one could use in such cases, and promised to request that an engineer officer be sent to take over the construction.

On the spot, as in Vilna, the author thought that the most striking defect of the camp was the complete absence of fortifications on the right bank of the Dwina. The village of Drissa lay opposite the point where the camp's left wing met the river, but being made of wood and without a wall it afforded no means of defense. No defensive position of any kind was to be found beyond the bridges, where the camp's provisions, principally an enormous quantity of bagged flour, had been stockpiled in makeshift sheds without walls; these could as easily be set on fire as be ruined by the weather.

In the event of a French attack, Phull's plan was to leave 50,000 of the 120,000 men he hoped to muster inside the camp, which at a pinch they could have defended, and with the remaining 70,000 to advance against whatever part of the enemy force had crossed the river to attack the camp from behind.

If the enemy crossed the river with excessive strength and thus was seriously weakened on the left bank, Phull meant to break out of the camp and overwhelm this weakened part. The whole advantage of the camp, therefore, was that it afforded easier and more direct communication between the two sides of the river, while the enemy could link his separate forces only by means of a single, somewhat distant bridge. But this advantage was hardly decisive, certainly not of a kind on which one could stake the success of a battle fought by 120,000 men, deprived of all means of retreat, against a superior force. In any event, the contemplated counterattack on one bank or the other required favorable ground. This was not the case on the left bank, where the camp's front was surrounded by woods and morass, which did not even permit observation of the enemy. Furthermore, some degree of defensive strength was also needed on the other side, so that, if one wished to attack on the left bank, a small detachment could protect the magazines on the right. But again this was not possible, the ground there being level and entirely unfortified.

Had the Russians not abandoned this position on their own, their force, whether 90,000 or 120,000 strong, would have been surrounded by 300,000 Frenchmen, attacked from behind, driven into the half circle of fortifications, and forced to capitulate.

Phull held fast to his idea of a fortified camp because in his onesidedness he could think of nothing better. A battle in the open field promised no success at all because the forces were too unequal; therefore he wanted to make up the difference by a more artful and concentrated defense. But as is often the case in strategic speculations, he did not think through the causes whose effects he wished to exploit; and having left the simple path of direct resistance for a more complex course, without incorporating any new defensive principle into his scheme, he was merely leading the Russian army toward a swifter and surer catastrophe.

It was only thanks to Phull's rigidity and lack of realism, which made it impossible for him to let go of his plan before it led to disaster, that the Russian army escaped.

When the author returned from Drissa on June 28, he found that imperial headquarters had moved to Swanziani, three days' march from Vilna. War had broken out, and the army had begun its retreat. General Barclay's headquarters was now two days' march nearer to Vilna.

The author now had to report to the emperor on the situation he had found at Drissa. General Phull was naturally present during the report, and, as may be imagined, the task was not an easy one. What had to be said against the camp at Drissa struck at its fundamental character and at General Phull personally. The author was the general's adjutant; the general had received him most cordially at Vilna and recommended him to the emperor. Besides, the author's mission had not been to present a critique of the fortified camp as such, only to report on the present state of its works. On the other hand, the failures and defects that he had discovered in the camp's overall conception weighed so heavily upon him, in view of the gravity of the situation, that he felt it absolutely necessary to call attention to the danger into which the army and the Russian cause were being drawn. The emperor, for his part, had already had his confidence somewhat shaken at Vilna, as we have seen, and now wished to have it restored by means of an unconditional and closely argued endorsement of the whole operation. The author, having thought over these circumstances, decided to confine his report, which he accompanied with a written memorandum, to the terms of his order, but to hint at the difficulties that one might have to face. The result of the meeting was that the emperor once more suspected that he might be embarking on an enterprise that had not been fully thought out. A few days later the prince of Oldenburg (husband of the future queen of Württemberg and thus the emperor's brother-in-law), who was present at headquarters and whom the emperor treated as a trusted friend, told the author that the emperor seemed to sense that his report had not been entirely frank. The author replied that he had wanted to call attention only to the most significant elements of the plan that were not yet fully resolved, and that, in so doing, he was indeed conscious of a number of other difficulties, which one ought at least to consider in order not to be surprised by them later on. The prince said that the emperor intended to discuss these matters once more with the author at greater length in private. Nothing came of this, presumably because the emperor now began to discuss the camp with other officers who were better known to him, and who expressed their objections with less reserve.

At about this time, as we were approaching the Drissa camp, Lieutenant

General Count Lieven arrived at headquarters. He had been the Russian ambassador to Berlin, and had been kind enough to assist the author's entry into Russian service. The author called upon him. With respect to the military situation, Count Lieven's thoughts and feelings were the same as the author's. {He had never distinguished himself in war and was not considered a good soldier.} But in Berlin he had often discussed Russia's position with the more capable officers there. They believed that Bonaparte would be ruined by the sheer immensity of the Russian empire, provided Russia could bring this factor effectively into play—that is, conserve her resources until the last moment and refuse peace on any terms. Scharnhorst in particular expressed this opinion {and championed it}. Count Lieven was utterly taken with it, and naturally discussed it with the emperor. In words that the author had already heard him use in Berlin, he said that the first pistol shot should be fired at Smolensk. Although this expressed a misconception, since continuous resistance during the retreat was essential to this kind of defense, its central principle was of the utmost importance and could hardly fail in its effect, provided one did not shrink from evacuating the whole country as far as Smolensk and began the war in earnest only from there.

The author told General Phull of Count Lieven's idea and tried to lead him toward a bolder conception than that of his camp at Drissa. Phull, however, was of all men the slowest to grasp and appropriate the ideas of others; he insisted that Lieven exaggerated, but gave no reasons for thinking so.

This conversation with Phull depressed the author once again about the conduct of the war, a feeling that was further deepened by the course of events over the next days.

General Barclay, who commanded the army from his headquarters a day's march to the rear, only reluctantly obeyed the uncertain authority that was guiding operations. The enemy did not press him, which allowed him to stop and rest at times when, according to the overall plan, he ought not have done so. Phull feared that the enemy would reach Drissa before the army. The author was repeatedly sent to General Barclay's headquarters to urge greater speed, and, although Colonel Wolzogen was with General Barclay and acted as mediator, he was nevertheless rather badly received each time. In several encounters the Russian rear guard had had some success against the leading French detachments, and this gave the troops and their commanders a certain self-confidence, which General Barclay, a very calm man himself, hesitated to disturb by a rapid retreat. {Besides, he was rather pleased to be able to express his disagreement. Colonel Wolzogen also thought that the concern and hurry of imperial headquarters was exaggerated and introduced a new idea by telling the author that if one aims for a Torres Vedras, one must first have a Bussaco.}[12]

---

[12] Wellington defeated Masséna at Bussaco before retreating to Torres Vedras.

The author did not share General Phull's apprehensions, regarded them as a sign of weakness, and very much disliked his missions to General Barclay. But, while he admired the latter's composure and evident independence, {the sham learning that Colonel Wolzogen introduced into the matter disgusted him as a sign of confusion and a glittering play with concepts. He was equally troubled by General Barclay's lack of good will and refusal to obey orders.}

The author thought that in such a great and vital enterprise it was essential to stay close to reality, to have the exact state of affairs in all its details clearly in view, and that decisions should be made only on that basis. Historical inferences could certainly stimulate ideas about issues far in the future and may clarify them if there is time, but they could not lead an army in the field. Insubordination and dissension at a time of critical military decisions foretold inevitable disaster.

These impressions presented themselves to the author most forcefully at Widsy, a town that lies roughly halfway between Vilna and Drissa. While imperial headquarters was there, it was reported that the enemy had turned the army's left flank, from which it seemed to follow that our line of march would have to be altered to avoid having isolated columns overwhelmed by superior forces the following day.* General Phull, with whom the author was quartered, was suddenly sent for by the emperor, with instructions to bring the author with him. We found the emperor in a small study; in a larger adjoining room were Prince Volkonsky, General Arakcheev, Colonel Toll, and the captain of the guard, Count Orlov. Colonel Toll, a member of the general staff, soon became quartermaster general of General Barclay's army, a position in the Russian service equivalent to that of assistant chief of the General Staff—the chief of staff being concerned with general matters, while the quartermaster general focuses on tactics and strategy. Although Colonel Toll did not yet hold this position, he was more or less accorded the status that was due it.

Count Orlov was Prince Volkonsky's adjutant, but since the prince had nothing to do with the direction of the campaign, this young officer could count for very little.

Prince Volkonsky informed General Phull of the recent report and told him that the emperor wanted to know what ought to be done now. Since the author of these memoirs had selected the encampments on the march to Drissa, he had also been summoned, so that General Phull might deliberate with him and Colonel Toll about how to proceed.

---

* Here as elsewhere in this account of the campaign, the author has not assembled detailed information about dates, locations, and numbers of troops. Whoever seeks this kind of historical data in these recollections will be disappointed. It is rather the author's intention to add some color to the picture that posterity has of these events, by describing the impressions they made on him at the time, and the reflections to which they gave rise.

General Phull immediately declared that the present difficulty was the result of General Barclay's insubordination. Prince Volkonsky seemed to agree, while observing quite naturally that what mattered now was to choose some course of action. Here Phull revealed his true character. Thrown into obvious confusion by unexpected events on the one hand, and on the other driven by a long-suppressed bitterness to that irony that was always typical of him, he now announced that, since his advice had not been followed, he could do nothing to remedy matters. He said this while pacing rapidly up and down the room.

The author was beside himself at this exhibition. However little he might have agreed with General Phull, he was naturally identified with him in the eyes of the others. Everyone considered him Phull's protégé, who was captivated by his ideas and convinced of his abilities. It was, indeed, as if Phull's behavior were his own.

The humiliating part that the author, through no fault of his own, was here condemned to play was a trivial detail in a very serious situation, but he may perhaps be forgiven if this should at first have agitated him more than anything else. In the end we cannot cut ourselves off completely from our self-esteem; and while we may overcome it on some occasions, the wound is still painful at the moment it is inflicted.

Prince Volkonsky and General Arachkev awaited the outcome of the discussion with evident impatience but without displaying the slightest desire to become involved themselves. At any moment the emperor might have entered and demanded to know the results of the conference. Under these circumstances the deliberations passed into the hands of the three more junior officers. Colonel Toll, Count Orlov, and the author gathered round the map laid out on a table to determine how matters stood. Count Orlov, a young officer of quick intelligence but with no experience of large-scale operations, began to make some extraordinary proposals that we other two did not consider feasible. Colonel Toll proposed a change in the following day's march, which was reasonable in itself but might easily have led to confusion, since there was no longer time to issue the necessary orders. The author thought the situation less grave than had been supposed, assuming that everything was in fact as indicated; furthermore, he doubted the report of the French flanking movement, and was therefore of the opinion that one should let matters run their course and not change the plans. In a council of war, whoever wishes to do nothing will usually carry his point, and this was no exception. Colonel Toll acceded to the author's view, and it was decided to advise the emperor that it would be best to leave everything as it was. The emperor opened the door. General Phull and Colonel Toll were admitted, and the conference came to an end. The next day the report turned out to have been false; we reached the camp at Drissa without seeing enemy forces, except those that were harassing the rear guard.

The episode convinced the author with the greatest possible clarity that nothing good could come of this method of command. The emperor's confidence in General Phull seems also to have received a severe shock: the emperor no longer sent for him, as he often had before.

The author now attempted to make General Phull aware of the emperor's loss of confidence and of the other disadvantages of his position, so that he might extricate himself. He told him frankly that, although he too doubted General Barclay's ability to lead a large army against Bonaparte with success, Barclay nevertheless seemed a calm, determined man and a competent soldier; that the emperor's confidence in General Barclay seemed to increase from day to day; and that if General Phull could persuade the emperor to offer General Barclay the supreme command, at least unity and coherence of movement could be achieved. The author was certain that he could rely on General Phull's honorable feelings; however one-sided and self-absorbed he may have been, he had no trace of egotism in his character. He possessed the gentlest and noblest heart in the world.

On July 8, when imperial headquarters reached the Drissa camp, the emperor sent for General Phull to inspect the camp with him and some officers from his entourage. Phull explained the purpose of the various earthworks in detail, not without falling into one or another minor inconsistency. The emperor seemed to seek confirmation of Phull's views from the other officers present. But for the most part he encountered only doubtful faces. Colonel Michaud, the emperor's aide-de-camp, had served in the corps of engineers of the Sardinian army before entering Russian service and was therefore a technical expert, besides being regarded as a very knowledgeable and capable officer. He seemed the least satisfied with what he saw, and it was he who shortly afterwards strongly criticized the Drissa camp and brought the emperor to a decision.

At first it seemed as if the plan had not been given up entirely, for the author was sent the next day to inspect the ground on the right bank, in order to decide where to meet the enemy, should he attempt to outflank the camp by crossing the river.

But in the meantime the campaign as a whole was taking a turn that did not favor General Phull's plan. When the moment came for General Bagration to take the offensive against the French rear, that is, at the start of hostilities, no one had the courage to give the order; instead, it was decided, either in light of General Bagration's views or because of a prevailing feeling of weakness, that he should retreat along a line that allowed him to join up with the First Army. In this way one of the major calamities that might have arisen from Phull's plan—the total destruction of the Second Army—was avoided.[13]

The emperor thus saw that events had half ruined the plan of campaign on which he had at first relied, and that the army assembled at Drissa was one-sixth weaker than he had hoped. He heard criticisms of the Drissa camp on all sides, and he had lost confidence in his original plan and in its author. He recognized the difficulty of commanding an army in this manner, and General Barclay argued vigorously against fighting a battle at Drissa and demanded above all that the two armies be united, in which he was entirely right. Under the circumstances the emperor decided to give up supreme command and place General Barclay temporarily at the head of the whole army, while he proceeded to Moscow and from there to St. Petersburg, to speed the reinforcement of the army, look after its supplies, and raise a militia that would bring a greater proportion of the population under arms. The emperor could not have made a better decision.

General Phull felt himself to be in a very difficult position; the emperor no longer spoke with him, the members of the imperial entourage began to avoid him. The author once more urged him to anticipate the breach by going to the emperor himself and advising him to place overall command of the army in General Barclay's hands. The general resolved to do this, though not without a pang, which did him the more honor. He went at once to the emperor, who received him warmly, and in his subsequent decisions seemed merely to follow the general's advice—though this could hardly have been the case, for the changes were made without much controversy and lengthy discussions.

Because it had now been decided not to fight at the Drissa camp and because it was impossible for General Bagration's army to concentrate there, Prince Alexander of Württemberg, the emperor's uncle and a senior general, who was present at headquarters in his capacity as governor of Vitebsk, proposed to occupy a strong position near that city, which he had already identified and which he described as impregnable. It was therefore agreed to march to Vitebsk.

The French army had still not passed Drissa. The route to Vitebsk over Polozk was still open, and as the enemy did not yet press very hard, one could hope that this march, which owing to the position of Vitebsk was in fact a flank march, might be completed in safety, behind the protection of the Duna. In Vitebsk one could at least hope to combine with Bagration. In any case it was on the way to Smolensk, from which the great road to Moscow

[13] The total destruction of the Second Army would have occurred if the camp, defended by the First Army, failed to tie down a majority of the French, in which case Bagration, attacking from the rear, would have been overwhelmed.

afforded a natural line of retreat, well suited to a junction with Bagration and with reinforcements from the interior. These reasons, probably more than Prince Alexander's claims about the strength of the position at Vitebsk, convinced General Barclay that this was the only feasible course. Evidently this was true, and the author was relieved and overjoyed when he saw events taking this turn.

Needless to say, the Russian army was still very much at risk and the general state of affairs anything but favorable; but the human spirit is so constituted that salvation from the nearest of many evils is seen as a great blessing, and the brightest hopes are entertained at the first sign of improvement in one's circumstances.

The emperor had resolved to leave the army. But he ordered his headquarters to remain with it, in part to avoid attracting too much attention and arousing fears among the troops that he was abandoning them completely, in part because he could not foresee the future course of events and wanted to preserve the option to return. He offered General Phull the choice of remaining at imperial headquarters or leaving for St. Petersburg. General Phull chose the first, as any soldier would under the circumstances; as long as other officers of his rank remained at headquarters, this did not seem beneath his dignity. But General Barclay found this retinue of high-ranking officers very disconcerting and ordered that during the retreat the imperial headquarters remain a day's march ahead of the army, which placed it in the same category as heavy baggage and galled the officers attached to it. Gradually the emperor called away the senior officers for this or that special assignment, and General Phull came to feel that he could not decently remain in such a position and departed for St. Petersburg.

In General Barclay's headquarters the two most important staff appointments, chief of the general staff and quartermaster general, had also changed hands. Lieutenant General Labanov had been given command of the guards, which constituted the Sixth Corps and had been commanded until now by Grand Duke Constantine, who left the army with the emperor. Labanov was succeeded as chief of staff by Lieutenant General Marquis Paulucci, who had distinguished himself in the war against the Turks and Persians. He had a restless mind that poured forth a torrent of words. Heaven knows how anyone could have concluded that his qualities suited him to high command in war. He combined a confused mind with a disreputable character, and it soon became clear that no one was prepared to work with him; his appointment lasted only a few days. He was called to St. Petersburg and later named governor of Riga, taking over from General Essen the defense of that vital spot. His place on General Barclay's staff was taken over at Polotsk by Lieutenant General Yermalov, who had previously served in the artillery.

He was about forty years old, with a character at once ambitious, violent, and strong-willed, though not without understanding and cultivation. He was certainly preferable to his predecessors, because he could be expected to make sure that the supreme commander's orders were respected, and to bring a certain energy to the management of affairs, which was seen as a salutary complement to the gentle, not very vigorous manner of the commander in chief. But since he had never given much thought to large-scale military operations or arrived at clear views about them, when it came to deciding and acting he felt out of place. Therefore he confined himself to the general management of the army and left questions of tactics and strategy to the quartermaster general.

This office, as we have seen, was at first held by General Muchin, a Russian to the bone, who understood not a word of any foreign language and consequently could have read only Russian books. He had been chosen for his office because he was an expert in making maps and surveys, a duty that in relatively unsophisticated armies is commonly held to be the epitome of military science. It was inevitable that such a man would soon reveal his incapacity; he was replaced by Colonel Toll.

Colonel Toll was a man some thirty years old, who shone among his colleagues on the general staff as a particularly knowledgeable officer. He possessed a fair measure of talent and great determination. For some time he had occupied himself with the study of major military operations, and being well versed in the recent literature in the field, he had become pretty much lost in the most recent ideas of all, those of Jomini. He was therefore fairly well acquainted with the subject; and if he was far from having thought things through for himself and lacked the creative intelligence necessary to conceive a comprehensive and coherent plan for the war, his knowledge and ability were adequate to the needs of the moment and sufficient to prevent others from acting in an excessively antiquated manner. {In battle he did not distinguish himself.}

Colonel Toll did not have General Barclay's full confidence, however, in part because the general's rather cold temperament was not easy to overcome, in part because Colonel Toll lacked the degree of personal tact that is indispensable in such circumstances. He was well known for his rudeness toward both superiors and subordinates.

Colonel Wolzogen had remained at General Barclay's headquarters. This officer would have been exceptionally well qualified for the post of quartermaster general by virtue of his technical knowledge, which probably exceeded that of any other officer in the Russian army at that time, and because of his resourceful character; but his natural intellectual powers were sometimes obscured by a kind of unfortunate staff-officer pedantry, which made him less well suited to that office. Whoever wishes to engage in an activity like war should have a trained intellect but not be bound by book learning; if

he follows preconceived ideas that are not stimulated by the force of immediate circumstance, that are not drawn from his own flesh and blood, then
the flood of events will smash the structure of his ideas to the ground before
it is even completed. He will always remain unintelligible to men with instinctive abilities and will never gain the confidence of the most gifted among
them, who know exactly what they want to do. This was the case with Colonel Wolzogen. His command of Russian, moreover, was such that everyone
at once recognized him as a foreigner. By nature he was strongly drawn to
politics. He was too clever to suppose that a foreigner with alien ideas could
win the degree of confidence and authority over the mass of the Russian army
that would enable him to assert himself openly, without reserve. But he believed that most people were so weak and confused that one able man could
lead them wherever he wished, if he handled them with some dexterity. This
attitude lent a secretive note to his character and conduct, which most Russians interpreted as a propensity for intrigue. It was enough to raise their
suspicions; they did not consider what his goals were or whether, under the
circumstances, they could be anything but to do the best for the army and
for the cause we all served. If one wishes to lead or influence others without
their being aware of it, one must have an insinuating personality. Colonel
Wolzogen had nothing of the kind; rather, his manner was dry and grave,
and in the end he failed to achieve a position commensurate with his intelligence. He was passed over for the post of quartermaster general and decided
to make the campaign as a member of General Barclay's entourage, where
he hoped at least to be able to do some good from time to time. How far he
succeeded in this, whether he occasionally prevented bad decisions, I am
unable to say. But his influence could not have gone further than this, since
from this time until the change of supreme command very little happened as
a result of positive decisions on the Russian side.[14] Although General Barclay
displayed no particular confidence in him, Colonel Wolzogen continued to
be an object of suspicion to the Russians; he was viewed, almost supersti-
tiously, as an evil spirit who brought misfortune to the high command.

The author had taken advantage of the presence of Count Lieven at Drissa
to obtain an appointment as general staff officer of a field command, and
hoped to be attached to the rear guard. General Lieven and Colonel Wolzogen arranged this with General Barclay, who issued the necessary order
during the march to Polozk, without having first consulted General Yermalov
or Colonel Toll. Understandably, both men took this very badly, just as they
resented the appointment of Lieutenant Colonel von Lützow to the staff of
the fifth corps, which was accomplished in a similar manner. A rather un-

[14] Barclay was replaced as commander in chief by Kutusov on August 29. See p. 137, below.

pleasant scene with Colonel Wolzogen followed; but the appointments were not withdrawn. *

In this way the author came to be attached to General Count Peter Pahlen, who commanded the rear guard covering the retreat along the right bank of the Dwina.

Count Pahlen was considered one of the best cavalry officers in the Russian army. He was not yet forty years old, simple in his habits and open in his character, without great intellectual power or scientific knowledge, but with common sense and refined manners. He had served with distinction, was brave, calm, and determined, qualities that in his position must rank among the highest. Because he spoke excellent German and was more German than Russian in his character, this appointment was doubly agreeable to the author. But he was unpleasantly surprised when he found himself assigned to Count Pahlen's corps as the senior staff officer (first quartermaster). The author had expressly requested to be posted only as second staff officer or adjutant, since he knew virtually no Russian. Colonel Toll, however, may not have been displeased that an appointment arranged by Colonel Wolzogen was obviously unsuitable from the start.

Count Pahlen received the author with rather refined indifference and at once asked whether he spoke Russian, to which the reply could only be in the negative, a month's study at Vilna having barely led him to the mastery of a few of the most necessary phrases. The author suggested that Count Pahlen employ him as his adjutant rather than as his chief of staff, which, however, the count refused.

Thus the author found himself once again in a false position, and nothing remained for him but to resolve to gain the respect of the Russians by avoiding neither fatigue nor danger.

Part II

COURSE OF THE CAMPAIGN

In the middle of July the Grande Armée *resumed its advance from Vilna.
The Russians detached a corps under Wittgenstein to cover the roads*

---

* Leo von Lützow, younger brother of the well-known free corps leader [Ludwig von Lützow], served in the Prussian foot guards before 1806. In 1809 he entered Austrian service, and following the peace he went to Spain in 1810. He was captured in 1811 at the capitulation of Valencia but escaped to the south of France, and from there made his way on foot through Switzerland, southern Germany, and then through northern Germany, Poland, and Russia, passing through the middle of the French army while doing so. He joined the Russian army at Drissa, where he was posted to the general staff as a lieutenant colonel. The author knows of no other German officer who fought in all three of these wars, with Austria, Spain, and Russia against France.

leading north to St. Petersburg, while Barclay retreated eastward on the Moscow Highway. During the retreat Clausewitz served with the Russian rear guard, first under Pahlen, then under Uvarov. On August 4 Barclay reached Smolensk, where he met Bagration's Second Army, and assumed tenuous command over their combined forces. An attempt at a counteroffensive failed to halt the French, however, and on the 18th, amid bitter dissension in the high command, the Russians resumed their retreat, reaching Wiäzma on August 27. Two days later Kutusov took over the supreme command from Barclay, who retained his posts as minister of war and commander of the First Army.

On the 29th [of August], a day's march short of Giatsk, Barclay believed he had finally found a position where, with the reinforcements that had arrived, he could offer battle. He strengthened it at once with some earthworks. On this day, however, Kutusov arrived as commander in chief. Barclay again assumed command of the First Army, and Kutusov ordered the retreat to continue for the time being.

This change of command had been talked about for only a few days before Kutusov's arrival, proof that his appointment had not already been arranged when the emperor left [the army], in which case Kutusov would also have arrived sooner. In the army it was believed that Barclay's indecisiveness, which had held him back from fighting a regular battle, and the mistrust he began to encounter as people started to consider him a foreigner, had finally convinced the emperor to give supreme command to the man who, among native Russians, had the greatest reputation.

As far as dates are concerned, it seems likely that the abandonment of the offensive at Smolensk finally decided things. This occurred on August 7–8; three weeks later Kutusov arrived. In the meantime, unfavorable reports of Barclay were probably sent to St. Petersburg, chiefly at the instigation of Grand Duke Constantine, who was still with the army at Smolensk and had been won over to the idea of an offensive. The reports must have reached St. Petersburg in mid-August, which explains how General Kutusov, with a little effort, could arrive at headquarters two weeks later.

In the army there was great joy over his arrival. In the opinion of the Russians, everything up to then had gone very badly; any change therefore held out hope of improvement. Nevertheless, Kutusov's reputation in the Russian army was not unmixed; one party considered him an outstanding commander, another did not. All, however, were agreed that a true Russian, a disciple of Suvorov, was better than a foreigner and at this moment absolutely essential. Barclay was not a foreigner: he was the son of a Livonian pastor who had also been born there; he had served in the Russian army from his youth, and there was thus nothing foreign about him except his name

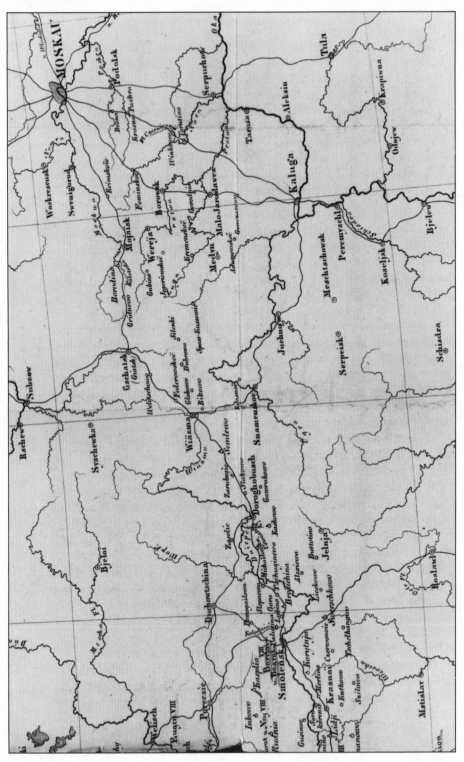

MAP 2. Smolensk to Moscow. Reproduced from the "Operationskarte für den Feldzug von 1812 in Russland," in Clausewitz, *Hinterlassene Werke*, 7 (Berlin, 1835).

and perhaps also his speech, for he spoke Russian badly and habitually preferred German instead. Under the circumstances, this was sufficient for him to be considered a foreigner. The fact that Lieutenant Colonel Wolzogen, who had only been in Russia for five years, remained close to General Barclay without becoming his adjutant or serving on the quartermaster general's staff made him appear to be Barclay's intimate advisor and further underlined Barclay's foreign character. Wolzogen himself, a serious man who lacked the affability that Russians value, was pursued with real hatred. The author heard one officer who returned from Barclay's headquarters bitterly say of Wolzogen that he sat in the corner of his office like a fat, poisonous spider.

Since, according to the Russians, things were going as badly as possible, it was believed that the treacherous advice of this foreigner was to blame for everything; no one doubted that Barclay had only been following Wolzogen's secret promptings. The ill will and mistrust that Colonel Toll and General Yermalov bore toward Colonel Wolzogen, because they believed he had sometimes opposed their views and caused much damage by his bad advice, may have been the main inspiration for this attitude. In particular, Wolzogen had played a part in the decision to abandon the offensive at Smolensk, chiefly because he was convinced that the main enemy force was on the Poreczie road. {At the time the author was struck by Wolzogen's poor judgment in this matter.} But people gave him far too much credit in believing that he possessed Barclay's confidence. Barclay was a fairly cold character, not very susceptible to suggestion, and such men as a rule do not submit to the will of others; nor was Wolzogen satisfied with General Barclay and with his own position at headquarters, which he accepted only because he believed that on occasion he might still do some good or prevent some evil. Least of all should people have suspected his intentions. It was truly primitive, worthy of a Tartar, to suspect an officer, who was the emperor's adjutant and possessed his confidence, of being a traitor, on no rational grounds whatever, simply because of his name.

This mistrust of outsiders was first aroused by Barclay and Wolzogen and spread throughout the cruder elements of the army until it touched all foreigners, of whom, as is well known, there are many in the Russian army. Many Russians who did not believe the foreigners were actually traitors nevertheless imagined that the household gods might be offended by their presence, which thus brought the army bad luck. But this was only a vague, muffled feeling in the army, which the author recalls because it was so characteristic and shows how the Russians viewed the campaign up to that point. Individually, foreign officers did not suffer because of it, because the people who knew them and could judge them clearly were always convinced that *this* officer, at least, was an honest fellow. The author, for instance, was almost always accorded the best reception and could take pleasure in the friendly manner of his comrades.

Kutuzov's arrival awakened new confidence in the army; the evil genius of the foreigners was exorcised by a true Russian, a Suvorov on a somewhat smaller scale, and no one doubted that a battle would follow at once, which would mark the culminating point of the French offensive.

But if Barclay had been stumbling backwards away from Bonaparte from Vitebsk to Wiäzma, like a man who has lost his balance and cannot regain it, Kutuzov, too, was unable at first to get the army back firmly on its feet. He marched on through Gzhatsk, which like Wiäzma was set on fire, and on September 3 took up a position at Borodino that seemed to him good enough for a battle and which he immediately began to fortify a little. In fact, the position at Borodino was chosen by the same eyes that had chosen all of Barclay's positions, the eyes of Colonel Toll, and this one was by no means the best among the many that this officer had thought suitable for a battle.

Kutusov, fifteen years older than Barclay, was almost seventy years old and no longer in possession of the physical and mental vitality that are sometimes found in soldiers of his age. In these respects he was Barclay's inferior, but he was certainly his superior in natural ability. As a young man Kutusov had been a tough trooper but had also shown considerable intelligence, cunning, and dexterity. These qualities always make a good general. But he had lost the disastrous battle of Austerlitz against Bonaparte, and the memory had never quite left him. His present situation, at the head of the whole Russian army, with the entire military might of the nation in his care, charged with leading hundreds of thousands of men against an opponent of equal size, over immense distances, and in so doing save or lose the Russian empire itself—these were conditions he had never faced before, and to which his natural abilities were not equal. The emperor sensed this and thought once again of taking supreme command himself, only this time from St. Petersburg, and without the assistance of such an awkward person as Phull.

At the center, however, at the head of the two Armies of the West, Kutusov still had to act as an independent commander, and his was certainly one of the most glorious tasks known to history, namely to lead 120,000 Russians against 130,000 Frenchmen commanded by Bonaparte.

In our opinion, Kutusov's performance in his role was anything but brilliant and far beneath what could have been expected of him in view of his earlier achievements.

The author was not close enough to this commander to be able to speak with complete confidence of his personal conduct. He saw him only for a moment at the battle of Borodino and can only report the impression that prevailed in the army immediately after the battle, which was that in the various phases of this great drama he counted for nothing. He seemed to possess no inner vitality, no clear view of prevailing conditions, did not actively intervene, did nothing himself. He allowed those who were in immediate control to go their own way, and as far as the particular parts of the fighting were concerned seemed to serve as no more than an abstract authority. The author concedes that he may be mistaken and that his judgment is not the result of his own direct observation, but in the years since then he has never had reason to revise the impression he formed of General Kutusov, and is now even more convinced of its accuracy. If it is a question of individual, personal influence over events, Kutusov counted for less than Barclay, a fact that must be attributed mainly to his more advanced age. Nevertheless, Kutusov was worth more than Barclay as head of the entire enterprise. Slyness and cunning stay with men even in old age, and they stayed with Prince Kutusov; with their help he understood his own position and that of his opponents better than Barclay had with his more limited insight.

The outcome of the campaign, which at the start could have been guessed only by someone with great vision and knowledge of a kind found only in exceptional minds, was now so plain to see that a clever man could grasp it easily. Bonaparte had entangled himself in such a terrible situation that events began to work for the Russians of their own accord, and success would follow without much outside assistance. Kutusov would certainly not have fought the battle of Borodino, which he probably did not expect to win, if it had not been pressed upon him by the court, the army, and the whole country. Presumably he regarded it only as a necessary evil. But he knew his Russians and understood how to treat them. With astonishing boldness he presented himself as the victor, announced everywhere the impending destruction of the enemy army, gave the impression, up to the last moment, that he intended to defend Moscow with a second battle, and did not hesitate to bluster and boast. In this way he flattered the vanity of the army and the people; with proclamations and religious addresses he tried to work on their feelings and thus created a new kind of confidence, artificial to be sure, but based on a fact, namely the miserable situation of the French army. The frivolity and hucksterism of the old fox were in fact more useful than Barclay's honesty would have been. The latter would have despaired over the outcome of the war, because he still did so in October, when most people were regaining hope; he would have found no resources within himself, and his anxiety would have deprived him of the support that others offered, for he even came out against the march on the Kaluga road.[15] In his sad and troubled face, every soldier would have read the desperate condition of the army and the state, and the mood of the commander might perhaps have communicated

[15] See pp. 165–66, 170, below.

141

itself to the army, the court, and the people. In short, Barclay—simple, honorable, personally energetic, but without ideas and incapable of fully grasping the major issues of the war—would have been overwhelmed by the moral power of the French victory at Borodino, while the frivolous Kutusov responded with brazen arrogance and endless boasting and so sailed with good fortune into the enormous gap that was already opening up in the French armada.

When Kutusov assumed supreme command, General Yermalov was the chief of staff and Colonel Toll the quartermaster general of the First Army of the West, and in a sense also of the combined armies, because until then the commanding general of the First Army had also functioned as supreme commander. At least the orders issued to both armies jointly came from these two individuals. As soon as Barclay left the supreme command, their official responsibilities were again limited to the First Army. With General Yermalov this was also true in practice, because Prince Kutusov was accompanied by General Count Bennigsen, who now assumed the post of chief of staff of the combined armies. Very likely Bennigsen had begged this appointment in St. Petersburg, because he must have seen that he would not be given command of one of the two armies, and as chief of staff he could move into the top position if things did not work out with the old prince. Little by little he gained some influence, though not through any special favor of his chief, who presumably was somewhat suspicious of him. In the army this peculiar appointment made a queer impression. But since the prince was not accompanied by a quartermaster general, Colonel Toll continued to perform these duties; whether he was actually appointed to the post or acting merely as deputy the author does not know.

As in the past, therefore, Colonel Toll selected the army's positions and determined the relevant tactical measures, and so the position at Borodino and the deployment of the troops there is presumably mainly his work.

Before we discuss this battle we want to comment briefly on the retreat toward Moscow.

The Russian army did not want to withdraw in the direction of St. Petersburg, but into the interior of the country, because there it could be reinforced most effectively and the pursuing enemy would have to face opposition from all sides. As long as the enemy still had great superiority in numbers, it was necessary to look to the protection of Moscow, because the French could always move toward the city in force, just as one had to protect St. Petersburg with Wittgenstein's corps when the main army left the St. Petersburg highway. To avoid further weakening of the army by detaching a second force, the army logically retreated toward Moscow. Had the rapid decline of the French army been foreseen, it would have been possible to choose another road into the interior. Instead of retreating from Smolensk toward Moscow, the retreat could, for instance, have taken the road to Kaluga and Thula. One could have predicted that as soon as the French lost their decisive superiority over the Russians, they would no longer be able to detach a force toward Moscow, and that with their single line of communications it would be even more difficult for the entire army to bypass the Russians and march toward the capital. If we consider that at Borodino no more than 130,000 French troops faced 120,000 Russians, no one will doubt that a Russian retreat in a different direction—for instance, toward Kaluga—would have eliminated Moscow as a French objective. But when the retreat from Drissa began, first toward Vitebsk, then toward Smolensk, no one thought that the French forces would melt away so quickly, and it was perfectly natural to continue to withdraw toward Moscow in order to cover and retain the city as long as possible.

At Smolensk the proportion of the two main armies was 180,000 to 120,000, and as one's estimate might easily be off by 20,000 men it was conceivable that the French might be as strong as 200,000. Under these circumstances the Russian generals could hardly be blamed if they were not yet prepared to maneuver, that is, to defend Moscow by indirect means. But even had they decided to do so at Smolensk, it might already have been too late. If changing the lines of operation of a large army is far more difficult than is usually thought, it is doubly so for a large force pressed by a superior enemy in sparsely populated Russia. The army could rest only in camps; it always had to remain concentrated. It was entirely dependent on supply depots. The depots had been prepared on the Moscow Highway and would first have had to be moved; everything in the way of ammunition, supplies, reinforcements, and so forth, that was on that road or was heading in that direction would have had to be shifted rapidly in the new direction. It seems very doubtful that there was still time to do this when the army was at Smolensk.

This suggests that the reproach some writers raised after the fact against the Russian leadership—not to have gone from Smolensk to Kaluga—was insufficiently thought through. Had they wished to choose this direction, they would have had to have made the decision much earlier. The indirect defense of Moscow became logical only later; earlier on it would have meant a great risk, which a general who did not even possess extraordinary authority could never have been expected to take.

One of these writers (Buturlin) regrets that General Barclay had not been familiar with the principle that in war an objective is always covered *best* by means of a position on one side or the other. The young always have principles handy. If an objective is covered by means of a flank position, everything depends on the size of the theater of operations, on the relative strength of the opponents, and on psychological factors—in short, on more or less every element in war. If the axiom is to hold good, it would have to take account of all these elements; if we accept such bare principles, it would be quite natural to object to what actually happened and to think that the problem was simple, whereas in reality difficulties of all kinds narrowed one's choice of action.

But at the time Barclay and his staff never considered a maneuver away from the center, a move that the enormous dimensions of Russia would have facilitated. The Russian empire is so large that one can play hide and seek in it with an enemy army; and this fact must be the basis for its defense against a superior enemy. A retreat deep into the interior draws the enemy army along, but leaves too much territory behind for it to occupy. After that nothing prevents the retreat that first proceeded from the frontier to the interior from being continued further, from the interior back to the frontier, where we and the weakened enemy force would come out again together.

The flank march on the Kaluga road, and a further retreat in that direction, [would have been] something of that sort, though things actually turned out even better in the end. Earlier on, however, no one had thought of retreating toward Kaluga and at such a sharp angle. The idea arose only after the battle of Borodino. Before then the Russian generals and their staffs had never even considered it, and I do not recall it being mentioned by any other officer. But at the moment when an emergency might have led to such a possibility, that is, when people began to realize that Moscow could no longer be covered, it was already too late, because as we have noted, the necessary preparations [for such a diversion] had not been made.

Let us now turn to the battle of Borodino. This battle is of a kind that really requires little explanation, because the outcome corresponded exactly to existing circumstances. One hundred twenty thousand Russians, among them 30,000 cossacks and militia, deployed in a mediocre position, faced 130,000 French troops under Bonaparte. What could be expected from a test of strength in this confined space, with equal courage on both sides, other than a slight shift in the balance to the disadvantage of the Russians? We have never understood why people were so eager to have the battle of Borodino explained to them. Some could not grasp why Kutusov withdrew, since he had won the battle; others, why Bonaparte had not destroyed the Russians.

Russia does not possess many locations suitable for defensive battles. In those areas where there are still great swamps, the country is so heavily wooded that it is difficult to find space to deploy large bodies of troops. Where the forests are not so dense—between Smolensk and Moscow, for instance—the ground is level, without significant mountain ranges, without deep valleys; the fields are not enclosed and consequently can be easily crossed; the villages have wooden houses and are not suitable for defense. In addition, even here one can rarely see very far, because smaller stands of trees are everywhere. In short, the choice of good defensive positions is limited. If someone wants to fight a battle without delay, which was now the case with Kutusov, and therefore has to find a location within a few days' march, it is obvious that he must take what he can get.

Colonel Toll could not find a better position than Borodino, a position that, like a handsome but weak horse, promises more at first sight than it can deliver. The right wing resting on the Moskva River, which is too deep to ford, the front covered by the Kolotscha stream, which flows through a fairly deep valley—at first glance all that seems promising, and probably impressed Toll. But unfortunately the highway from Smolensk to Moscow does not run at right angles to the Kolotscha, but for some distance runs parallel to it, and after crossing the stream, diverges at a shallow angle toward the hamlet of Gorky. Consequently, if the army is drawn up parallel to the stream, it is positioned at an angle to its line of retreat and exposes its left flank to the enemy. This was particularly dangerous here, because two miles from the Moscow Highway the Old Moscow Road runs through the hamlet of Jelnia and leads to the rear of the position. Moreover, any position where a road bends sharply, as here, is weak, because as the enemy advances he has already half turned its flank, and the line of retreat is threatened from the beginning, which greatly weakens resistance. It is true that the attacking enemy is similarly exposed, but he generally has the advantage in such an unusual situation because his troops are advancing and have been organized for movement, which is less true of the defense. In this respect as well, then, the left flank was too exposed to be further weakened by a line of retreat that was not perpendicular to the defensive front. This meant that the right wing, parallel to the Kolotscha, was very well placed, but that the center was already some distance from the stream and that the left flank had to be bent back at a sharp angle. The whole assumed the form of a convex arc, and the French attack, consequently, that of an enveloping curve, its fire concentric against the defense—in this confined area, and considering the enormous mass of artillery, a very important factor.

The area that was occupied by the left wing of the Russian army presented no particular advantages. A few gently sloping hills, perhaps twenty feet high, together with stretches of small trees and shrubs, formed such a confused whole that no one could say which side would have the advantage. But the best part of the Russian deployment, the right wing, could achieve nothing. The entire position drew the French to attack the left wing and permitted them to ignore the right. To attack the right meant squandering one's troops; it would have been better for the Russians to have extended the right wing along the Kolotscha to the neighborhood of Gorky, and the rest of the terrain running to the Moskva River might have been occupied with a few units, or merely observed.

145

The left flank, as has already been noted, was bent back, unsupported by favorable terrain. It was therefore strengthened with earthworks, and the corps of General Tutschkov, reinforced by Moscow militia, together about 15,000 men, was stationed on the Old Moscow Road far to the rear and hidden, so that it threatened the right flank and rear of any enemy force that attempted to turn the Russian left. The plan was very good, we think, but failed because the numbers and distances did not stand in a proper relationship to the whole, as we shall discuss later on. The earthworks were constructed on the left flank and in the center, one of them as an advance redoubt some two thousand paces before the left flank. These works were only constructed after the army occupied the area. They were located in sandy soil, open to the rear, without any kind of reinforcement, and so could only be considered separate points of somewhat heightened defensive strength. None was able to withstand a serious assault, and in fact most of them were lost and recaptured two or three times during the battle. Nevertheless, it must be said that they contributed to the substantial, vigorous Russian resistance, and on the left flank they formed the only positional advantages the Russians possessed.

At the beginning of the battle, before the Russians shifted their troops from the right flank, their front consisted of about five infantry corps deployed in two lines, behind them the cavalry, again in two lines, with 4,000 cuirassiers behind them, plus the 15,000 men under General Tutschkov, hidden to the rear of the left flank, which could also be considered a reserve. One can say, therefore, that the Russians were deployed in two lines, with a third and fourth line of cavalry behind, and that four-ninths of the whole were in reserve. If we take note that the Russian front extended only about eight thousand paces, that the five corps forming the two front lines were about 40,000 men strong, making 20,0000 men in each line, and if we further consider the great number of guns (six for every thousand men), then we see that the deployment of the first two lines was very dense. If we further note that the corps of Bagavout and Ostermann were eventually moved from the right flank, where they served no purpose, to strengthen the rest of the front, we can see that on this day the Russian army fought in a position that was perhaps unequalled in narrowness and depth. The disposition of the French army was equally compressed and therefore in comparable depth. Its enveloping front was longer than that of the Russians, but that was made up for by their larger numbers. This compression is the most important characteristic of the battle. It explains:

First, the very solid and obstinate Russian resistance. The battle began at six in the morning, lasted until four in the afternoon, and during those ten hours the Russians withdrew no more than 1,500 to 2,000 paces on the left flank, the area where they gave up the most ground. Only Tutschkov's corps, which engaged in a separate fight, was driven back further. The Russians retained their cohesion throughout these ten hours of fighting. Evidently both [the solid defense and the little ground lost] were the consequence of their compressed formations. It is only where space permits the cavalry to exploit the successes of infantry and artillery, and to enlarge on it, that troops begin to flee, which leads to disorder and significant loss of ground.

Second, the high density of troops explains the enormous casualties. According to Buturlin, the Russian army lost 50,000 men in two days, of whom few were prisoners. In the army at the time the losses were thought to be only 30,000, which seems more probable to us; but even this—one quarter of the whole—is an unusually high percentage.

Colonel Toll strongly favored deep formations, that is, a short front and correspondingly stronger reserves. He repeatedly discussed this conception with the author, who always regarded it as of great significance, as the best means of changing from the defensive to the offensive, and of depriving the attacker of the advantage of staying with his *final* [planned] *disposition*, and thus of surprise. We do not doubt, therefore, that the unusual depth of the Russian position should be primarily credited to Colonel Toll.

But we cannot concur with the use Colonel Toll made of the principle in this battle. We believe the battlefield should have had [still] greater depth, that is, cavalry and reserves should have been kept further back. We think the time has passed when a battle could be considered a single act, with the victory gained by one thrust, through the clever coordination of all parts of the machine. Perhaps there never had been such a time, but theory usually favored this idea. The surprise maneuvers with which Frederick the Great won at Leuthen and Rossbach, together with his so-called oblique order of battle, have long been the basis of this conception. But if we consider how slowly all major battles develop, how much time a tactical evolution now requires, that the weakening and wearing down of opposing forces in the fire fight must precede the decision, and that the decisive moves can therefore only be executed late in the process, then it seems certain that a reserve far to the rear, which in a sense is not even on the battlefield but may be thought of as a newly arrived corps, can always be used to achieve the decision.

The resulting advantages are:

1. That these reserves remain out of range.
2. That it is easier to keep them hidden from the enemy.
3. That they can be employed more easily for envelopments and previously unplanned movements.

Here we cannot discuss the idea as fully as it deserves, but we do want to describe it more closely by noting that we have a distance of three to five thousand paces in mind. Further, we must admit that the particular location will usually exert a significant influence on the intervals and will often make a long interval impossible.

In the position at Borodino, however, where Colonel Toll had so strongly embraced the idea of deep deployment in succeeding battle lines, the other element—that of the distance between them—had been unduly neglected.

The cavalry was positioned three to four hundred paces behind the infantry, with the distance from it to the main reserve barely a thousand paces. In consequence, the cavalry as well as the reserve suffered greatly from enemy fire without being able to do anything themselves. If one further recalls what an unusual number of guns the Russians had and that the Russian artillery takes up much more space than any other because of its many small ammunition carts, then one can imagine how crowded everything was with one unit crammed against the next. To this hour the author remembers the impression this density made on him.

Had the cavalry been placed a thousand paces behind the infantry, it would have been equally and better able to act against any significant success of the French horse. Had the Guards and General Tutschkov been placed back twice as far as they were, they would not have suffered from enemy fire until they themselves could fire, and could have been used with greater surprise and in every respect more effectively.

The author has discussed this aspect of the battle of Borodino at such length because he believes this issue is of great contemporary importance and plays a greater or smaller role in every battle, especially on the side of the defensive, and because it distinguished the battle of Borodino more than the other tactical dispositions that occurred in it, which we believe hardly offered anything new but to which we will now turn.

With a united force of 130,000 men, Bonaparte advances on the position of Borodino. Some distance away he crosses the Kolotscha with most of his troops and chooses the obvious option of concentrating on the left flank, which Poniatowski's corps is to outflank and envelop. On September 5 a preliminary struggle developed for the advanced redoubt before Bagration's front. After stubborn resistance, the Russians withdrew in the evening to avoid committing too many forces to this side issue.

At six o'clock on the morning of the 7th the real battle began. To the left of Kolotscha, Eugene,[16] with approximately 40,000 men, was to attack the Russian center. To the right of the stream, Davout and Ney were to attack the left flank with about the same number. Junot, the Guards, and part of the reserve cavalry—together another 40,000 men—stood in reserve behind Davout and Ney. Poniatowski, with his 10,000 men, was to advance on the Old Moscow Road and envelop the left flank. Poniatowski's advance brought

[16] Eugène de Beauharnais, Napoleon's stepson and viceroy of Italy.

Tutschkov into play earlier than the Russians had expected. Similarly, at the beginning of the action, Bagration felt compelled to draw Carsnitzu's division further forward. Tutschkov's units were not heavily engaged until the fighting elsewhere had lasted for some hours.

Since Poniatowski was prevented by Tutschkov from carrying out his order to envelop the left flank, one can say that Tutschkov's corps was still acting as a reserve. Poniatowski had only 10,000 men; Tutschkov still had about 12,000 after Konownitzin's division had been detached, more than half of whom, however, were militias and cossacks. Here as elsewhere, therefore, the struggle remained in balance for hours.

When Poniatowski could not overcome his opponent, he was reinforced by 10,000 men under Junot, whereupon Tutschkov was compelled to withdraw about a mile, in the course of which he was fatally wounded. Eventually his forces took up new positions so far to the rear as to cause concern for the Russian army's left flank and line of retreat.

At the center and on the left, the battle began around six o'clock and for some hours was maintained by violent artillery fire and by the Russian *Jäger* regiments, two in each division. Most of the *Jäger* formed skirmish lines before the corps front and, protected by all sorts of minor terrain features, defended themselves vigorously. It may have been eight in the morning when the village of Borodino, on the French side of the Kolotscha, defended by a *Jäger* regiment, was already taken, and men were struggling for possession of the [great] redoubt before the Russian center, that the Russians decided to launch an attack against the French left flank.

On the Russian right General Platov, with some 2,000 cossacks, had been looking for a ford across the Kolotscha, had crossed the stream, and was surprised to encounter little or no opposition on the other side, where he had expected the whole of the enemy's left wing. He observed the left wing of Eugene's force advance toward the village of Borodino, and nothing appeared easier than to attack these units in the flank, and so forth. We say "and so forth" because in most cases people do not know what such a flank attack should really achieve. To run down the apparently unprotected reserve artillery of the enemy, and to capture munition carts rolling back and forth, often seems much more significant in imagination than it is in reality. In short, Platov sent the prince of Hesse-Philippsthal, who served as a volunteer on his staff, to General Kutusov to inform him of Platov's discovery and to suggest that a powerful force of cavalry be sent across the stream to attack the unprotected enemy. The prince, perhaps even more in favor of the plan than Platov but a young officer with little experience, reported the plan to Colonel Toll with such enthusiasm that at first it really seemed promising. Colonel Toll was won over and at once rode to Prince Kutusov, who had halted at the little hamlet of Gorky. The author, at that time senior quartermaster gen-

MAP 3. The battle of Borodino. Reproduced from Dmitrii Buturlin, *Atlas des plans, légendes et tableaux d'organisation de l'histoire militaire de la campagne de Russie en 1812* (Paris, 1824).

Russians (morning of September 7):
1. Konownitzin; 2. Stroganov; 3. Moscow militia; 4. Vorozov; 5. Neverovski; 6. Konlebakin; 7. Paskevitch; 8. Sievers; 9. Liekechev; 10. Kapzewitch; 11. Pahlen; 12. Bakhmetiev; 13. Tschogolokov; 14. Korff; 15. Olssuviev; 16. Duke Eugen of Württemberg; 17. Uvarov; 18. Prince Karl of Mecklenburg; 19. Douka; 20. Imperial Guard; 21. Depreradovitch; 22–24. Cossacks; 25–28. Chasseurs.

French Bivouacs (night of September 6):
A, B. Poniatowski; C. Nansouty; D. Montbrun; E. Latour-Maubourg; F, G, M. Davout; H, J. Ney; K, L. Junot; N. Grouchy; O. Eugene; P. Italian Guard; Q. Ornano; R, S. Imperial Guard.

French (morning of September 7):
T. Zayonczek; U. Kniesewicz; V. Kaminiecki; W. Compans; X. Dessaix; Y. Friant; & Girardin; a. Ledru; aa. Marchand; b. Razout; c. Wolwarth; d. Junot; e. Wolff; f. Nansouty; g. Montbrun; h. Latour-Maubourg; i. Delzons; k. Morand; l. Girard; m. Broussier; n. Italian Guard; o. Grouchy; p. Ornano; q. Curial; r. De Laborde; s. Legion of the Vistula; t. Walther; u. Old Guard.

PLAN
DE LA BATAILLE
DE BORODINO
Livrée le 26 Août 1812,
ENTRE L'ARMÉE RUSSE
Commandée par le Général en Chef
Prince Golénitscheff Koutousoff,
ET L'ARMÉE FRANÇAISE
Commandée par l'Empereur Napoléon.

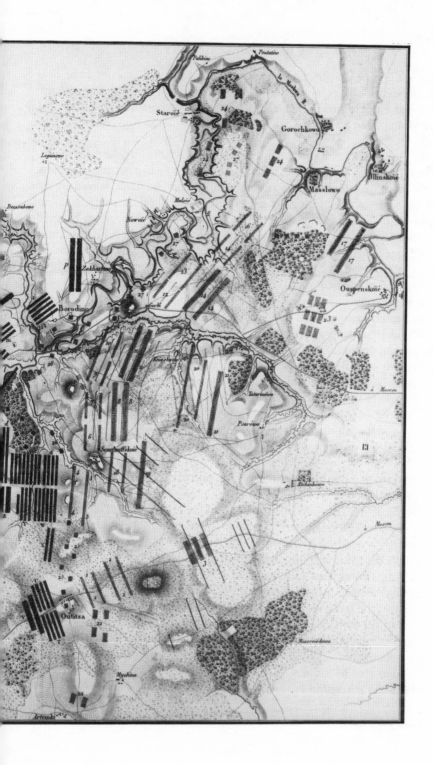

eral of the First Cavalry Corps under General Uvarov, happened to be near the prince with other members of Uvarov's staff when Colonel Toll rode up. Toll had just returned from the left flank and now reported to the prince that everything there was under control, Prince Bagration having repulsed all attacks (in the first two hours of combat it could hardly be otherwise). Just then it was reported that Eugene had been taken prisoner in the great redoubt, which had been lost and recaptured. Enthusiasm rose like blazing straw; several voices suggested that the news should at once be made known to the troops; some calmer heads among the generals thought the report was so improbable that one ought to await confirmation. Nevertheless, it was believed for about half an hour, even though Eugene was not brought to headquarters, an absence that was explained by the fact that he was severely wounded. Today we know that it was General Bonami, not the viceroy of Italy, whom the French had left behind, badly wounded, in the redoubt.

It was during this wave of enthusiasm and the happy feeling that things were beginning to go well that Colonel Toll presented the proposal of the prince of Hesse to Prince Kutusov. It was evident that Toll, carried away by the general optimism, believed that an energetic diversion by cavalry against the enemy's left flank would have an impact and perhaps decide the battle. He suggested using the first cavalry corps, consisting of 2,500 men of the light horse of the Guards and stationed to the rear of the right wing, which had not yet been engaged. Prince Kutusov, who had been listening to the reports and discussions like someone who did not have his head screwed on straight, and who only now and then said, "C'est bon, fait-le,"[17] also responded to this proposal: "Et bien, prennez-le."[18] The prince of Hesse had volunteered to guide the corps through the ford to the decisive point. General Uvarov was therefore ordered to follow him, and to attack the French army in the flank and rear when he had reached the chosen spot. This order was certainly unexceptional, and it was not possible to go into great detail; but according to our understanding of war we cannot find it totally sufficient. The operation was not fully understood. If, despite the superior strength of the enemy, it was decided to pull a corps of 2,500 men out of the order of battle and remove it from central control, one should at least have tried to insure that the force would be effective in its mission. It was apparent from the order that General Uvarov should attack any cavalry of equal or inferior strength that he might encounter; but it could also be expected that he would meet infantry and—if he hoped to constitute a real threat—strong infantry units supported by artillery. We know what happens when one arm of the service is to fight against two. It is true that General Uvarov had twelve pieces

17 "Good, do it."
18 "Fine, take it."

of light artillery; but among the large number of guns employed in this battle, that did not signify much. In our opinion General Uvarov should have been ordered to attack whatever force he encountered, not so much with the intention of fighting a successful engagement as of tying down a significant number of troops and thus of weakening the French attack. Under the circumstances, even if his force were completely defeated it should not have been regarded as a failure. A mission of this sort is always problematic, and to carry it out always demands much self-denial and devotion to the common good; but it cannot be expected that a general will proceed in this manner without specific orders. On the contrary, he will usually seek victory and avoid defeat.

Between eight and nine in the morning, when it was decided to make this diversion, the battle was still in its opening phases and no one could predict its outcome. Twelve hours of daylight still lay ahead, and in view of the enemy's firmness and determination new challenges might be expected up to the last moment, so that one could well say that the day should not be praised before its end. A diversion of 2,500 men could not possibly have a decisive effect in a battle against 130,000. At most it could provide a partial, momentary check on the enemy's intentions, perhaps cause him some surprise. Had this taken place at a decisive moment, when both sides were exhausted and any new threat was bound to be more effective, the diversion might have achieved something. But early in the day the enemy could obviously counter this isolated thrust with superior strength, eliminate General Uvarov, and then return to the main task.

Later on we shall discuss the offensive that the Russians might have implanted in their defensive battle; for the present we follow General Uvarov on his raid.

He forded the Kolotscha above Starroie, then turned left toward Borodino, but was forced to diverge somewhat to the right by marshy brooks running into the stream. It was between eleven and twelve o'clock when he reached the brook that runs past Borodino into the Kolotscha. To his left lay the village of Borodino, occupied by Eugene's troops, in front of him was the brook, which ran through narrow but marshy meadows. On the near side of the brook stood two regiments of French cavalry and a body of Italian infantry, perhaps a regiment or a reinforced battalion. The cavalry at once withdrew over the dam that crossed the brook about two thousand paces above Borodino, but the infantry was bold enough to remain and formed a square with its back to the brook. General Uvarov ordered his men to attack. In vain the author suggested that the square first be placed under fire by the light artillery; the Russian officers feared it would then retreat and they would not get any prisoners. The hussars of the Guard were therefore called forward and ordered to charge. They made three ineffectual attacks; the Italians maintained discipline and their tight formation and returned a steady fire. As is usual in such cases, the hussars turned back some thirty paces from the square and drew out of range. General Uvarov discontinued these not very brilliant attempts, ordered the artillery to open fire, and at the first volley the enemy withdrew across the brook. The whole business then came to an end.

Borodino itself could not be attacked with cavalry; horsemen could only cross the brook on the dam, on the other side of which some 4–5,000 infantry were positioned in the open spaces between the undergrowth that covered the hilly ground. Cavalry stood behind them. In Borodino we could see a few strong columns of troops, and beyond the village toward the center large masses of infantry and cavalry, which we had to assume were the Guards, stood at rest behind the battle line. General Platov with his 2,000 cossacks was fifteen minutes to the right of Uvarov, looking for a ford through the swampy brook. By the time General Uvarov arrived opposite Borodino, several hours of the most intense fighting had already passed, and the Russians began to view the matter with different eyes than they had between eight and nine in the morning. They sensed that only now the whole weight of the giant was beginning to press on them, and that they might not be his match. The corps of Bagavout and Ostermann, which had formed the inactive right wing, were already employed to strengthen the center and the left, and even the Guards had sent some of their units forward. The Russian reserves were shrinking severely, while the French Guards remained motionless in thick columns like a dark thundercloud. The Russians could no longer think of another offensive beyond General Uvarov's move; all eyes were now turned on him. An adjutant, an officer of the general staff, and an imperial adjutant all rode over one after another to see whether anything at all might be achieved there. If we are not mistaken, even Colonel Toll appeared for a moment, and of Lieutenant General Osarovski's presence we are more certain. All rode back, convinced that Uvarov could do nothing. On the one hand, it was no trifling matter for the cavalry to cross the brook under enemy fire; on the other, one saw such large units of troops in reserve on the far bank that 2,500 horse could not possibly achieve a success that would influence the course of the battle.

Under these circumstances the author thanked God for having been reduced to a zero. He was not even able to take part in the exchanges in Russian between General Uvarov and the various officers that were sent to him. From the outset he had been convinced that this diversion would fail, and now saw that if anything at all was to be salvaged it could be done only by a young fire eater who had his reputation to make, not by General Uvarov.

Several hours passed while people were talking back and forth, until suddenly heavy firing began on the far side of the brook on the French left, and soon word came that Platov had at last found a passage and was now in the bushes with his cossacks. Soon we could see these troops—remarkable in that sometimes they are exceptionally brave and at other times exceptional cowards—careening about between enemy infantry and stands of trees without making a serious charge. It almost seemed as though they were merely skirmishing. The enemy units opposite us feared that the cossacks might force them into the swamp and marched off to one side. At this, the cossacks of the Guards, who were attached to Uvarov's corps, could restrain themselves no longer. They streamed over the dam like a rocket with a long tail, and like lightning were among their brethren in the woods on the other side.

Uvarov could certainly have followed them, but he had no wish to be squashed against the dam if he were thrown back, or to lose cohesion and retreat in all directions, as cossacks do on occasion. As in any case he had already sent back all the emissaries of Kutusov, Bennigsen, and Barclay, he remained in place while awaiting further orders. Soon the Guard cossacks returned to the near bank, having lost a considerable number of killed and wounded.

It was under these circumstances that we watched the battle develop, and I still find it interesting today how it gradually took on the character of weariness and exhaustion. The infantry units became so reduced that perhaps no more than a third of their original strength was still engaged; the rest had been killed, wounded, were evacuating casualties or reforming in the rear. In short, large gaps had opened up everywhere in the line of battle. The enormous number of guns that both sides had brought to bear—over six hundred—now were heard only occasionally, and even these single shots seemed to have lost their original thundering, forceful tone and sounded weak and hoarse. Almost everywhere cavalry units had taken the place of infantry. They charged in a weary trot, riding back and forth, and in turn occupied and abandoned the earthworks.

Toward three o'clock in the afternoon it was evident that the battle was dying down, and that, as almost always, the decision now depended on who still held the last trump card—the stronger reserves. From our position we could neither determine this nor identify the general positions of the two sides. The reports that reached us were not exactly disquieting, which somewhat surprised the author, because the Russian center had already fallen back here and there, from which one might guess at the situation on the left flank.

At three o'clock General Uvarov was ordered to return to his former position. We moved off and reached the rear of Gorky between four and five o'clock, where we reformed.

The course of the battle could not have been simpler. Because Tutschkov prevented the envelopment of the left flank, the French attacked straight ahead and pushed in the Russian center and left with the weight of their numbers.

As the original right flank of the Russians was not attacked, and almost all troops there were gradually moved elsewhere, the flank essentially ceased to exist. The original center of the line of battle, from Gorky to Seminovsky creek, now became the right flank, and the rest of the battle line the left. Half of Bagration's army—Raevski's corps—must be considered part of the right wing, because it had defended the redoubt in the center and met the first threat of Eugene.

The main French assault was directed against the Russian left flank. Step by step they committed the corps of Davout and Ney, 40,000 men; the corps of Junot and Poniatowski, 20,000 men; and three cavalry corps of 10,000 men, together 70,000, while the Guards—approximately 20,000 men—stayed in reserve without taking part in the fighting. On their left flank, the Russians had Tutschkov with 15,000 men; Bagration with three divisions, a cuirassier division, and a cavalry division, making 25,000 men; about 10,000 men taken from the reserves; and 5,000 men from Bagavout's corps, together some 55,000 men exclusive of cossacks and militia. The result [of this un-equal encounter] was that the Russians were forced out of their positions and had to give up a few thousand paces of ground—an outcome that had already been assured by noon.

The Russian right flank was now attacked by Eugene. In the course of the attack he received no other support than one charge on the redoubt in the center by the second cavalry corps, which formed the link between his troops and Ney's. Consequently the French amounted to 40,000 men here, but the Russians gradually committed the corps of Raevski and Doctorov, 20,000 men; Ostermann with 10,000; one division of Bagavout's corps with 5,000; three cavalry corps and one cuirassier division with 12,000; together 47,000 men, with 6,000 reserves who did not really take part in the battle. The result was that here the battle continued throughout the morning without the Russians losing ground, and that the main French attack, which took the redoubt in the center, was not launched until the afternoon, when the village of Seminovsky on the left flank had already been lost and the redoubt could no longer be strongly supported.

In this way the battle continued until about four o'clock in a terrible fire fight with constant movement back and forth. In these ten hours French superiority in numbers, and probably also in tactics, forced the Russians to give up some ground, surrender their earthworks, and retreat to a new position in which their troops were pressed together even more; their left wing was withdrawn even further, so it was now parallel to the Moscow Highway, and no more than two thousand paces from it, while the Old Moscow Road was now practically in French hands.

Although in the Russians army it was still thought necessary to express doubt about the outcome of the battle, and much was still said of the need to remain on the battlefield, which had not really been lost yet—thus of winning the victory by persevering—in reality the issue was already decided, and Kutusov was clever enough to remain in no doubt about what he should do next. The superiority of the French, already evident before the battle, had increased during it, with the Russians losing more men than the French. In the ten hours of conflict the balance by no means remained perfectly even; it had perceptibly shifted to the disadvantage of the Russians.

No improvement could be expected from renewing the action. The Russian front had already been forced back, its line of retreat had been threatened; the next phase of misfortune would have been a complete defeat. At present the army was still in good order, and could retreat without becoming disorganized. Kutusov decided to begin the retreat that night, and his decision undoubtedly followed the dictates of good sense.

On the other side, Bonaparte could expect Kutusov's retreat. Had he been mistaken and had Kutusov still been in position on the 8th, he would have had to renew the attack, and it cannot be doubted that he would have done so. It is another question whether on the 7th, when there was still time and a large French force was still intact, Bonaparte should not have made greater efforts to raise his victory to the level of a total defeat of the enemy. That certainly would have been in the spirit of the conduct to which he owed such great success in the world. By renewing the attack with all his forces, he might possibly have gained new successes and reached the point where a massive cavalry pursuit could have completed the destruction of the Russian army. But if we take account of Bonaparte's situation that afternoon, note the magnitude of the battle, how large were the forces committed to it, and how surprisingly quickly they had shrunk to the point where he had to fear they would not be sufficient, we can see that from now until peace negotiations began, the preservation of his army would appear to him as his main objective. He had won the battle, he could hope to enter Moscow; to gain more by risking his last resources seemed to him neither necessary nor advisable.

It should not be objected that, according to the usual polarity of interests, one of the two commanders necessarily had committed an error, because if the continuation of the battle was against Kutusov's interest, it logically had to be in the interest of his opponent. Polarity refers only to the ends, not the means. Both men may wish to seek battle, or to avoid it. Had Bonaparte been certain of destroying the Russian army he would surely have committed more of his resources. But the Russians are brave fighters; they were still in good order; the terrain, though open for Russian conditions, was not open enough to be really suitable for cavalry. Finally, the Moscow Highway is so broad that the Russians could march over it in four columns and still keep their artillery with the infantry and cavalry, so that in effect they were all moving in combat-ready formations on one and the same road, which enormously facilitated and secured their retreat. All of this promised no easy gains, but rather heavy casualties. One must also remember that opposing commanders never have exactly the same field of vision; each always knows his own situation better than that of the other, and their conclusions can therefore never be exactly identical.

We confess consequently that we find no cause for surprise and astonishment in the outcome of the battle of Borodino, but rather a perfectly natural course of events.

Now a few more words about the dispositions of the two sides.

As we have already indicated, perhaps too exhaustively, both sides were very much compressed. Poniatowski's flanking movement [on the far right of the French line] was actually a minor measure that could not have had too much impact, because his force consisted of only 10,000 men, and Bonaparte could not have expected much from it. The main attack was therefore a perpendicular thrust or pressure on the enemy front; but because the Russian front was convex, French pressure on it took a concentric form and so achieved some of the effects that are usually associated with an envelopment. That Bonaparte chose this simple approach proved that he expected significant resistance, because the simple form is essentially the less daring form, but of course also the less decisive one. Had he instead merely threatened the enemy center, which because of the terrain was infinitely stronger than the left flank, and had he tried to envelop the left flank with 50,000 men instead of 10,000, the battle would have been won sooner, and the victory presumably would have been more decisive. But that would have been a riskier form of attack, because the mass of French forces would have moved to one side of their line of retreat, which would have increased the difficulties in case of a setback.

Kutusov should have told himself that, occupying a not very strong position, he had no reason to expect a victory over an enemy who was his superior in morale and numbers. To gain a victory he would have had to employ the remaining advantages of the defense—his knowledge and control of the ground and the potential of surprise. In short he would have had to combine his defensive position with strong offensive measures.

If this offensive was to carry out a surprise and therefore a short advance, the convex position of the Russian army made it necessary for the attack to be launched from the same flank where the French attack was expected. That was undoubtedly on the left, and it was one of the advantages of the Russian position that this could be foreseen with certainty.

We think, therefore, that Kutusov should have prepared to defend the area to the right of the Moscow Highway as far as the Moskva, indeed he should have made his preparations as obvious as possible by siting many earthworks there, but he should have occupied this part of the line of battle only thinly to meet the preliminary attack; that he should have combined the remaining forces on the right wing, General Tutschkov's corps, and some of the cavalry of the center and left, into a force of 50,000 men, and hidden it a good mile or more behind the left flank, which the woods and underbrush in that area would have made easily possible; and that he would keep the Guards as reserves behind the defensive part of the position [the right] and to protect the left flank against the first enemy actions against it. If after the opening phase of the battle, that is after the first few hours, the hidden Russian reserves were then to move against the enemy's right wing, the success they could achieve beyond what might be expected from their numbers would depend on the degree of surprise attained, as well as on other accidental circumstances. But in any case, they could not be deprived of their share in the battle. Who would advance or retreat would still be decided by the greater force, but the Russians would have retained the advantage of facing the enemy in an enveloping arc.

Now enough of this!

The Russian army retreated on the night of September 7–8 and, as we said, in four parallel columns on the Highway. It moved only five miles, to the rear of Mojaïsk, which is sufficient proof that the troops retained discipline and combat readiness to a degree unusual after a lost battle. The author can also testify that he observed no trace of the disorganization mentioned by an otherwise impartial writer.* The number of Russian prisoners may have reached a few thousand, the number of lost guns between twenty and thirty. The French trophies were therefore insignificant.

From now on, the retreat to Moscow proceeded continuously, but by very easy marches. The distance between Borodino and Moscow is seventy miles, which were covered in seven days. On the 14th the army passed through the city.

The rear guard had been placed under the command of General Miloradovitch and consisted of about 10,000 infantry and about as many cavalry, among them General Uvarov with his corps. The French did not press hard. Murat with a strong cavalry force formed the advance guard. Usually the two sides did not engage until the afternoon, drawing up in line of battle, skirmishing and firing on each other at long range for some hours, after which the Russians would withdraw a little further and both sides would make camp. This march, like the last phase of the preceding battle, also bore the character of a certain weariness and strategic impotence.

Only one day proved an exception. On September 10 Miloradovitch had moved to within two miles of the main body of the army when, an hour

---

* Chambray. [I.e., Georges de Chambray, *Histoire de l'expédition de Russie*, 2 vols. and atlas (Paris, 1825).]

before sundown, the French appeared with infantry and artillery as well as cavalry. Miloradovitch could not take evasive action without uncovering the main camp, and because the ground seemed not unfavorable he decided to risk battle. The Russian infantry, drawn up among trees on a low ridge, defended itself vigorously, and after it was forced to withdraw it continued to fight for another hour in a very unfavorable position at the foot of the ridge. Here too the French attacks, though initiated with energy, had a feeble quality about them. The engagement lasted until eleven o'clock, and Miloradovitch retained a position close behind the battlefield.[19]

Kutusov has also been criticized for directing his retreat from Mojaïsk to Moscow. It is said that he could have taken the road over Vereya to Thula [near Kaluga] instead.

But on the Vereya road he would not have found a single piece of bread. Everything that an army needs in its rear area—all the men and equipment, moving back and forth, that give it life—were on the Moscow Highway. The road to Vereya, running off at an angle, naturally was more open to the enemy. Its condition was not as good, the connection with Moscow ceased to be direct and easy—all these were difficulties that called for particular attention from a defeated army. In any case, here too the march toward Kaluga would scarcely have fulfilled its intention [to divert the French from Moscow]. The French army was now within sixty-five miles of Moscow. Bonaparte would not have hesitated to detach a force of 30,000 men to occupy it, which under the prevailing circumstances he could have done with impunity. Moscow would have been lost and Kutusov would then have been accused by short-sighted Russian critics of having given up the capital needlessly by this unrealistic flank march. Instead, Kutusov adhered to his natural line of retreat, as any other commander would probably have done in his place.

Here we want to add a few general comments on the retreat of the Russian army and the pursuit by the French, which might contribute to a better understanding of the outcome of the campaign. In the major provincial cities between Vitebsk and Moscow, the Russians everywhere found stores of flour, cereal, biscuits, and meat. Enormous caravans carrying foodstuffs, shoes, leather, and other necessities reached them from the interior. This meant that they had a mass of wagons available, whose great number of teams were fed without difficulty because hay and oats were in the fields, and even in peacetime the Russian haulers feed their draft oxen in the meadows that are everywhere in Russia. All this enabled the Russian army to camp wherever it wished, as long as it was near water. The summer had been unusually hot

---

[19] Clausewitz does not mention that his horse was wounded during this action. See his letter to his wife, November 4, 1812, in *Correspondence*, 301.

and dry; this part of Russia is not rich in rivers and streams, the smaller streams had mostly run dry, and we know how little one can rely on wells in the villages under such conditions. In general, then, water was scarce, and Colonel Toll thought himself lucky when he could find a campsite near a small lake.

Because the retreat from Vitebsk to Moscow was basically one uninterrupted movement, except for the halt at Smolensk, and because from Smolensk onward the goal always lay pretty well directly to the rear, the entire retreat was an extremely simple movement, with very little maneuvering, and without much need to fear the enemy's maneuvers. If one gives way and retreats in a straight line, it is very difficult for the enemy to turn one's flank, divert one from the intended route, and so forth. Added to this, the theater of operations has few highways and few major terrain features, which reduces the impact of geography on strategy.

Every soldier knows from experience that such factors, which greatly simplify a retreat, preserve the strength of men and horses. In this retreat there were no long assembly periods, marches back and forth, detours, surprises—in short, there was little or no tactical art and effort. Even outpost duties did not trouble the army much, because the cossacks performed them routinely.

Whenever two roads ran near each other, the army marched in divided columns. When side roads became difficult, the main force remained on the very broad Moscow Highway, because feeding the troops did not require separating them over long distances. The march began at a convenient time, people made themselves as comfortable as possible, and there was sufficient food for man and beast. It is true that bread was usually lacking and that one had to content oneself with very bad biscuits, which however were not unhealthy and proved as nourishing as bread would have been. Porridge, meat, and spirits were plentiful. There was seldom grain for the horses, but Russian horses are used to feeding on hay, and on this occasion the author saw for the first time that hay is more nourishing than we usually think. Hay of excellent quality could be found everywhere. The Russians give their horses fifteen to twenty pounds a day and rejected the sheaves of ripe oats that were lying in the fields, because they thought them less wholesome.

Only the cavalry of the rear guard (which was the larger part) was worse off, especially because it could rarely unsaddle. The author scarcely remembers a single light cavalry regiment unsaddled during the retreat, and toward the end all the horses had saddle sores.

All of this shows that on its ten-week retreat the Russian army remained physically in very good shape. Its numbers were reduced only by the casualties it suffered, and it lost few men from sickness and straggling. This is also shown clearly by the ultimate success of the campaign.

After Wittgenstein was detached [in mid-July], Barclay and Bagration were at first 110,000 men strong. The reinforcements that gradually joined them might have amounted to some 30,000 men. When the army marched through Moscow it was 70,000 strong. Its loss had therefore been 70,000 men, most of whom, as can easily be seen, were casualties. The opposite was true of the French. Just as the Russians, benefiting from special circumstances, found themselves physically in an unusually favorable situation, which could hardly have been equalled in the most highly cultivated country, so the French found themselves in an unusually unfavorable situation.

It is always difficult to supply an advancing and pursuing army, because by the time stores are collected the army has moved on, and now a mass of wagons is needed to bring the supplies forward. These difficulties increase as the population and economic resources of the area decrease. The attacker has only two ways of improving his situation. Now and then he can capture stores of the retreating army, and he does not need to remain as concentrated as his opponent. He can divide his forces to a greater extent, which makes it easier for them to live off the country. But in Russia these two expedients were not available. The Russians usually burned their stores and even most of the towns and villages they left behind, and the theater of operations was thinly populated and its road net poorly developed. In order not to do without the second expedient altogether, Bonaparte always moved his army in three widely separated columns, of which those on the left and right of the Moscow Highway usually amounted to a mass of some 30–40,000 men. These side columns, as we learn in detail from some French authors, had to contend with so many difficulties that they generally did not reach camp until after nightfall, and only with tremendous effort.

Difficulties of supply therefore were bound to arise very quickly on the French side, and it is well known that they did.

The cavalry suffered greatly. Usually the Russians had swept the nearer fields clean and the French had to forage at some distance, which reduced the quantity of fodder.

The water supply also proved to be a major problem. Even the Russian rear guard usually found all wells dry and the smaller streams fouled and had to rely on whatever rivers and small lakes might be in the area. But because scouts could be sent out, they had some leeway in choosing where to camp, and the difficulties were not as great as they were for the French pursuers. The French advance guard could not scout ahead and generally had to take up a position just behind the Russian rear guard. Besides, no detailed map of the country existed other than the so-called Podoroschka [route and station] map, which the French had enlarged and translated. But because of its small scale, the Russian original left out many villages and even more small terrain features.

The author still vividly recalls the oppressive lack of water during this campaign. Never had he suffered such thirst; the filthiest puddles were emptied to quench the fever, and washing was often out of the question for a week. How this affected the cavalry can be imagined, and as we have said, the French must have suffered doubly. It is well known in what wretched condition the French cavalry reached Moscow.

It became the custom of the Russian rear guard to burn villages as they were leaving them. Usually the inhabitants were already gone, whatever food and forage remained was quickly used up, and the only things left were the wooden houses, which in this region are not worth much. Under these circumstances no great care was taken to protect them from being burned or torn down, and that by itself was sufficient to cause the destruction of most of them. What had at first been thoughtlessness and carelessness gradually became policy, which was often extended to small and large towns as well. The bridges were also torn down, and the numerals were hacked out of the mileposts, which eliminated a useful source of information. As very few inhabitants remained, the French must often have found it difficult to know where they were on the highway.

These difficulties impeded the French advance and burdened and wasted the energies of man and beast. The French needed twelve weeks to march the 530 miles from Kowno to Moscow, and of the more than 280,000 men who began the march, not more than 90,000 reached the capital.

On September 14 the Russian army passed through Moscow, and the rear guard was ordered to follow the same day. At the same time General Miloradovitch was told to conclude an agreement with the king of Naples,[20] which would grant the Russian army a few hours to complete the evacuation of the city. Should this be rejected, he was to threaten resistance to the end at the city gates and in the streets.

Miloradovitch sent a flag of truce to the French advance guard, requesting a meeting with the king of Naples, who, one knew, was in command. After a few hours we were informed that General Sebastiani had come to the outpost line. General Miloradovitch was not pleased, but he went to the outpost and had a fairly long talk with Sebastiani, at which we members of his staff were not permitted to be present. Eventually both men rode together part of the way toward Moscow, and from their conversation the author could see that General Miloradovitch's request had not been rejected. When Miloradovitch expressed the hope that Moscow might be spared as far as possible, General Sebastiani responded quickly, "Monsieur, l'empereur mettra sa garde à la tête de son armée pour rendre toute espèce de désordre absolument impossible,"[21] and so forth. He repeated this assurance several times. The

---

[20] Joachim Murat, commander of the French advance guard.

[21] "Sir, the emperor will place his Guards at the head of his army to make any sort of disorder absolutely impossible."

author thought it worth notice, because these words implied the strongest wish to take control of an undamaged city. On the other hand, General Miloradovitch's statement, which gave rise to Sebastiani's reassurance, did not indicate that the Russians intended to burn Moscow.

It may have been three in the afternoon when we entered Moscow, and between five and six when we took up positions beyond the city.

Moscow seemed more or less abandoned. A few hundred people of the lowest classes met General Miloradovitch and begged for his protection. Here and there in the streets we encountered other groups, watching us sadly as we passed by. The streets were still crowded with wagons leaving the city, so that General Miloradovitch had to order two cavalry regiments to ride ahead and clear the way. The most painful sight was long rows of wounded soldiers, who lay along the houses and were vainly hoping to be moved away. All of these unfortunates probably died in the city.

As we passed through Moscow we turned into the road to Riäzan and then halted about a thousand paces beyond the city.

General Sebastiani had promised that the first units of the advance guard would not enter Moscow until two hours after we had left. General Miloradovitch was therefore surprised to see two French light cavalry regiments deploy against us just after we had halted. He immediately sent an emissary to the king of Naples with a request for a meeting. But once again he did not appear, perhaps because he regarded it as beneath his dignity, and Miloradovitch again had to be content with General Sebastiani. He complained forcefully about the French following too soon; but Sebastiani had no difficulty in answering, because our move through the city had been delayed by a number of accidents and taken longer than the French expected. But as a result of their talk both sides now faced each other at close distance without fighting. From our location we could see uninterrupted lines of small Russian coaches leaving the city gates, emptying Moscow more and more, at first without being interfered with by the French. The cossacks still seemed to control the districts of the city nearest to us, and the French advance guard paid attention only to our rear guard. In the outskirts of the city a few wreaths of smoke were already rising, the result, the author believed, of the confusion that existed there.

During the second meeting of General Miloradovitch and General Sebastiani, the author experienced the painful pleasure of hearing German commands in typical Berlinese as the two leading uhlan regiments were deployed. And really, they were Prussian units, of which one, the Brandenburg uhlans, had been stationed in Berlin. He used the opportunity to send word to his family through one of the officers.

As we had moved through Moscow, the author anxiously awaited to discover in what direction the retreat would continue. General Uvarov had fallen ill and his cavalry corps had been integrated into General Milorado-vitch's command. The author now served in a subordinate capacity on his staff, and by chance had not learned the direction the retreat would take. He was pleasantly surprised to see that at least it was not due east, toward Vla-dimir, but south toward Riäzan. He associated this decision with certain dis-cussions among general staff officers at army headquarters. On several occa-sions after the battle of Borodino, when the author had reported to him on some business, Colonel Toll had said that in his opinion the retreat beyond Moscow should not continue in the old direction, but turn south. The au-thor concurred wholeheartedly and employed an image that by now had be-come habitual in his mind: in Russia one could play hide and seek with the enemy, and by always retreating might in the end return to the frontier to-gether with him. This playful idea, which the author employed in the quick informality of conversation, referred primarily to the spatial element, to the advantage afforded by the enormous dimensions of the country, which made it impossible for the attacker to cover and strategically control the areas be-hind him simply by advancing. In developing this idea, the author had reached the conclusion that a very large western country could be conquered only with the help of internal dissension. Colonel Toll had not paid much attention to this aspect; he primarily emphasized the economic resources of the provinces to the south of Moscow, the greater ease of reinforcing the army, and of threatening the enemy's right flank from there. But in these talks he also showed his concern that he would not succeed with his idea, which the senior generals would strongly oppose.

The more junior officers of the general staff also frequently talked about this matter. If it was not thought through to complete clarity, it was at least fully discussed.

We mention this to suggest that the march toward Kaluga, which subse-quently became famous as a peak of intellectual brilliance, did not suddenly spring from the head of the commanding general or of one of his advisors, like Minerva from Jupiter's helmet. In any case we have always believed that ideas in war are usually so simple and obvious that the merit of devising a strategy cannot constitute the essence of generalship. The ability to choose among five or six possibilities the one that promises the best result; the pen-etrating intelligence that quickly surveys and eliminates a mass of vague con-siderations, and with mere instinct reaches an immediate decision—these might more correctly be regarded as the cardinal talents of the commander, and they are something quite different from mere invention.

But the main thing is always the difficulty of execution. Everything in war is simple, but the simplest thing is very difficult. The military instrument resembles a machine with tremendous friction, which unlike in mechanics, cannot be reduced to a few points, but is everywhere in contact with chance.

Besides, action in war is like movement in a resistant element. A movement made easily on land becomes very difficult under water. Danger and exertion are the elements among which the mind operates in war; but in one's library these elements are not known. In the field one always falls short of the goal one has set for oneself, and it already demands unusual ability not to fall below mediocrity.

Having expressed this belief, we feel we do not minimize the merits of the Russian high command when we assert that by itself the idea of continuing the retreat toward the flank was no great achievement, and that its importance has been exaggerated in the literature.

If everything is to be correctly understood, we should even say that the success of the campaign in no way resulted from this idea, or was significantly associated with it. Changing the direction of the retreat would have been valuable only if it had become a means of driving the enemy out of the country. But that was not the case here, because the French would have had to leave the country anyway, as soon as they could not conclude a peace. Today we know that had Kutusov retreated toward Vladimir, Bonaparte would neither have been able to follow him, nor to have wintered in Moscow. He had to withdraw no matter what, because he had fallen victim to the illness of strategic consumption, and had to use the last strength of his sick body to drag himself out of the country. We mention this only to clarify the causal connections. The move toward Kaluga always remains meritorious because at the time the Russians did not know the condition of the French army, and still thought it was capable of continuing the offensive. Besides, Kutusov's flanking position on the road to Kaluga had the further advantage of threatening the line of the French retreat and thus contributed to the ultimate outcome; but it is by no means to be regarded as the primary cause.

The author does not know how Colonel Toll succeeded in having his views accepted. The account Colonel Buturlin gives in his history of the campaign may be generally correct, but we very much doubt that when Prince Kutusov took the road to Riäzan he already intended to continue to the Kaluga road. He could more easily have gone to Kaluga directly from Moscow, and however well the flank march over Riäzan was organized, and however well it succeeded, at the beginning it must have seemed a very risky undertaking.

When Colonel Toll [first] had the idea of withdrawing to Kaluga, before the army reached Moscow, it was probably only with the thought of diverting the enemy from the capital. In practical terms it was always easiest for the army to change to the new direction in Moscow itself. Kutusov chose the Riäzan road because, as the middle road [between the Moscow Highway due east and the Kaluga road to the southwest] it was so to speak the compromise wisdom of the council of war. Most likely Colonel Toll convinced him to turn toward Kaluga only later on, when it became apparent that the move could be made without difficulty. During the first few days the French were so busy settling into Moscow that they pushed out troops beyond the city very slowly, and only on the road to Riäzan. The cossacks, who were roaming over all the roads, reported that the area around Podolsk was still entirely free of the French; besides, the road there was more or less covered by the Pachra River and its fairly deep banks.

On September 16, the third day after we had left Moscow, the decision was made to march along the French flank. On the 17th and 18th we did so, and gained the Podolsk-Thula road. Very likely this had been the goal of the flanking march, for we remained at Thula for a day. Only when the old prince saw how nicely everything was developing could he be convinced to march one additional day to the Old Kaluga Road.

The maneuver succeeded so perfectly that the French lost sight of us for a few days.

During this march we saw Moscow burning day and night, and although we were thirty miles from the city the wind occasionally carried ashes all the way to us. Even though the burning of Smolensk and of many other towns had accustomed the Russians to sacrifices of this kind, the burning of Moscow saddened them and increased their anger at the enemy, on whom they blamed the fire as a true expression of his hatred, arrogance, and cruelty.

This leads us to causes of the fire. The reader will already have noted that the Russian command seemed to display care for the preservation of the city rather than the intention to destroy it. Very likely this reflected its true intention. The army immediately regarded the fire as a great misfortune, a true calamity. Rostopchin [civil governor of Moscow], whom the author had occasion to see several times in small groups a week or so after the event, defended himself tooth and nail against the charge that he was responsible for the fire, an idea that began to be current at the time. The confusion and everything else that the author had noticed in the streets of Moscow when the rear guard moved through the city, and the fact that pillars of smoke first rose in the outskirts, where the cossacks still held sway, convinced him that the fire was the result of the confusion and of the cossacks' habit of plundering thoroughly and then burning every place they had to abandon to the enemy.

The author was firmly convinced that the French were not responsible, for he had seen how much value they attached to controlling an undamaged city. That the Russian authorities were the culprits seemed to him at least unproved. Not a single piece of evidence pointed in their direction, and the vigorous and determined denials of Rostopchin, who would have had to have been the main actor, seemed to remove all doubt. Had Rostopchin set the fire as a great sacrifice that one was compelled to make, he would not have denied responsibility so vigorously. For all these reasons the author was long unable to convince himself that Moscow had been burned intentionally. But since then new evidence has appeared, and especially since the not very satisfactory defense that Count Rostopchin has published, the author has not only come to doubt his former view, but is now nearly convinced that Rostopchin ordered the burning of Moscow on his own responsibility and without the prior knowledge of the government. Perhaps his [subsequent] disgrace, his long absence from Russia, is the result of such high-handedness, which a Russian autocrat seldom forgives.

Probably the government had intended only the evacuation of the city, the departure of the administrative agencies and of the most important inhabitants, if it planned anything at all, which would have been possible only if people were already thinking about evacuation at the time Smolensk was given up. But in any case, even if Rostopchin had thought of this measure on his own, he would have needed the approval of the government. Of course, once you have thought of the measure, going through with it is already a little easier.

It is unlikely that the government, especially the emperor, had wanted to burn the city and had ordered it. It does not agree with the emperor's tender-hearted nature, and it is equally foreign to a government that is not supported by the fanaticism of a large popular assembly. On the other hand, the responsibility Rostopchin assumed was enormous, because however few preparations were necessary, in the end he needed a number of agents who heard his orders in person. If it was indeed he who was responsible for the fire, one can only imagine that a combination of passion and bitterness, which he did seem to feel at the time, gave him the strength for such a decision, the implementation of which would have exposed him to every conceivable danger and brought him neither gratitude nor honor.

Count Rostopchin's personality is not such as to make us believe that strong sentiments, enthusiasm, or raw fanaticism triggered this act. He had the character and education of a deft man of the world, grafted onto a forceful Russian nature. He and Kutusov were decided enemies; Rostopchin loudly accused Kutusov of falsehood in making the whole world believe to the last moment that he would risk yet another battle to save Moscow.

In any case, it must be one of the strangest phenomena of history, that a deed, which people believe enormously influenced the fate of Russia, appears like the fatherless offspring of an illegitimate union. In all probability the veil will never be lifted.

That the burning of Moscow proved highly detrimental to the French cannot be denied. If the fire made the possibility of peace negotiations seem even more remote in the czar's mind, and if it became a way of enraging the Russian people further, this probably constituted the main damage it caused to the French. On the other hand, it is exaggerating the significance of a single act to regard the burning of Moscow—as the French usually do—as the main reason for the failure of the campaign. The fire certainly deprived the French of resources they could have used, but their most important need was for *soldiers*, and these they would not have found in an undamaged Moscow either.

An army of 90,000, of exhausted men and horses, at the point of a narrow wedge driven 550 miles into Russia; to its right an enemy army of 110,000; on all sides a population in arms; forced to face the enemy in all directions, without depots, without adequate supplies and ammunition, depending on a single, devastated line of supply and communications—that does not add up to a situation one can tolerate through a winter. But if Bonaparte was not certain he could maintain himself in Moscow through the winter, he had to begin his retreat before winter came. Whether Moscow still stood or had been destroyed would not significantly influence that issue. Bonaparte's retreat was inevitable; his entire campaign failed the moment Emperor Alexander refused to sue for peace. All his moves had been designed to bring about a negotiated peace, and Bonaparte certainly did not deceive himself on this point for a moment.[22]

When we come to the end of our account, we shall add a few comments on Bonaparte's plan of campaign. We will therefore postpone until then what might be said about this phase of it.

After the loss of Moscow a mood of grief and dejection prevailed in the Russian army, which led men to see an early peace as the only way out. Not that the army had lost courage; on the contrary, rightly or wrongly it was still filled with a soldierly sense of superiority and pride, which served to encourage people. But there was little confidence in the government's conduct of affairs, the sense of the great sacrifices the country had already made was overwhelming, and in this crisis people did not seem to expect the government to act with firmness and energy. That peace would soon come was therefore thought not only probable but also desirable. What Prince Kutusov thought about this was perhaps known to no one, but he gave himself the appearance of strongly opposing any peace negotiations whatever.

We can see from this how little the army understood the meaning of these

---

[22] Compare Clausewitz's statement in one of his early discussions of Napoleonic war, written in 1804: "If Bonaparte should someday reach Poland, he would be easier to defeat than in Italy, and in Russia I would consider his destruction as certain" (Carl von Clausewitz, *Strategie aus dem Jahr 1804, mit Zusätzen von 1808 und 1809*, ed. Eberhard Kessel [Hamburg, 1937], 42). In *On War*, p. 615, he was to write: "The Russians could expect to grow much stronger in the course of the campaign. . . . Tremendous things were possible; not only was a massive counterstroke a certainty if the French offensive failed (and how could it succeed if the czar would not make peace nor his subjects rise against him?) but the counterstroke could bring the French to utter ruin. The highest wisdom could never have devised a better strategy than the one the Russians followed unintentionally."

great events. And yet we were already near the culminating point of the French offensive, near the moment when the entire burden that the French had lifted but could not carry would fall back on them. General Barclay was the second most senior commander in the army, and as minister of war must have been best informed about the war. And yet at the beginning of October—only fourteen days before the French began their retreat—when the author and a few other officers who were being transferred took their leave from him in the vicinity of Voronova, he said, "Gentlemen, you should thank God that you are being called away from here. Nothing good can come of this."

We thought differently; but of course we were foreigners, and it was easier for us to be objective. However much we were troubled by the turn of events, we were not, like the Russians, directly affected by the agony of a deeply wounded, suffering fatherland whose very existence was at stake. Such emotions will always affect judgment. Our only fear was the prospect of peace; in the calamities of the moment we already saw the means of salvation. But we were careful not to express this view openly, which would have made us suspect and disliked.

In St. Petersburg the turn of events was correctly interpreted, and to the emperor's credit, it must be said, not only at the last moment, but already earlier on.

The reports the emperor constantly received from the army on the enemy's daily losses, written, perhaps, more with the intention of making things seem better than out of true conviction; Wittgenstein's early victory at Kliastichi; the first battle of Polotsk, which was undecided, despite the superiority of the French; the capture of Saxon units at Covrin; the approach of the Moldavian army and of Steinheil on the left and right wings; the withdrawal, caused by circumstances rather than plan, deep into the interior of the country, far beyond Smolensk—all this had given some first rays of hope to people in St. Petersburg. Removed as they were some hundreds of miles from the bloody battlefields, the devastated villages and towns, the painful retreat of the Russian army, and the triumphant advance of the enemy, their judgment was calmer and firmer. It must be considered great good fortune that Emperor Alexander had not remained with the army.

In St. Petersburg, invigorated by the first favorable indications of possible success, fortified by the advice of energetic counselors, among whom Baron vom Stein certainly figured, the emperor decided not to listen to any peace proposals, to build up the armed forces everywhere as much as possible, and to conduct the overall policy of the war from St. Petersburg.

We have seen that falling back in the center and then operating against the enemy's flanks had been the original Russian conception of the campaign, though not on the scale on which it actually happened. Now circumstances had taken the French deep into the country, while their right wing was still at the frontier and their left had halted at the Duna River. For the two main reinforcements of Russian regulars, the Moldavian army and the Finish divisions, the most natural line of advance was against the two wings. It was therefore equally natural—but no less meritorious for that reason—for the emperor now to revert to the original plan of the campaign and execute it on a larger scale. It was decided to deploy two armies in southern and two in northern Lithuania, in the rear of the *Grande Armée*—Tshitsagov, Sacken, Wittgenstein, and Steinheil—where they would overwhelm the inferior French forces, then advance toward the center's main line of communications, cut the *Grande Armée's* strategic lifeline, and block its retreat.

This decision was taken in St. Petersburg at the beginning of September, and the dispositions were drafted immediately. At that time the outcome of the battle of Borodino was not yet known, but it is obvious that the dispositions were made more on the assumption of defeat than of victory, and that was sensible. Up to this point the emperor's conduct deserves the highest praise. But it was impractical, and demonstrates a lack of military experience, for the dispositions of the four armies to have been so detailed. The outcome shows this clearly: not one of the plans could be carried out. It is to be noted, and is characteristic of Russian administration, that the forces that were supposed to be moved to Riga and to Wittgenstein's command never reached one-half of the totals specified in St. Petersburg. Taken together, such discrepancies mean that if we compare the dispositions issued in St. Petersburg with what actually took place and could take place, the result is almost ludicrous. Colonel Michaud of the General Staff, who had become the emperor's personal adjutant and at the time counted for much, probably had the principal share in drafting the dispositions. He was a well-versed officer, formerly in the Piedmontese service, but he may not have had the clearest ideas about the conduct of operations, and at least was not experienced in such duties.

Immediately after the evacuation of Moscow, General Miloradovitch gave up command of the rear guard, which was transferred to General Raevski, and the units making up the rear guard were changed. For the author this meant that he was transferred to headquarters as an officer available for new assignment. When he reported to General Bennigsen, he found an order of the emperor appointing him chief of staff of the garrison of Riga. The post had been held by another former Prussian officer, Lieutenant Colonel von Tiedemann, who had been killed in an attack on August 22. The emperor found it advisable to fill the post with a German officer and had remembered the author. The order had lain for some weeks at headquarters and in the confusion of day-to-day business could have been overlooked, had not a younger officer been kind enough to advise the author of its existence.

The appointment under General Essen in Riga certainly promised the author a more satisfying field of action than would a division or cavalry corps of the main army, where his ignorance of the language meant that with enormous effort he could only render the most mediocre service. This fact had made the campaign doubly difficult for him, and he looked forward to his new duties with pleasure. After several delays, and provided with proper travel documents, he left Krasnoï Pachri on the mail coach on September 24 to travel by way of Serpuchov, Thula, Riäzan, Yavoslov, and Novogrod to St. Petersburg, where he planned to re-equip himself and then proceed to Riga.

But scarcely had he reached Serpuchov on the Ocha River when militia men stopped him because he could not speak Russian. His passport, a whole bag full of official Russian documents, his Russian appointment, his uniform—nothing sufficed to allay the suspicion of the militia officers. A German—or, what was worse, a Frenchman, as most believed—with a Polish servant seemed to them too doubtful a business. They forced the author to return to headquarters in the company of a Russian officer who was just on his way there. So as to avoid a repetition of the experience, the author decided to wait for a courier whom he could accompany. After a few days he learned that the former Prussian officer, Count Chasot, and the former Saxon officer, Baron von Bose, who had served on the staff of the prince of Oldenburg, were being sent to St. Petersburg to begin organizing the Russo-German Legion. They were accompanied by a Russian guide, and the author decided to join them. Despite the guide we were again nearly taken for spies and arrested in a few small towns. Count Chasot became so ill on the trip that we often had to stop at night and were on the road for over fourteen days. We did not reach St. Petersburg until the middle of October.

When we reported to the prince of Oldenburg, the emperor's brother-in-law, who had returned to Yaroslav as governor and proved to be an efficient and energetic administrator, his wife, the grand duchess Catherine, did us the honor of receiving us. The French had not yet begun their retreat, but the conviction that they would soon be forced to go back had suddenly spread, and only a few people still believed in the possibility of a new French offensive to the south of Moscow. The grand duchess was eager to have news of the army. She questioned us with much intelligence and sense, and we could see how seriously she reflected on everything that we were able to tell her. She asked the author what he thought Bonaparte would do now. Would it be a simple retreat, and what road would he take? The author replied that he had no doubt that the French army would soon retreat, and that he was equally certain that they would take the same road on which they had come. The grand duchess already seemed to have formed the same conviction. She left us with the impression that she was a woman made to rule.

Because we shall now turn away from the main army, we will permit ourselves a few comments on Bonaparte's retreat.

We have never understood how people could so stubbornly stick to the idea that Bonaparte should have returned by a different route than on the one on which he had come. What could he have lived on, except his depots? What good was an area that still had foodstuffs to an army that had no time to lose, that always had to bivouac in concentrated masses? What officer would have been willing to ride ahead of the army to organize the collecting of food, and what Russian officials would have obeyed his orders? The army would have been starved out in the first eight days.

A force that is retreating in enemy country usually needs a route that has already been prepared for it. A force retreating under very unfavorable circumstances needs it twice as badly. A force that must withdraw 550 miles in Russia will need it three times as badly. By "prepared route" we mean a route protected by one's troops, on which one will find supply depots.

Bonaparte's march to Kaluga was a necessary beginning of his retreat, which did not imply the eventual choice of another road back to the frontier. From Tarutino, Kutusov was three days closer to Smolensk than Bonaparte was from Moscow. Bonaparte therefore had to begin by threatening Kutusov in order to make up his lead before he began his real retreat. Of course he would have preferred to compel Kutusov to withdraw to Kaluga, and he attempted to do this by suddenly changing from the Old to the New Kaluga Road and threatening Kutusov's left flank. But neither this maneuver nor his attempt to advance on Kutusov at Maloyaroslavetz seemed to have an effect, and so he desisted, thinking there was no longer time to sacrifice 20,000 men of the limited forces he still possessed in a general battle, and then to have to retreat anyway.

That Bonaparte's retreat began as a pretended new offensive directed toward the south was for him, as we know the man, also of great value.

Once Bonaparte ran into Kutusov he was of course compelled to march on the New Kaluga Road for a time, until he reached the Old, but this did not cause the same difficulties, because this stretch of the road ran between his main forces and his detachments on the Moscow-Smolensk Highway. He prepared this move by advancing Poniatowski on the right, who began his move by retaking Vereya. Bonaparte shortened this part of his route as much as possible. From Maloyaroslavetz he did not march straight to Viasma because this stretch was too exposed to the enemy, but made a detour over Borovsk and from there marched directly over Vereya to Mojaïsk. Who can doubt for a moment that only the most pressing reasons motivated this decision.

By the time the author arrived in St. Petersburg [in mid-October] the military government in Riga had changed hands. Marquis Paulucci, of whom we have already spoken, had relieved General Essen of that command. The author strongly disliked being attached to this peculiar man; at that moment news arrived that the French retreat had begun, and it could be foreseen that Riga would cease to play a role in the war; he therefore asked the duke of Oldenburg, who was in St. Petersburg organizing the Russo-German Legion, to appoint him as the Legion's senior staff officer, a position for which he had already been considered earlier. Because this post would carry no duties while the corps was being raised, he then asked the duke to obtain leave from the emperor for the author to serve with General Wittgenstein's army until the Legion became operational. The emperor granted this double request, and on November 15, after waiting about a week while the dispatches he was to take with him were prepared, the author left St. Petersburg, by way of Pskov and Polozk, for Czasniki, which he reached a few days after the battle of Smoliantsy.

A certain air of self-satisfaction reigned at Wittgenstein's headquarters, a proud sense of accomplishment, which contrasted somewhat with the atmosphere at imperial headquarters.

Wittgenstein had successfully covered St. Petersburg, which, in addition to the rewards received from the emperor, brought him much flattering praise from the capital and further enhanced the nimbus of glory that already surrounded him. There was indeed every reason to be satisfied with General Wittgenstein's operations. In spirit and morale he had always shown himself equal, and often superior, to his opponent; he had carried out his mission; in this theater the French had completely failed, not merely because of the force of circumstances, but because of the performance of Russian arms.

If we count the original strength of the three French corps deployed against Wittgenstein, those of Oudinot, St. Cyr, and Victor, plus Doumerc's cuirassier division, their total comes to 98,000 men. To oppose them, Wittgenstein certainly had no more than 75,000. Thus he effectively neutralized the offensive power of a superior enemy force without losing any ground; on the contrary, he achieved such a significant advantage that he was now ready to participate in the operations of cutting off the French army planned in St. Petersburg. Such an outcome, gained against French troops and Bonaparte's generals, deserves the name of a creditable campaign.

General Wittgenstein was a man of some forty years, full of good will, with an enterprising, adventurous spirit. Only his judgment was not unfailingly clear, and his energy sometimes flagged.

His chief of staff was Major General d'Auvray, a Saxon by birth, now somewhat over fifty, who had long been in Russian service. He was a good-natured man of excellent character, had a good mind, and was broadly educated. Honest and full of good will, he was always driven by concern for the best interests of the state. But he was somewhat lacking in day-to-day military gifts. He rode badly and did not know how to speak sharply and take harsh measures, which is sometimes absolutely necessary.

Major General Diebitsch was quartermaster general. A Prussian by birth, he had entered Russian service as a young man from a Prussian cadet school, and by serving in the Guards and the general staff had risen rapidly to the rank of colonel; in the course of this campaign he became a general at the age of twenty-seven.

He was the prime mover in Wittgenstein's command.

As a young man he had worked hard and acquired a sound knowledge of his profession. Fiery, brave, and enterprising, decisive and bold, with great firmness and natural intelligence, somewhat brazen and imperious, a leader of men, and very ambitious—this was General Diebitsch, and these qualities could only propel him rapidly toward his goal. Since he was open and honest, with a noble heart and without trace of intrigue, Generals Wittgenstein and d'Auvray were soon won over by him. One can see that Wittgenstein's headquarters—whose three most important figures were men of good character, honest zeal, and good will, without any hidden purposes—was not lacking in understanding and enthusiasm; and the same qualities will be seen to have shaped the events of Wittgenstein's campaign, if we consider them in a fair and realistic light.

When the author reached this army, it had just repulsed the last effort by the French marshals to mount an attack near Smoliantsy. This engagement was viewed as another victory, and indeed one heard talk of seventeen such pitched battles in which Wittgenstein's army had participated. But this was only a way of suggesting the constant activity that had prevailed in this theater of operations. The victory of Smoliantsy was regarded merely as a defensive action, in which the pursuit of the enemy did not play a significant part.

According to the emperor's instructions, Wittgenstein was to drive Oudinot entirely out of the area, push him back to Vilna, and then leave it to Steinheil's army to neutralize him. Without pausing over the strange confusion reflected in these highly impractical instructions, we will only note that this had not happened. Oudinot had retreated toward Victor between the Dnieper and the Dwina; only his Sixth Corps, still a few thousand men strong, diverged toward Vilna; Steinheil had not been able to form a separate command, and could do nothing better than attach himself to Wittgenstein.

Wittgenstein's army was only some 40,000 men strong; Oudinot and Victor's forces were estimated to be at least as large. Some troops also had to be detached to oppose Wrede. Consequently, Wittgenstein would be fully occupied if he prevented the French from doing more than hold their ground.

Besides, Wittgenstein was also instructed to occupy the Ulla River below Lepel, and then await further developments.

In short, Wittgenstein had no reason to leave the area around Czasniki.

He therefore stayed in place for a week following the action at Smoliantsy. On November 20 he learned that the marshals opposing him were moving toward the Berezina, which indicated the approach of the main French army, about which nothing was known except that it had arrived at Smolensk in very weakened condition. Wittgenstein decided to have his advance guard, on the road between Chereya and Kholopenichi, follow the enemy closely, and to march with his main force to Chereya, where he would still be in position to cover the Ulla while lying in wait behind the river, should Bonaparte choose that line of march.

On the 22nd he learned of Tshitsagov's arrival near Borisov. Tshitsagov suggested he move close enough so that they could cooperate, and on the 24th Wittgenstein marched to Kholopenichi. Here he learned of the engagements at Krasnoï; that Bonaparte had passed Orsha on the 19th; and that Kutusov had halted for several days and sent only an advance guard of 20,000 men in pursuit, a day's march behind the French. At the same time news arrived of a very costly engagement on the eastern bank of the Berezina on the 23rd, fought by the advance guard of Tshitsagov's army under Pahlen.

The threads were now drawing together into the decisive knot. Tshitsagov blocked the French approach to the Berezina at Borisov, and in an area of perhaps a day's march above and below that point.[23] One could be fairly certain, based on a knowledge of local conditions, that the French were in no position to force a crossing there. It was therefore believed that they would have to turn right or left and take either the road to Lepel or to Bobruisk. Under the circumstances it seemed more likely that they would turn left toward Bobruisk because Wittgenstein barred their route to Lepel. But Wittgenstein, whose area of responsibility included Lepel and the Ulla, had to keep this obligation in mind and had to maintain a position from which he could move his army either on the Lepel-Borisov road or behind the Ulla. Consequently he could not cross the Berezina and unite with Tshitsagov.

The surest way for Wittgenstein to secure a part for himself in the events now unfolding would obviously have been for him to have advanced straight up the road to Borisov on the 25th and 26th. Had Bonaparte turned left, Wittgenstein would have been nearer to him; had Bonaparte remained on this road or advanced toward Lepel, Wittgenstein could have attacked him and seriously upset his plans.

But Wittgenstein had just faced two French marshals, whose combined strength he judged nearly equal to his own. If one of them had now turned toward Borisov, he would still have remained on the left bank of the river and could still have supported the other. The so-called main French army,

---

[23] The region around the Berezina, in which the action Clausewitz is describing takes place, is shown at the lower center of Map 1, above.

advancing under Bonaparte's personal command, was according to some reports still 80,000 strong, and even those who judged most conservatively thought it must include 60,000 able-bodied men. We should not be too surprised at this overestimate. That the French had suffered enormous losses was of course known; but one felt one had made a sufficient reduction in assuming that of the 300,000 men who had passed this way only three months before, 60,000 now remained. The last official reports on the enemy's strength were received before the engagements at Krasnoï; Kutusov had badly overestimated it then, and the enormous French losses suffered in and after these actions could not be known with certainty. Observation by reconnaissance was very difficult, because one could not clearly distinguish those in the massed retreat who were still bearing arms from those who were not. In short, it is both understandable and excusable that Wittgenstein's headquarters believed it was facing 90–100,000 men, whereas we now know them to have been only about 30,000.

Wittgenstein could expect no help from Tshitsagov, who was tied down in a fairly extended defensive position and who, moreover, received such a sharp slap in the face on his first attempt to cross the Berezina that one could assume he would not make a second. The main Russian army had given up close pursuit; even the advance guard was now two days' march behind the French. Wittgenstein was thus quite isolated and could count on no support whatever during the first day of battle, and on only doubtful support during the second. To go forward blindly under these circumstances seemed like Curtius's leap into the abyss.[24]

Had Wittgenstein marched from Kholopenichi to Borisov on the 25th and the next day attacked the enemy wherever he encountered him, he would not have found the abyss as deep as was feared. He might have been beaten by Bonaparte, but he would certainly have delayed his passage by a day and might have made it impossible on the following day as well. But sacrificing oneself for the good of the whole, which sounds fine in books, is nevertheless something on which one ought not to rely in the real world, or at least only in those few cases in which, on higher authority, it becomes a positive duty.

From General Diebitsch we would have expected a bold, selfless rush forward; how far he wished to do so, but could not, remains unknown to us. But it was plain to see that at this moment opinion was divided in Wittgenstein's headquarters.

Wittgenstein did what most men in his place would have done, and it cannot be deemed an absolute error. On the 25th he left Kholopenichi on the road from Lepel to Borisov, keeping Lepel occupied in order to protect

---

[24] Curtius was a mythical Roman hero who, in obedience to an oracle, saved his country by leaping fully armed into a bottomless pit that had opened in the center of the Forum.

the route to the upper Berezina and the Ulla. When his advance guard did not come into contact with the enemy on the 25th, General Wittgenstein recognized that Bonaparte had not turned right, and on the 26th he marched west toward the road between Borisov and Kostritsa, which was only a few hours away, and about ten miles from the point where the French intended to cross the river.

At Kostritsa General Wittgenstein learned that the French were making preparations to cross at Studenka. Tshitsagov had occupied the surrounding country as far as Zembin, and a successful crossing in the face of opposition seemed very doubtful. On the 27th, however, General Wittgenstein decided to advance along the road and attack the French from the rear while they were trying to break through Tshitsagov on their front.

The author was not at Wittgenstein's headquarters during these days, but rather with a detachment that remained behind to cover the left flank, and returned to the army only on the evening of the 28th. Therefore he did not personally witness the battles with Victor on the 27th and 28th and cannot understand on the basis of actual observation why General Wittgenstein marched not for Studenka, but down the Studensk road, although the former was known to be the enemy's crossing point. The decision unquestionably reflects a certain timidity, an excessive concern to preserve the army from harm; and on this score General Wittgenstein cannot be absolved from having contributed to Bonaparte's escape. On the 27th, to be sure, he could no longer have prevented the crossing as such; but the enemy's losses would have been much greater.

In these two days Wittgenstein took some 10,000 prisoners, including an entire division. He soothed his conscience with this brilliant result and placed the chief blame on Tshitsagov, who had prematurely abandoned the right bank as far as Zembin.

Admittedly, this general seems to have shown no great talent for command in 1812. But everyone believed that the enemy would turn south toward Bobruisk. A message to this effect even arrived from Kutusov. The notion that the presence of Wittgenstein's army would prevent the enemy from turning north was probably the main cause of this preconceived opinion. But even after his premature move on the 27th Tshitsagov still had time to oppose the crossing, and the chief responsibility for the miscarriage of the Russian plan must lie with him.

Never was there a better opportunity to compel an army to capitulate in the open field than here. The Berezina, bordered partly by swamps, partly by dense forest, affords places to cross—and of continuing the march after crossing—only at a few points. The enemy had only 30,000 men left, about as many Russians stood on the west bank, as many again were on the east, and 10,000 were coming up on the French rear. To this must be added the total disorganization of the enemy, the presence of 40,000 unarmed stragglers, hunger, disease, and the exhaustion of all physical and moral powers.

Undoubtedly chance favored Bonaparte somewhat, in that he found a usable crossing point at Studenka, close to Borisov. But his reputation as a soldier had made the real difference, and he now benefited from capital built up long before. Both Wittgenstein and Tshitsagov were afraid of him, of his army, of his Guards—just as Kutusov feared him at Krasnoï. No one wanted to be defeated by him. Kutusov believed he could reach his goal without taking that risk; Wittgenstein did not want to sacrifice the glory he had just won; Tshitsagov did not want to suffer a second repulse.

Bonaparte was armed with this moral power when he saved himself from one of the worst situations in which a commander ever found himself. But of course moral power was not everything; the strength of his intellect and the military qualities of his army, which could not be entirely subdued even by the destructive forces of nature, were here destined to shine once more in all their brilliance. After he had overcome the crisis, Bonaparte said to his entourage, "Vous voyez, comme on passe sous la barbe de l'ennemi."[25]

Bonaparte had saved French honor, and even added to it; but the outcome was still a further step toward the complete destruction of his army. We know how much of this force arrived in Kowno and that the battle of the Berezina was the last blow that led to this result. It is the same with respect to the entire retreat. Apart from himself, his senior generals, and a few thousand officers, Bonaparte saved nothing worth mentioning from the entire army. When it is said that he carried out the difficult retreat, it must be understood only as a phrase, and that is also true of the individual episodes of the campaign. Eugene escaped at Krasnoï by a detour, but with only half his troops. Ney also escaped by an even more roundabout route, but (as his own secretary declares) with no more than 600 men out of 6,000. Nominally, the Russians failed to cut off the French—Eugene and Ney at Krasnoï, Bonaparte at the Berezina; but they nevertheless cut off very substantial masses of men. This is even more true for the campaign as a whole. Despite many opportunities, the Russians rarely get in front of the French; when they do so, they always let them through; in every battle the French are victorious; in each they are allowed to achieve the impossible; but—when we come to the final reckoning, the French army has ceased to exist, and, except for failing to capture Bonaparte and his general staff, the campaign was the most complete success. Should the Russian army be given no credit whatever for this outcome? That would be a very unfair conclusion.

Never before had a strategic pursuit been conducted with the energy and effort shown in this campaign. To be sure, the Russian generals were often

[25] "You see how one passes under the beard of the enemy."

timid at the moment when they should have taken hold of the fugitives, but even so the energy of the overall pursuit was marvelous, considering the scale of the operation. To follow an enemy over five hundred miles in fifty days, at the end of a difficult campaign, in the ice and snow of Russia in November and December, over side roads that had hardly been used or main roads utterly ruined, despite terrible supply problems, is perhaps unexampled in history; to sum up the whole effort in a word, one need only say that the main Russian army left Tarutino with 110,000 men, and arrived at Vilna with 40,000. The remainder were left behind dead, sick, wounded, or exhausted. This effort did great honor to Prince Kutusov.

When Kutusov finally decided to take his enemy by the throat at Krasnoï, blocking the way to the Dnieper with half his army under Tormassov, only to hold back at the long-awaited moment and allow the dreaded fugitive to escape with a modest squeeze, many thought they saw only extreme weakness or dangerous indifference to the reputation and success of Russian arms— but, of course, they pondered the matter in their studies, rather than on the battlefield of Krasnoï itself.

If one considers the winter in all its harshness, the general paralysis of physical and moral powers, an army led from bivouac to bivouac, plagued by sickness and hunger, its path strewn with dead, dying, and exhausted men—then one will understand that to accomplish anything at all was extremely difficult, and that only the strongest impulses were capable of overcoming the inertia of the mass.

Kutusov saw how his army was melting away in his hands and that he would have difficulty bringing any significant part of it to the frontier. He foresaw that the success of the campaign would be enormous in any case and even, with great acuteness, the total destruction of the enemy: "Tout cela se fondera sans moi"[26] were his words to his entourage. Could, or rather should, the more rapid destruction of the enemy have been so important to him as to cause him to endanger a greater part of his own force? We do not wish to deny that personal anxiety over once more being soundly beaten by Bonaparte was one of his strongest motives. But if we set this motive aside entirely, are there not enough other reasons to explain Kutusov's caution? Nor should we overlook the fact that he believed the enemy still to be far stronger and more powerful than he was.

Kutusov decided not to attack with his entire force but rather to pursue the enemy relentlessly with large and small detachments, to harass and exhaust him—which, he believed, would be sufficient to bring him down. Most commanders in his position would probably have thought the same.

Only in one case can Kutusov be accused of an unquestionable error. He knew that Tshitsagov and Wittgenstein would bar the enemy's way at the

[26] "All this will happen without me."

Berezina and bring him to a halt, as laid down in the czar's plan. Under these circumstances, he should just at that time have remained within a day's march of the enemy. If the two days' halt at Krasnoï was unavoidable, he ought to have made up the lost time by two forced marches in order to arrive at Borisov on the 27th, which the French reached on the 25th and 26th; instead he was four days' march away, at Krugloë. His advance guard reached Borisov on the 28th, while his main force took the direct route for Minsk over Uscza. Because the issue here is not a greater or lesser degree of success, but rather the support Kutusov owed his subordinate commanders, his conduct must be judged differently from that at Krasnoï.

From the Berezina, Tshitsagov took the lead in pursuing the French, followed by Miloradovitch; Platov and several other cossack bands stayed close to the French flanks, at times even reached their front. Under these circumstances, Wittgenstein was of no use on the main road, which in any case was in terrible condition. He left it at Kamen and headed toward Niemenzin, which lies on the bend of the Vilia north of Vilna. For this reason we witnessed only a fraction of the famous retreat; but during this stretch, some three days' march, all its horrors were heaped up in almost unbelievable measure. The sufferings of the French army have been described so often that the author considers it superfluous to add any new strokes to the picture. In truth, he felt he would never again be free from the impressions of this terrible spectacle, to which we now had to accustom ourselves. We wish to recall only one point. One should not forget the hardships that the Russian soldier, too, had to endure. In the middle of an uncommonly harsh winter, the corps were generally forced to bivouac, since the few wretched villages that lie near the road, such as exist in this part of Lithuania, could accommodate only a few troops, and most had to be assigned to the cavalry. Had all the troops been quartered in houses, they would have had to be divided into much smaller columns. Provisions were also very scarce, forage parties could not be sent too far ahead, and the steady forward progress did not allow food to be brought in from great distances on our flanks. Therefore the road taken by the advance guard was always marked by dead Russian soldiers who had succumbed to cold and fatigue. Wittgenstein also lost a good third of his troops in the last four weeks of the campaign, for he had above 40,000 men at Czasniki and scarcely 30,000 at Vilna.

General Wittgenstein was ordered by headquarters to turn toward Samogitia and the lower Niemen, so as to cut off Macdonald, who, it seemed, had not yet left Kurland.

Bonaparte had in fact not thought to order this general to withdraw; the order was issued only from Vilna, by the king of Naples,[27] and handed to a

---

[27] Murat assumed command of the *Grande Armée* following Napoleon's departure for Paris on December 5.

Prussian officer who happened to be there. This officer, a rather unreliable man in any case, was delayed by mishaps, and excessive anxiety caused him to take the circuitous route over Tilsit and Teltsch, so that he arrived at Mitau only on December 18.

Macdonald had experienced the most painful uncertainties. Another Prussian officer had been sent by General Yorck to General Krusemark at Vilna, which he left again on the 6th, as the first fugitives from the main army were arriving; he had reached General Yorck on the 10th with news of the emperor's retreat and the dissolution of the French army. Relations between Marshal Macdonald and General Yorck were already on a very poor footing, and Macdonald thought it beneath his dignity to take particular notice of these reports. At any moment he expected to receive official instructions from Vilna and in the meantime declared that the rumors already circulating were fatuous inventions of ill will. Macdonald's anxieties were all the greater because two-thirds of his corps consisted of Prussians, and he no longer fully trusted General Yorck.

On December 18 the officer arrived from Vilna with the order to retreat and at the same time confirmed the worst news. On the 19th Macdonald left, his forces divided into four columns. Two consisted of Grandjean's division and of six battalions, ten squadrons, and two batteries of Prussians under General Massenbach; the other two comprised the remainder of the Prussians under Generals Yorck and Kleist. The first two columns, with the marshal himself, left a day earlier than the others and remained a day's march ahead. The corps followed a common route over Janischki, Schawlia, and Koltiniani; from there the last two columns proceeded through Tauroggen and Piktupöhnen, while the first two moved toward Tilsit by way of Pojour, Coadjuten, and Rucken, the marshal with them.

The march proceeded fairly rapidly; the first two columns, which left on December 19, reached the area around Piktupöhnen, 140 miles from Mitau, in eight days. The move was made more difficult by heavy snow, severe cold, and bad roads. Under these conditions General Yorck and the other two columns, which left Mitau only on the evening of the 20th and carried a great deal of baggage with them, fell two days' march behind Marshal Macdonald. He reached the area around Koltiniani only on the evening of the 25th, by which time the marshal was already in Wainuti, twenty-eight miles away.

That General Yorck fell behind was hardly deliberate, but seems rather to be explained by the prevailing conditions.

Wittgenstein, having rested his corps for some days at Niemenzin, left there on December 17, in the direction of Georgenburg on the Niemen, by way of Wilkomir and Keidany. In addition to his usual advance guard under General Scheppelov, he had sent two small additional detachments, mainly cavalry, farther ahead. The first, under Major General Kutusov, consisted of

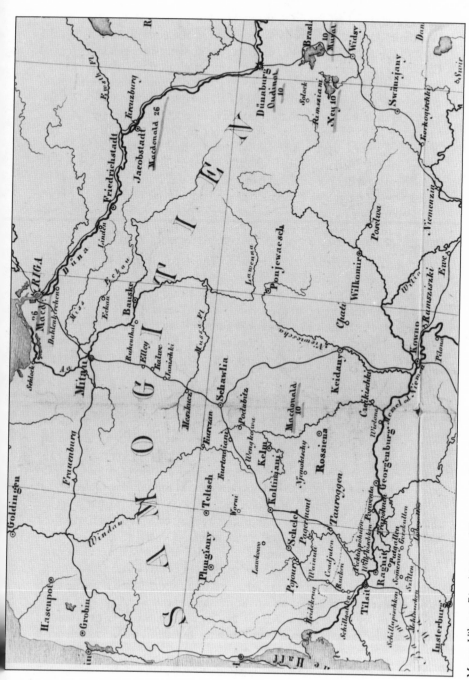

MAP 4. Vilna to Riga (vicinity of Tauroggen). Reproduced from the "Operationskarte für den Feldzug von 1812 in Russland," in Clausewitz, *Hinterlassene Werke*, 7 (Berlin, 1835).

4,000 cavalry and infantry. On the 20th, while General Wittgenstein was in Wilkomir, it was already six days' march ahead at Georgenburg, the crossing point of the river. The second, of which the quartermaster general, General Diebitsch, had temporarily taken command (and on whose staff the author now served), consisted of the regiment of Grodno hussars, three regiments of cossacks, 1,300 horse altogether, and a light infantry regiment, which, however, had shrunk to only 120 men, and six pieces of horse artillery.

On the 20th this detachment already stood at Koltiniani, in the direction of Memel, seven days' march ahead of Count Wittgenstein. Up to that time General Diebitsch had been able to learn nothing of Macdonald's movements and did not doubt that he had taken the route to Memel in order to cross the Kurland Spit;[28] in which case he would have been safe. Diebitsch intended to press forward across Samogitia and occupy Memel. On the 23rd, having passed Teltsch and only two days' march from Memel, he suddenly learned that Macdonald had by no means withdrawn but was in fact approaching down the road from Schawlia. This report seemed scarcely credible; but others confirmed it, and consequently General Diebitsch at once turned back and marched to Worni. Here he heard on the 24th that Macdonald's rear guard stood in Wengkowa, and he decided to lie in wait for it the next day at Koltiniani. He broke camp early and reached this point by ten in the morning, when some Prussian sutlers belonging to Massenbach's command were found. They declared that a rear guard of two squadrons of hussars and two light infantry companies was still behind, but that the rest of the column had already passed. General Diebitsch deployed his men to cut off the retreat of this rear guard.

The author, who had two brothers with the Prussian corps, of whom the older was a major and commanded its light infantry, could assume with fair certainty that, as a good outpost officer, he would be in command of the entire rear guard. The thought of perhaps seeing him here taken prisoner was even more painful than that of being opposed to him all day under fire. It was thus an indescribable satisfaction to learn from other captured stragglers that the rear guard consisted of four line infantry battalions, two squadrons of cavalry, and a battery, under the command of General Kleist.

General Diebitsch, at the head of 1,200 men and far from other support, had little chance of seriously damaging this rear guard. Like a player at ombre, however, he wished to play a low trump in order to see how the cards lay. He asked the author if he would ride to General Kleist under a flag of truce to parley. The author replied that as a Russian officer he would of course undertake any duty assigned to him, but that he would prefer it if

[28] A sandbar sixty miles long connecting Memel and Königsberg. It afforded a line of retreat comparable to the more southerly route actually taken by the French army.

General Diebitsch would send an officer from Livonia or Kurland, who could speak German equally well, and would probably make a less disagreeable first impression on General Kleist than would one of the officers who, to the great displeasure of most Prussian generals, had left the Prussian service for that of Russia at the outbreak of the war. General Diebitsch understood and sent Major von Rönne on this mission.

Rönne was to indicate to General Kleist that his direct line of march was blocked by a substantial force; that means might be found to come to an understanding and avoid useless bloodshed; and that General Diebitsch therefore wished to confer with General Kleist.

Major von Rönne returned with the answer that General von Kleist could not engage in talks because he was not in command; that General Yorck himself was still in the rear, and was expected that evening; until then the situation might be allowed to remain as it was. It was now clear that instead of the rear guard, we had cut off the main body of the Prussian corps from Macdonald.

General Diebitsch must have thought himself lucky to have been brought to this by chance. He could expect only insignificant military advantages; but the possibility of reaching an understanding with the Prussians was of the greatest significance.

The position of the various forces on this day was as follows:

Generals Yorck and Kleist, with 10,000 men, three miles east of Koltiniani.

Opposing them, General Diebitsch, with 1,200 men, at Koltiniani.

Macdonald, with some 4,000 men, at Wainuti, twenty-eight miles from Koltiniani on the western road to Tilsit.

Grandjean, with 6,000 men, at Tauroggen, eighteen miles from Koltiniani, and the same distance from Wainuti, on the eastern road to Tilsit.

General Kutusov,[29] with 4,000 men, at Piktupöhnen, on the road between Tauroggen and Tilsit; he had also occupied Tilsit.

General Scheppelov, with Wittgenstein's real advance guard, 4,000 strong, at Wielona, still a day's march from Georgenburg.

Finally, Count Wittgenstein, with some 15,000 men, one day's march further back toward Keidany.

On the next day, the 26th, when General Yorck was to continue his march through Koltiniani, these dispositions were changed to the extent that each corps advanced one day's march toward its objective. Only General Kutusov remained where he was, as a result of which his outpost at Piktupöhnen, commanded by General Vlastov, was attacked by the Prussian cavalry from General Grandjean's advance guard and, with the loss of two weak battalions

---

[29] Nephew of the field marshal.

and a few guns, driven back to Tilsit, where General Kutusov received the beaten troops.

Kutusov now withdrew to Ragnit, nine miles above Tilsit on the left bank of the Niemen; and both Piktupöhnen, which is a kind of pass, and Tilsit were occupied by the French.

Macdonald was with his force at Coadjuten, a day's march northwest of Piktupöhnen.

We can see that General Yorck was indeed cut off from all immediate support; but a detachment of 1,200 cavalry was in no position to contest his passage seriously. It is true that he was two long marches away from either Grandjean at Piktupöhnen or Macdonald at Coadjuten, during which the Russian cavalry would have taken a large part of the many wagons he had with him and would have caused him other losses as well, because his own cavalry was too weak to keep General Diebitsch entirely at bay. Nor could he know whether other Russian detachments, or Wittgenstein himself, might not arrive. But under other circumstances such considerations would not have caused General Yorck a moment's hesitation.

On the 25th Macdonald began to grow very uneasy about his position. On the one hand, it was reported that Tilsit and Piktupöhnen were already occupied by the Russians; on the other, he lacked any news from General Yorck. So as not to leave Yorck entirely in the lurch, he made only a short march on the 26th, eight miles from Wainuti toward Coadjuten, and on the 27th another of the same length to Schillgallen, on the way to Tilsit. He arrived in Tilsit only on the 28th and remained there on the 29th, although he had reason to be concerned about his own further retreat. In the course of these four days he felt that General Yorck would surely be able to reach him, and he waited anxiously for news. Several attempts to send him orders even by means of strong patrols failed, because they were blocked by the Russian cavalry.

Let us return to General Yorck. With his corps he reached General Kleist toward evening, and by means of the officer whom General Diebitsch had again sent to him he informed General Diebitsch that he was prepared to meet him between the outposts. The meeting took place at nightfall.

Here we must pause for a moment to consider General Yorck and his position.

General Yorck was a man of some fifty years, distinguished by bravery and military competence. In his youth he had served in the Dutch colonies, that is, had seen the world and broadened his mental outlook. A violent, passionate will that he hides under seeming coldness, enormous ambition that he hides under constant resignation, and a strong, daring character distinguish this man. General Yorck is an upright person, but he is morose, melancholic, and secretive and therefore a bad subordinate. Personal attachment is rather foreign to him; what he does, he does for the sake of his reputation and because he is naturally competent. The worst is that under a mask of bluntness and rectitude he is basically very cunning. He boasts when he has little hope, but much more readily seems to consider a cause lost when actually he sees little danger.

He was undoubtedly one of the most distinguished men in our army. Scharnhorst valued his extreme usefulness, during a period when few had shown themselves useful, even more because it was combined with a great dislike of the French, and had always tried to remain on a friendly footing with him, although a suppressed enmity against him may always have raged in Yorck. From time to time it seemed about to burst out, but Scharnhorst behaved as though he noticed nothing and pushed Yorck into every position where a man of his kind could prove useful.

When the war with Russia broke out, the French requested the appointment of General Grawert [to command the Prussian contingent of the *Grande Armée*], an old and infirm man of very limited intelligence and character who, moreover, had never been disinclined to favor French interests in Europe. The king believed he had to accede to the emperor's view. Scharnhorst, who had by then left the government but still kept his hand in play, arranged General Yorck's appointment as second commanding general of the Prussian corps. Scharnhorst indicated to the king that General Grawert, being an old and in addition a weak man, could easily give in too much to the French; that in such a position one needed a man of character and determination; and that no one was better suited to it than General Yorck. He was therefore attached to Grawert's corps with the rank of lieutenant general, in essence as a kind of supervisor for General Grawert.

Within six weeks Grawert became so ill and mentally enfeebled that he was obliged to give up the command to General Yorck. Thereafter it did not take long for relations between General Yorck and Marshal Macdonald to become strained. Macdonald's campaign in Kurland was certainly not the sort to inspire admiration. While he and the Seventh Division held an idle position on the Duna, the Prussians remained in a disagreeable situation before Riga and had to sustain the fighting there more or less alone during the six months of the campaign. General Yorck was not an indulgent judge of others, for bitterness was the predominant feature of his character. The result was that he was just as dissatisfied with Macdonald's overall conduct as with that part which affected the Prussian corps and, on the other hand, was perhaps too proud of what the Prussian troops accomplished at Riga. His cold, reserved, mistrustful demeanor, and the remarks of those around him, did not long leave the marshal in doubt about Yorck's feelings, and a cloud of dissension gradually arose between them. The provisioning of the troops, which was first handled by a Prussian and later by a French commissary, after which it had become much less adequate, brought the suppressed resentment into the open. Yorck complained of the lack of forage, and Macdonald declared that Yorck's horses were bursting from overfeeding. The affair grew bitter in the course of a short correspondence, in which the marshal formally accused the general of a lack of zeal and good will for their cause. This breach, which occurred at the end of November, was reported by both men to Vilna, by Yorck to the Prussian ambassador, General Krusemark, by the marshal to the duke of Bassano [the French foreign minister]. General Yorck also sent one of his adjutants to Berlin to inform the king of these circumstances. This adjutant had not yet returned when Yorck was to hold his first conference with General Diebitsch.

Although General Yorck received special instructions on being appointed to the Prussian corps, it is nevertheless certain that these included nothing by which the step he was now contemplating could be justified.

As early as September, General Essen [military governor of Riga], in order to test General Yorck, had urgently invited him to a meeting at the outposts, to which Yorck agreed. But Yorck's behavior seems to have been too forbidding, for General Essen did not have the courage to explain himself fully and nothing was actually discussed. The Marquis Paulucci [Essen's successor] was a man of bolder speech, which by the beginning of December was in any case justified by events. On December 5 he formally called on General Yorck to defect. The latter rejected this demand but offered himself as a mediator should the emperor wish the marquis to make proposals to the king of Prussia. Proposals of a general kind were then put forward in this indirect way, which General Yorck sent on to Berlin through his adjutant, Major von Seydlitz.

All these circumstances must be mentioned in order to place General Yorck's conduct in a clear light. He was too level-headed to allow himself to be guided in this matter by his animosity toward Marshal Macdonald; that would have meant using enormous means for a small end and would have led him far beyond his goal. On the other hand, it is not inconceivable that had friendly relations existed between the two generals—and had Yorck been a man as good-natured as Macdonald himself, a man truly devoted to the person of his superior—such considerations might perhaps have forestalled the remarkable event that now followed.

How the king and the Prussian people felt toward the French could have been no secret to General Yorck; but whether those in Berlin thought that the catastrophe the French had just suffered had entirely shifted the balance, and whether they would consider the present moment sufficiently favorable for a sudden change of roles—about these things General Yorck could only have the gravest doubts.

If he reflected on the character of the king,[30] he must have anticipated the greatest aversion to any sudden change of course. {Nor was the Prussian ministry of the kind to reach a forceful and at the same time very unusual decision.} Scharnhorst, the most determined enemy of the French and the man who would have advised such a course and supported it to the hilt, had left the ministry and was living in Silesia. Baron Hardenberg had shown that he knew how to steer dexterously among rocks and shoals, but whether he could reach a truly courageous decision, and possessed the ability to inspire courage in others, remained very much in doubt. If General Yorck, by himself and at his own risk, now came to a decision that was to turn Prussian policy in an entirely contrary direction, it would be one of the boldest undertakings in history. Count Haugwitz had in effect conducted himself in somewhat similar fashion when he concluded the Vienna treaty in 1805, but on that occasion Count Haugwitz acted in the interest of the more powerful party and knew the Prussian ministry would oppose the French only with reluctance. Besides, an act of diplomatic boldness is never resented as strongly as a military one; the former at most costs a man his office, the latter, as a rule, his head. If the king was truly determined to adhere to the French alliance, he had virtually no alternative but to bring Yorck to trial. {How close the government was to taking this step! and how difficult it was for General Yorck to foresee that, apart from an outright decision for or against France, a third alternative existed: to remain in an ambiguous position until the moment for an open decision was even more favorable! It was only this third alternative that forestalled the first, and saved General Yorck.}

The author begs the reader's pardon for having discussed at such length and with so many digressions the conditions surrounding the apparently unimportant meeting between Generals Yorck and Diebitsch; we believe we have only now gained the perspective from which the great implications of this event can be surveyed, and return again to Koltiniani.

General Yorck and General Diebitsch met there on the evening of the 25th. The latter had deployed his troops to conceal their strength as much as possible, but he was honorable enough to speak frankly of the forces he did and did not have—adding that he did not imagine he could block Yorck's way, but that he would do everything possible to take away his supply train, his artillery wagons, and perhaps some of his guns. This was of course the least weighty of the considerations General Diebitsch could put forward; the main subject of discussion was the total destruction of the French army and the fact that the emperor had instructed the Russian generals not to treat the Prussians as true enemies but, in view of the amicable relations that had once existed between the two powers and the likelihood that these would soon be

---

[30] 1835 edition: "If he reflected on the state of affairs in Berlin."

renewed, to arrange whatever friendly accommodation the Prussians might desire. Accordingly, General Diebitsch declared that he was prepared to enter into a neutrality agreement with General Yorck and, for this purpose, to give up whatever military advantages he might possess.

General Yorck made no definite reply. He showed himself inclined toward an agreement of a kind that would not diminish the honor of his corps; but he felt that at present such a step would not yet appear militarily justified. It was agreed that the troops would remain in place during the night; the next morning General Yorck would first reconnoiter and then march toward Lawkowo, as if to turn the left flank of General Diebitsch's detachment, but that General Diebitsch was to face him again at Schelel.

At the close of the conference General Yorck said to General Diebitsch: "You have quite a few former Prussian officers with you. Do send one of them to me from now on; it will give me more confidence."

General Diebitsch asked the author whether he would undertake future assignments of this kind, to which the author naturally declared that he was at his service.

It was late when we returned to Koltiniani, perhaps ten o'clock at night. General Diebitsch discussed the situation with the author and asked him what he thought of General Yorck's intentions, and what kind of man he was. The author could not avoid warning General Diebitsch of General Yorck's secretive character. He feared that Yorck might use the night to overwhelm us and force his way to Macdonald; he therefore urged the utmost vigilance.

General Diebitsch placed two regiments of cossacks opposite General Yorck, with the third in the rear, toward Schelel, and kept the hussar regiment in Koltiniani itself, which is a reasonably large village. The hussars were kept in a state of readiness, and the orderlies at headquarters were also ordered not to unbridle their horses. We had dismounted at a house, laid ourselves down on the straw fully clothed, and had scarcely closed our eyes when pistol shots were heard from the rear of the village. They were not single shots but a general fire, which lasted some minutes. We leapt up, and the author said to himself: It is Yorck attacking our rear; you judged him right. We mounted. Two squadrons were sent to the road toward Schelel but found no enemy, only the cossack regiment covering the rear. From the cossacks it was learned that a troop of enemy cavalry had suddenly appeared among them and thrown them back into the village. It was a patrol of fifty Prussian dragoons, which General Massenbach had sent from Schelel to Koltiniani under Captain Weiß, with a message from Marshal Macdonald to General Yorck. The patrol was ordered to break through by force, but it found the enemy too strong and, after driving the cossacks back into Koltiniani, turned about and vanished before it could be pursued. We learned this only later from Prussian officers; for the moment we were left completely in the dark.

General Yorck made his reconnaissance on the 26th but found it inadvisable to march in the direction agreed upon, shifting instead toward Schelel, on the road to Tilsit. The bad roads and the desire to avoid useless wear and tear to his men and horses were the reason for this; but General Diebitsch was naturally suspicious and believed General Yorck tried to gain a day's march toward Tilsit. A series of parleys ensued, in which the author always took part.

The first time the author went to General Yorck, on the 26th near Schelel, the general would not see him for fear of compromising himself. He reprimanded the outpost officer who accompanied the author for allowing him to proceed so far without special permission. The author therefore did not meet with General Yorck, although this was merely a charade, since the general sent the Russian lieutenant colonel Count Dohna out to discuss matters with him.

Count Dohna had left Prussian service for the Russian army in 1812 at the same time as the author; he belonged to the Russo-German Legion and had received permission to go to Riga to take part in the campaign. He was attached to General Levis, who had followed General Yorck with 5,000 men from the Riga garrison but still remained several days' march away, and had sent Count Dohna ahead as a negotiator. The author was greatly pleased to meet one of his closest friends at this juncture.

From what Count Dohna said it was evident that General Yorck meant what he had said, but that he also wished to postpone matters for another few days, during which he could not remain as if nailed to the ground; he would therefore push on toward the Prussian border.

One could easily understand General Yorck's concern, because apart from the fact that he was awaiting the return of an adjutant from Berlin, who did arrive on the 29th, it made a better appearance militarily if he attempted once or twice to reach Macdonald. Had the latter remained in Tauroggen and Wainuti, where he was on the 25th, or had he returned there on the 26th, the convention [of Tauroggen] would not have come to pass. But as Macdonald continued on his way, leaving the Russians between the two forces, able to prevent Macdonald's messages and orders from reaching Yorck, Yorck could assume the appearance of having been abandoned by Macdonald.

General Diebitsch understood this; but on the other hand, he did not yet feel entirely sure of General Yorck. If Yorck were to maneuver him back toward Tilsit and then suddenly break out and disappear, Diebitsch would have played a poor part and might even have been placed in a questionable light.

General Diebitsch therefore did all he could to bring General Yorck to a decision and constantly protested against a further withdrawal; General Yorck in turn sought to appease him and continued his march toward him, although always in very short stages. Thus Diebitsch proceeded on the 26th to Schelel, on the 27th to Pagermont, and on the 28th over Tauroggen to Willkischken, which was only nine miles from Tilsit. Macdonald had entered Tilsit with his last detachment on this day, where he intended to await Yorck, who had reached Tauroggen. Actually, nothing whatever now stood in the way of their union except a thin screen of cossacks.

The matter would have had to be given up as lost were it not that General Yorck had already been badly compromised by reason of his slow progress and his frequent negotiations. If he considered his own interests, he could scarcely back out now.

At midday on the 29th the author was again sent to General Yorck at Tauroggen, whom he had left there only the night before. This time he brought with him two documents, which were regarded as decisive.

The first was addressed to General Diebitsch by Wittgenstein's chief of staff, General d'Auvray, and began by reproaching him for not having brought the negotiation with General Yorck to a conclusion. The current disposition of Wittgenstein's army was then described, from which it was clear that the advance guard under General Scheppelov was to be at Schillupischken on the 31st, and Wittgenstein himself at Sommerau.

Schillupischken lies on the western road leading from Tilsit to Königsberg. The road proceeds through wooded country in which it forms numerous narrow passages for some eighteen miles. As early as at Schillupischken, where the road crosses a small stream, it forms a pass. Sommerau, where General Wittgenstein meant to be, lay only four miles from Schillupischken. If Wittgenstein really carried out his march and if Macdonald waited for General Yorck in Tilsit, where the latter could not arrive before late evening on the 30th, it became very uncertain whether Wittgenstein and Macdonald might not reach the forest at the same time. Wittgenstein, of course, was significantly weaker than Macdonald and Yorck, but they could not know this for certain; if they did not yet need to consider themselves entirely cut off, their further retreat was nevertheless precarious. These circumstances would certainly carry weight with General Yorck. General d'Auvray's letter therefore included an instruction to make General Yorck aware of them, along with the explanation that, should he fail to take account of them and decline to put an end to his indecision, he would be treated like any other enemy general, and a friendly agreement would no longer be possible under any circumstances.

The second document was the following letter from Marshal Macdonald to the duke of Bassano, which Wittgenstein's troops had intercepted.

Stalgen le 10 Décembre 1812

Mon cher Duc!

Vous ne me donnez pas de vos nouvelles, j'en envoye chercher; un officier qui arrive de Wilna nous débite des absurdités de cette ville; il assure pourtant avoir vu passer S. M. l'Empereur se rendant, dit-il, à Kowno où V. E. la suivra.

Je ne puis croire à tout ce que je viens de lire dans les bulletins russes que je vous adresse, quoique l'on cite des personnages que je savois faire réellement partie du 2me et 9me corps; j'attends d'un moment à l'autre que vous m'éclairiez. Enfin la bombe a crevé avec le Général Yorck; j'ai cru que dans des circonstances telles que MM. de l'état-major prussien les accréditent, sans les repousser je devois montrer plus de fermeté. Le corps est bon, mais on le gâte; l'esprit est prodigieusement changé, mais quelques grâces, des récompenses, et je le remonterai aisément, pourvu toute fois, que les officiers que je signale soient promptement éloignés; ils ne seront pas regrettés, les deux tiers de l'armée les détestent.

Au nom de Dieu, mon cher Duc, écrivez moi un mot que je sache quelles sont les positions que l'on va prendre; je me concentre d'avantage.

Milles amitiés, je vous embrasse.

Macdonald[31]

[31] The letter reads as follows:

Stalgen, 10 December 1812

My dear Duke!

Since you give me no news of yourself, I am sending for some. An officer arriving from Vilna brings some absurd reports from that town; but he assures us that he saw His Majesty the emperor passing through on his way to Kowno, where Your Excellency is to follow him.

I cannot believe everything I have been reading in the Russian bulletins I am sending you, although they mention the names of men who, I know myself, do belong to the Second and Ninth Corps; I await clarification from you from one moment to the next. The bomb has burst at last with General Yorck. I had thought that under the circumstances, which are uncontested by the gentlemen of the Prussian staff, I ought to show more firmness. The [Prussian] corps is sound, but it is being spoiled. Its spirit is prodigiously changed, but a few favors, some rewards, and I will easily restore the situation, provided the officers I designate are promptly removed. They will not be regretted; two-thirds of the army detests them.

The first of these two letters would have made no impression on a man like Yorck; but as a military pretext it meant a good deal, should the Prussian court wish to excuse itself to the French.

The second letter must at least have reawakened all the bitterness in General Yorck's heart, which Yorck's consciousness of his own guilt toward Macdonald had perhaps diminished somewhat in recent days.

When the author entered General Yorck's room, the latter cried out, "Keep away from me, I want nothing more to do with you. Your damned cossacks have let a messenger from Macdonald through, who brings me an order to march on Piktupöhnen and join him there. All doubt is now at an end. Your troops do not advance, they are too weak, I must march, and I won't have any further negotiations, which would cost me my head." The author replied that he did not wish to dispute the general but begged for a candle, because he had some letters to show him; when the general hesitated, the author added, "Surely Your Excellency will not place me in the embarrassing position of departing without having carried out my mission." General Yorck then called for candles and for his chief of staff, Colonel Roeder, who entered from the antechamber. The letters were read. After a moment's reflection General Yorck said, "Clausewitz, you are a Prussian. Do you believe that General d'Auvray's letter is honest, and that Wittgenstein's troops will really reach the places named by the 31st? Can you give me your word of honor?" The author replied, "Your Excellency, I guarantee the honesty of the letter, based on my knowledge of General d'Auvray and the other men at Wittgenstein's headquarters. Whether these dispositions will really be achieved I can, of course, not guarantee, since Your Excellency knows that in war with the best will in the world one must often fall short of the line one has set oneself." The general remained silent for a few moments of serious reflection, then held out his hand to the author and said, "You have me. Tell General Diebitsch that we confer early tomorrow morning at the mill in Poscherun, and that I am now firmly resolved to separate myself from the French and their cause." The meeting was set for eight o'clock in the morning. When this was settled, General Yorck said, "I won't leave things half way; I will bring you Massenbach as well." With this he called in a cavalry officer from Massenbach's command who had just arrived. Much like Wallenstein, he asked, pacing up and down the room, "What say your regiments?" The officer immediately burst with enthusiasm at the idea of leaving the French alliance and said that the troops felt likewise. "It's easy for you to

---

In the name of heaven, my dear duke, write me a word so I may know what positions to take up; I am concentrating myself still more.

A thousand greetings; I embrace you.

Macdonald

talk, you young people," replied Yorck, "but this old man's head is shaking on his shoulders."

Happy and relieved, the author hurried back to [Willkischken][32] and the following morning accompanied General Diebitsch to the mill, where they found General Yorck in the company of Colonel von Roeder and his first adjutant, Major von Seydlitz. Apart from the author, only Count Dohna accompanied General Diebitsch, so that the negotiations were conducted by men who were all native Prussians.

The convention itself is widely available in print; we will merely say that by its terms the Prussian corps was declared neutral, and neutral territory was assigned to it in Prussian Lithuania, on the Russian frontier. Should the convention prove unacceptable to either monarch, the Prussian troops would be allowed unimpeded withdrawal by the shortest route, while pledging themselves, in the event the Prussian king rejected it, not to serve against Russia for two months.

Already on the 26th, General Yorck had sent one of the king's adjutants, Major Count von Henckel, who was with the corps, from Schelel to Berlin to bring the king up to date on the situation. He now dispatched Major von Thile from his staff with the convention.

At the end of his accompanying letter, General Yorck wrote:

If I have done wrong, I willingly lay my head at Your Majesty's feet; I would perish with the glad assurance of at least not having failed as your faithful subject and as a true Prussian.

Now or never is the moment when Your Majesty can tear yourself free from the impudent demands of an ally whose intentions toward Prussia, should fortune have favored him, were shrouded in such darkness as must provoke anxiety. This view has guided me; let heaven grant that it may lead to the welfare of the fatherland.

By this time General Massenbach was in Tilsit with six battalions and one squadron; two other squadrons camped along the road to Insterburg, and seven more were attached to Bachelu's brigade near Ragnit. On the 30th General Yorck sent an officer to Tilsit to inform General Massenbach of the step he had taken. At the same time, to relieve him of all responsibility, he ordered Massenbach to leave Tilsit and rejoin the Prussian corps. He also forwarded through him the letter in which he informed Marshal Macdonald of his decision.

General Massenbach did not hesitate an instant in obeying General Yorck's order. At first the circumstances seemed especially favorable, since only his six battalions were in Tilsit, and Grandjean's division was quartered

---

[32] The manuscript has "Schillupischken," which must be an error.

some distance away. On the night of the 30th, however, as he was about to carry out the order, several regiments of Heudelet's division arrived by chance from Königsberg, and others, including Grandjean's division, were expected.

General Massenbach believed these measures might be directed against himself and decided that under these circumstances it would be better not to break camp during the night, but to wait for the following day, assuming that by then the suspicions against him would have been allayed. This reasoning seems not entirely valid: if the French were already suspicious of him, they would have remained so the following day. It is true, however, that it was easier to take appropriate measures by day, and the only thing to be feared was that by then suspicion might have become certainty. But this was not the case; the French troops had not been assembled to be used against Massenbach, and the latter was able to cross the Niemen at eight o'clock on the morning of the 31st and march toward the Russians.

General Macdonald, having at last been informed of these circumstances by letters from Generals Yorck and Massenbach, which were forwarded to him after the event, behaved very nobly. He dismissed Lieutenant von Korff, who commanded a detachment of thirty horse at headquarters and who had been unable to accompany Massenbach, with expressions of friendship and gifts for his officers and men.

Among the Prussian troops the convention was greeted with the greatest enthusiasm.

What caused General Yorck to delay his decision for so long is in part apparent from our account. Lack of resolve seems to have had least of all to do with it. He hoped that the military position of his corps would deteriorate and that additional Russian forces would arrive, which would do more to justify his decision. In this he succeeded, partly because General Levis had advanced far enough to make contact with Diebitsch and partly because those elements of Wittgenstein's army that had cut across Marshal Macdonald's retreat could play a good role in any legal defense of General Yorck. Furthermore, General Yorck wanted to await the arrival of his adjutant, Major von Seydlitz, from Berlin, who was expected at any moment. This he also achieved, because Seydlitz arrived in Tauroggen early on the 29th. Whatever he reported about the political part of his mission has not become known. Presumably it was decided in Berlin that the time had not yet come to give up the French alliance, and one did not wish to do so without first consulting Austria. Therefore the answer was probably negative, that is, silence. Had anyone in Berlin imagined that General Yorck would take the bold step that he did, they would presumably have prohibited it directly, in which case General Yorck would not have dared to act. But this fortunately was not the case; and because Major von Seydlitz, in whom General Yorck had great confidence and on whose personal impressions much depended, was also convinced that Prussia could and should now free itself from the French yoke, he saw conditions in Berlin in light of this preconceived opinion and to this extent influenced General Yorck. Yorck recognized that he was still risking a great deal, but at least his hands were not completely tied.

From another perspective one must say that, in human terms, a decision of the kind General Yorck made requires time to ripen, and that, if the period of ripening can be called indecision, it was in all likelihood overcome by the last dispatches brought to him by the author. As his guilt increased every day, it finally required only a slight nudge to remove any idea of retracing his steps.

The conduct of General Diebitsch throughout was worthy of the highest praise. By conferring upon General Yorck as much confidence as his own authority allowed; by always showing himself to be unprejudiced, frank, and honorable, with only the common interest, and nearly as much for Prussia as for Russia, at heart; above all by rejecting all thought of triumph, all the pride of the victor, all the vanity or rudeness of the Russian—he made it easier for General Yorck to reach a decision that was bound to be very difficult and which under less favorable circumstances would probably never have come to fruition.

The author looks back with pleasure on a little scene that took place at Willkischken. On the night of the 28th, when the author had just returned from seeing General Yorck, General Diebitsch, greatly perturbed, entered the room and told the author he had just received word that a cossack patrol, a noncommissioned officer and six men sent to Ragnit with a letter for General d'Auvray, had been taken by the enemy. This letter, or rather note, included a brief report, written in French no less, describing how far matters had progressed with General Yorck; if it were to fall into French hands it would do General Yorck the gravest damage. General Diebitsch was beside himself at the thought of being responsible for Yorck's misfortune. He pleaded with the author to return at once to General Yorck and tell him honestly what had occurred. The task was not a pleasant one, but the author willingly undertook it; the sledge had just come to the gate when the leader of the cossack patrol arrived and informed General Diebitsch that he had been attacked by the enemy and his men scattered. "And the letter?" cried the general at once. "Here it is," replied the cossack calmly and handed it to the general, who embraced the author and wept with joy.

As soon as Marshal Macdonald learned of the Prussian defection, he marched from Tilsit to Melauken, at the edge of the forest. On this road he met neither Wittgenstein nor Scheppelov, but only a few regiments of cossacks belonging to General Kutusov's forces. They naturally gave way, and he reached Melauken easily, although hotly pursued by Diebitsch and Kutusov.

Because he had mistaken the name, General Scheppelov had marched on the 31st not to Schillupischken but to Szillen, on the road from Tilsit to Insterburg. Since Macdonald did not use this road, this proved entirely useless. General Wittgenstein was furious with this general, who was deprived of command of the advance guard. But Wittgenstein himself might easily have reached Schillupischken in good time by the 31st since he was already in Löbegallen, only some twenty-three miles away, on the 29th. But he only reached Sommerau; the very poor roads, the exhaustion of the troops, and the need for rather dispersed quarters may well excuse the lack of forced marches, but the main reason was that energy was beginning to flag and that one began to think, in the face of such an enormous success, that no further effort was required, and that one would do better to spare one's own men.

Even so, Count Wittgenstein followed hard on Marshal Macdonald's heels to Königsberg, prevented him from concentrating his forces there, and destroyed any thought of the French perhaps defending East Prussia; in this way the question of whether or not to cross the frontier, much debated at the main Russian headquarters, was for all practical purposes decided. Once Wittgenstein arrived at Königsberg it was necessary to support him, so Tshitsagov was ordered to follow over Gumbinnen. Both then pursued the French as far as the Vistula.

At this point Tshitsagov, as the older commanding general, was given supreme command of the forces pressing forward into Prussia. Wittgenstein was so offended that he remained behind in Königsberg under pretext of illness. The situation was soon mended, however. Tshitsagov remained before Thorn, and Wittgenstein, after leaving 10,000 men at Danzig, continued with the rest of his forces, which might have amounted to another 10,000 men, over the Vistula to Konitz, where he remained several weeks; he later proceeded to Berlin, which he entered at the beginning of March.

Even if Wittgenstein naturally did not act without express orders from Kutusov and the emperor, he nevertheless provided the first impetus for extending the campaign as far as the Elbe, and so pulled the whole army along with him.

Although General Yorck, as we have seen, had been adroit in preparing the king by means of two separate letters for the step he wished to take, the king was nevertheless disagreeably surprised by Yorck's convention. He found himself pushed near the abyss by the independent action of his general. The moment for a change in policy seemed not yet to have arrived, and if it had in fact arrived, it nevertheless seemed unnecessary and illegal that the decision was made by a general. This line of reasoning was natural in Berlin, where the full extent of the French army's destruction was not yet recognized. Nor could one grasp the overall consequences for the war that followed from General Yorck's withdrawal from the operations, so that his action could only be seen as pointless and high-handed.

Nevertheless, calm consideration of the circumstances and consultation with Baron Hardenberg may already have given the king the idea that it was neither Prussia's duty nor interest to hold fast to France during the storm of misfortune that she had brought on herself.

It was therefore decided at this difficult moment to avoid as far as possible any explicit declaration, and to maneuver as carefully as one could.

General Yorck's conduct was to be formally disapproved, the treaty rejected, General Kleist placed in command of the corps, an investigation of General Yorck opened, and a new contingent of troops promised to the French; Prince Hatzfeldt was to be sent to Paris with all these decisions. These were all steps that in themselves could have no great effect on the political balance but which would have to satisfy the French for the moment.

One of the king's adjutants, Lieutenant Colonel von Natzmer, was sent to Yorck's corps with these instructions. It was of great significance that at this moment Yorck's corps stood behind Wittgenstein, so that Lieutenant Colonel von Natzmer had to pass through the Russian troops. He could not do this secretly, nor did he have orders to try; rather, he reported to Count Wittgenstein and asked for permission to proceed to General Yorck. Count Wittgenstein asked what his mission was, to which Lieutenant Colonel von Natzmer replied that he had orders to relieve General Yorck of his command and transfer it to General Kleist. "In that case, sir, you will not pass my lines," said Count Wittgenstein. "Have you any further instructions to carry out?" Lieutenant Colonel von Natzmer declared that he had a letter for the czar. "Ah, with the greatest pleasure I shall allow you to deliver it!" A small sledge drove up, a Russian officer joined Lieutenant Colonel von Natzmer, and they departed for the emperor in Vilna. This occurred in the middle of January, and General Yorck remained in possession of his doubtful command. In Berlin more was learned every day about the destruction of the French. The idea of resistance grew hourly, and within a month of Lieutenant Colonel von Natzmer's departure no doubt remained as to which side one ought to take. The king left Potsdam for Breslau. Wittgenstein entered Berlin on March 7. Yorck followed him and arrived on March 17; the same day, it was announced in Breslau that an investigation had found General Yorck blameless and that he was therefore restored to his command; the king's proclamation to the Prussian army and people also occurred on this day.

This brief look at the consequences of the Russian campaign, at the conclusion of the movement that had been carried out by hundreds of thousands of men, was necessary to understand fully the significance of Yorck's convention.

Had Yorck rejoined Macdonald, the latter, together with Heudelet's division from Königsberg, would have assembled a force of 30,000 men behind the Niemen. Because the main Russian army had stopped at Vilna and because Tshitsagov had orders not to cross the border, while Wittgenstein only had about 20,000 men left, including troops from Riga, it is unthinkable that Wittgenstein would have crossed the Niemen on his own authority, offered battle to Marshal Macdonald, and pushed the war into the heart of Prussia. According to the history of the campaign by Colonel Buturlin,* Count Wittgenstein was originally ordered from Vilna to Gumbinnen, but because of the poor roads near the Niemen he was forced to turn north. But one cannot ascribe much authority to this unintelligible, or rather unintelligent, passage of the work. The routes to Gumbinnen and to Wilkomir are too divergent to imagine them being used for the same purpose. In Vilna one scarcely contemplated pushing a corps of 20,000 men forward 140 miles into Prussia. According to the author's recollection of Wittgenstein's headquarters at this time, it was Wittgenstein who fought for the successive advances toward Königsberg to cut off Macdonald, and then the pursuit of the marshal to the Vistula. But Wittgenstein himself was only drawn from one step to the next by Macdonald's late arrival [at Tilsit], by the isolation of General Yorck, by the negotiations with him, and finally by the conclusion of the convention and the danger in which this placed Macdonald. It would have been a different matter if 30,000 men had been waiting for the Russians behind the Niemen or even the Pregel. It is nearly certain that the Russian campaign would then have reached its conclusion at the Prussian frontier.

Although we are not inclined to see the events of this world as resulting from individual causes but always take them as the complex product of many forces, so that the loss of a single component can never produce a complete reversal {but only a partial transformation relative to the significance of the component}, we must nevertheless recognize that great results have often arisen from seemingly small events, and that an isolated cause, strongly exposed to the workings of chance, often brings forth universal effects.

This is true of Yorck's convention. It would be unreasonable to believe that, had it not been for the decision General Yorck reached at Tauroggen on the evening of December 29, Bonaparte would still occupy the French throne and the French would still rule Europe. Such great results are the effects of an infinite number of causes, or rather forces, most of which would have retained their strength even without General Yorck; but it cannot be denied that the decision of this general had enormous consequences and in all likelihood very considerably speeded up the final outcome.

* Part 2, p. 423. [Clausewitz refers to Dimitrii Buturlin, *Histoire militaire de la campagne de Russie en 1812* (Paris and St. Petersburg, 1824). Werner Hahlweg (*Schriften*, 2, part 2: 913n) has noted that the correct reference is to page 422.]

Finally, the author would like to offer his opinion on Bonaparte's plan of operation in this much-discussed campaign.

Bonaparte wanted to conduct and conclude the war in Russia as he had conducted and concluded all his campaigns. To begin with decisive blows and to employ the advantages he gained from them to achieve further decisive battles, always placing his winnings on the next card until the bank was broken—*that was his way*, and it must be said that he owed the tremendous success that he had achieved only to *this way*; his degree of success was scarcely conceivable by any other means.

In Spain this approach had failed him. The Austrian campaign of 1809 had saved Spain because it prevented him from driving the English out of Portugal. Thereafter he was forced on the defensive in Spain, which cost him enormous effort and, in effect, crippled him in one arm. It is extraordinary, and perhaps the greatest error Bonaparte ever made, that in 1810 he did not go to the peninsula himself to end the war in Portugal, after which the war in Spain would also have gradually been extinguished, for undoubtedly the Spanish insurrection and the [British] campaign to aid Portugal supported each other. Still, it would always have been necessary for Bonaparte to leave a substantial army in Spain.

It was entirely natural, and probably also justified, that in the new war with Russia it was his principal objective not to become involved in a similarly protracted and costly defensive struggle in a still more distant theater. Above all, he needed to end the war in one, or at most two, campaigns.

To defeat the enemy's army, to destroy it, to occupy his capital, to drive the government to the farthest corner of the country, and then in the chaos that followed to win the peace—that until now had been the operational plan of all his wars. In Russia he had the vastness of the country against him and the disadvantage of two widely separated capitals. These circumstances would diminish the *psychological* effects of his victories, a loss that he probably hoped would be made up by two other factors: one was the weakness of the Russian government {its lack of energy and ability}; the other, the dissension that he might be able to sow between the nobility and the crown.[33] This is why he was so disturbed when he found Moscow abandoned and destroyed. From Moscow he had hoped to influence opinion in St. Petersburg and the rest of Russia.

That under these circumstances Bonaparte should have attempted to reach Moscow in one thrust was only logical.

The effects of Russia's vast territory and of a possible popular war—in short, the weight of a great state with all its powers—could only make them-

[33] The 1835 edition adds: "In both cases he deceived himself."

selves felt gradually and might prove overwhelming if he did not master them at the first attempt.

If Bonaparte really had to count on two campaigns to win the war, it still made a great difference whether or not he reached Moscow in the first. Having occupied the capital, he might hope to undermine preparations for further resistance by employing the power that remained to him, the power to impress, to lead public opinion astray, to turn people's feelings against their duty.

If Moscow remained in Russian hands, it might become the center of such powerful means of resistance that, in the next campaign, Bonaparte's own necessarily weakened forces would no longer be adequate. In short, with the capture of Moscow he believed *he had turned the corner.*

These seem to us the natural conceptions of a man like Bonaparte. It is simply a question of whether one can say such a plan would not work in Russia and whether another might have been better.

We do not believe so. To defeat the Russian army, disperse it, and occupy Moscow was a goal that could certainly be achieved in one campaign; but we believe that this goal omits one further, essential consideration: *to remain strong even in Moscow.*

We believe that Bonaparte neglected this last consideration solely out of that arrogant recklessness that was characteristic of him.

He reached Moscow with 90,000 men—and should have reached it with 200,000.

This would have been possible had he managed his army with greater care and attention. But such attitudes always remained foreign to him. He might have lost 30,000 fewer men in battle had he not taken the bull by the horns every time. A more thorough preparation for the campaign, better organization of his supply services, and more carefully planned marches to avoid bringing together such huge masses of men on a single road would have prevented the shortages that prevailed from the beginning and would have limited the army's losses.

Whether the deployment of 200,000 men in the heart of the Russian empire would have had the moral effect necessary to bring about peace is of course an open question; but it seems to us that, at least before the fact, one might be permitted to count on such a result. It could not be foreseen with certainty, it was perhaps not even likely, that the Russians would abandon Moscow, burn it down, and engage in a war of attrition; but once this happened the war was bound to miscarry, regardless of how it was conducted.

It must be regarded as a second great failing that Bonaparte had given so little thought to preparing for his withdrawal.

If Vilna, Minsk, Polozk, Vitebsk, and Smolensk had been fortified with fieldworks and palisades and each place garrisoned with 5–6,000 men, the retreat would have been easier in more than one respect, particularly through better food supply. We need only note the seven hundred oxen the cossacks captured near Smolensk on November 9. If we further consider that the French army might have reached Moscow in greater strength and therefore would have left it stronger as well, then its retreat would not have been the plunge into the abyss that it became.

What of the other plan, which after the event some critics held to be more reasonable or, as they prefer to characterize it, more methodical?

Bonaparte should have halted his advance at the Dnieper and Duna, or at least concluded the campaign with the occupation of Smolensk; then establish himself in the occupied territory and secure his flanks to achieve a better base of operations; arm the Poles, to increase his striking power; and march on Moscow in the following campaign, with a better start and more staying power.

This sounds persuasive if we do not examine it too closely and if we do not compare it with the prospects offered by the plan that Bonaparte adopted.

According to this idea, he should occupy himself in the first campaign with the conquest of Riga and Bobruisk (which are the only fortified places in the relevant territory), and for the winter establish a defensive line from the Gulf of Riga along the Duna to Vitebsk, from there to Smolensk, and then along the Dnieper roughly to Rohatschev, then behind the Precipiez and Mukhavets Rivers to the Bug—in all a line something over nine hundred miles long.

That would have meant ending the campaign without having defeated the Russian army, which would have remained more or less intact, with Moscow not even threatened. The Russian forces, which were still weak at the start of the campaign and which would nearly double during its course, would thus have had time to prepare and during the winter begin an offensive against the vastly extended French defenses. To play such a passive part was not to Bonaparte's taste. The worst of it was that any victory he achieved under these circumstances would remain without positive effects since, in the middle of winter or even in late fall, there was nothing for the victorious force to attempt, no objective toward which it could advance. He could therefore do nothing but parry the blows of the Russians, without returning them.

Let us now think of the practical problems of executing such a plan! Where should he station his army? In quarters? For fairly substantial bodies of troops that would be possible only near large towns. In camps? That was impossible in winter. But if he divided his forces among the towns, the open territory between them would never belong to him, but to the cossacks.

The losses that the French army would have sustained in the course of a winter probably could not have been made up by arming the Poles.

And, looked at closely, arming the Polish people would have presented great difficulties. First of all the Austrian provinces would necessarily have been excluded, as well as those that remained in Russian hands; furthermore, again because of Austria, the Poles could not have been armed on the basis they desired, namely as a step toward the restoration of the former Polish kingdom, and that would seriously hamper their enthusiasm. But the main difficulty would be that a country suffering the presence of a huge foreign army is in no condition to make a major military effort of its own. Extraordinary efforts on the part of a state's citizens have their limits; if they are called for on one side, they cannot be made available on the other. If a peasant and his cattle must remain on the road all day, transporting a foreign army's supplies here and there; if his house is full of soldiers; if the merchant must give up his stores for their subsistence; if the needs of the moment are always pressing everywhere—then it is hardly likely that voluntary offers of money, goods, and personal service will provide the means to raise additional forces.

Setting all this aside, however, we will concede the possibility that such a campaign might have achieved its goal and prepared the ground for further gains in the following campaign. But we must also consider matters as they appeared from Bonaparte's perspective: that he found the Russians only half prepared; that he brought a huge preponderance of force against them; that he might gain a victory that would give his whole enterprise that cataclysmic rapidity so essential to paralyzing the enemy; that he could be fairly certain of reaching Moscow in one stride, with the *possibility* of having peace in his pocket in three months. If we consider all this, and compare these possibilities with the results of a so-called methodical campaign, it seems very likely that Bonaparte's plan held a greater probability of ultimate success than the other, and that his was the correct way—not the *more daring*, but in fact the *more cautious* of the two. In any event, it is clear that a man like Bonaparte would not have hesitated over the choice.

The dangers of the moment always exert the most powerful influence on men, and therefore it often happens that an action seems audacious that in the end proves to be the only road to safety and which is therefore the most prudent course. Mere intelligence is rarely sufficient to allow men to rise to this level of insight; it is for the most part a natural boldness of character that equips an individual to discern such prudent paths. This boldness was so much a part of the great conqueror that he would have chosen the most audacious course from pure inclination, even if his genius had not also shown it to be the wisest.

We repeat, everything that he was he owed to his daring and resolute character; and his most triumphant campaigns would have suffered the same censure as this one had they not succeeded.

SIX

From "Strategic Critique of the Campaign of 1814 in France" (early 1820s)

As its title indicates, this work is not a history of the campaign but rather an analysis of the strategic and operational decisions made by both sides during the allied invasion of France, which ended with Napoleon's abdication.[1] Clausewitz's purpose is to evaluate these decisions and to extract general insights from them. When he speaks of principles, however, he does not mean absolutes, as he himself makes plain. "Grundsätze" to him are not laws or rules, but considerations that generally apply, that should always be taken account of, but that do not invariably hold true. If the work is not history, its analysis must nevertheless rest on the most accurate reconstruction of events possible. For his treatment of Prussian and allied decisions, Clausewitz could draw on an exceptionally well-informed if scarcely impartial source, his close friend Gneisenau, who had served as Blücher's chief of staff in the campaign. Their friendship did not prevent Clausewitz from criticizing some of the Prussian decisions. For information on the French he must have relied on several histories, although he cites only one author, Koch, and does not mention the title of the work. A reference to "Koch, Part II," however, makes it certain that the work in question is General Jean-Baptiste-Frédéric Koch, Mémoires pour servir à l'histoire de la campagne de 1814, 2 vols. (Paris, 1819), a widely used if often criticized account by a participant. That Clausewitz does not refer to A.J.F. Fain's Manuscrit de mil huit cent quatorze, which after its appearance in 1823 became the standard work, may suggest that he wrote before it appeared.

The "Campaign of 1814" is a work of some twenty-nine thousand words, divided into two parts, of which we reprint here the introduction to part I and the opening chapter of part II. In these two sections, as in the work as a whole, Clausewitz scarcely enters into details of battles and engagements. Once the opposing forces confront each other, he believes the outcome is more or less determined by their relative strengths, their situation, purpose, and the attitude of their commanders. The drama of combat, the core of much military history, is raised by Clausewitz to the drama of ideas and emotions. This ten-

---

[1] Clausewitz also wrote a briefer survey of the campaign, "Übersicht des Feldzugs von 1814 in Frankreich," *Werke*, 7: 325–56.

dency to pass over the occurrences in battle reflects a general attitude that is only occasionallly abandoned—for instance, in his account of the battle of Borodino in 1812. Few historians of war have written as little about actual combat as Clausewitz did. What primarily interested him when he explored the history of a campaign, he wrote at the very end of his life, were not tactical events but the strategic intentions of the opposing sides and how they were translated into action.[2] His main concerns in the "Campaign of 1814" are the decisions that lead to combat and result from it. Psychological factors, which incorporate both the troops' morale and their commanders' abilities and points of view, form a crucial element in this analysis, even if he finds it an element difficult to evaluate and quantify.

In the "Campaign of 1814," Clausewitz's neglect of battle is mirrored by a corresponding and more surprising neglect of politics, the relevance of which to all aspects of war he could normally be expected to emphasize. Here Clausewitz is doing less than justice to the political complexity of the campaign, perhaps in order to develop the operational problems as clearly as possible. His preliminary observation that "the actions of the allies are not untouched by diplomatic considerations" may seem an insufficient acknowledgment of the difficulties of a war in which Austria sought a negotiated peace while Prussia aimed for decisive victory and Britain and Russia vacillated between them. Nor does Clausewitz mention the political and dynastic considerations that tied Napoleon to Paris and insured that if he lost the city he would lose the war. In this work, however, Clausewitz is not interested in the exigencies of coalition warfare, a subject on which he has much to say elsewhere, but in testing strategic ideas against historical reality.

The introduction to part I discusses the campaign of 1814 as an exceptionally clear example of Napoleonic warfare and of strategic thought in action. To Clausewitz, the manifold uniqueness of this historical episode reveals the workings of timeless elements. The first chapter of part II, which is followed by chapters discussing the specific phases of the campaign, treats the campaign as a whole—first from the point of view of the invading allies, then from the point of view of Napoleon, fighting for his political survival. The rigorously symmetrical analysis is a bravura piece of historical reconstruction and evenhanded interpretation. The entire work illustrates how Clausewitz thought through the phases and elements of a historical episode and the use he made of history for developing and testing his theories—in this case, theories that concern plans and decisions rather than such more basic elements as the political nature of war or the social and psychological dynamic of organized violence.

---

[2] Peter Paret, "An Unknown Letter by Clausewitz," *Journal of Military History* 55 (1991).

Part I
Plan of the Campaign after the Battle of Leipzig

INTRODUCTION

No campaign exemplifies the processes of strategic thought as clearly as does the campaign of 1814 in France. To begin with, it belongs to a period in which the element of war moves rapidly and freely. Although the actions of the allies are not untouched by diplomatic considerations, which like some foreign matter douse the fire of violence, the whole concept of war and of its purpose is not as thoroughly politicized as was the case in most recent wars before the French Revolution. Both sides are driven by a great purpose and neither is prepared to engage in those temporizing measures with which belligerents in former times used to spin out a campaign in a reasonable and acceptable manner. Second, the campaign of 1814 is characterized by large forces and important results that are concentrated in a brief time span and a very limited geographic area. Third, the offensive and the defensive are sharply delineated. Fourth, inevitable as well as accidental circumstances lead to the repeated division of forces, which favors the use of strategic maneuver. Fifth, operational bases, lines of communication, arming the people are all part of the strategic intentions of one side or the other. Finally, the psychological factors that play such an important role in all wars, but which in the early stages tend to be still unformed and masked, are here very much in evidence. The opposing commanders and armies know each other's character and condition, so these factors can be included in their strategic calculations from the start.

Every campaign plan chooses one path among a thousand. The greater the belligerent states and the forces they mobilize, the greater the number of potential combinations, and—to be candid—it becomes impossible to consider them all. For that reason it is usual to draw up a complete plan, leaving it to judgment and instinct to identify what is appropriate in it and what is erroneous. In many cases any further analysis of the strategic rationale becomes unnecessary. The mere listing of the essential facts will enable common sense—that is, a mind that is not corrupted—to identify at once what is true and right. Such a mind possesses something akin to musical sense: it easily identifies a false argument as though it were dissonant. That is how things work in practice. But here, where we try to illustrate the application of theory by a historical example, we must for once trace the thread of ideas fully and accurately. We must draw up a clear plan, based on our principles, and in a sense invest the plan with that inevitability that pertains to philosophic truth. No one needs to remind us that we find ourselves in a realm that is ill-suited to absolute truth, and we are far from regarding our principles and the results derived from them as absolutes. They differ from the usual arguments in this field only because they originate in a striving for the absolute, and because our conclusions evolve directly from principles, and our principles directly from the phenomena.

This method of analyzing the subject in forms that pertain to the exact sciences is opposed to a way of reasoning that is all too common in military theory. Usually the theorist does not worry about establishing a logical point of departure; he argues backwards and forwards on the basis of whatever point of view he finds particularly agreeable, takes the closest object as the most important, and so sketches a kind of panorama of his subject without beginning or end, in which pro and contra, if and but, whirl and draw their curlicues through the sky. Not what we have argued but the manner in which we have argued may, we believe, benefit theory. Of course, to repeat what we have often said, here as in all practical matters theory has the function to form the practical man and to educate his judgment, rather than to assist him directly in the execution of his tasks.

Part II
Execution of the Opposing Plans, or the Actual Events of the Campaign

CHAPTER 1. GENERAL OBSERVATIONS

On the part of the *offensive*, the campaign is divided into the following six major phases:

1. The advance and meeting of the two allied armies under Schwarzenberg and Blücher, through the battle of La Rothière, to their first separation.
2. Blücher's operations in the Marne valley.
3. The advance of Schwarzenberg's army along the Seine, its retreat to the Aube, to the battle of Bar-sur-Aube.
4. Blücher's march to Schwarzenberg's army, his second separation, his advance on the Aisne, the battle of Laon, up to the renewed advance of the united armies on Paris.
5. The new attack by Schwarzenberg's army, the battle of Bar-sur-Aube, the renewed advance to the Seine until the second withdrawal to the Aube and the battle of Arcis-sur-Aube.
6. The combined advance on Paris and the battle of Paris.

The main phases of the *defense* are:

1. The pretended defense of the rivers in eastern France, retreat and concentration of the various corps until Bonaparte assumes command.
2. Bonaparte's march to the Aube, battle of La Rothière, retreat to Troyes.
3. Bonaparte's march to the Marne, his attacks on Blücher's corps.
4. Defensive operations of the French marshals on the Seine until Bonaparte's arrival.
5. Bonaparte's advance on the Seine, his encounters with separate enemy corps, his renewed march on the Marne and Aisne, the battle of Laon and his attempt on Rheims.
6. Second concentration of the marshals on the Seine.
7. Bonaparte's second march on the Seine, the battle of Arcis.
8. The advance against the flank of Schwarzenberg's army.
9. The operations of Mortier and Marmont on the Marne, and their retreat to Paris.

These various offensive and defensive moves will be traced in separate chapters, but first we want to consider the campaign as a whole.

THE OFFENSIVE

Up to the battles of Brienne or La Rothière, allied operations were simply designed to bring about a major battle. When this is the case, criticism has nothing to contribute. Schwarzenberg and Blücher sought the point of their meeting in the direction that Schwarzenberg had taken; they found it at Brienne. Bonaparte concentrated his forces and advanced on the combined allied army.

Instead of following up the resulting victory with the pursuit and destruction of the enemy's main force, Blücher left Schwarzenberg and moved to the Marne valley. To do the former would have been natural and simple and therefore correct. The cause of the separation must be sought in Schwarzenberg's ponderous and indecisive leadership. The extent to which this was the result of Prince Schwarzenberg's personality cannot concern us here[3]— enough that Blücher and his advisors felt or thought they knew that nothing would be achieved as long as they stayed with the main army and that they

---

[3] Clausewitz does not feel it necessary to spell out his implication: that Schwarzenberg's indecisiveness reflected not only his personality, but also political conditions. Austria did not favor Napoleon's destruction in the field. Almost to the end, Metternich looked for a negotiated settlement of a kind that might have been made more difficult by a major battle, even a decisive victory.

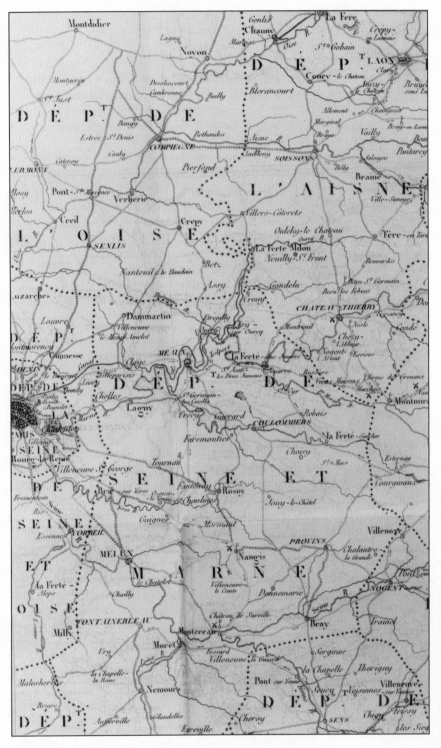

MAP 5. The Campaign of 1814 in France. Theater of operations (eastern France). Reproduced from A.J.F. Fain, *Manuscrit de mil huit cent quatorze* (Paris, 1823).

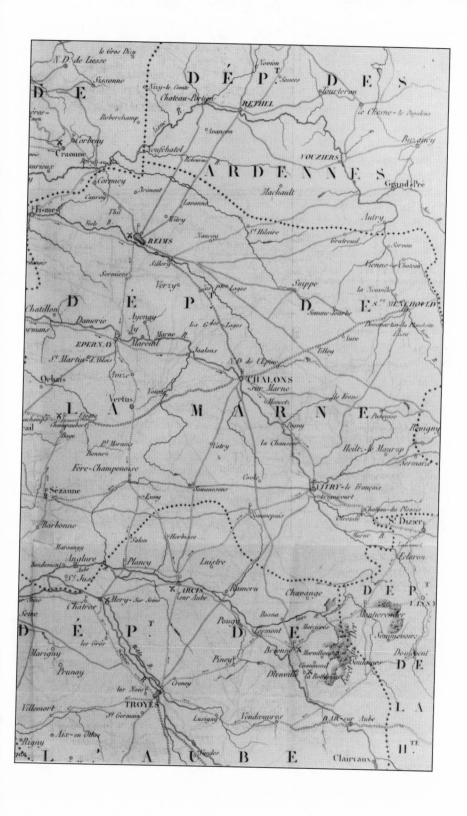

wanted to be independent in their own theater of operations. The forces of the four corps (Sacken, Langeron, Kleist, and Yorck) that Blücher could assemble on the Marne might amount to about 50,000 men. Since Bonaparte seemed to have no more than 70,000 in place and would have to detach some troops to observe the main allied army, Blücher did not believe he risked being crushed by a superior force. With his will, courage, and enterprising nature he intended to remain on the offensive as far as he could: a few victories would sweep the main army forward.

Three weeks later similar reasons led Blücher to quit the main army once more. All eyewitnesses agree that this benefited the common cause; in certain cases such subjective reasons may therefore overcome objective considerations. But even subjectively, Blücher's first departure seems not to have been motivated as strongly as was the second. It is true that the main army moved forward very slowly, had spread out its forces in an excess of caution, and may well have felt a certain dread at the thought of a direct march on Paris. Nevertheless, it had continued to advance, the victory at La Rothière must have somewhat raised its spirit and determination, and it could be expected that in the end Blücher's energy would carry it forward and thus bring about the most salutary results. Therefore we cannot refrain from describing Blücher's departure as premature and consequently in error. The catastrophe that overtook him on the Marne certainly did not follow inevitably, but still it was a natural consequence of his leaving Schwarzenberg. The main reason why we regard any unmotivated separation as an error is that we can never know with certainty whether the opponent will also divide his forces or divide them to the same extent, which obviously was not done here. Bonaparte left only 25,000 men under Victor and Oudinot against Schwarzenberg's 120,000 and moved with some 40,000 against Blücher, who, if he concentrated his entire command, would have no more than about 50,000. Under these conditions it is at least not improbable that Blücher would be beaten even if he had all his units together. Victory might have been doubtful, but casualties would have been less if the allies had remained together, and with their great superiority in numbers they surely could have created an entirely different situation than could the risky battle that Blücher accepted.

But his defeat was not the only injury that flowed from Blücher's march to the Marne. How much time was lost by this digression from the straightforward advance on Paris, what energies were expended unnecessarily by marching back and forth through hostile areas, and finally how far was Schwarzenberg's indecisiveness fostered by the uncertainty that always accompanies a separation of forces! Several days passed before it was realized in the main army that Bonaparte had moved off; then it was not certain how many troops he had taken with him; several days before he returned, people feared that he had already come back. All these uncertainties, and then the other: had Blücher perhaps suffered a total defeat, which would of course profoundly deepen the indecisiveness of the supreme command? And that is what happened. A division of forces was permissible only if one was determined to make up any defeat Blücher suffered by defeating Victor and Oudinot and by trusting on one's superiority to march on Paris, whatever might take place elsewhere. But how far removed from such determination was the supreme command if it could not even bring itself to pursue the beaten enemy with its united might at La Rothière?

Bonaparte had correctly figured that he would be back at the Seine before his marshals reached Paris. Since they had enough space to evade the allies and besides were helped by the important geographic barrier of the Seine, the numerical superiority of the main army posed less of a threat: even with the greatest superiority it demands a good deal of ability and enterprise to strike significant blows if the opponent has the scope and intention to evade your advance.

The next major move after Blücher and Schwarzenberg had separated is their reunification. Both have lost a battle, both feel the need to join together because then they have the strength to defend themselves. This demonstrates that one is never stronger than when all forces are combined.[4] Hardly has Blücher returned than the anxious supreme command wants to persuade him to retreat further to Chaumont, Langres, to the Rhine. Instead Blücher's sense of independence causes him to quit the main army for the second time. He might combine with 50,000 men under St. Priest, Winzingerode, and Bülow and move with a force of 100,000 to the Marne or the Aisne. Schwarzenberg's retreat is already under way. To bring it to a halt at once is out of the question. Under these circumstances nothing is more deserving of praise than the decision to leave again. The general retreat is inoculated with a new, if weak, dose of the offensive, and the effect is immediate. Bonaparte reacts to Blücher's move. His arm, which is ready to strike, pulls back and prepares to parry. Thereupon the main army does come to a halt. It is true that the king of Prussia contributed to the decision to end the retreat, but that is no reason to think that the halt was not ultimately caused by Blücher's action. Even if Schwarzenberg's retreat had continued for another few days, Macdonald and Oudinot on their own would never have induced him to return all the way to the Rhine.

At this second separation the difference between the opposing strengths had lessened. Bonaparte left some 30,000 men on the Seine, so that he retained only 40,000. Schwarzenberg had formed a new southern army, which

---

[4] A comment directed at the still popular concept that it was good policy to divide one's forces to cover as many "key points" as possible.

left him with no more than 80,000 to 90,000 men. But Blücher now opposed Bonaparte's 40,000 with 100,000 men.

The new separation had the very natural consequence that Blücher was forced to fight Bonaparte on his own. But the new ratio of forces deprived Bonaparte of any possibility of victory. Thus this second division of the allied armies, which was essential for psychological reasons, also held out fewer disadvantages with regard to their physical strengths than had the first. The new ratio of power rendered any anxiety pointless.

Let us return once more to the time when Schwarzenberg began to withdraw. When his corps are defeated on the Seine, he learns of the forces the French have assembled at Lyon, he orders Blücher to rejoin him, but at the same time decides to form an army of 40,000 on the Rhône, to which he must contribute some 20,000 men, and also decides to retreat to Langres to protect his flank. This move would have carried him back to the Rhine.

Here two false ideas support each other.

Because Schwarzenberg believes himself too weak to master Bonaparte, he feels he must concern himself about the security of his left flank and his base of operations; and because he is excessively concerned about their security and weakens himself, he feels still less of a match for the emperor.

With 150,000 men, the combined strength of Schwarzenberg and Blücher, it surely would have been possible to crush 60,000, that is, to defeat them in a major battle and drive them back beyond Paris. This done, any victories on the Rhône would be immaterial.

But the greatest error was that in the decision to retreat, the 50,000 men who could have been assembled on the Marne were ignored. To face Bonaparte as long as possible with united forces and, if he sought a major battle one wanted to avoid, to evade in the direction of Vitry and Chalon and join up with Winzingerode, St. Priest, and Bülow—surely this would have been a simple, practical idea.

After Blücher and Schwarzenberg separated, the general situation had not changed, but the offensive element of the allied army (Blücher) had torn loose from the main force, gained new energy and dash, and thus the inert mass was pulled forward again. Though with redoubled caution, Schwarzenberg again marched to the Seine and advanced along it. As soon as he suspected Bonaparte's return, he concentrated his forces for the battle of Arcis on March 20. He could have done exactly the same four weeks earlier, when Blücher was still with him. At that time his strength would have been greater by 50,000 to 60,000 men, and Bonaparte perhaps only by 10,000 to 20,000.

Now what might have caused Schwarzenberg's entirely different decision in March? His new southern army had reached Lyon and probably already recognized its superiority over whatever opposition it might encounter, but the decisive engagement did not take place until March 19, and on the 20th the main army could not yet have known the outcome. The battle of Laon had pretty well revealed Bonaparte's weakness; still, he had managed to get away in fairly good shape. Both of these events certainly somewhat changed Schwarzenberg's outlook, but the strongest reason for giving battle may have been—as so often in the clash of psychological motives [*innern Bewegungsgründen*]—a tiny spring: the disagreeable sense of always having retreated before Bonaparte without so much as one attempt at resistance.

Bonaparte breaks off the battle of Arcis and decides to try his luck with a strategic threat against the opponent's flank and rear. The most natural response to this maneuver was an advance by the united allies; this occurred and was the best move of the whole campaign.

THE DEFENSIVE

It was Bonaparte's intention to unite his forces on the Marne—we have already discussed this plan. As soon as he sees the allied army concentrating on the Aube, he turns against it, a perfectly natural response. He believes the allies to be still dispersed, in which he is correct, and therefore attacks Blücher on January 29 at Brienne. On the 30th and 31st he waits for Marmont and intends to fight a decisive battle.

The question arises whether this was sensible. Bonaparte still had the possibility of withdrawing all the way to Paris, he could take up two defensive positions behind the Seine—once at Troyes, the second time between Nogent and Montereau—he could therefore figure on gaining at least fourteen days if the allies were to continue their advance with determination. In those two weeks he might still have been reinforced by 15–20,000 newly organized troops; he could have ordered Mortier and Macdonald to join him, which would have meant a further reinforcement of 20,000 men. In short, rather than fight at La Rothière with 50,000 men, he could have fought before Paris with 90,000, and it may be assumed by then that the allies would have suffered significant losses. To be sure, if he lost the battle before Paris he would also lose the city, as in fact happened. But it is obvious that it was the fault of the allies that their victory at La Rothière did not carry them to Paris, and one may argue that if they did not reach the capital in consequence of their victory at La Rothière, they would have been even less likely to do so without this victory. In other words, considering the circumstances, the allies would not have pushed Bonaparte back to Paris; on the contrary, their indecisiveness would soon have brought them to a halt and would have taken Blücher to the Marne.

The only argument that can be raised against this line of reasoning is that their victory at La Rothière made the allies reckless, and that it was their recklessness that caused them to divide their forces. Perhaps this is really what happened, but it would be an excessively risky detour to success for a defender to expose himself to defeat merely in the hope that victory would cause his opponent to take chances and act foolishly.

Bonaparte sacrificed his possible advantages in order to exploit the fresh courage and heightened spirit which fortifies any army—especially one as proud and vain as the French—when it moves in unison against an advancing enemy. Nor did he want to risk his reputation in Paris by a two-week-long retreat. And for someone of his personality and character, it was always more natural to confront danger boldly than to avoid it cautiously, to oppose a threat with passion and energy rather than with prudence and cunning.

After the defeat at La Rothière led to a division of the allied forces, instead of having the bad effects that might have been expected—the total dispersion of the French—it was the most natural thought for Bonaparte to attack one part with his combined might.

Bonaparte could hardly have recognized or guessed the subjective causes of the separation of the allies after the battle of La Rothière. Even the moves of Yorck, Kleist, Kapzewitsch, and Winzingerode toward the Marne, which made it the natural area of concentration for Blücher's army, would have been difficult for him to evaluate because presumably he had no exact information on the marches of most of these corps. Bonaparte could explain the division of the allies after the battle only as a sign of confidence: they assumed the campaign had already been won and now tried to reach Paris more quickly by a wide envelopment, either to take the city by surprise or at least to carry the war into its vicinity unopposed.

So for Bonaparte it was not a question of attacking with superior force an enemy who had split up because he lacked decisive and united leadership. Rather, he believed he was putting a spoke in the allies' wheel of victory. He was countering the advantages that his opponents wanted to draw from their victory and exploiting mistakes they were apparently committing out of bravado and recklessness.

Based on this view of his opponents, Bonaparte's decision undoubtedly deserves greater praise than it would if he had believed them to be confused and disunited. Certainly few commanders would have acted as he did; the great majority would at once have rushed to Paris.

Bonaparte did not consider himself as severely defeated as his opponents appeared to believe, and he wanted to exploit their mistaken assumption and the division of forces that resulted from it by attacking one of their armies with relative superiority. The only question was: Should he attack Schwarzenberg or Blücher? It would have been simpler to strike at Schwarzenberg because no additional marches would have been necessary: Schwarzenberg's army, divided into several corps, faced him across the Seine. He might have done at once what in the end he felt compelled to do. Nevertheless, Bonaparte appears to have been right in deciding to turn first against Blücher. Unlike Schwarzenberg, Blücher would not have allowed himself to be immobilized by a small force while the main French army struck a blow elsewhere. Consequently, he had to be attacked and crippled if Paris was not to be endangered. In any case, as the more enterprising leader he should be given priority, and because he was much weaker than Schwarzenberg success seemed more likely. Finally, a rapid move after Blücher, the sudden appearance on the Marne when it was believed that Bonaparte was still stunned by his defeat, would be a surprise akin to a sudden raid—and as it turned out his move had that effect. Here then is a case where the simplest action was not the best. Bonaparte's maneuver on the Marne is the best thing he did in the entire campaign.

After he had defeated Blücher's corps, should he have returned to the Seine or should he have pursued Blücher? This is the kind of question that often arises in war. In general, it is quickest and most effective to exploit an advantage at the point where it was gained: no time is lost on marches and the iron is struck while hot. But one must always consider whether elsewhere more can be lost than may be gained here. The answer to this question depends on the relation of the defeated part to the whole, both in the physical and in the psychological sense. In the present case, if we consider only the factor of numerical strength, it would be foolish to believe that by further pursuing Blücher Bonaparte could have induced Schwarzenberg to retreat. Schwarzenberg's 120,000 men could surely have defeated the 25,000 men of the French covering force. But if we include the psychological relationship in our analysis, if we consider that Blücher was the enterprising element in the allied army, that Schwarzenberg's exaggerated caution was clearly revealed in his timid advance, that the French forces on the Rhône caused him to fear for his left flank, and that a retreat across the Meuse by Blücher would have convinced him that his right flank was lost, then it appears certain that to continue the pursuit of Blücher would have benefited Bonaparte more than turning against Schwarzenberg. It might easily have led to the total dispersion of Blücher's army, and a retreat to the Meuse, Mosel, and Saar. The continued exploitation of his victory over Blücher, whatever Schwarzenberg might do, would have been in the same spirit as Bonaparte's original attack. However, all of these considerations are based on psychological and moral factors, which in war cannot be known with certainty, and therefore we should not regard Bonaparte's contrary decision as a true error.

When Blücher left Schwarzenberg for the second time, Bonaparte followed him at once. Again he might have turned more quickly against Schwarzenberg, and his reasons for not doing this might have been similar to the ones he followed the first time; but if we look closely, the circumstances were no longer the same. Now Blücher could assemble an army of 100,000 men at the Marne or the Aisne. This concentration would not be prevented merely by following him; and it was inconceivable for 40,000 men to achieve a decisive advantage over 100,000. On the other hand, Schwarzenberg was not in the process of advancing as he was the first time, but was retreating. His army, reduced by the detachment of the prince of Hesse-Homburg to Lyon to some 80–90,000 men, was discouraged and downcast. Continued pressure would undoubtedly have driven it to the Swiss frontier. Bar-sur-Aube is approximately halfway between Basel and Paris; Schwarzenberg's army would have reached Basel before Blücher could have combined with Bülow and marched on Paris, if, indeed, Blücher could seriously have considered such a move in these circumstances. Courier after courier would have been sent to recall him, so that he might protect the Rhine and form the pivot for a grand strategic swing through Switzerland. The battle of Dresden and its consequences would have been imprinted on the mind of every strategist.[5]

Instead of this almost certain success, based on the anxiety of the allied high command, of which he was aware, Bonaparte sought a battle at Laon that he could not win and had to count himself fortunate that he was not totally destroyed. After this failure, having done nothing to protect Paris, he again, as we have seen, moves against Schwarzenberg's army, which he confronts at Arcis. This move was a mistake, as everything is that is done without a definite plan, and it was a particularly bad mistake in view of the seriousness of the situation, from which only the most stringent economy of time and strength might have saved him.

That the battle of Laon was a defeat and could not be won shows that Bonaparte's strength no longer sufficed for the kind of defense waged by offensive means that he had practiced so far. A battle with all his forces in a defensive position before Paris was his last remaining option east of the capital. By concentrating all his corps he might still deploy 70–100,000 men. It is true that the allies were advancing with 150–160,000 men, and in our opinion this number can hardly be defeated by 70,000. But since in the end 30,000 men under the marshals dared to fight before Paris, 70,000 men under Bonaparte should have had even less hesitation to attempt this last possibility. Instead of resorting to this natural measure, Bonaparte invents an advance in the rear of the allies that can only be described as vain bluster. By itself following the opponent's advance means little, because it takes considerable time before such a measure becomes effective and therefore is not suited to times of immediate need. Besides, only a force with far better lines

---

[5] The battle of Dresden (August 26–27, 1813) was Napoleon's last great victory, in which an inferior French force badly defeated a poorly integrated allied army under Schwarzenberg.

of communication than its opponent can advantageously follow his advance, and that was far from being Bonaparte's situation. He was primarily based on Paris, while his opponents' base was the Rhine and all of Switzerland. Finally, such a move demands a clear numerical superiority because it always uses up a good deal of strength, and because a defeat with fronts reversed is extremely dangerous. Bonaparte regarded it as a last attempt to impose himself through a most unusual step. But a maneuver with nothing in its favor except being unusual is like a phantom in the corporeal world. This march into the blue is undoubtedly Bonaparte's worst move in the war, and its effects bear this out. The united allies marched on Paris, and Bonaparte revealed the absurdity of his flanking move by immediately following them, marching day and night, and still arriving there twenty-four hours too late.

Political Writings

History was the foundation on which Clausewitz based his political ideas. In this he was not exceptional. For a variety of reasons, Germans of his generation were inclined to think and write about politics in historical terms. At the most superficial level, the past provided a reservoir of facts that could be used to support theoretical arguments. More significantly, the constitutional traditions of the Holy Roman Empire, like the English common law, were rooted in precedent and historical experience. The diversity and particularity of the past had been an important weapon in the arsenal of those who had sought to defend local customs and autonomy against encroachment by the centralized state. With the triumph of the latter, this mode of argument had gradually been adopted by its supporters. Apologists for absolutism liked to present it as the triumph of reason over disorder, and therefore as a natural and inevitable historical development—a conceptual leap that Clausewitz himself, although a defender of the modern state, would reject. Furthermore, the fact of historical change was congenial to the idea of reform, whose immediate necessity may have arisen suddenly and unexpectedly but whose moral justification depended in part on a new understanding of the past, an understanding entirely at odds with the fixed idea of "tradition." Finally, these intellectual and rhetorical habits were generally agreeable to Germany's rulers, who were more inclined to tolerate political discussion when the immediate frame of reference was the past rather than the future.

All of these impulses were strengthened by the French Revolution, which seemed to confirm both the possibility of cataclysmic change and the dangers of political rationalism. All are evident in varying degrees in Clausewitz's political writings. Had they appeared when they were written, they would probably not have struck contemporaries as unusual in form.[1] Nevertheless, Clausewitz regularly drew attention to his reliance on historical arguments, which he associated with common sense, impartiality, and realism, in contrast to the abstraction, self-interest, and unrealism of those he opposed. And, while the contrast may have been overstated, he was not wrong to make it.

---

[1] With the exception of a brief letter on the Polish uprising of 1830–31 (p. 371, below), none of Clausewitz's political writings were published during his lifetime. Most were intended for limited circulation or simply to clarify his ideas. Some remained fragments. Two, "Our Military Institutions" (1819) and "On the Basic Question of Germany's Existence" (1831), were rejected by the periodicals to which they were sent, evidently for political reasons. The circumstances surrounding the composition and publication of each piece are described in the introductions that precede them.

Clausewitz felt the weight of the past in two seemingly contradictory ways: as a source of constraint, and also of instability. On the one hand, historical experience limited the range of possibilities available to modern society and thwarted the plans of those who imagined the Revolution had proven that men could freely transform their political surroundings. On the other hand— and it is here, above all, that Clausewitz found himself at odds with the conventional wisdom of the Restoration—existing political forms could never be other than transitory expressions of profound social, economic, and cultural forces. Institutions were therefore to be judged by their capacity to express the balance of existing social forces accurately, to manage change, and to adapt and change themselves. Clausewitz's sensitivity to the static and dynamic elements of the past was combined with a keen eye for the play of chance and personality, which is also evident in his historical and theoretical work. The result is a body of political writings of considerable complexity, in which Clausewitz's natural skepticism, awareness of the past, and respect for action and commitment contend on more or less equal terms.

It is in his treatment of political actors that Clausewitz's skill in balancing continuity and contingency, character and circumstance, is most striking. Clausewitz judged individuals by the same standard he applied to institutions: personal success depended on penetrating the logic of the age, harmonizing one's effort with it, grasping its real possibilities; failure resulted from shortsightedness or excessive devotion to abstract principles divorced from experience. Nowhere are these values more evident than in his retrospective accounts of the reform era, the *Observations on Prussia* and the essay on Scharnhorst, included in part I among his historical works. Had either been published during Clausewitz's lifetime, however, their political implications, rather than their qualities as scholarship, would have made the most immediate and forceful impression on their readers.

It is not simply that Clausewitz sometimes judged respected figures harshly. He also cast an unaccustomed light on politics as such. In an age when most biographers confined themselves to recounting their heroes' public conduct, for instance, Clausewitz's emphasis on Scharnhorst's "character" was unconventional. That creative individuals may exist at odds with their societies was already a familiar idea as applied to artists and men of letters. To see it applied with equal force to soldiers and statesmen was at least unusual, the more so since Clausewitz portrayed this sort of tension as running through the whole effort of reform. In other contexts, particularly when writing about international relations, Clausewitz tended to treat states as organic entities, acting out of a sense of self-interest that could almost be taken for granted. His essays on the reform era, in contrast, illuminate the way that interest was formulated in practice, a process that cannot be understood if the unity of the state is allowed to obscure the multiplicity of competing interests that it embraces.

In Clausewitz's view, the Prussian reforms were an inspired response to the challenges of the age rather than an inevitable or even probable expression of deep historical forces. They grew out of a political struggle that could have ended differently: Scharnhorst might have been defeated by the opposition of more pedestrian colleagues. If he was not, it was less because of the inherent excellence of his ideas than because those ideas were grounded in history and experience, and because he possessed the ingenuity to overcome the apprehension of others. Scharnhorst's mind, in Clausewitz's presentation, never strayed far from real events, which he would painstakingly compare to similar events in the past. In this way he determined what, in any situation, was ephemeral and what was fundamental and enduring. He was also able to persuade less gifted men to follow him, by portraying his ideas simply as intelligent modifications of past practices. His intellectual distinction and political success thus flowed from a common method. Scharnhorst's knowledge of the past honed his political instincts and gave him a sense of what was possible; it provided him with the means to manipulate the "imperceptible levers" of public life in order to lift his fellow men off the "sandbar of prejudice";[2] and it insured that his ideas and conduct always displayed that "naturalness" that Clausewitz prized above all.

For the most part, however, Clausewitz found these virtues sorely lacking in the politicians of his day. Despite his almost unreserved praise for the reformers' accomplishments, his view of politics is generally pessimistic. All too often the fate of nations would be in the hands of small-minded men like those who, after 1806, could conjure up no better response to Prussia's defeat than a sheepish admiration for the victor. The forces of chance and friction weigh as heavily in the council chamber as on the field of battle. For this reason, politics could no more be a science than war could be.

This realization did not prevent Clausewitz from harboring political ambitions of his own, any more than the unpredictable nature of war prevented him from becoming a soldier. His interest in politics dates from his earliest maturity. His surviving papers leave no doubt that, at a time when his professional energies were being consumed by the tactical exercises appropriate to a twenty-three-year-old lieutenant of infantry, his mind was already turning to the life and death of states.[3] A few years later, as Scharnhorst's assistant at the War Department, Clausewitz had a share in the success of reform in Prussia, and in the immediate aftermath of Napoleon's defeat he was given several diplomatic assignments. As prospects for advancement in the peace-

---

[2] "On the Life and Character of Scharnhorst," above.
[3] Notes on History and Politics (1803–1807), below.

time army began to fade, he hoped to exchange his military career for an ambassadorial appointment. This effort, however, was finally frustrated by doubts about his political views: some highly placed figures feared that Clausewitz was a secret Jacobin, a man who could not be trusted with the highest interests of the state. In the end he was unable to match the achievements of his mentor, Scharnhorst. But he was nevertheless a member of Prussia's political elite, and a figure of some significance in the life of the state. The successes and disappointments of Clausewitz's career thus provide one possible context in which to evaluate his ideas.

Hans Rothfels was the first to examine the question systematically, in a monograph entitled *Carl von Clausewitz: Politik und Krieg,* and in the introduction and notes to an important edition of Clausewitz's writings, *Politische Schriften und Briefe.* For Rothfels, Clausewitz was above all a Prussian patriot, whose values found their most emphatic expression during the crisis that confronted Prussia at the start of 1812. After being allowed a precarious neutrality under the Peace of Tilsit five years before, Prussia was finally forced to join France in its impending crusade against Russia. Rather than acquiesce in an alliance he regarded as shameful, Clausewitz abandoned Prussia and, in common with several dozen of his fellow officers, sought service with the czar. He also sought to justify his action. The resulting "Political Declaration," addressed to Frederick William III, combined a rigorous insistence on the preeminence of the national interest, even over the king himself, with an emotional fervor comparable to any of the patriotic outpourings subsequently inspired by the Wars of Liberation.

These events mark the middle, rather than the end, of Clausewitz's career; even in 1815 his exaggerated devotion to Prussia had moderated a good deal and would continue to do so, as Rothfels was of course aware.[4] Nevertheless, Rothfels emphasized the first part of Clausewitz's life at the expense of his later development, which seemed to Rothfels to be marked by feelings of disappointment and depression that partly derived from Prussia's failure to fulfill the demanding mission Clausewitz had once attributed to it.

Peter Paret expanded on Rothfels' interpretation without entirely rejecting it, first in his monograph *Clausewitz and the State,* which contains the fullest discussion of Clausewitz's political writings in the literature, and subsequently in three articles devoted to Clausewitz's political career and ideas.[5]

---

[4] *Politik und Krieg* concludes in 1815. Rothfels discussed Clausewitz's later work primarily in his notes to *Politische Schriften und Briefe,* which do not offer the kind of connected analysis presented in his earlier book; nor do they seriously qualify his emphasis on Clausewitz's early career and experiences.

[5] Paret, *Clausewitz and the State,* 286–306, 343–50; "Bemerkungen zu dem Versuch von Clausewitz, zum Gesandten in London ernannt zu werden," *Jahrbuch für die Geschichte Mittel- und Ostdeutschlands* 26 (1977): 161–72; "Die politischen Ansichten von Clausewitz," *Freiheit*

For Paret, Clausewitz was less a frustrated patriot than a disillusioned reformer, whose youthful idealization of the Prussian state gave way to a more dispassionate, realistic view of its strengths, interests, and weaknesses. If Rothfels found the center of gravity of Clausewitz's politics in the first half of his career, Paret found it in the second half, particularly in the essays and memoranda in which Clausewitz defended the achievements of the Prussian reformers against conservative criticism. In them he expressed ideas about social equity and governmental responsibility that approached the limits of acceptability in his day, and helped to explain, if not to justify, the suspicions of Jacobinism that fell on him. In personal terms, moreover, the result is seen to be not depression and disappointment, but emotional detachment and intellectual independence, without which Clausewitz's later achievements in the areas of history and theory would have been impossible.

One aspect of this interpretation was challenged in turn by C.B.A. Behrens in an important review of Paret's book entitled "Which Side Was Clausewitz On?"[6] While Paret regarded contemporary perceptions of Clausewitz's liberalism or even radicalism as significant evidence about his position, Behrens discounted those perceptions as parochial and backward-looking. She sought instead to evaluate Clausewitz's ideas in light of a broader tradition of European liberalism to which, she thought, they did not measure up. His inconsistent support of parliamentary government, his ambiguous and occasionally hostile attitude toward the constitutional movement of his time, the hardness of his response to Polish demands for self-determination in 1830, above all his unqualified acceptance of the power of the state—these to Behrens suggested a man who, had he been spared an early death in 1831, would have drifted ever more firmly into alliance with the forces of reaction. The year 1848, she concluded, would have found Clausewitz on the side of those who crushed the revolution and steered Germany down the path of illiberalism.

In politics the question of where someone stands is usually the first to come to mind. The answer, however, should depend heavily on circumstances. As Paret observed in a response to Behrens in the foreword to the revised edition of his book, views that might make someone a moderate or even a conservative in the House of Commons could easily inspire charges of Jacobinism in Prussia.[7] These kinds of intellectual distances are worth keeping in mind: it is difficult to think of any significant political figure of the 1820s in Germany or elsewhere who, had he somehow been transported to the year 1848,

---

ohne Krieg?, ed. Ulrich de Maizière (Bonn, 1980), 333–48; and "Gleichgewicht als Mittel der Friedenssicherung bei Clausewitz und in der Geschichte der Neuzeit," *Wehrwissenschaftliche Rundschau* 29 (1980): 83–86.

[6] *New York Review of Books*, October 14, 1976, 41–44.

[7] Paret, *Clausewitz and the State*, ix–x.

would have been considered a liberal in that setting. In politics, Clausewitz wrote for his own place and time not simply by default, but as a matter of conviction. If he saw those times differently than others did, he did not transcend them, and did not wish to. In politics, he was the opposite of a visionary.

The form of the question is also important. The metaphoric spectrum of "left" and "right" on which the idea of choosing sides depends was only just gaining currency in Germany at the time of Clausewitz's death. It takes for granted an ideological structure that did not exist, and for that reason it may not be the most direct route to understanding Clausewitz's position. Politics as he experienced it was a highly disorganized business, in which personal relationships and pragmatic loyalties predominated, and in which other, more ideologically coherent forms of organization were not just absent but positively despised, even by those who in other respects were critics of the status quo. Political writers of Clausewitz's generation could not and did not feel a need to choose a side with the consistency that would be expected of their successors twenty years later. Neither, however, did they feel themselves entirely adrift. Clausewitz's politics made sense to him and to his opponents, who, whatever else they may have thought of him, never accused him of incoherence.

To the extent that German political writing in Clausewitz's day acknowledged a single orienting principle, it had less to do with the political formulas the Revolution inspired—"left" and "right," after all, are part of its rhetorical legacy—than with the fact of the Revolution itself. Clausewitz, in common with many of his contemporaries, offered no clear answer to the question whether the Revolution was a good thing or not. He never expressed the slightest doubt, however, that the Revolution was not an accident.

Clausewitz attributed the Revolution to the intersection of two basic causes: a centuries-long decline in the role and condition of the French nobility, whose standing vis-à-vis the middle class and the peasantry had ceased to correspond to its contribution to the life of the state; and administrative abuses by the French monarchy, in which the nobility was implicated to the extent that the abuses were a prop to its privileges. The latter, the spark igniting the explosion, were largely a matter of chance; similar abuses had not occurred in Germany because its princes had been unusually firm, thrifty, and prudent. The social transformation from which the Revolution derived its fundamental power, however, was neither accidental nor unique to France. It continued to operate at varying rates throughout Europe, and one way or another it would play its part in shaping the future.

This transformation constituted an important argument for greater civil and social equality. Although Clausewitz was not one to imagine that the true and the good always coincided, he often attributes a kind of moral authority to deep-seated historical processes. This tendency of his thought may have been reinforced by the methods of German idealism and historicism, to which Clausewitz was indebted in many ways. But it probably derived first of all from the instinctive realism with which he approached every problem: since social productivity and personal potential were in fact becoming more equal than they had been in the past, rights and opportunities should be more equal too.

The glacial shifting of the social balance that Clausewitz believed had helped cause the French Revolution also demonstrated to him that the basic assumptions of contemporary conservatives were false. If the Revolution had been a transient catastrophe, now defeated and relegated to the past, it was at least conceivable that the extraordinary means required to master it—the reorganization of the Prussian army and administration, the abolition of serfdom, the resort to universal service, and so forth—could safely be rolled back. But since the underlying cause persisted, the political will and spirit of innovation necessary to meet it would have to persist, too.

It is in the international arena that Clausewitz's political ideas begin and end. Whatever one might make of the Revolution as an expression of political ideals, there was no denying that it marked the revival, after a hiatus of eighty years, of French ambitions in Europe. Clausewitz's earliest notebook entries are directed toward this issue, and it is never far from his mind thereafter. He believed the balance of power in Europe had acquired its present form in response to the growth of French power, and its preservation is the closest thing to an absolute political value one can find in his work.[8] That he should have felt this way is attributable in part to his personal position: it was his own society that would have been most at risk if the French bid for hegemony had prospered. It also reflects his understanding of the historical and psychological forces that had produced the modern world.

Clausewitz never wrote about men in a "state of nature" and considered the attempt to derive political principles from such speculative notions misguided. But he shared the general Enlightenment view that, to the degree that politics was rooted in human character, the natural individualism of mankind should favor the decentralization of power—a tendency toward republicanism that he regarded at least for a time as particularly pronounced among the Germans.[9] Alongside this, however, were equally natural human desires for security, community, and power itself. Clausewitz may have been too sanguine in his assumption that all polities must seek to increase their power and influence; but the historical record appeared to him to bear this

[8] Clausewitz's conception of the balance of power is analyzed in more detail in Paret, "Gleichgewicht."

[9] "The Germans and the French," below.

out.[10] Whether this sort of conduct would persist forever was impossible to say. For the moment, however, conflict seemed inherent in the idea of sovereignty itself. That being so, the existing international system expressed a balance among competing values—security and autonomy, authority and diversity—that was reasonable enough to command allegiance when compared to the available alternatives: anarchy, or the domination of a single state over all the others.

Clausewitz's view of that system in operation was untainted by ideology. Although a life-long opponent of French expansionism, he accepted France's right to pursue its interests to the fullest extent, and he regarded war as a normal instrument of international relations: it is finally by war or the threat of war that equilibrium is maintained. In theory the demands of the system were universal and unremitting. In practice, however, they weighed most heavily on states like Prussia, which could preserve their independence only by husbanding their resources with the utmost efficiency. There were no moral grounds on which to regret that the interests of small or weak states would sometimes be sacrificed to preserve the balance of power. Yet it was obviously of paramount importance not to become one of those states.

When the French Revolution began, most outside observers believed it would weaken France.[11] The effort to reverse the growth of absolutism that seemed to be getting underway there in 1789 was precisely the kind of thing continental statesmen had learned to associate with passivity and decline. That it should have had the opposite effect was surprising at first, perhaps unreasonably so, since the idea that the people constituted an enormous source of raw energy was commonplace in itself. Still, the Old Regime—with its inelastic economy, its rigid and expensive military institutions, its intricate hierarchies—offered no means for government to exploit those reserves. The Revolution had. Indeed, so far as Clausewitz could see, the political passions of the French people had found a real focus only after they were harnessed to the perennial ambitions of the French state. That state in turn had derived unprecedented strength from a movement that had, to all appearances, been bent on its destruction. To lose sight of this seemingly paradoxical but, as Clausewitz would come to regard it, entirely natural dialectic was to court disaster.

The amoral reality of international power defined the domestic political possibilities open to Germany or any other society. It also demanded that those possibilities be investigated as disinterestedly as possible. Clausewitz's

---

[10] Notes on History and Politics (1803–1807)," p. 249, below.

[11] T.C.W. Blanning, *The Origins of the French Revolutionary Wars* (London and New York, 1986), makes a convincing case that this misapprehension, which was matched by an equally misplaced French belief in the inherent decadence of Europe's monarchies, contributed to the outbreak of war in 1792.

sympathies were accordingly confined to ideas or institutions that took the facts of international life fully into account; but they were not otherwise limited by social or historical preconceptions. His insistence on what would one day be called "the primacy of foreign policy" set him at odds with those who believed constitutional government was a political goal surpassing all others. It also made his point of view anathema to those who considered the preservation of the social hierarchy an objective rivaling the safety of the state.

As a member of the reform party after 1806, Clausewitz had worked to dismantle what he regarded as an obsolete system and to create political institutions more responsive to the truly productive elements of Prussian society. In this sense social considerations loom large in his politics. Yet he could discern no inherent connection between the way a state treated its people and the way it conducted itself in relation to other states. In contrast to those, like Immanuel Kant, for whom republicanism, progress, and peace went hand in hand,[12] Clausewitz did not believe the spread of constitutional government would necessarily contribute to the felicity of Europe. This was not a reason to oppose it. In the pacific circumstances that prevailed after 1815, for instance, Clausewitz regarded constitutional government, including a representative assembly of modest dimensions, as feasible and salutary for Prussia.[13] A few years later, however, he professed not to care about the institutional structure of the state, provided it operated according to rational principles of efficiency and accountability.[14] There are no textual or biographical grounds for preferring one of these statements over the other, particularly since, from Clausewitz's perspective, they presented no fundamental inconsistency: political decisions should always be based on concrete conditions, never on theoretical preconceptions.

That they reflect a certain ambivalence about the political potential of the average citizen, however, is fairly clear. Clausewitz's doubts about representative government stemmed from two general sources. In his earliest writings, before there was any serious prospect of elective bodies gaining real importance in Germany, Clausewitz saw parliaments as desirable luxuries. Because of their size and location, countries like France or Great Britain could tolerate the inherent inefficiency of parliamentary decision-making better than smaller states in the middle of Europe.[15] As the constitutional movement in

[12] Immanuel Kant, *Zum ewigen Frieden. Ein philosophischer Entwurf* (Königsberg, 1795). The idea that democratic revolution was the road to peace—that princes, not peoples, made war—is prominent throughout Europe from the 1790s on. The issue is surveyed in Michael Howard, *War and the Liberal Conscience* (London and New York, 1978), esp. 25–51.

[13] "On the Political Advantages and Disadvantages of the Prussian *Landwehr*," below.

[14] "Agitation," below.

[15] "The Germans and the French" and Notes on History and Politics (1807–1809), below. Whenever Clausewitz considered the defects of deliberative bodies, it was the possibility of dead-

Germany gained ground, however, this pragmatic reservation became linked to another: a temperamental disdain for public politics, and specifically for the political intelligence and integrity of people who were not servants of the state.

German politics after the Wars of Liberation were less congenial to the progress of reform than the reformers themselves might have expected. That peace would afford their conservative opponents a chance to rally was anticipated, but not the ingratitude of those whose political aspirations had been awakened by the struggle against France. In place of restored harmony between the rulers and the ruled, based on the more equitable institutions reform had created, one encountered endless haranguing and demagoguery, impolitic demands by people with no political experience, absurd schemes that would have staked the nation's future on a theory—the sort of spectacle a contemporary Englishman might have regarded as simply the normal background noise of public life, but which Clausewitz found unnatural and debilitating.

In principle, public opinion was a force deserving of cultivation and respect. Clausewitz regarded it as the most significant source of strength left to the Prussian monarchy following its defeat in 1806.[16] He attributed superior political instincts to the common people as compared to the elite.[17] And in the "Political Declaration" he painted a stark picture of the wretchedness of a monarch bereft of public support—an image whose underlying logic is not much different from that espoused by the political activists Clausewitz would later oppose.[18]

At the same time, however, personal and historical experience showed that politics, even when confined to a narrow political class, was a divisive business. It seemed essential to limit the scope of that divisiveness, lest it threaten the unity of the state. Except in times of exceptional danger, when all available energies had to be called upon, Clausewitz regarded public affairs as the proper concern of legally circumscribed institutions whose exact nature was a matter of indifference to him, but in which opportunities for active participation would obviously have to be limited to those with a significant material and cultural stake in the country. The tacit, qualified support he offers to

---

lock and delay, rather than any supposed tendency toward weakness, ignorance, or misplaced humanity, that troubled him the most—a reflection of the role that speed had always played in maintaining Prussia's security. In *Observations on Prussia* Clausewitz would mock the exaggerated faith of Prussia's overaged generals in the magic word "mobilization." But he always considered speed and decisiveness in a crisis to be indispensable political virtues in Prussia.

[16] *Observations on Prussia*, p. 73, above; Notes on History and Politics, p. 277, below.

[17] "Scharnhorst," p. 95, above; cf. his comment on the mistaken tendency to judge French opinion on the basis of what was being said in Paris in "On the Basic Question of Germany's Existence," p. 384, below.

[18] "Political Declaration," p. 300, below.

representative bodies is thus never extended even by implication to more spontaneous expressions of public sentiment.

At the outset of the reform era, representative government had seemed to be the natural culmination of reform itself: one more means of binding the nation to the state. In 1809, when Prussia's failure to rise to the French challenge weighed heavily on him, Clausewitz could speculate privately that a parliament might not be a bad idea, since it would at least bring a few more reasonable people into the government.[19] It is hard to imagine him feeling that way later on. On the contrary, as it became clearer that parliaments might have more in common with newspapers and coffeehouse oratory than with state councils, Clausewitz's natural skepticism of all things abstract, unrealistic, and incoherent—fair characterizations of public opinion and its organs at the time, without question—prevailed. One can search his writings in vain for a kind word about newspapers, journalists, academic fraternities, and so forth, or for any hint that Germany's ubiquitous censorship, whose insidious pressure he surely felt himself, might have contributed to the political naïveté he always found so deplorable in his countrymen.

Clausewitz's considerable insight into the power of public opinion, in which he was somewhat ahead of his time in Germany, was not enough to reconcile him to the vagaries of participatory politics—a form of politics, needless to say, for which only the most tenuous social basis existed in Prussia. In social terms his sympathies were as broad as those of the activists he opposed. But those sympathies were not matched by any corresponding regard for the ramshackle institutions by which previously inarticulate elements of society were trying to make themselves heard. These seemed to him no less divorced from reality than the aristocratic politics of the Old Regime.

In his own eyes these apprehensions were vindicated by the attitude of educated Germans toward the revolutions of 1830, when public opinion in much of Germany exhibited a marked sympathy for the national rebellions in Belgium, Italy, and Poland, and corresponding hostility to the idea that Prussia (or any other power) should intervene against the revolutionaries. Many Germans seemed to find the Polish case similar to their own. They sympathized in human terms and felt sure the restoration of the Kingdom of Poland would be a useful precedent for Germany, which, like Poland, had seen its national aspirations thwarted by the persistence of *raison d'état* in European affairs.

Clausewitz regarded all this as the last word in folly. It seemed essential to him that someone "make it clear to the good people that something besides cosmopolitanism should determine our position on the Belgian, Polish, and

---

[19] Notes on History and Politics (1807–1809), p. 273, below.

other questions."[20] Early in 1831 he took it upon himself to try, and he submitted an article, "On the Basic Question of Germany's Existence," to one of Europe's most influential (and determinedly cosmopolitan) newspapers, the *Allgemeine Zeitung* of Augsburg. In it he scorned the notion that ideological affinities and moral considerations should determine a state's policy, or that the diffusion of a common liberal creed would secure the peace of Europe. This kind of thinking, Clausewitz believed, had spawned the religious wars of the past, and it was to the enduring credit of the modern world to have curbed it. In the lives of states, if not of peoples, the only thing that mattered to Clausewitz was power. Those who did not understand this could expect to be dominated and victimized by those who did.

It might seem, then, that the new possibilities opened up by the French Revolution and its aftermath finally meant little to Clausewitz. The underlying structure of the European state system had survived the Revolutionary era after all, and Clausewitz certainly expected the traditional interests of its members to continue to predominate within it. A dogmatic insistence on subordinating those interests to domestic concerns would therefore be a mistake. It made no difference whether those concerns involved the social pretensions of the nobility (as they had in the reform era), or the idealism of the bourgeoisie (as they did in 1830). But a similarly dogmatic refusal to take account of new forces—no less real for their newness—would be equally fatal in the long run.

And here Clausewitz's conduct provides some additional insight into his point of view. In its precision and detachment, as in its narrowness, Clausewitz's analysis of Germany's options in 1830 is scarcely different from what might have been expected of Kaunitz or Frederick the Great. It need hardly be said, however, that neither of those men would have thought to publish their reflections in a national newspaper, as Clausewitz tried to do on this occasion. In the end the article was rejected, a decision, Clausewitz must have felt, that merely confirmed his fears.[21] But even so, the attempt is significant, if only for what it tells us about his sense of who the audience for a political argument was. In 1812 it had been the king; twenty years later, for better or worse, it was the educated man on the street.

It is the kind of fact that is easily overlooked in an effort to tie up the loose ends and answer all the questions left open by Clausewitz's political writings. Taken as a whole, the works presented here constitute a reasonably consistent effort on Clausewitz's part to understand, and sometimes to influence, his political environment; but they fall short of offering the reader a unified the-

[20] Diary entry for February 21, 1831, in Schwartz, *Leben*, 2: 313.

[21] The reasons for the rejection are not known. The question is examined in detail on p. 377, below.

ory of justice, or legitimacy, or even of power, the aspect of politics that most fully engaged his imagination. In politics, as in the writing of history, Clausewitz was a transitional figure. He contemplated the growth of those habits and institutions that would later seem quintessentially liberal with nothing like equanimity, however firmly he may have grasped and approved of the social forces that were inspiring them. He was not a democrat, and had he lived longer he would not have become one. But he lived in what Tocqueville, to whom he has sometimes been compared, called "democratic times,"[22] and as he knew better than most, the times leave their mark on even the most independent personality. However much he may have disdained the understanding of ordinary citizens, he harbored no illusions about their potential significance. He did not shrink from the task of educating the people in the real nature of the power they would one day be wielding for themselves.

[22] Alexis de Tocqueville, *Democracy in America* (1835–40), book 2, chap. 20: "Some Characteristics of Historians in Democratic Times." One of the characteristics Tocqueville believed typified the historian in democratic times was a tendency to focus on impersonal social forces rather than individuals as the main drivers of historical change, an observation that applies as much to Clausewitz's work as it does to Tocqueville's.

SEVEN

Notes on History and Politics
(1803–1807)

Clausewitz's earliest surviving manuscripts date from his attendance at the Institute for Young Officers in Berlin and his subsequent service as adjutant to the king's cousin, Prince August. Following the Peace of Basel in 1795, Clausewitz had spent six years in the small garrison town of Neuruppin, a posting that afforded leisure and modest facilities for self-education, but little that would stimulate or give direction to his already well-developed curiosity. The opportunity to live and study in the Prussian capital was an important watershed, especially because it brought Clausewitz into contact for the first time with Gerhard von Scharnhorst, the Institute's director and the man who was to exert the greatest influence on his intellectual development. Scharnhorst's realistic, nonideological approach to politics, his distrust of dogmatism, and his belief that political understanding depended on a knowledge of the past pervade Clausewitz's early writings. Other influences are evident too. References to Montesquieu, Machiavelli, and other classic and contemporary authors testify to the breadth of Clausewitz's reading in the historical and political literature. In the broadest terms, these notes show us Clausewitz in his early twenties teaching himself the political calculus of the Old Regime, and then trying to apply it in an independent way to the new challenges of the present.

Most of the material that follows was first published by Hans Rothfels as an appendix to his important study, Carl von Clausewitz: Politik und Krieg.[1] *A few additional selections appeared later on in W. M. Schering's* Geist und Tat *(Stuttgart, 1941).[2] The original manuscript from which they all derive— a notebook ninety-eight pages long—has been lost, so it is impossible to say for sure how far these extracts represent the full range of Clausewitz's early ideas. In historical terms the range could hardly be greater. Despite their disconnected form, these private notes represent a sustained effort of reflection on European international relations since the Middle Ages. They also reveal a*

---

[1] "Historisch-politische Auszüge und Betrachtungen," 197–220.

[2] "Erste Aufzeichnungen," 6–19. Schering does not date his selections. The present work retains the order employed by Rothfels. Passages published by Schering have been inserted as seemed most reasonable in view of their contents. Unbracketed dates are in the original. Dates in brackets are inferred from the contents of the selection that follows. All ellipses, indicating gaps of unknown length, are in the published German texts.

consistent preoccupation with the logic of political power, and especially with the balance of power, whose threatened destruction in the wake of the French Revolution seemed to Clausewitz the dominant political phenomenon of the present—one that challenged his historical understanding, but which also cried out for reversal.

Although these notes do not refer to contemporary affairs and contain no practical proposals, their analytic tone cannot conceal their author's growing impatience with the drift of recent events. The years from 1803 to 1806 saw the dissolution of the Holy Roman Empire and the reorganization of southern and western Germany into a confederation under French control. That Prussia should have reacted passively to these ominous developments, allowing itself to become isolated and inactive at a time when energetic measures seemed essential, was to Clausewitz both an outrage and something of a mystery, to which he would still be returning twenty years later.[3] From the vantage of the Restoration it is likely that Clausewitz would have regarded his youthful comments on Prussia's and Europe's predicament as incomplete. His firsthand observations on Prussia's slow decline toward what he would later call the "catastrophe" of 1806 leave no doubt of his mastery of the nuances of power politics; but they lack the psychological subtlety of his mature work, in which power is rarely treated in isolation from those elements of human character that may modify, distort, or even prevent its use.

The final selection presented below was written under even more trying circumstances. In October 1806, Clausewitz was taken prisoner during the retreat of the Prussian army following the battle of Auerstädt. He spent much of the next year interned in France under easy but inevitably humiliating conditions. During this time he continued to record his ideas and impressions, accumulating a second manuscript forty-seven pages long. It too has disappeared, and it is again to Hans Rothfels that we owe our knowledge of it.[4] Most of its contents are of purely biographical interest and have not been included here. In one long entry, however, Clausewitz returns to the problem of political equilibrium in a way that, if nothing else, testifies to his determination to penetrate the hidden logic of events. The balance of power, Clausewitz now argues, can exist in two distinct forms: as a spontaneous expression of objective forces, as in the past; or as a conscious design, imposed by reason in the interest of autonomy and freedom. Both conditions favor the "development of mankind" and may even be natural to it, Clausewitz believes. They have constantly been threatened, however, by the historical tendency of power to become concentrated in large monarchies. This tendency need not continue indefinitely: the French bid for universal monarchy may fail, after all. But

[3] See especially *Observations on Prussia*, above.

[4] "Bemerkungen und Einfälle," in Rothfels, *Carl von Clausewitz*, 221–29.

even if it does, the result will not be a return to previous conditions but the further consolidation of Germany into one or two great states—a striking conclusion indeed, the more so for having been achieved at a time that proved to be the height of French power in Europe.

1803

Whether the Franks are like the Romans? Extraordinary! Why should ten years be considered evidence of a similarity that for so many centuries was never once suspected? When people talk about the French and the Romans they are talking about whole nations, which can be compared only in terms of their national characters, and here at least there is not the slightest question of similarity. But if we compare the French system, the character of French politics, with that of the Romans, the similarity in their positions requires us to answer: yes, they *are* alike, as *much* alike as the difference in their eras allows.

Rome wanted to conquer the world, or at least rule it; France marches confidently toward the same goal; it wants to crush its neighbors with its size and hold them in subjugation. This is the terrible result of this comparison!

As far as the happiness of other peoples goes, a second Rome must not be allowed to arise today; whatever new structure emerges from the present crisis, whole nations should not let themselves be chained to the victory chariot of one among them—who would deny this!!

Perhaps Europe's present condition should not cause us to fear a new Rome; perhaps the mighty strides with which France has approached her goal count for nothing, and the balance of power, already ruined, will reassert itself according to the immutable laws of nature, through new and terrible wars, or a peaceful exchange of territory. And yet a forgivable fear still lingers in our soul! Fear? Absolutely! Consider that France, exactly as she appears today, is merely an object of wonder and admiration—and cowardly idolatry—by the rest of Europe. No one can deny a nation the right to fight for its interests with all its strength, to free itself from slavery—not even *France* can be criticized if she plants her foot on our back and extends her realm of frightened vassals to the polar sea.

But must this inspire nothing but timidity? Greatness makes this sort of impression only on cowards. Among men of courage and strength, greatness inspires greatness in return, it awakens courage and noble pride, it sows the seeds of great deeds.

What, then, does this idolatry signify? Are we really such a cowardly race that we dare not measure ourselves against this proud conqueror? To believe this, *there* lies the cowardice! Have we really sunk so low that we consider it honorable to bow down abjectly before another nation, to lose ourselves in its glory and interests?

Shame and contempt on all those who are so timid and blind! Alas, more than one German is caught in this spell, shamelessly forgetting his nations's dignity, denying *his own nation*. A man who disparages the nation in order to make himself seem greater is more shameful than the simple soul who loses himself in the spectacle of great deeds or the contemplation of eternity. The first man stands in judgment over the nation, ever ready to appreciate the great achievements of its neighbor—and sets himself above his fellow citizens. Let him stand where he pleases; he can contribute nothing to the nation's recovery, its ennoblement, its survival—the nation casts him off like a useless limb, and leaves it to his conceit to make good the praise he might have won from his compatriots.

If we consider France, with her population, her wealth, her size, and her position so well suited to trade, we find only two countries in Europe—Spain and Italy—that compare to her; but if we consider France's political position, right in the middle of England, Spain, Italy, and Germany, and defended, moreover, by strong natural borders unassailable by most of these other lands, there is scarcely any country that can compare. It follows that France has a capacity to promote her interests that many, in their disgraceful forgetfulness, would call a *right*, but which the rest of us must resolve to hold in check.

If we consider the level of culture that France now possesses, as revealed by her constitution and the customs and spirit of the nation, it is clear that at most Germany and England can be considered comparable. Spain and Italy are held back by internal slackness. In the first case it is mainly the weakness and total exhaustion of the government that has undermined the nation for years, not by *destroying* its dignity and noble pride in its former power, but by binding them unnaturally to indolence and vice. Italy stands even lower; since German arms deprived it of world dominance, it has developed a taste for permanent dependence on foreign powers.

People may bring up the free Italian states of the Middle Ages. But what is there to say about a few small republics in comparison to the whole Italian people? Can a feeling of liberty and independence be called a national feeling when it is displayed not by the whole nation, but by a tiny colony, surrounded by a great, downtrodden mass? Could even the Italian republicans gain any sense of themselves as Italians, when they saw perhaps five-sixths of their nation under foreign rule? Besides: I could never be convinced that the spirit of the medieval Italian republics was a true, lofty spirit of freedom and independence and strength, an expression of moral principles. Sometimes it expressed the power of usurpation and democracy, as in Florence; sometimes the influence of shrewd commercial interests, as in Venice; and its preferred instruments were always intrigue and betrayal rather than martial virtue. We need only think of the way wars were fought, with rented soldiers and hired commanders.

[Italy] has fallen so low not merely through the force of political circumstances, but through internal moral collapse, a general decay of its values and spirit. The corrupt domination of Europe by its popes could only push the nation further down; and if an occasional powerful mind appeared among them, it is only thanks to the splendid soil of classical antiquity, which despite the general decline and without any cultivation and attention, now and then brings forth luxuriant plants and fragrant blossoms. It is the glowing fire and light of religion that makes them shine.

The arts and learning cannot free a nation from foreign domination. It must throw itself into wild, elemental struggle, staking a thousand lives against a thousandfold increase in its own life. Only then can it rise again from the sickbed to which foreign chains brought it. Among the rich Italians and Spaniards the foreign yoke seems to be a minor burden, so we should not look for much assistance from that quarter. Besides, the wealth of these lands has declined terribly thanks to the incompetence of their governments.

England, as little as it too may be compared to France, has too little direct involvement on the continent to be the main counterweight, and from the moment Europe relies primarily on England it will be ruined. Germany, perhaps at the same level of culture and internal prosperity as France, possesses such a notoriously intricate federal constitution that it can no longer bring its full natural weight to bear against her. Russia can have no significant impact unless Germany is already lost. What a prospect for Europe! Nothing remains but a coalition. And if we consider that coalitions have been constantly employed since the time of Louis XIV, always with some success, but consider also how much effort has been required to resist the power of France in this way, and then think how far our policies are from those of Leopold, Joseph, William of Orange, and Queen Anne[5]—what a prospect for Europe!

ON COALITIONS

In politics there are two kinds of coalitions: one that aims expressly to defeat or coerce the enemy, and another that aims to *weaken*, to *preoccupy*, both

[5] The Holy Roman Emperors Leopold I and Joseph I, along with King William III and Queen Anne of England, were the main opponents of Louis XIV.

the enemy *and* the state with which one is allied. Politicians who consider the second objective illegitimate sacrifice the state's interests, for which they are responsible, to their own sense of propriety. Those who conduct themselves in high office as they would in private life are true egotists. They see their own interests as the goal and the state as something extra. Who, for instance, could blame Russia and France if they allied with Austria against Prussia, so that both Prussia and Austria would be weakened?

Statesmen commonly make the mistake of forming coalitions in the hope of enjoying both advantages, and this does not work. Coalitions of the second kind are not appropriate under all circumstances. Austria cannot ally with Russia against Prussia in order to weaken both, because Prussia would aim its main blow against Austria. Weak states play a dangerous game with this sort of policy and can easily become victims of their own cunning. This is a role suited only to self-sufficient states, and indeed even they can play it safely only if they cannot be seriously threatened by the common enemy.

People who complain about the ineffectiveness of coalitions do not know what they want; what better way is there to resist a stronger power? History itself, the favorite stalking horse of all opponents of coalitions, must be brutally distorted to make it prove what these people always want it to prove. Apart from the unsuccessful coalition of 1792 I can think of scarcely one that *entirely* failed in its purpose. That they did not achieve everything they wanted is quite natural, for this is often the way life is. Furthermore, it should be noted that defensive objectives are ordinarily the last to be lost, which suggests that coalitions are the proper means to resist a superior power.

Italy, Holland, and Germany have had only coalitions to thank for their long-lived independence. The ones people usually talk about are the League of Cambrai against Venice, the Holy League of 1510 against France, the alliance against Charles V after the Treaty of Madrid in 1526, and finally the Seven Years' War; all these alliances prove the opposite of what they are supposed to prove.

The purpose of the *first* was not to overthrow Venice completely, but to humble her, and this was achieved. Venice had to pay dearly for peace with its various opponents. Spain gained a great deal, as did the pope; the emperor had no claim to make, since he had made no sacrifices; only France came away empty-handed, although it had made the greatest effort. But for France the alliance was also the most irrational imaginable,[6] and the fact that some-

[6] France's interests were opposed to those of its partners in the League of Cambrai: Spain, the empire, and the papacy. They had resisted the French invasions of Italy after 1494 and would soon join forces against her again in the Holy League described in the next paragraph. France thus fell victim to the "second kind of coalition" mentioned in the previous selection—one intended to weaken both an enemy and one of the partners.

one loses out in a coalition that makes no sense cannot possibly argue against coalitions in general.

The common *objective of the second coalition* was to drive the French out of Italy, in addition to which one ally sought a local advantage for itself.[7] The first aim was achieved completely, the second more or less, so the fact that this alliance ended in separate peace treaties cannot count against it.

The objective of the third was to oppose the superior power of Charles V; to guarantee the duke of Milan possession of his duchy; and to force Charles to give up the claim to Burgundy set forth in the Treaty of Madrid, and set free the sons of the king of France in exchange for some compensation in cash.

The war went entirely in favor of Charles V. Two French armies, one in Naples and another near Milan, were totally destroyed, Rome was taken by storm, the pope was imprisoned and brought to his knees; and yet the treaties of Cambrai and Bologna were certainly not *positively harmful* to the allies. The Treaty of Madrid was moderated, the Venetians and the pope lost nothing, and even Sforza [the duke of Milan] had his claim to Milan reaffirmed. The only penalty the Italian princes suffered was a contribution to pay for the war. . . .

Finally there is the *Seven Years' War*, which ignorant people constantly bring up to prove the futility of coalitions. No one takes into account that Frederick II survived because he concluded a countercoalition with England and some German princes, and also at one point with Peter III; or that the results of the coalition against him were such that, powerless and at bay in his victor's camp, he lost forever the desire for conquest, at least by force of arms. It is hard to believe that *without the Seven Years' War* Frederick would have let his victorious arms remain inactive for thirty years. He kept Silesia, but not the bold courage to expand his realm at Austria's expense. That was successfully wrung from him.

The idea of the balance of power had to develop first in Italy, where it first achieved concrete form, almost as a test case. Here were a number of small states, roughly equal in strength, forced together in a very small area, which, moreover, was the theater of war between the two dominant powers, Spain and France. Furthermore, culture had already created far richer and more varied connections among the Italian states than, for instance, in Germany.

What Germany would later become, namely the container for the small weights used to maintain the balance of power, Italy was before.

---

[7] Julius II and Leo X wanted to use the wars against France as leverage to expand their secular authority in Italy.

The balance of power *system* only reveals itself when the balance is in danger of being lost. As long as the natural weight of states is sufficient, without noticeable distortion or moral exertion, to keep everything in its place and the whole machine steady—that is, free of violent oscillations—there is no question of a balance of power *system*; the balance simply exists in itself. We see this in northern Europe, where Sweden, Denmark, Poland, and Russia existed from the days of Gustav Vasa to the Thirty Years' War without the dominance of any state, and without any effort to prevent such dominance.

Germany's constitution and her current political weakness derive mainly from three causes:

1. After the dissolution of the Frankish kingdom, Germany again became an electoral empire, while a hereditary monarchy was established in France.
2. Germany's geographical position was less favorable than that of France, Spain, and England, because it bordered Hungary, Poland, Bohemia, the Greek states, and finally Turkey, which led to innumerable wars.
3. Germany's territory was so large at a time when it was impossible to govern such a massive state—namely the Middle Ages, when the feudal system, with its tendency toward anarchy, had reached its height. At a time when civil constitutions were beginning to develop in Spain, France, and England, and their rulers were busy strengthening their internal power (the general requirement of the age), the German emperors were so embroiled in Italian affairs and so hampered by the dangerous intrigues of the popes that they could make only a minimal effort to expand their princely authority in Germany.

Though these reasons might seem sufficient, the German national character must contain a force that has contributed to this result.

1805

We must not fear—or rather, we must not hope for—the condition of total subservience, but that shameful, languid period in which our civil existence is not yet threatened, while the independence and dignity of the state have already been lost.

244

Why do so many men devote themselves to a diplomatic career when they are no better at it than anyone else who can read and write, lie without blushing, and suffer abuse without fainting? They don't know the first thing about their business if they imagine a state can remain untouched by the fate of its neighbors.

To me the chief rules of politics are: never be helpless; expect nothing from the generosity of another; do not give up an objective before it becomes impossible; hold sacred the honor of the state.

Neither Montesquieu nor Machiavelli, I think, noted that the tricks in which Roman methods of rule were so rich *included* a willingness to tolerate a free, often almost defiant manner of thinking and speaking among subject peoples. One might think that such talk would inevitably lead to action—but no! If men are allowed to speak they still feel free themselves and are satisfied to expend their inner strength in empty chatter; thus the most eloquent, tearful lament does not easily inspire the sort of desperate resolve that silence does. If tyranny grows so heavy that no man dares to talk, then misery swells and becomes the seed for great deeds. . . .

Bonaparte seems to have overlooked this aspect of Roman policy, and it may be the only one; I am glad of that and hope some good will come of it.

I know only two ways to insure that an advantageous alliance leads to advantages in war. The first is to concentrate all the forces committed to the war under a *single* commander; the second is to draw up a common strategic plan, based on the natural circumstances and advantages of each of the states involved, an alternative which we will analyze more fully some other time.

The first approach has been used from time to time in the past, particularly if the forces one state wanted to commit were too insignificant to justify a share in the leadership of the war; as often as not, however, the ministers involved would use all their cunning to dig up all their petty interests and forestall a unified command. They believe, falsely, that any concession that does not lead directly to a *political* advantage is a sign of weakness or incompetence; they do not consider and do not know how to value what they might gain indirectly, both materially and by increasing the probability of victory.

It is easy to see that things cannot always be done this way. But in that case people should at least choose the other course firmly, which is even more difficult. They hinder the uniform, harmonious operation of forces by bringing *conflicting points of view* into play and creating *divided interests*, and they seldom possess sufficient insight and skill to restore unity some other way, *through the proper deployment and coordination of these diverse elements*. This is the second, much more significant defect of our military alliances.

There is no doubt that this is an inexhaustible source of failure. For if it is endlessly difficult to satisfy all the interests at stake *without unduly violating sound strategic principles* and reducing the probability of success, nevertheless we clearly cannot expect the problem to be solved *merely by chance*. For how else, in practice, are politicians supposed to determine the way war is conducted? Whoever has the slightest real knowledge cannot reject an opinion based on a thousand experiences, which leads to another that is entirely convincing on its own.

The operational principles according to which military alliances should be concluded are easily stated, although no additional arguments or supporting examples will be presented here for those who do not accept them.

1. Whenever possible, the major armies of both powers should each have its own theater of operations.
2. If it is not possible to separate them so that each has its own theater, it is better to unite them as completely as possible.
3. If each has its own theater of operations, these should reflect as far as possible the following considerations:
   a. If the operation is offensive, the resulting conquest should remain in the hands of the power that carried it out.
   b. If it is defensive, the land endangered by an unsuccessful campaign should be that of the defender.

These principles cannot always be satisfied, but they should never be deliberately violated.

I do not think much of the petty secrets and stratagems of politics. I do not mean to suggest that policy can always be carried out in broad daylight, with its aims unconcealed; but however deep and cunning a plan may be, political methods must always be vigorous and worthy of the state when an important issue is at stake.

Simple and resolute methods are even more important in specific, practical negotiations, where the game of intrigue can at most serve the personal interests of the negotiators, by somehow making their task easier.

My belief in this idea has been strengthened above all by the Peace of Westphalia. I do not see that the Spanish and the Austrians achieved anything of much use by their ridiculous, endless intrigues, and the Swedes, who always employed open, firm, dignified language, supported by the sword, gained more for themselves and their allies than all the others.

[1807][8]

People talk all the time about the martial character of the Middle Ages and complain about the softness, cowardice, and political indolence of the modern world, because they see princes of the second rank paying unrestrained homage to those who are more powerful, while in the Middle Ages the most humble vassal defended his independence with his blood.

But it is a mistake to attribute to individuals that which lies in their circumstances. In the Middle Ages the vassal struggled with the prince, the subject with the vassal, the cities with the nobility, the lesser princes with the emperor, etc. This contest lasted for centuries, and finally ended not because men became less warlike (the appearance is undeniable but more a result than a cause of the struggle's ending), but rather because, unless an outside force intervened, the constantly shifting position of those involved had to lead to a loss of the equilibrium that bound the contestants together. Every social structure, unless it is ultimately subjected to the laws of reason, has a tendency toward monarchy. For what did each contestant strive? To dominate his opponent. But how is it possible for permanent equilibrium to prevail among the multitude of parts into which European society was divided under the feudal system? Once the balance is lost at several points, however, the result is not merely a tendency, but rapid progress toward monarchy. Will a universal monarchy result? I do not know, but I do know that if the number of contending elements were sufficiently reduced that mutual alliances became possible among them, and if European culture were sufficiently advanced that these alliances became a real necessity, then a self-conscious balance of power, established and preserved by reason, could emerge. This sort of equilibrium, maintained by design and effort, is different from the one that developed through the mere rubbing of forces against each other. This design, this effort, is the outside force we just now mentioned, which ought to govern the material forces involved.

To return again to the tendency toward monarchy: Do not greater vassals come from smaller ones, and lesser princes from these, and from these mighty kings? And once the equilibrium between prince and vassal is overthrown, isn't the independence of the vassal soon destroyed?

---

[8] The selection that follows dates from Clausewitz's internment in France (January to August 1807); see Rothfels, *Politik und Krieg*, 221n.

This trend has been halted, for entirely different reasons, in Germany and Italy. In Germany because at various times in the past—when the French monarchy emerged, when the English heptarchy arose,[9] when Ferdinand the Catholic united Spain under his scepter—Germany's inhabitants were still animated by an exceptionally warlike spirit and a love of independence. This highly developed martial and independent spirit might have done no worse than delay the establishment of a monarchy by fifty years, were it not for the simultaneous influence of two other developments. The first was the Reformation, which gave new strength to the spirit of independence by further dividing what wished to be united; the second is the emergence of the balance of power, which suddenly arrested and stabilized Europe's progress toward universal monarchy. The constitutions of Germany and Italy can therefore be regarded as political fossils.

It is truly remarkable that, in fifteen hundred years, no monarchy could establish itself in Italy, and it will be worth the effort to explore the reasons why. Apart from the invasions by Pepin and Charlemagne, Italy remained essentially free from outside pressure until the reign of Charles VIII. I realize the German emperors constantly waged war there, and were often victorious; but basically their power could never have done serious harm to the Italian states, and if these had not been so fragmented the German emperors could hardly have preserved even the shadow of the possessions that drew their armies there from time to time. Why, for instance, couldn't the Ostrogoths create an Italian monarchy; why not the Lombards, why not the Berengari?[10] Why not the king of Naples?[11] To explain a phenomenon that lasted fifteen hundred years we are certainly entitled to point to general causes. Two, it seems to me, are fairly obvious and perhaps also sufficient.

1. The remnants of the ancient Roman culture and constitution that survived following the barbarian invasions. These vestiges afforded Italy a head start in its development compared to the rest of Europe; Italy was rich in cities when these were still totally lacking elsewhere; it alone engaged in large-scale trade. These advantages allowed small cities and provinces to resist the general trend toward monarchy. The strength of these small states can be seen from their ability to resist foreign influence and hold the secular power of the papacy in check. But they had also used that strength earlier to preserve their independence. Yet their power seems to have had an entirely different char-

---

[9] A supposed confederacy of Anglo-Saxon kingdoms during the seventh and eighth centuries, whose reality is now generally denied.

[10] Berengar I, electoral king of Italy from 888 to 924, Holy Roman Emperor from 915, founded a line of Italian princes who were once viewed, incorrectly, as national kings.

[11] Apparently a reference not to an individual, but to the whole line of Neapolitan kings, first Hohenstauffen, then Angevine, finally Aragonese, who ruled southern Italy from the twelfth century until the establishment of the Habsburg viceroyalty there in 1503.

acter from that which German princes used for the same purpose. The latter were warlike and poor, the former peace loving and rich, and it is not the strength of their swords but the power of their money and the influence of their more refined political system that saves them.

2. The presence of the papacy in Rome—which is not to say that the pope wielded great influence over the souls of Italians by virtue of his office, or that his worldly power allowed him to direct Italian affairs as he saw fit. Much was lacking in both areas, for it is impossible to be less firmly seated on a throne, or less respected by the people, than many of the popes were. The significance of the papacy lies rather in the fact that, as head of the church, the pope was allied with all Christian monarchs, even before alliances among them were conceivable, so that a point of contact was established with the king of France, the German emperor, the king of Bohemia, etc., which early on created a kind of balance of power in Italy and kept things as they were. It is because of these divergent efforts by the Germans and Italians that both countries remained divided into a number of large and small states until political equilibrium emerged, as it did in Italy very early, if incompletely, and in Germany only in the sixteenth century. From then on it was no longer the effort of the small states, but simply the self-interest of the larger ones, that kept the former from being swallowed up.

It follows that once the balance of power is completely destroyed, small states must lose their independence. The bond that held them in their places as if by magic is loosened, and they again follow their natural tendency to coalesce in large monarchies. France actually wishes to increase this fragmentation, but only to subjugate the parts more completely. This, however, is not the only way small states can disappear. If France fails to achieve its goal, it is obvious that this state, having overthrown the balance of power, will have taken a burden on its shoulders that it cannot carry forever, and the result must be violent political oscillations that will again lead to equilibrium, but of still another kind. In this transition everything will move according to its natural weight, that is, the system will not be subject to a rational will, acting as an outside force, but each part will follow its own momentum wherever it may lead. This will be the moment when Germany will become a single monarchy, or divide at most into two large realms. This will certainly occur if France fails to subjugate Germany—an assumption whose probability, or lack of it, I will not judge here.

That this tendency of republican states toward monarchy is contrary to the tendency of men and even of individual states, and handicaps the development of humanity, cannot detract from the truth of these observations.

EIGHT

"The Germans and the French" (1807)

Clausewitz wrote the following essay in November 1807, following his return from internment in France, and it bears conspicuous traces of that trying experience. Like so many of his early notes, "The Germans and the French" is concerned with understanding the growth of French power since the Revolution and the corresponding decline in the positions of Prussia and Germany. Clausewitz had first sought an explanation by way of historical comparison and analysis. In 1803 he had asked himself "whether the Franks are like the Romans" and had decided they were, if only in the scope of their ambitions, which had been nourished by favorable geographical positions and fortunate political conditions.[1] But Clausewitz also sensed that geography and constitutional history were not sufficient to explain Germany's predicament. "The German national character," he suspected, "must contain a force that has contributed to this result."[2] Defeat and internment lent new weight to this supposition, which he explored systematically for the first time in the essay presented here.

Many of Clausewitz's observations in "The Germans and the French" will strike the modern reader as parochial and ill-judged. They reflect the strain of the author's personal humiliation and recall the worst clichés of German romanticism, on which Clausewitz drew as a way of interpreting his experience.[3] As clichés his comments are not without interest, if only for the contrast they offer to the national stereotypes of the future. Clausewitz finds the French to be natural conformists, lacking intellectual depth and emotional passion, but correspondingly facile in practical matters. The Germans, in contrast, are natural individualists, indifferent to social pressure, prone to pursue all questions to impractical depths, instinctively hostile to "the aims of government." These attributes have political consequences: the values and attitudes of the Frenchman make him easier to govern and more suitable as a "political instrument," while the German's distrust of authority makes the concentration of political power and the defense of the nation against outsiders more difficult. It is the Germans, not the French, who are the temperamental republi-

---

[1] P. 239, above.

[2] P. 244, above.

[3] On the relationship between Clausewitz's ideas and those of August Wilhelm and Friedrich Schlegel, see Paret, *Clausewitz and the State*, 134–45.

cans, Clausewitz believes, an inclination fatally at odds with their exposed geographic position.

Judgments like these are liable to stick in the mind, though for the most part they did not stick in Clausewitz's: his mature work is distinguished by a lack of chauvinism. The personal animus that colored his firsthand impressions of France and its people would fade, as would the need to denigrate Prussia's enemies. What would survive was a more vigorous sense of the interconnection between politics and culture, which would find a permanent place in his political writing, alongside more objective (or at any rate more traditional) considerations of geography, national wealth, and raison d'état. That the nation may indeed become the instrument of the state, and that some cultural values are more conducive to this result than others, was an insight worth having, and one that would continue to inform Clausewitz's politics.

It is not clear what end Clausewitz had in mind for "The Germans and the French." It has the polish of a work intended for publication and brings together a number of themes first broached in correspondence and private journals.[4] At one point Clausewitz alludes to his desire to test his convictions by expressing them to others. Had the essay appeared, it would have made a puzzling sequel to an earlier series of articles on the campaign of 1806, in which Prussia's defeat is attributed to the strategic and operational failures of the army and the genius of Napoleon.[5] In a logical sense, however, the work is incomplete, since Clausewitz does not propose any means of exploiting the peculiar qualities of the Germans to achieve national regeneration. The only morally convincing conclusion would have been a call to defy the conqueror, a call whose immediate futility the author certainly understood. In any event, the manuscript remained unpublished until Schwartz included it in his biography seventy years later.[6]

In considering Germany's present condition and recent history, we are at once forced to ask ourselves: Is the cause of everything that has happened a matter of necessity, or chance? Must the German national character lead to this—is the role we are playing in accord with our moral powers? Or is it

---

[4] See Clausewitz's letters to his fiancée, Marie von Brühl, January to October 1807, in Karl Linnebach, ed., *Karl und Marie von Clausewitz: Ein Lebensbild in Briefen und Tagebuchblättern* (Berlin, 1917), 76–149; and his "Journal einer Reise von Soissons über Dijon nach Genf," in Schwartz, *Leben*, 1: 88–110.

[5] Carl von Clausewitz, "Historische Briefe über die grossen Kriegsereignisse im Oktober 1806," *Minerva* [Hamburg, ed. J. W. von Archenholz], January, February, and April 1807; reprinted Bonn, 1977, ed. Joachim Niemeyer.

[6] Schwartz, *Leben*, 1: 73–88; reprinted in *Politische Schriften und Briefe*, 35–51.

merely the result of temporary moral decline and surmountable slackness? Or, finally, are there other chance circumstances that have brought us to this point?

If, on the other hand, the French now dominate Europe, if they have subdued Germany, which held them off for centuries, and achieved moral supremacy on the battlefield everywhere in recent years, then it is equally natural to ask: Does the cause lie in that nation's essential character, in the impetus it received from the Revolution, or in still more accidental circumstances, for instance the talent of its present leader? That *chance* helped create the present relationship of these two nations cannot be denied without the most extreme prejudice. But even so, it is not irrelevant to ask whether their national characters have contributed significantly to it; rather, the answer is essential. For the character of a nation, even insofar as its original, fragile nature may be affected by changing customs, is not as easily reshaped as philosophers and moralists seem to think; yet the underlying human relationships between two nations can have many important consequences for the future.

To proclaim the French men of a higher spiritual type, who have their more southerly clime to thank for their greater intellectual aptitude, is to cut the knot with an arbitrary assertion that actually says nothing at all in the absence of more precise evidence and detailed knowledge of both nations. Yet people keep saying this because the French have lively, nimble minds, which impresses most Germans but is a very one-sided and paltry standard of mental power. In society one often finds such mental agility in people of very high rank, who are intellectually quite mediocre. In this respect the impression the French make on us is like a card trick, half voluntary, half unwitting. Even the French language, to a German who understands it only a little or not at all, somehow seems vaguely sophisticated and clever, because he is accustomed to hearing it only from the upper classes and considers it a sign of great culture. A child who speaks French—how adorable; a servant who speaks French—how proper!

I have spent ten months in France, and have also had other occasions to meet many Frenchmen. Constant, almost involuntary comparison of my countrymen with the French, of our language with theirs, has left me with such a clear impression of these two nations and their moral relationship that I would be hard-pressed to erase it again. To the extent that my weak knowledge of the past has allowed me to compare this impression with the histories of these and other nations, I have found it generally confirmed, and unfortunately I cannot conceal from myself how far the German national character has contributed to our present condition, and how fully it explains it, in combination with a few chance circumstances. Because I want to be certain of my views, however, I cannot refrain from expressing them to others.

The main ingredient of the French character, which defines the whole most clearly, is a sensitive, lively, but inconstant and hence not very deep sensibility. In the French this sensibility is entirely analogous to intelligence. A Frenchman's attention will easily be drawn to something, and his mind then demonstrates its agility; but his attention span is limited, so his understanding remains on the surface. There he grasps the smallest nuance quickly; but he rarely drinks deeply of the essence of things. This characteristic is conspicuous in his language and literature.

From this flashing, inconstant sensibility—which seldom rises to the level of real passion—ideas that seldom lead to deep meditation, and the liveliness that the French aptly call *pétulance*, the primary and secondary elements of the French character follow quite naturally, just as the nation's customs follow from its spirit.

Thus the Frenchman has a limited—but within those limits, very nimble—intelligence, and since a typical, superficial social encounter always remains within a narrow range of ideas, he is able to impress a German in these circumstances.

A lively but limited intelligence reasons eagerly about everything, but in part it clings to the surface, in part it can be diverted easily, like a stream, into channels where its rationalizing does no harm.

The more people focus on external appearances, the less they delve into the realm of abstractions, the nearer they hold to the world of the senses, the more limited will be the circle of ideas in which they move, the less their minds will diverge, and the more their views will coincide. The fruit and leaves on a tree look the same to everyone. For the most part the Frenchman grasps commonplace things, things closest to the realm of the senses, and remains content with that. It is not difficult to see the effect of this peculiarity among the French themselves. Originality of mind is so rare in France that the expression *un original* has become a mark of ridicule; the language has lost the inner vitality and flexibility that make the expression of true individuality possible; it has been filled up with ready-made ideas from which everyone serves himself without embarrassment. The commonplace expression is the best, and *cela ne se dit pas* has become the first rule of speech.

This intellectual superficiality nourishes the French wit, which encompasses a hundred forms of mental play. From it arose their obsessive concern with the external forms of art and the mechanical rules of aesthetics—though I cannot get involved here in a discussion of their literature.

I have said that the reasoning of a limited intelligence can easily be diverted into safe channels, so that it does not sweep everything along to destruction. This is actually quite natural: one can simply go along and keep its limited demands satisfied.

As long as the kings of France were careful to preserve the outward symbols of national happiness—national fame, personal dignity, a brilliant court, and so forth—the French found their government quite satisfactory on the whole, though Louis XIV squandered a monstrous sum, totally out of proportion to the strength of the state, on fortresses that were mostly never finished. But when weak monarchs ignored these matters and gave in to decadence, they found the nation to be a stern judge. We now see clearly how eager the people were for the outward forms of freedom during the Revolution, and how little they grasped of true republicanism. Bonaparte, who is concerned about the happiness of France only insofar as it is compatible with his lust for power, but who has taken care to satisfy the nation's vanity and superficial rationalizing with his victories and his newspapers, finds the French to be loyal subjects once again. But the limitations of the French spirit do not just make them more tractable politically. They also concentrate their minds within a narrow sphere and make the French *more adept at political life*. Their very lack of individuality contributes to *esprit de corps* and, more broadly, to *national spirit*; and precisely for this reason *the French are better suited to be political instruments of their government*.

So much for their spirit, now something of their character.

Vanity is a prominent feature of the French national character, which we hardly need to emphasize, since it is well known to everyone with common sense, even foreigners. This vanity is not connected with a high level of emotion but rather with their shallow, restless sensibility. Because of the peculiarities of the French intellect, this vanity readily expresses itself as arrogance and ostentation. It is not that the French are poor show-offs, but rather that boastfulness itself signifies a limited mind. The inclination to remain on the surface, the lack of depth of feeling, give rise to the desire to wear one's virtues like an embroidered robe, to protect them from every blemish that might rob them of their glitter in the eyes of others. Thus the great importance of the *point d'honneur* among the French. I do not disparage this, for there is something poetic about it. But that it is not primarily an expression of a high moral nature is shown by the [recent experience of] the nations of the old world, and the greatest men of the new. It is an accidental virtue, born of vice.

The *courtliness* of the French is the most direct proof that for them external customs count for more than inner values. The least important Frenchman I knew in France never spoke to me without the courtly overture: "*Comment va la santé de Monsieur?*"[7] But then he immediately allowed himself the question: "*Qu'est-ce que fait donc votre pauvre roi, pourquoi ne fait-il pas le paix?*"[8] or something of the sort, which could only give offense. If the

---

[7] "How is the gentleman's health?"

[8] "But what, then, is your poor king doing, why does he not make peace?"

German, because he is better-natured, is also more courteous at heart, that is not the Frenchman's fault; but if nature has denied the French that congeniality that fills our hearts with good will and true courtesy toward others, why must they seek it in external forms? Because they tend to focus on the surface of things.

The *cruelty* of which the French are capable, of which the Revolution offered unprecedented examples—what else is it but emotional sensitivity combined with a lack of depth? Love and loyalty need time to take root in the hearts of even the most passionate men; but hatred and vengeance can be ignited in an instant. And the Revolution itself has demonstrated how different this hatred and vengefulness are from the passionate fervor that all southerners feel. Who in France has pursued a passion or an enthusiasm with real determination? No one, from the king and Mayor Péthion to Moreau; nor has any idea been fully worked out, from the most unlimited freedom to the most unbending despotism. Bonaparte found the French to be obedient subjects, for which they excuse themselves on the grounds that he fought off the hydra Revolution; but Barrère, one of its most appalling offspring, lives in society and among friends in Paris.

An *irrepressible, tempestuous courage* is the result of a lively sensibility and an intellect that places great store in outward signs of respectability. This gallantry is the finest characteristic of the French.

I will say nothing here of the well-known frivolity and facetiousness of the French. They are too closely connected to these fundamental characteristics to require any further comment.

This vanity, then, provides the government with a powerful lever for leading the nation, often with only the slightest effort; the nation's shallowness of feeling permits it to follow any path, the monarchy or the republic. The French insistence on the *point d'honneur* makes them temperamentally suited to war, their courage leads them to victory, and all these factors again lead to the conclusion that *through them the Frenchman becomes an outstanding political instrument.*

Customs, all things that have to do more with surface than substance, please the Frenchman above all; thus he prefers wit, humor, and intellectual games to meditation, amusements to work, play to passion. This is most broadly demonstrated by their manner of living, in which amusements have a much greater part than among northern peoples, and by particular customs that are broadly representative. For instance: the many plays, which are more heavily attended in their small towns than our large cities; the municipal promenades that exist even in the small towns, carefully maintained at public expense and eagerly attended even by people of the lowest classes; the French aptitude for games; the multitude of coffeehouses, social circles, and associations in every town; the importance of social formality; the conversational character of the French language; their love of dancing, balls under the open sky, of games and similar pastimes that we consider childish and which would shame a youth, but which in France will be played for hours without inhibition by a fifty-year-old businessman, and for which space and facilities will often be maintained at public expense.

Since it is through customs that the land and climate shape national character everywhere, so in France it is the land that makes this devotion to amusement possible, and presumably created it, since little labor suffices to maintain life in their fertile land. It is for this reason that the Frenchman is exceptionally thin, and while he has a great inclination to epicurism he is rarely a glutton, and is usually satisfied with remarkably little, provided it is tasty. Thus the Frenchman works less than the German. Other southern peoples work even less, but this is the result of sloth, which is far removed from the French *pétulance*. The Frenchman craves activity, but of a kind as unstrenuous as possible—hence games.

On the whole the French are bad businessmen, as their history shows; nowhere else do we find so many men living off their investments as in France. Anyone, in Paris or wherever, who has scraped together a small sum by industry and effort invests it at interest and spends the second half of his life in peace and bland contentment in some small town. The Frenchman is a good manager of small ventures, but he is no speculator in large affairs. He is penny-pinching, but not greedy; in the world of commerce, as of the intellect, far-reaching speculation is the distinctive expression of a more comprehending mind, and the hunger for riches is a deeply rooted, enduring, almost passionate feeling.

The trifling character of French customs, the shallow pleasures, the satisfaction with a little, the small scale of enterprise and wealth, the richness of the soil—all mean that the government can seldom risk offending the most sensitive elements of society. If it is relatively adroit and knows how to soothe these petty concerns, however, it can take the most forceful steps without serious opposition, as is obvious today. The complaints of a few speculators hardly compare to the uproar present-day restraints on industry would create in other nations, particularly Germany. Here too we get the same result: *the peculiar customs of the French make them good instruments of their government.*

If we turn now to the Germans, we find that their spirit, their character, and their customs are almost completely the opposite.

The German is indeed more *phlegmatic*, as they say, which is supposed to imply that his feelings are less keen, his intelligence less lively, his mental processes slower. As far as intellectual liveliness and agility go this is undeniable, for the German is the opposite of *pétulant*—but keenness of feeling obviously depends on other things besides mere liveliness, a quickening of the blood. For it is undeniable: the German is capable of very refined feelings, he is in general only too soft-hearted (which in politics is often thought to signify weakness and lack of character), and in any case he is more emotional than the Frenchman. But German emotion is calmer, more ember than flame, so it expresses itself more slowly and pierces the heart more deeply.

The German intellect has the same tendency. It pursues a firmly held idea more steadfastly, and thus farther, and instead of taking immediate pleasure in the correspondence of its ideas to reality, as the French mind does, instead of being constantly attracted and held by external appearances, it delves deeply into the nature of things, into abstractions, and strives for complete understanding. Who could mistake this spirit in the German language and literature? There it is utterly splendid; for among the intellectual riches with which nature has endowed man, the capacity for abstract analysis is certainly the highest, and it will always be the most magnificent ornament of the German character.

But while it elevates the human being, it often damages his usefulness in practical, particularly political, life. The higher the spirit soars, the more independent the nature of the individual, the more he struggles against mundane political forms. Because of the natural inequality of men, government must exploit *prejudices, passions, even weaknesses* to unite and lead them, for up to now no state has been governed by purely rational means. But this is the least of the problem. In the end, reflection would lead to roughly the same techniques that the pragmatic statesman employs instinctively—but the path of abstract inquiry is strewn with so many pitfalls, and it is so hard to be sure of avoiding error, that few of those who venture onto it, leaving the mundane word of experience behind, remain on the road to truth. The unbelievably rationalistic spirit of the Germans derives from this philosophical tendency, and, in contrast to the French, it is not confined to narrow limits that the government can easily circumvent; rather, it extends to the farthest limits of thought. The deeper the intellect penetrates, the more it must fear one-sidedness, not as an inevitable consequence of depth, but as a danger that dogs the pursuit of it. This one-sidedness, the enemy of all political and indeed all practical institutions, is the true mark of the inquiring German spirit. Hence the great number of philosophical systems, each revolving within its own limits, and insisting on the correctness of *its* boundaries. This is true not only among scholars and philosophers, but among the mass of common folk, who also talk about the great questions of the human mind, even if it is all a lot of hot air. But of course each group has its own standard: a noble, powerful striving for certainty and a very forgivable one-sidedness on the part of the nation's great thinkers may become nothing more than partisan nonsense when attempted by a pamphleteer. Wherever the necessary intellectual power and tools are lacking, it is natural that the spirit of study and inquiry should lead to mere carping.

Thanks to this spirit, which pervades everything and subjects even the most perfect political achievement to penetrating criticism, transforming the whole population into a standing army of nay-sayers, it is certain that in Germany, more than anywhere else, even the most outstanding accomplishment will find its detractors; that there are no circumstances under which the nation will willingly unite; and consequently that Germany does not have what in other lands are called national heroes, national achievements.

But this is only part of the whole picture. The more opinions diverge because of this tendency to abstract thought, and the more people lose themselves in the realm of ideas, the greater the differences among individuals become, and the more difficult it becomes to achieve that consensus we call national consciousness—a consciousness that is not easily reconciled with the degree of originality that so distinguishes the German race from the French. As in all other respects, here too the languages are totally representative.

Nevertheless, *national consciousness* is something entirely different from *national character* and *nationality*, and it is a great error, however long-standing and widespread, to suppose we do not possess the last two because we lack the first. The very intellectual tendency we have been describing, which destroys our national consciousness and makes us cosmopolitans, is actually part of our nationality. We have too few healthy prejudices; the pure spirit of criticism that dwells in us always finds good side by side with evil. We therefore give other nations their due, while dwelling on our own failings—which destroys national consciousness, whose greatest strength lies in prejudices. But of course our rationalism does not simply destroy healthy prejudices; its misuse *fundamentally* undermines our character, about which a few words will be said below.

The spirit of the Germans is ill-suited to the citizens of a great, unified monarchy. If there is a form of government to which it is least hostile it is republicanism, in which the spirit of criticism would find itself at home, and in which lawful participation in government would restrain its natural cosmopolitanism and bind the public's interests more closely to those of the fatherland. But the German's true element, in which he can follow all his natural leanings, is the recently lost [imperial] confederation, and it is no idle fancy to suppose that the German national character is one of the chief reasons the country preserved that constitution for so long.

Unfortunately, large republics are unacceptable on the continent, and in any case Germany's geographic position precludes such a constitution. Germany, of all countries, has the most contact with its neighbors, and it plays too important a role in the political affairs of Europe. Therefore we can only wish her the greatest uniformity of political activity and political institutions.

Political partisanship, which in other countries may be beneficial, must in Germany—the target of constant foreign interference—always lead to great divisions that would cause the collapse of the regime. It is self-evident that a nation with such a spirit is less suited than the French to be led by the hundred small expedients of government. Anyone who thinks he can control public opinion in Germany as in France, with a few mercenary journalists, is badly mistaken. Here each man wants to go his own way, and a writer from Bamberg has as much authority with the public as one from Berlin.

In more than one respect the German character would be highly suited to wind a unifying bond around the German nation. We are *warm, loyal*, and *honest*, as long as we do not oppress ourselves with clever rationalizations. But this oppression weighs upon the German heart more than it should. This eternal sophistry is the cause of our unfortunate skepticism. No one trusts anyone else's ability, nor the abilities of the nation. Earlier, among German communities that were less mature, where this evil was less pronounced, political bonds appeared that were so intimate as to be unique in history; I have in mind the Swiss confederation. But constant arguing, however worthwhile it otherwise may be, can only remain far removed from such noble and trusting simplicity.

We are much less vain than the French, so we are less capable of the kind of enthusiasm that springs from vanity, and which—whatever the philosophers say—sets great forces in motion within the machinery of the state. I have already remarked how little we are moved by petty expedients, and here is the place to say more about this. For it is vanity above all that makes such measures work. The reproach directed at Germany's governments—that they fail to make enough use of trickery to move the masses—seems to me doubly correct. First, because our governments reflect the German spirit, which wants nothing to do with such measures and is actually repelled by them, which often looks like mere laziness, though it is not; second, because in the past a few minor attempts have made so little impact that, without exactly knowing why, we retreat from them even more.

Etiquette will never have as much importance to the Germans as to the French or other nations. "What's the point? It's all *vain and useless*," says the common man. "*One must not control and degrade men by such base means*," says the philosopher. In Germany, if a public festival is coming up, the money to pay for the lighting will be given to the poor; if a monument to a famous man is supposed to be built, schools and hospitals will be proposed instead. All this, it seems to me, shows how little vanity the German has, how far he sees into the essence of things.

It is for just this reason that we are more *self-sufficient* than the French and put more weight on our own consciences than the approval of others. A Frenchman, having given in completely to public opinion, will think himself fit to do nothing on his own; the German often defies public opinion completely. This is supposed to be a virtue, with only good effects, but this is not so. Someone as accustomed to arguing as the German will often soothe his conscience with sophistry. The views of other people are not affected by our own rationalizations, however, so it is a genuine failing that we pay so little attention to them. Here, as everywhere, good borders on evil. Who would believe that, of all the [fortress] commanders who capitulated in shame before the eyes of the world [in 1806], not even one saved himself from public humiliation by a willing death? They all soothed their consciences with the same rationalizations that led them to surrender in the first place.

Because Germans are more guarded about their feelings, there is less of that mutual stimulation that gives rise to enthusiasm. This is why, although we have richer and deeper feelings than the French, we seem to have *less*.

In their habits, the Germans are distinguished by enterprise and hard work, in part because the land generally requires more effort to work, in part because constant activity is inherent in the German's character. His earnestness makes him uninterested in amusements and games, and the source of this earnestness, his inclination toward deep inquiry, also inspires the wide-ranging ventures that occupy his enterprising spirit, the constant striving for greater prosperity that is so important to the Germans compared to the French. If someone in Germany earns ten or fifteen thousand taler through hard work, he does not retire from further labor and place limits on himself; rather, success is a spur to new effort, and neither the weakness of old age nor the approach of death prevents him from expanding his business and advancing from prosperity to riches. The German businessman pursues his economic objective with the same enormous energy the German philosopher uses in plumbing the depths of knowledge. On the other hand, the German is less thrifty than the Frenchman, and his body requires more ample nourishment.

Doesn't all this naturally lead to the conclusion that the constraints of social forms and positive laws, and the sacrifices required for the state's existence, are more of a burden to the German than to the Frenchman? That as a result the German often feels he has cause to complain about the conduct of his government? That he is highly critical and opposes the aims of government with all his might? Who can deny this? Don't we struggle against this tendency all the time, under the names egotism and selfishness?

What, finally, is the result of our inquiry? That the Frenchman, with his limited nature, modest aspirations, and personal vanity, is more easily pressed into a uniform whole, more amenable to the aims of government, and hence a generally superior political instrument to the German, with his boundless spirit, his manifold originality and individualism, his inclination to reflection, and his ceaseless striving toward a higher, self-imposed goal.

Anyone who considers the histories of both nations cannot fail to find still greater and broader support for my claims.

It was in France that the feudal system, based on the concept of individual worth, first disappeared and was transformed into a unified monarchy. A weak king, Charles VII, could dare to deal feudalism the final blow, because he was strengthened by *the patriotic enthusiasm of his vassals.* And Louis XI [Charles's son] could risk negotiating with these vassals, an idea that would have occurred to no other prince in Europe at that time. Even before the struggle with feudalism ended, it was always the nobility as a whole that obstructed the monarchy in France, while in Germany it was the determination and mighty courage of individuals. Finally, at a time when the feudal system in France was entirely destroyed and nothing remained but empty, formal privileges and external trappings, secured not by law but by the principle of honor,* empty forms intended to flatter the vanity of the great, at just this time feudalism in Germany was following an entirely different path, leading to true territorial sovereignty for the most powerful vassals. And while a French peer might take pride in appearing before his king with his head covered, the independent German prince, with that peculiar German tendency to look only at the essence of things, did not refuse his emperor a courtier's humble service at his coronation.

In France chivalry was more romantic than in Germany; in France the crusades were supported more universally. And most of the great kings of France—Charles VIII, Francis I, Louis XII, Henry IV—eagerly took up whatever chivalrous project presented itself, while Louis XIV became the very epitome of superficial splendor.

How far the French remain at the level of first impressions, which in politics is often the most practical approach, is evident in their Parlement [of Paris]. A superior court, which by definition had no right to make constitutional law, was long viewed by the nation as the only bulwark against arbitrary tyranny, *simply because it had always shown itself to be a stalwart, honest, and intelligent tribunal.* But this very Parlement reveals how far the French may be ruled by appearances, for no Parlement or other court could exercise the least authority or political power in the presence of the king.

The same decisive superiority that the French seem to have over the Germans in practical politics also seems to have been possessed by the Romans over the Greeks, just as there is no denying that the Greeks possessed a finer and richer individuality, a kind of superiority no one would deny the Germans when compared with the French.

---

* [William] Robertson, *History of Charles V.*

If I possessed more historical knowledge than I do, I would allow myself a comprehensive comparison of these four nations, or rather of these two analogous relationships, for I am convinced the correspondence between them would lend historical support to my argument. But I must be satisfied to draw attention to a few points which, by the way, everyone knows as well as I do.

The Greeks developed earlier than the Romans, who never matched them, even later on, in any of the arts of peace. They were always superior to the Romans in intellectual riches. Even in the art of war the Greeks stood at least on the same level. I consider a direct comparison of Greek and Roman tactics fruitless, because, owing to the effect of other factors, we can conclude nothing about Roman tactics from a few successful battles; on the other hand, Hannibal, using the Greek phalanx, was long victorious over the Roman legions. Nevertheless, the Greek states played a leading role in the world for barely 150 years, namely, from the first Persian war until the reign of Alexander the Great. The Macedonians were great only with and because of Alexander, while the Romans were for 800–900 years (from the time of Alexander to the migrations of the fourth century) the greatest people on earth.

NINE

Notes on History and Politics
(1807–1809)

Following his return to Prussia in the fall of 1807, Clausewitz resumed the practice of recording his thoughts in the notebook he had begun to keep before the war.[1] *Now, however, his reflections increasingly revolved around Prussia's immediate problems and the steps that might be taken to reverse its defeat. Some of his earlier concerns reappear in a markedly different light. His remarks a few years before on the cross-purposes of coalitions, for instance, had deprecated the idea of applying private moral standards to politics. In his comments "On the Russian Manifesto Following the Peace of Tilsit," on the other hand, he finds Russia's conduct toward its erstwhile Prussian ally to be captured with "algebraic" precision by just such a moral analogy: Russia is like a man who steals from someone he had tried unsuccessfully to save from another thief.*

If the notes written before Prussia's defeat reflect a general preference for firmness, energy, and clarity in foreign affairs, those written afterwards express a desire for action almost for its own sake, without regard for the revolutionary risks it might entail or the coercive measures that might be necessary to bring it about.[2] *Time was not on Prussia's side after 1807, in Clausewitz's judgment, for both psychological and strategic reasons. To delay resistance seemed to invite further deterioration in the morale of the population, which would eventually grow used to oppression. Delay would also afford Napoleon the opportunity to defeat his enemies one at a time. Even the failed Austrian campaign of 1809 was better than passivity—it diverted French resources from the war in Spain, inspired pride and hope in Germany, and reminded Napoleon that fortune might not always favor him as it had so far. Above all, Clausewitz wants to detach the question of resistance from disputes about the adequacy of the means available to carry it out. And here he sounds a note*

---

[1] On the provenance of the following material, which represents the balance of the selections published by Hans Rothfels and W. M. Schering, see p. 237, note 2, above.

[2] Clausewitz was personally prepared to go very far in search of a more active role than that afforded by his position as Prince August's adjutant. Following the Austrian declaration of war on France in April 1809, he tried to secure a commission in the Austrian army; when this plan was ruined by Austria's defeat, he briefly investigated the possibility of joining the British service instead.

that would echo throughout his later work: that decisions about the goals of policy should not be confused with decisions about the means of achieving them. That the ends and means of politics must interact was obvious; but "where only one goal is possible, the available means are the right ones."

These entries reveal an increasing sensitivity to internal divisions within the government, expressed most vividly as intense irritation at the selfishness of politicians. He is also increasingly aware of what might be called the psychology of subjugation. The collective response of the Prussian people to defeat was more complex than the simple hatred and desire for action that Clausewitz felt. Many preferred to identify with the conqueror, to blame themselves, to withdraw emotionally, to develop self-defeating rationalizations for inaction. In retrospect, Clausewitz would assign these impulses disproportionately to the upper classes in Prussia—a sociological interpretation inspired by his later experiences as a member of the reform party, trying to make headway against the inertia of tradition. It is not in evidence here, where the focus falls on human nature in general.

Despite their often violent language and biting sarcasm, these notes reveal the germs of deepening political understanding: that the unity of the state was itself a political achievement, which might be undermined or destroyed by personal conflicts or factional strife; and that success in such an ambiguous environment depended on special qualities of mind and character—qualities in which Clausewitz always felt deficient himself. Clausewitz's notes break off just as he was becoming directly involved in Prussian politics for the first time, as Scharnhorst's assistant in the War Department. But a strong sense of the significance of all these personal and psychological elements would color both of his major retrospective accounts of this period.[3]

[1807][4]

To me there is no more discouraging observation than this: that the most exalted social institutions, however many centuries they may survive and function, still carry the seeds of their own destruction within them. What is wiser than Lycurgus's constitution for Sparta? For centuries it secured domestic peace and a noble, manly existence for that state. Yet it made Sparta's continued survival impossible when the Romans were coming to power.

What is more lofty than the founding of a great religion? Yet there is not

[3] See "On the Life and Character of Scharnhorst" and *Observations on Prussia*, above.

[4] This selection dates from the fall of 1807; much of its contents were incorporated in a letter to Marie von Brühl, October 5, 1807, in Schwartz, *Leben*, 1: 294.

one that would not be undermined and destroyed by precisely the same principles that originally made it strong and great.

What is nobler in purpose and means than the founding of a monastic order, to lend religion new dignity, luster, and strength through a life of perpetual sacrifice? And yet haven't the monastic orders fallen into disrepute not merely through decadence, but by their very nature?

In speaking of the principles behind these phenomena, we mean those that define them as civil institutions, as political instruments. In its elemental purity religious feeling will always live in the human heart, but no particular religion can last forever. The beneficial influence of virtue on human society will never change, but this universal spirit cannot be encapsulated in a narrow legal code, which must collapse sooner or later, once the stream of time washes away or alters the conditions on which it was based. Renunciation and penitence will always inspire sympathy and wonder, but reason will not always be disposed to acknowledge them as the only goal of the citizen's life.

This view is most disturbing to those who have devoted themselves to civil life, in contrast to those who have fled the real world for that of imagination and devote themselves to timeless art. Even if most works of art fade from view along with the times in which they were created, a few luminous works remain suspended above the horizon, as if torn free from everything ephemeral. While the priest of art carries in himself the exalted and gratifying sense that his life's purpose is elevated above the norm, existing not in time and space but in eternity—with no goal too remote, nor the realm of heaven and the spirit too high—the ordinary citizen must remain within the narrow limits of conventional life in order to lay the foundation stones of the social edifice. He anxiously draws boundaries around himself in time and space and measures his achievement by modest standards of permanence and completeness. Always he must *distinguish, divide, classify, choose,* and *exclude, even* while boldly reaching out toward that divine unity that is the highest object of our reason, and all we know of the world's purpose, without ever knowing how well or badly he serves its ends.

I have not spoken of *science*, which is set apart from both the *arts* and *practical life* in this way: *that it carries its object within itself.* It is thus independent of time and space, but also of all the goals of life. The arts seek an infinite goal; practical life seeks a finite goal; whoever enters the realm of science must have no goal at all. For a goal would be nothing more than a preconceived opinion, which is entirely alien to science. The essence of science is *analysis*; the essence of the arts is the *force of synthesis*.

Those in the political world (which I always think of as the opposite of the artistic) who disdain these limits and wish to rise to the level of art have not studied history and fail completely. The world thinks of them as dreamers, and if this impression unjustly denigrates the imagination, let those who would set the imagination on the throne of a kingdom where it ought to obey answer for it, for it is because of them that the abuse occurs.

But I am getting distracted by other issues even though I must still draw an important conclusion. *That the citizen who works and builds only for the short term should not waste his time, should not be satisfied, with* [political] *salvation that points only toward the distant future.*

On the Occasion of the Russian Manifesto Following the Peace of Tilsit[5]

Out of sympathy for human weakness, and also because not all mistakes are committed from evil motives, we watch in silence while Alexander, defeated more in his feeble spirit than in the field, turns anxiously to his poor, cowardly advisors to save him and surrenders himself to shame and misery.

We register this distasteful impression in silence, for why waste words on a sight familiar enough in all times, though none has given in to it the way ours has.

Yet the Russian counselors expect too much of their fellow men if they think that, having achieved high office, they can remain free of blame for displaying the most unheard-of impudence and cowardice, and turning *their backs* on danger with heads bowed low! That is more than a noble heart can bear in silence, and it is not for nothing that nature has given us the power to vent our rage in ridicule and curses.

Anyone, I think, will feel this way who reads Alexander's manifesto, in which the great deeds of his army, the glorious outcome of the war, the recovery and return of provinces his ally lost, his dignified refusal of aggrandizement at that ally's expense, and the noble expansion of his kingdom to secure borders are all spoken of shamelessly and blindly. I say *blindly* because when a man hopes to deceive others he may well deceive himself.

It was once customary to clothe policy in the guise of legality on those occasions when it could not go around naked in the world. *This* policy, if it really is one, goes around in moral rags through which its nakedness is all too visible. *This logic* looks like a broken theorem, *this glory* a dunce cap,

---

5 This manifesto sought to justify the Russian treaty with France, concluded on July 7, 1807. Under its terms Russia lost no territory but entered into alliance with France, agreeing among other things to conform to the continental system and accept the creation of the Grand Duchy of Warsaw, which brought a French army permanently to its own frontier. Prussia's Polish provinces were incorporated into this new state. Prussia signed a separate treaty two days later, by which it lost all its territory west of the Elbe. The czar's manifesto was promulgated in St. Petersburg on August 9, 1807, and was published in several German newspapers in October.

this friendship a poisoned potion. Are we supposed to bow down before this union of foolishness and crime?

1. When Alexander sent his brave army to help his friend and ally Frederick of Prussia, that unlucky prince had only lost the lands west of the Elbe and the Mark. Silesia and West Prussia still held out, thanks to their many fortresses and by any concept of war this left him in effective possession of Silesia, East-, West-, and South Prussia, more than two-thirds of the kingdom. Whom, then, should common sense blame for failing to defend these fortresses and for the loss of the territory between the Vistula and the Niemen? The Prussian army, at most 30,000 strong, or the Russian army, five times stronger? What Prussia regained in the war thus hardly equalled what she lost because of the Russians. Are we cheerfully supposed to overlook this?

2. What was the emperor's purpose in going to war against France? To secure Germany's independence, to protect Prussia? It seems to me, then, that the return of a few Prussian provinces as part of an honorable peace is no more an act of generosity than the original Russian aid was; on the contrary, I think it was the only significant element of the treaty. Or maybe the tacit plea to the enemy not to threaten Russia any more was the most essential part? But to confess as much, *that* ill-becomes pride.

3. Russia generously declines to enrich herself at Prussia's expense—have the Russian counselors forgotten that Prussia, not France, was their ally? Obviously! Otherwise it seems to me there could be no more question of this than of deciding whether a man draws a sword in a duel to wound himself or his opponent. It is a form of indirect conquest to make Prussia pay for half her provinces with the loss of the other half, just as it is a negative form of generosity not to *rob* the man one has gone to help.

4. That Russia should boast of renouncing her claims to the property of her blood brother in fact shows without a doubt that she was capable of considering the idea, since whoever pleads innocent in the absence of a charge accuses himself; but while there was no chance this passage [in the treaty] would be overlooked, the Russian counselors, with incredible inconsistency, assert their claim to *the artificial extension of the Russian frontier* right after this hypocritical boast, and expect the reader to forget in the second line what he read in the first, to forget that Prussia's destitution must pay for this conquest.

We could also describe this great event, like the *a* and *b* of an algebraic problem, by way of the following story.

An honest man is attacked by a thief, threatened with death, and robbed. When he is already lying on the ground half-naked, another man leaps to his aid—who gets beaten up in turn and takes to his heels, but not before hastily compensating himself for the blows he has received by stealing from the unarmed victim.

Machiavelli would turn away in disgust from such a policy!

And why did this sudden change of heart occur? Because up to the moment of peace the emperor Alexander followed his own ideas or, more precisely, his own feelings. None of this can mislead me about the emperor's character. This monstrous policy entered his soul through fear and uncomprehending anxiety and overcame the honest disposition and noble impulses that are unmistakable in him. With each new setback in the field he felt that he was not cut out to resist the superior power and talent of the enemy. As the danger seemed to his deceived senses to grow larger as it drew nearer he looked around in fear—and there behind him, waving wildly, stood the sons of misery: "Why wear ourselves out in this effort," they say. "If we swim with the current we will become great and mighty without so much as thinking about it. We can give Your Majesty no other advice than to make peace and an alliance with France, for we know no other way to save ourselves."

A little insight, some knowledge of history and human nature, were enough to conjure up this ghost before the emperor's eyes, and a man weak in the ways of politics will inevitably be startled by it. A few steps closer and it won't vanish completely even to the most jaundiced eye. Alexander strode too boldly and imprudently onto the path of treachery, just as he wandered too boldly and carelessly onto the path of heroism! He forgets that great crime, like great virtue, requires energy, the *only* thing they have in common.

If France should become lord of the German lands, secure in her position for the long term, she would never allow Russia to share in this dominion, nor to grow too powerful in Asia, just as the overweening pride of Rome forced the Syrian king to leave Greece for his homeland, where Rome soon looked to find him. When Russia finally collides with France—then at least Alexander won't be looking to his present advisors for salvation.

But to declare Germany lost is too hasty. Individual talent is a matter of chance, which cannot last beyond a human life, and besides, only the spirit of two nations can determine their relationship. If these two nations are compared, there can be no question of French dominance. Such a view would be *incredibly petty*, lacking both depth of feeling and insight. Everything history teaches us shows that we are closer to acting as a unified nation than the French, who have now passed that point [in their development], and for just that reason are farthest from it.

No book on earth is more necessary to the politician than Machiavelli's; those who affect disgust at his principles are idealistic dilettantes. What he says about the princes' policies toward their subjects is certainly largely outdated, because political forms have changed considerably since his time. Neverthe-

less, he gives some remarkable rules, which will remain valid forever. . . .
But this author is especially instructive in foreign affairs, and all the scorn
cast on him (to be sure, often out of confusion, ignorance, affectation) has to
do with his teaching on the treatment of the citizenry, insofar as it is justified
at all. Frederick II, who wanted to demonstrate and exercise his literary abilities in his response to Machiavelli, wrote the "Anti-Machiavelli" as a young
man, and the whole essay, published in 1740, quite bears the imprint of a
young academic who is delighted for the first time to be able to write in the
professorial mode. In his foreign policy Frederick II was a most obedient
student of Machiavelli, and if he did not suppress his "Anti-Machiavelli"
later on, that too was a Machiavellian refinement. Voltaire said it well: "*Il a
craché dessus pour en dégouter les autres.*"[6]

Given that the policy Machiavelli advocates toward other powers is designed primarily for states too weak to act in a straightforward manner; that
measures which appear to be aimed at a state's own subjects may only be
intended for use against other princes, because the author did not always
have the courage to spell out his principles; and finally that in Italy and the
small states with which he was always concerned, entirely different domestic
policies were required then than now—if we consider all this, we will be
unable to accuse Machiavelli of more than this: with a certain lack of decency, he called things by their proper names. You kindhearted moralists,
just look at yourselves in the mirror—look at how your principles, your moral
egotism, are so utterly changed when reflected back by the real world. Look
at how you heap proud disdain and sentimental revulsion on Machiavelli's
impure theories and admire the effects of these impure theories among his
students with every indication of adulation. And you sensitive politicians,
have you learned anything yet from experience? The twenty-first chapter of
Machiavelli's *Prince* is the basic code for all diplomacy—and woe to those
who fail to heed it![7]

1808

Today a state is torn from its moorings and cast down from the heights, and
tomorrow the obituaries appear; tomorrow comes the autopsy of the friend
who died today. Such is the spirit of Germany's political journals and pam-
phlets. They just seem to lie in wait for the passing of the great and sacred,
in order to take possession (with most unseemly haste) of the sad legacy of

---

[6] "He spit on it to repel the others."

[7] Chapter 21, "How a Prince Should Act to Acquire Reputation," advises against neutrality
for a prince caught between two powerful rivals.

biographies, discussions, reflections, prophecies, and whatever other weeds
may spring up from the grave.

If you are not so *stupid* as to be without all feeling, if you don't mean to
be slaves to prejudice, then what do you think you're doing, you rabble?

No nation has ever responded to repression by another with anything except hatred and enmity. We alone suffer from this asininity, this fool's wisdom, which imagines itself wearing a crown while dragging the chains of a
slave.

In Reference to Well-Meaning German Philosophers

Presumptuous philosophy deserves contempt and derision when it seeks to
raise us high above the activities of the day so that we can escape their pressures and cease all inner resistance to them! When it promotes a *lifeless* faith
in the cosmic order and its higher goals, a frigid sophistry standing as a spec-
tator over God's work, in place of the consuming ardor that is his instrument!

That individual generations are nothing but insignificant tools of providence; that they can realize their value only in the work accomplished
through them; that it does not matter if the tool breaks down a little sooner
or later; they do not exist to observe the world; by constantly striving for rational goals they *are* the world—*that*, I think, is the highest standpoint, beyond
which there is no other.

What wretched comfort this foolish faith in the future offers! It is today
that makes tomorrow, the present that creates the future. Those who wait
foolishly on the future will find it mangled by their own idle hands.

The times belong to you; what they will become they will become through
you. Do you want to pass on to your children, to your children's children,
the burden of raising the fatherland once more from the abyss, in which so
much that might make for greatness is rotting to no purpose—why not do it
yourselves?

Don't you think your children and your children's children will look back
across the generations to their ancestors? You want to teach your children to
be worthy of the great task of liberation—make yourselves worthy first. The
corrupting breath of vice cannot instill virtue. Set a good example for your
children—that, above all, is the education they need. Do not seduce them
with the indolence you call wisdom. Face the rising generation fortified with
self-sacrifice, armed with strength! Then they will be what you are waiting
for, then you have a right to pass on the unfinished work to their hands.

Stop trying to stifle the fire in your breasts, as if it were a form of corruption! That fire is God's holy instrument; it does not consume you for nothing! Why shouldn't it too burst forth in flames to attack the hostile element: Fire ignites fire, flame feeds on flame—once your fire penetrates the whole nation, it will burst forth in leaping flames and rid the age of the foul vapors that the plodding pace of events has left hanging over us.

POLITICAL CALCULATION

The truth of a political or moral argument is only a matter of probability, and thus is persuasive in varying degrees among different men. Yet this sort of difference is not as harmful as another—namely, that one man, to avoid getting lost in a labyrinth of alternatives, will reject all the possibilities that can still exist alongside a highly probable outcome, while another will continue to consider them all. The first man arrives quickly at a firm conclusion, the second never does. The conduct of the first is always guided by the most likely case. He may be wrong, since the most likely case is not the only possibility; but error is always *unlikely* for him, and his ratio of success will be high. The other man, because he cannot see and evaluate every possibility simultaneously, soon finds himself with no other guide for action except *his desires*. His intelligence then gives up, and he is an easy prey for his enemies.

This is why ordinary men do not act rationally in a great crisis until, finding themselves on the horns of a dilemma, they no longer see any way out except by a daring leap. This gives them courage, conviction, and energy. But their decisive attitude is lost whenever the remotest of false hopes are awakened. These false hopes are the true sappers of energy, of moral electricity, and before our eyes a person's inner strength will sink from its artificial height with unbelievable speed, and collapse into their former pitiful state, where the lurking specter of cruel fate can take hold without difficulty.

I recognize clearly what makes a great man in the practical or, even more, in the political world, because I feel I lack it myself: it is a high degree of orderly, focused activity directed toward a great goal. Not many men are even capable of setting a great goal for themselves, that is, of *seriously* adopting it, of sacrificing lesser but more immediate and certain advantages to achieve it. There is of course no shortage of big talkers. I know such men; I also know them to act, even to act in a more or less orderly way. But I still miss that unity of effort in their activity, that constant renewal of energy in themselves and others, that diligence in seizing *every means* available—in short, that supreme determination to succeed as quickly as possible, which seems to me so solid, constant, strong, and firm. I understand this lack quite well, for I feel it in me. Perhaps I would feel it less if I were in a position to act. Most probably I would find it less in others, too, if they were in a position to act freely and entirely on their own account. Nevertheless, under any circumstances a feeling of incompleteness remains if we do not pursue a goal with all possible effort, so that, even if it has moved beyond our reach and is no longer attainable, it still represents our greatest happiness, pointing steadily toward some universal purpose.

Once weak men are subjected to a tyrant's rule, they are always ready to mistake what are merely the workings of tyranny for their own failings. But that is the most abject position people can be in, when they can no longer get justice even from themselves. This natural process has long been noted by tyrants, among whom the art of making the weak into instruments of the tyranny that holds them down has always been highly developed.

The weak recognize all their failings except their own weakness. Yet I have known some who recognize this too, and although this does not make them any more capable of remedying it, I still prefer them by far because they trust in a higher power outside themselves and submit to it, which often gives them a kind of courage, while the others, who are merely respectful to their enemies, to whom they attribute the powers of gods or devils, believe all people are like themselves and are therefore incapable of real trust. They have their own kind of courage, namely, the kind that suffers everything and does nothing.

1809

Shallow men consider it a miraculous intellectual effort if they distinguish, in the person of the ruler, between his private and his public identities, and nothing has led to more vulgar and awful misunderstandings. Because a king once possessed a private fortune, separate from the public treasury, they think he also has a private sense of honor with which the state need not be concerned. The interests of a prince can of course be distinguished from those of his subjects, and if this at first seems illogical, consider Bonaparte's example. But the person of the prince cannot be separated from his rank, because the rank is not a quality of the person, from which he can step back whenever he likes; rather, the person is the property of the office and equally inviolate. Honor is an attribute of the individual and can never be divorced from him. Therefore the public honor of the king is indivisible from the personal; it is the most magnificent ornament of the crown. A nation that purchases material advantages at the expense of its honor must be in such decline that without great upheavals it cannot continue for long among other nations. For the honor and dignity of a nation are the final product of its whole moral condition. But where can the dignity of a nation be more painfully wounded than in the honor of its monarch, in which its own honor is, so to speak, concentrated? An honorable, noble nation will be outraged and eager for revenge if even one of its members is harmed. How much more must this be so if the offense is directed against one who is sacred to it, one who represents the entire nation? Among states and nations where the heartless sophistry of the prophets of misery does not prevail, where the heart is still a source of warm and noble feelings, the moral identity of the nation is not represented only by the intellect of the ruler; rather, his entire personality represents the identity of the whole people. The person of the monarch must therefore be the nation's most sacred trust in every way, which no one can insult without insulting the nation itself. How, then, could a nation desire that, in exchange for material advantages, its ruler should sacrifice his honor? That would be no different than if the nation gave up its own honor for the same reason—which occurs, let me say it once more, if the nation is approaching a great revolution or its own destruction.

To develop and express one's opinion with precision and clarity in councils of state, war, or government is one of the most pointless tasks anyone can undertake. The effort is wasted on those who can and will understand him, that is, those who share the same view; on the others, too, but for different reasons, since everyone brings his particular point of view, his system, with him. Good heads, open-minded and ready to learn about the matter under discussion, are by nature absent. Instead, everyone returns to the house he came from, or acts like he does, and the truth is told to the wind. It is no different with princes than with their advisors. It is something else entirely, however, to address an assembly of several hundred educated men, among whom a few good heads still exist despite the corruption of the electorate: some of the first rank, many who through passion and imagination will achieve a higher level of effectiveness than they normally would.

These good heads, however, are not like ministers or councilors who are driven along like mill horses by the machinery of state; they still bring a certain open-mindedness with them. Here the speaker has an audience that listens and thinks about what he says. If he wins a majority among the best of them, the mass will soon follow, and now the obstinate, entrenched stupidity that couldn't be shaken by a thunderbolt of truth is overwhelmed and swept away by the tide of the majority.

There are certain political pessimists who shrug their shoulders when people talk about the *possibility* of success in a war with France. Unless we have a better constitution, leading to a different form of government, they do not entertain this possibility. I want this, too, and believe that in the long run (that is, over many generations, for over one or two, fortunately, a great ruler can prevail) we cannot sustain ourselves in our dangerous position without it. Germany must look to a more noble and appropriate constitution for its citizens and states in order to secure its future existence.

In the present crisis, however, to await this slow rebirth (slow because with us at least there is no violent revolution waiting at the gate) seems ridiculous to me.

War, great danger, great misfortune are capable of raising the ordinary man above his commonplace existence, that is, of causing him to disregard the comforts of his normal life, whether he has already lost them or not. National hatred, deep outrage at the wickedness and violence of the oppressor (which in our case is certainly no empty presumption) come into play and can substitute for religious or political passion or for extreme attachment to the old ways—at least when there is no positive hatred of the government, nor a dislike of former conditions. Finally, there is the play of luck, which dominates in every war. If all these advantages are not enough for those whose genius consists in cutting everything from whole cloth, who shape their means according to abstract principles and only see success when it is already obvious in the means—then I ask, if these half-measures seem contemptible, what better do they have to offer in the present emergency?

They want a revolution—I have nothing against it; but won't this revolution of state and society be more easily accomplished if all elements are active and in motion, as happens in war? Where, otherwise, is the prospect of a healthy revolution, the prospect of salvation? We must act in the real world. I am for action. Where a choice of goals exists, it is appropriate to reflect and consider the means; where only one goal is possible, the available means are the right ones. Fortune favors the brave. Those who are fixated by specific formulas and do not recognize or know how to seize opportunities in the passing stream of events count for nothing in the real world.

What particularly annoys me about these people is that they are always talking about *broad views*. Their broad views are *narrow* views. If someone needs to solve an algebraic equation, he is a narrow fellow indeed if, being unfamiliar with algebra and unable to solve the problem in the scientific way, he does not persevere by means of numbers, examples, experiments, and whatever mother wit he may possess.

This observation was made before the Austrian war [of 1809] and pertained to its cause. It was written down *after* the war, however, and I think it remains true despite the outcome and valid for all circumstances in which another war is conceivable.

People will say the Austrian war achieved none of its promised results and only made matters worse. By no means. The people of Austria (at least the Germans) raised themselves to a level of patriotism they had not shown for some time, and those traces will not be easily erased (so says our knowledge of the human heart). The army fought so bravely at Wagram and Znaim that it won the respect of the enemy and gained new self-confidence. In the Tirol a spirit of heroism and Spartan courage developed that is an invaluable example for Germany and Switzerland. If Schill was an isolated spark whose brief existence drew all eyes to him and momentarily aroused everyone's feelings,[8] then the Tirolese are a mighty firebrand, which has already cast its light on us and by whose heat we can warm ourselves. North Germany, although in no way active, was in such an excited state during the war, in which its chains loosened a little, that at least it did not progress further into subjugation. Which is the better way to make a disobedient child obey—by keeping a tight rein on him, or by letting him run wild from time to time and then forcefully disciplining him? The first way, certainly; the other is bound to make a rascal of him. The analogy is easily applied.

Generally speaking, all the seeds produced by this war must eventually survive and propagate. Peace is like the snow of winter, under which they sleep and slowly develop; war is the heat of summer, which germinates them rapidly and brings them to maturity. Such seeds are evident even in chance events: the Danube destroyed the enemy's bridges; a minor wound has shown the emperor that fortune will not always protect her favorite from profane bullets—one of his most outstanding commanders was killed[9]—and while it might seem too clever to claim that these seeds are real and capable of further development, the living principle underlying the whole, overarching logic of existence (the law of probability) cannot be denied. Everyone can view these advantages in his own way, as more or less significant, but whoever claims they are meaningless cannot or will not think clearly.

[8] Major Ferdinand von Schill, commander of the Second Brandenburg Hussars, conducted a short-lived independent campaign against the French in the spring of 1809, in an attempt to force Prussia to come to Austria's aid. Schill's regiment was eventually defeated; Schill was killed, and eleven surviving officers were tried and executed by the French.

[9] Jean Lannes died of wounds suffered at the battle of Aspern-Essling in May. Clausewitz's curious insistence that Napoleon's luck might be running out may be partly explained by the fact that Lannes was the first of Napoleon's marshals to be killed by the enemy.

So much for the benefits of the war as war; now for the consequences of its results. These seem unfortunate if we compare them to what would have followed a victorious war, but they should be compared instead to what would have followed from the peace in preference to which the war was fought. The consequences of a long peace would have been the defeat of Spain and a war later on against the undivided power of France. How totally different would that war have been, how totally different the likely result? Is it not entirely natural to fight a war that is absolutely unavoidable in concert with an ally? . . . And if war were in fact avoidable?—Oh, if that is so, then a balance of power existed in Europe when the war broke out, and I have been wrong from the beginning.

PRUSSIA AFTER THE PEACE OF 1809[10]

Prussia's position from the peace of 1807 to that of 1809 has clearly been equivocal and still awaits a *final* resolution. This resolution can only come from the man who decides everything. If Napoleon's intentions toward Prussia were benevolent, he would have made them public already. After the Peace of Tilsit, nothing would have prevented him from binding Prussia to France as firmly as he bound Bavaria and Saxony; and if this did not accord with the feelings of the monarch and the Prussian people, they could not have freed themselves any more easily under the circumstances than Bavaria and Saxony could, that is, by nothing short of a universal national war against France. Instead of securing this advantage for himself, Napoleon left Prussia in a state of uncertainty, thus giving her the chance and the temptation to take part in the enterprises directed against him by Spain, Austria, and England. Even if the emperor never believed Prussia could be a threat to him in such circumstances, he still must have had a reason not only for keeping her in a state of uncertainty and fear for so long, but also for the peculiar harshness with which he treated her, which could only lead to bitterness. This reason is most probably the desire to provoke Prussia to attack him again. Being convinced that her weak government would never be a serious threat to him, he hoped to find a suitable pretext either to dissolve the state entirely or to make it even more wretched and dependent. Prussia's conduct during the last war was highly ambiguous, which certainly did not increase the emperor's benevolence. For the moment he is still occupied in

[10] The Treaty of Schönbrunn (October 14, 1809) ended the war between Austria and France. Its terms resembled those imposed on Prussia at Tilsit. Austria lost about 20 percent of its population, all of its Polish territories, and access to the Mediterranean. Austria's defeat heightened Prussia's already great vulnerability to French pressure.

Spain, he has work to do in Holland and the Tirol, and he will presumably postpone a decision on Prussia. Perhaps conditions will arise that will provide a pretext for action against her. If not, there are plenty of materials on hand, even for a manifesto with all the customary sophistry, not to mention the kind of worthless article the filthy Paris newspapers are accustomed to provide in place of declarations of war. If we then ask what Prussia has to expect, we would have to be completely prejudiced and narrow-minded (as indeed many Prussians are) if we did not anticipate the total dissolution of the state or a higher level of subjugation, both combined with physical suffering.

Anyone who still doubts this should think about the demands for contributions (legal, no less) that France has yet to make, of the impossibility of paying them, and of the consequences of this refusal, which in the end can and must have *no* other results than those that befall any other bankrupt—humiliation and physical misery!

Thus the question now arises: Should Prussia submit without resistance? There are plenty of people for whom this is no longer even a question; but I believe that Prussia, that is, the government, must meet force with force. It would be absurd to deny that war between a nation of five million and a French army is *possible*. But the nation, people say, is wretched, it is corrupt, soft, and powerless.

Suppose it is. As an excuse for the government this is pure sophistry, because the government itself need not be soft and powerless—indeed it shouldn't be, since it sets the example for the people; it should lead them, and not be led by them. Certainly governments have made ample use of force against their own people for much narrower goals and lesser purposes: therefore a benevolent government like Prussia's (which can be in no danger of being misunderstood in this regard) might vigorously employ all the means of compulsion at its disposal to hold the people to their most sacred duty. I have no wish to recall the hideous example of the guillotine, which drove men to the frontiers to defend France in the first years of the Revolution.* There is such a thing as compulsion, even fearful compulsion on the part of government, that is not tyranny. The government must employ it if the nation becomes wretched enough to betray itself in a crisis, or worthless enough to shrink from its most sacred duty.

Who can doubt for an instant that the energy of the government would immediately be transmitted to the people—that, in the moment of supreme danger, the call to fulfill the ultimate duty of citizenship would not arouse tremendous enthusiasm. The feeling of leaving a narrow, prosaic life be-

---

* This is true for two reasons. First because those who did not enter the National Guard cast suspicion on themselves, and second because people found more personal security in the army than at home.

277

hind—not painlessly, not playfully, but driven by an all-powerful destiny—of taking up a truly poetic existence, full of idealism and dignity, would take hold of our educated youth, as has already occurred in a number of cases. Hatred of the oppressor would pervade the lower classes, the activity of the government would quickly inspire confidence; what else is needed to invigorate and unite the power of five million people?

Suppose, further, that all this is not enough, that our army, badly led, is beaten; courage struggles vainly against despair; misfortune tramples it under foot; the state is destroyed, and the enraged conqueror prepares to enslave the nation. Would blood have been shed in vain then? Won't this glorious death lift the courage of our descendants? It is a narrow and petty mind that cannot take these things into account. Isn't it in the nature of human passion to pursue a goal all the more tenaciously, the more we have already sacrificed on its behalf? Just as the passion of a gambler grows with defeat, so the love of independence will grow along with the sacrifices we make for it.

Woe to the nation if, out of shortsightedness, we now accept dishonorable, shameful terms. This submission, which people praise as wisdom, is obviously poison; it will undermine the strength and vitality of the nation for generations, and the range of its effects is beyond the power of our limited understanding to measure.

Suppose, finally, the nation proved incapable of liberating itself under the leadership of the government, that our soldiers fled like cowards from the ranks, that the army, easily beaten, simply added to the trophies and arrogance of the enemy, that we were destroyed, having merely exposed our shame more clearly to the light of day. I mention this dishonorable supposition only to satisfy that cold egotism that has for so long been stifling the last sparks of respect for human character. I myself declare such a supposition absolutely intolerable—and yet suppose, finally, the most debased and abominable conditions of peace anyone can imagine: then I am still convinced that the king must meet force with force, that he should not perish except in struggle.

What infamous doctrine is it that teaches men to sacrifice the moral to the material, to give up virtue for physical comfort? What teacher can say this to his students or tolerate it from them, what king can say it to his people? It is a cowardly sophistry to speak of the ruler's duty to sacrifice his own honor and that of the nation for its material well-being. The king is the representative of the nation. Whatever he does, whatever is admired in him—in that the nation has an involuntary, perhaps unmerited share in the eyes of the world and posterity. The monarch who succumbs with shame defiles the nation and renders it miserable; the monarch who is gloriously vanquished exalts the nation, and his exalted name is balm on the nation's wounds.

TEN

Letter to Fichte (1809)

In June 1807, the philosopher J. G. Fichte published an article on Machiavelli in the Königsberg journal Vesta.[1] *Its purpose was to defend Machiavelli against the vulgar misconceptions that, then as always, were attached to his name, and to argue that Machiavelli's unsparing approach to political power was the only one adequate to Germany's present circumstances. Those circumstances were indeed grave. By June 1807, Königsberg had become the last redoubt of the Prussian monarchy. On the 14th, the battle of Friedland would bring an end to all hope of further resistance against the French. Like the Italian states of the sixteenth century, Germany had become the battleground for the great powers on its periphery, and it was entirely natural to have sought inspiration in the work of the great Florentine republican.*

Clausewitz read Fichte's essay early in 1809 and found it so stimulating that he wrote the author the letter reprinted here.[2] *By then, as he says and as is evident from his early notebooks, he was already familiar with Machiavelli's ideas. In politics, above all in international affairs, Clausewitz believed Machiavelli's work contained enduring insights. Machiavelli's conception of the state as an amoral, autonomous agent and his understanding of politics as a realm in which force and expediency prevail over law and conscience are Clausewitz's as well. He admires Fichte's efforts to defend these ideas against those who saw states as being animated and legitimized by some spiritual mission— a point of view that was both wrong and dangerous from Clausewitz's perspective, because of the ease with which the realm of the spirit could become a refuge in time of defeat. In military affairs, on the other hand, Machiavelli had not risen so far above his own time: although his natural gifts made him a shrewd judge of men and events, his understanding of war in general was too dominated by the achievements of the ancients to be of permanent validity.*

Fichte, too, had been unduly impressed by past experiences of war. His

[1] "Ueber Machiavell, als Schriftsteller, und Stellen aus seinen Schriften," *Vesta: Für Freunde der Wissenschaft und Kunst* (June 1807), 17–81; in *Johann Gottlieb Fichtes nachgelassene Werke* (Leipzig, 1924; reprinted Berlin, 1962), 3: 401–53.

[2] The letter was first published in J. G. Fichte, *Briefwechsel*, ed. H. Schulz (Leipzig, 1925), 2: 520–26; reprinted in *Verstreute kleine Schriften*, 157–66. Clausewitz wrote to Fichte anonymously, so no reply exists. Quite apart from its political import, the letter sheds considerable light on Clausewitz's relationship to German idealism. See Paret, *Clausewitz and the State*, 167–79.

uncritical acceptance of some of Machiavelli's military opinions—particularly his deprecation of artillery—seems to have been the immediate inspiration for Clausewitz's letter, which begins with an abrupt denial that questions such as how much artillery an army needs can be resolved at the level of theory. Experience, Clausewitz believes, must be the guide. But he agrees with Fichte that some kind of revivifying force is needed if Germany is to save itself and goes on to locate that force not in new military forms, but in a renewal of the fighting spirit of the people, which, given time, will create appropriate techniques of its own.

Clausewitz's argument that military recovery had to begin by taking account of the state of mind of the ordinary soldier, indeed of the ordinary citizen, was in accord with the practical reforms in which he was then becoming involved. It also harmonizes surprisingly well with the notion that the moral improvement of individuals was a prerequisite to national revival. This attitude was associated at the time with an apolitical quietism that Clausewitz openly despised. Here, however, he casts the issue in a somewhat different light: spiritual strength is not a compensation for political failure, but a direct and immediate source of political and military power.

In contrast to Fichte, however—though, it may be noted, like Machiavelli himself—Clausewitz did not regard the moral freedom or excellence of the individual as a legitimate goal of politics, however desirable it might have been on other grounds. States could draw on the spiritual resources of their citizens, and to that extent had an interest in cultivating and protecting those resources. But they remained self-interested automatons, indispensable to the social order but still in perpetual tension with other values and aspirations in which power played no part.

To the gentleman who wrote the essay on Machiavelli in the first volume of *Vesta*.

I have read this essay, and while I am not the man of profound insights into the art of war, and still less the man of influence on whom you call to study Machiavelli's book on the art of war, I believe I am without prejudice, the more so since I have seen the traditional military forms and opinions among which I grew up come apart like rotten timber and collapse in the swift stream of events. Six years of intensive reflection on war had also prepared me to read it. Since I read Machiavelli's *Art of War* a few years ago and it is not now at hand, I am not in a position to present a rigorous argument on specific points. Nevertheless, I hope you will allow me to offer a few observations that it may please you to consider in relation to your own reflections. Today more than ever it is vital that a broad, sound view of war, beyond the petty maxims of the practitioners, should become the common property of every citizen, so that all those striving toward understanding may communicate with each other.

Artillery, like every other weapon, has certainly been badly employed here and there, mainly by the Prussian army in 1806, less so by the French, who do not have much artillery judged by present standards.

It is difficult, however, to work out the best ratio [of guns to infantry] on theoretical grounds except by sophistry, and small differences probably do not matter. To overlook artillery entirely would almost certainly have decisive disadvantages, for when guns are concentrated in large numbers it is impossible to do anything against them. Their effectiveness since Machiavelli's day has probably doubled at least. Augerau's corps at Eylau was destroyed by the Russian artillery alone, which Napoleon, stubbornly abandoning the usual rule, had them charge. In this as in other matters, experience alone can lead us to the truth. So much, for now, on the artillery.

There can be no doubt that the art of war in Germany is in decline. It must be animated by a new spirit if it is to serve us, and justify the toil, effort, and sacrifices that any war requires. You will allow me, in the following remarks, to indicate what has to happen, and also, in that regard, [to speak of] the relevance of Machiavelli's work.

I have often found Machiavelli to be a very sound judge of military matters, with some new insights, as for instance when he shows, in the case of Fabius Cunctator (in his *Discourses on Livy*, I think), that his major operations were not designed primarily in light of circumstances.[3] He adopted a delaying strategy not because he found it especially appropriate to existing conditions, but because he was a temporizer by nature. For when Scipio wanted to go to Africa [to attack Carthage], he opposed the plan. If Fabius had become king, Rome would have been ruined.

But so far as Machiavelli's book on the art of war itself is concerned, I recall missing the free, independent judgment that so strongly distinguishes his political writings. The art of war of the ancients attracted him too much, not only its spirit, but also in all of its forms. The Middle Ages could easily develop an exaggerated regard for the Greek and Roman art of war. At that time war had fallen into profound decline and become a kind of craft, as is best shown by the hired armies and generals of the period.

Before the period of the Swiss,[4] warfare found its fullest development

---

[3] Fabius Maximus Cunctator was a Roman commander during the Second Punic War (218–201 B.C.), who is remembered for the strategy of harassment and attrition with which he met the invading Carthaginians under Hannibal. The word "Fabian" is coined from his name.

[4] In the fourteenth century the Swiss began employing pikemen in massive squares, a formation that resembled the phalanx of the Greeks, and proved effective against cavalry. The technique was widely imitated, and marked the beginning of the renewed ascendency of infantry on European battlefields.

among the heavy cavalry of the knights, and it was here that it was diverted toward small engagements and personal combat by the constant increase in defensive weaponry. It is therefore splendid that Machiavelli believed, as I have read in Johannes von Müller, that in the early Middle Ages (before firearms were widely used) the art of war was far more at home among people who seemed to have none of it, than among those who wore themselves out refining it. The Swiss, to whom the examples of ancient Greek and Roman tactics were unknown, rediscovered a superior way of fighting for no other reason than because, owing to their poverty and the geography of their country, they had to go to war on foot, with no defensive weapons but courage; and because the isolated Swiss cities, blissfully ignorant of the wrong-headed practices of others, were better instructed by their own common sense.

Returning, then, to the degeneration of warfare into a craft, which, as we have said, was by no means confined to the Middle Ages but was even more pronounced in some later periods, I believe that, unlike Machiavelli, we should not cling to methods that were successful in the past, reviving them in one form or another, but rather seek to restore the true spirit of war. We should begin not with the form but with the spirit, and wait confidently for it to destroy the old forms and create better ones.

This true spirit of war seems to me to consist in mobilizing the energies of every soldier to the greatest possible extent and in infusing him with warlike feelings, so that the fire of war spreads to every component of the army instead of leaving numerous dead coals in the mass. To the extent that this depends on the art of war, it is achieved by the manner in which the individual is treated, but even more by the manner in which he is employed. The modern art of war, far from using men like simple machines, should vitalize individual energies as far as the nature of its weapons permits—which, to be sure, establishes a limit, for an essential condition of large forces is to have the kind of organization that permits them to be led by a rational will without excessive friction.

But we should not go further and, as was the tendency particularly in the eighteenth century, turn the whole into an artificial machine in which psychology is subordinated to mechanical forces that operate only on the surface, which seek to defeat the enemy with mere forms and afford the individual the least possible opportunity to use his intellectual powers. The history of nearly all civil wars, particularly the Swiss war for independence and the wars of the French Revolution, show that infinitely more is achieved by stimulating individual energies than by artificial forms. Modern weapons, far from contradicting this approach, are highly favorable to it. The ancients could not dispense with the phalanx and the legion, and these are unquestionably more artificial than the simple, modern deployment in two or three lines. Except for light troops, battle in the ancient world only occurred between these generally quite clumsy masses of men. In modern war mass armies are only used when the objective requires it; they can also be divided into smaller forces.

The number of light troops, that is, those who fight as individuals, is now much greater than among the ancients, relative to the size of the army; and in some forms of war, especially in the most beautiful of all, the war that a people wages on its home ground for liberty and independence, it may be worthwhile to double this number. Despite what people say, the proper use of our main weapon, the firearm, is by no means a matter of mere mechanical technique, for the effect of infantry fire is endlessly variable, not just among skirmishers but in battles fought by troops in line, depending on whether the infantry is more or less accustomed to danger and to use its weapons in an appropriate way. The fire of French infantry proved superior to that of the Prussians, despite the better technique employed by the latter, for just this reason.

It is said that the most important advantage the ancients possessed in motivating the fighting spirit of the individual came from the hand to hand combat to which every battle generally led; and it would be prejudice to deny this completely. But it is nevertheless clear enough now that, as important as firearms are to paving the way to victory in modern war, the decision can only be secured by an enthusiastic advance with cold steel. To be sure, among the ancients the value of the individual warrior had more to do with their civil constitution than with their manner of fighting, which is the more difficult to deny since the peoples who distinguished themselves in war were also distinguished by their civil conditions, compared to those they defeated, but not by any greater inclination to personal combat. And if, in view of this, the lack of individual valor in modern times stems from deliberate neglect of the true spirit of war, a false tendency to resort to dead forms of warfare, then we can surely see the two wellsprings we have to clear again so that the warlike spirit will return to us and make us feared among our neighbors. First, civil conditions, which are a matter of political arrangements and education; second, the appropriate use of military potential, for which the art of war is responsible.

If we follow the above principles and organize our army with the greatest simplicity, placing at the head of each formation men with an instinct for war, with great energy and an enterprising spirit; if the supreme commander proceeds with an attitude of trust in them, if he himself is a bold warrior who cares only for the martial spirit and knows how to inspire it through sacrifice;

if, therefore, the powers of the whole army are further developed, then martial virtue will soon be instilled in the very fabric of the army, by example from above and by constant contact with danger. In any case, the instinct for war that already exists in some men for other, for instance political, reasons will not be stifled by great mechanical forces, as usually happened before. *Then preconceived views on weapons and on the basic forms of war will disappear by themselves*, for, as we know, the natural enemy of mannerism in every art is the *spirit*.

I confess that I have a very elevated conception of the superiority of that form of war in which martial virtue animates every part of the army, and in which the main purpose of the art of war is the fullest possible employment of this spirit. I believe this form of war will dominate any other, however intelligently conceived the latter might be, not to mention that, by its nature, it would most closely approach war in its most complete form. And if it is self-evident how far this form of war is especially appropriate to our present circumstances, then I believe that we must strive for it above all, and seek our salvation there.

You will forgive me this outspoken communication, which I make in all modesty, and only because of the sacred zeal that now binds us all together. If there is but a spark of truth in it, its pale glimmer will not escape the great philosopher, the priest of this holy flame, to whom a beautiful privilege has granted access to the innermost essence, the spirit of every art and science.

Königsberg, January 11, 1809

I have only now read the remainder of your vindication of Machiavelli, and although it is not immediately relevant here, and I cannot believe it would give you particular pleasure, my natural candor forbids me to conceal the great satisfaction that your splendid essay has given me, whose results entirely agree with those at which I have arrived in my own quiet reflections, and which I have previously been unable to speak aloud as my own conviction.

For most people, keeping their opinions to themselves, which they like to think of as wise discretion, or at least as distinguished egotism, is merely wretched fearfulness or sheer stupidity.

ELEVEN

From the "Political Declaration" (1812)

Among Clausewitz's political writings, the "Political Declaration" most closely approximates a political act in its own right. It was written in February 1812, in anticipation of Prussia's impending alliance with France, and presents an unflinching defense of those in the reform party who, like Clausewitz, were preparing to abandon Prussia. It is addressed to the king, and also to posterity, to whom the author looks for vindication.

In some respects, the "Declaration" is a highly personal document. The German title, Bekenntnissdenkschrift, suggests a confession of faith, and the first section concludes with a catechistic affirmation of Clausewitz's belief that "a people courageously struggling for its liberty is invincible," and that "even the destruction of liberty after a bloody and honorable struggle assures the nation's rebirth." At the same time, the "Declaration" was a party document. Several copies circulated in draft form among the military reformers, Gneisenau and Boyen both suggested revisions,[1] and knowledge of the essay's existence and import became fairly widespread within the government, further aggravating the animosity that already existed between those who favored accommodation with France and those who opposed it.

The "Declaration" is a work of some twenty thousand words, divided into three sections, of which the first two are presented here. The first and shortest section is an impassioned call to resistance for its own sake, as a moral imperative—the only honorable course open to those who do not deliberately delude themselves about Prussia's prospects. The second section, longer and less emotional in tone, is an attempt to justify resistance in political terms, by analyzing the transformation of Prussia's international position since the Peace of Tilsit and comparing the likely consequences of a French alliance with those that might result from open defiance. Having already denied that the choice between submission and opposition can be based on calculations of political expediency, Clausewitz nevertheless emphasizes that Prussia's cause, although desperate, is not hopeless. Rebellion against France, if carried through with

---

[1] These are indicated in the apparatus that accompanies the most accurate of several published versions, in *Schriften*, 1: 678–751.

genuine determination, might succeed and could do no worse than plant the seeds for the future regeneration of the country.

The final section, omitted in the translation that follows (along with a few transitional paragraphs at the end of part two), is a detailed and optimistic assessment of Prussia's capacity to wage the war on which, in Clausewitz's judgment, its survival depends. Here the emphasis falls on the latent power of the nation in arms, whose mobilization would provide the most direct means of tapping all the resources of state and society, and would also be a natural expression of the political and moral revival the "Declaration" was intended to help foster.

In the final analysis, Clausewitz's argument turns on his belief that, regardless of Prussia's conduct, its ultimate dissolution was settled, a point of view already evident in the last surviving entry from his early notebook. If true, this would indeed have rendered moot the arguments of those who favored the French alliance as a way of surviving the present crisis. Strictly speaking, Clausewitz's attempt to divine Napoleon's intentions has proven to be mistaken: Napoleon had not decided on Prussia's destruction prior to the Russian campaign. Nevertheless, his general argument seems sound enough. For Prussia, the best possible outcome of an alliance with France would surely have been a status similar to that of the members of the Confederation of the Rhine. Although the consequences that might have flowed from a French victory in 1812 can only be imagined, it is almost inconceivable that they would have included greater independence for France's junior partners.

At the same time, however, it is no trivial distinction to note that the stakes in 1812 involved the autonomy of the state, and not its existence. Clausewitz regards existence and autonomy as morally indistinguishable; his opponents did not. Neither, for the most part, did his allies. In staking out such an unyielding position, Clausewitz set himself apart from most of those in the reform party for whom he wished to speak. Few of them would have subscribed to the ethically demanding conception of the state's interest presented here, or endorsed Clausewitz's call, should the worst happen, for a sacrificial war of self-annihilation as an example to future generations. Although Clausewitz's characteristic realism shines through in much of the "Declaration," the idealized conception of the state that gives the work its exceptional energy scarcely resembles the real Prussia whose interests he wished to defend. Clausewitz would soon retreat from the more extreme formulations of this essay. But "independence" would remain a capital political virtue in his eyes, the dominant consideration in his interpretation of international relations generally, and an attribute whose sacrifice, although no longer synonymous with extinction, would always be viewed as a sign of decay.

MOTTO

Of course I know the value of rest, the attractions of society, the joys of life; I too want to be happy like anyone else. But as much as I value these things, as little would I purchase them at the cost of baseness and dishonor. Philosophy teaches us to do our duty, to serve our fatherland loyally even with our blood; to renounce our ease, yes, to sacrifice our very existence.

—Frederick II, in his *Posthumous Works*

This brief work is intended to justify, in the eyes of the world, the political opinions of those who considered opposition to France a necessity, who had to give way before the majority, and who were denounced as fanatics, or dangerous revolutionaries, or reckless babblers, or self-serving intriguers.

As they leave the stage, abandoning their happiness and everything to which they have been loyal because it is impossible for them to serve energetically and honorably an enemy they despise from the bottom of their hearts, who can blame them if they wish to appear to be men of calm reflection and cool, mature judgment. Out of consideration for the government, their opinion could never be spoken aloud; it was kept from the public by a foreign tyranny. We seek to present it here just as opposing views have been presented.

A king who knows best of all that these men have served him unselfishly, that his cause was cherished most warmly in *their* hearts and that they were not the least able of his servants, will surely allow them this satisfaction.

When Prussia has thrown herself completely into the arms of France, when the men whose creed is set down here are no longer officially her subjects (however much they remain so in their hearts), it will be possible for this work to appear without compromising the government. Perhaps then it will still be able to kindle some sparks in the minds and hearts of the people, which might one day be useful to the state.

First Declaration

The moment for a new war in the north is approaching. Perhaps the outbreak will be delayed a few months. It is impossible for the storm to blow over completely, however, though many like to deceive themselves.

All those in other lands who care about the Prussian state (and there are unquestionably many) anxiously await the fate that will befall her in this new catastrophe.

It is not just Prussia's fate, however, but also her conduct that attracts great and universal interest. Everyone would wish that Prussia might at least have fought with honor and perished gloriously.

It is to these sympathetic friends above all that this brief work is directed, as the declaration of a private opinion that few, but nevertheless some, of my fellow citizens share; but also to the rest of my fellow citizens, as a formal protest against any kind of participation in [the policies that] will be decided on, and in what might ensue and will one day be deeply regretted and expiated.

Perhaps these lines will also stimulate a feeling of duty and honor in some breasts, perhaps they will cast a ray of light into a few minds, banish the specter of fear, show the danger that really exists, and distinguish it from what does not.

Since 1794 Prussia has fought a single conflict that did not last nearly long enough and was pursued with far too little effort and determination to justify total despair. On the contrary, Europe must expect that this state will rise up once more against complete subjugation and destruction, and in a struggle for life or death show itself worthy of Frederick's name.

The name Frederick II, which is in the mouth of every Prussian, rightly leads the world to expect that worthy sentiments still exist among us; a sense of duty, virtue, and honor that, far from being blunted and weakened by hardship, has instead grown more resilient and filled us with noble anger. In fact, it is mere vanity to go on about honor and fame when both were acquired long ago and are not endangered; and we might as well have spared the rest of the world all the phrases with which we have too often belabored them. How contemptible and base all this boasting will seem when everyone sees how we shrink from danger, untroubled by honor and shame.

It seems incredible that the very men who were the instruments of Frederick's deeds, and others who ceaselessly invoke his name, approve only of what *he* did, and despise everything not done in his manner—that these, because of the shameful cowardice they openly display, are totally unworthy heirs of the heroic generation that brought Prussia the respect and sympathy of the world.

I do not intend to draw a complete picture of the public mood and opinion in Prussia. I lack the necessary knowledge for that, because I am only familiar with the capital and the upper classes; yet since I am formally repudiating the public opinion that surrounds me, I am perhaps obliged to touch briefly on its most important characteristics.

The idea that France can be opposed has almost completely disappeared in Prussia. Everyone believes in the necessity of an unconditional *alliance,* of throwing ourselves on their mercy, and finally of sacrificing the dignity of our own ruling house. They accept this progression of evil with a shrug—blushing deeply, their eyes on the ground.

This is the prevailing *mood*. A few still stand out because of the audacity with which they insist on the security and peaceful enjoyment of their property, on the necessity of sacrificing everything to this, even the rights of the king, even the honor of the king, even the safety and freedom of the king!

This, with few exceptions, is public *opinion*. The various classes, and within them individuals, differ in the way they acknowledge and express it. The upper classes are corrupt; court and government officials are the most corrupt.

Unlike the others, they do not merely want peace and security, they have not merely given up the idea of doing their duty in the face of danger. They also pursue those who do not despair with an irreconcilable hatred.

For what else is it but despair if we prefer our present condition, and the still harder times to come, to resistance?

Anyone who does not despair of keeping the state on the path of duty and honor, who does not agree that his duty can only be the most unconditional, shameful submission—he is a traitor; and he can count on being hated, persecuted, publicly accused, denounced before the king—and betrayed to the French ambassador by officials who have forgotten their duty.[2]

Thus the true patriots, the only ones who honestly wish the king well, are scorned by the public and, thanks to the insanity and wickedness of self-serving weaklings and worthless libertines, denounced as members of a conspiracy against the state and the king.

Who has not heard of the almost laughably persecuted *Tugendbund*? Those accused of being its leaders and most active members are hardly aware of its existence. It takes the most bald-faced lies to make this pipe dream seem real, like a carnival ghost, in order to frighten the court and the people of Berlin. But when it comes to terrifying an anxious public, this sort of trick is good enough.

Personal hatred, envy, and vindictiveness are easily combined with this political approach, and men who are shameless enough to confess this cowardly creed and preach its foul principles from day to day are probably incapable of feeling shame at denigrating the personal worth, heart, and character of those with whom they ought to be quarreling on purely political grounds.

But let us look away from these sorry signs of national corruption, which, like ulcers, are outward symptoms of an inner sickness from which the whole body, poisoned and broken down, can perish all too easily.

---

[2] It was owing to such intrigues that Scharnhorst was forced to resign as head of the War Department in June 1810.

Those who have not been driven by the corruption of their hearts and principles to such professions of fear and despondency as are now in vogue are not lost forever. They could and would raise themselves if a helping hand were held out to them.

As devoted as we are to the government, we cannot deny that in the main it is lack of confidence in the government that causes general discouragement. Equally, the government has little confidence in its subjects and even in itself. Its total lack of faith in itself and others is the general cause of our public opinion; and the constant influence of weaklings, profligates, and shirkers on this opinion is the cause of the public mood.

I formally renounce this opinion and mood, which many have assumed as if they had arisen from an unselfish concern for the common weal, or were even identical to it.

I renounce the facile hope of being saved by chance.

The sullen waiting upon the future, which a dulled sensibility refuses to recognize.

The childish hope of taming the tyrant's anger by voluntarily disarming, of winning his trust through craven submission and flattery.

The false resignation of a repressed intellect.

The foolish mistrust of our God-given abilities.

The sinful neglect of all responsibility for the common good.

The ignominious sacrifice of every honor due to the state and people, of every personal and human dignity.

I believe and confess that a people can value nothing more highly than the dignity and liberty of its existence.

That it must defend these to the last drop of its blood.

That there is no higher duty to fulfill, no higher law to obey.

That the shameful blot of cowardly submission can never be erased.

That this drop of poison in the blood of a nation is passed on to posterity, crippling and eroding the strength of future generations.

That the honor of the king and government are one with the honor of the people, and the sole safeguard of its well-being.

That a people courageously struggling for its liberty is invincible.

That even the destruction of liberty after a bloody and honorable struggle assures the people's rebirth. It is the seed of life, which one day will bring forth a new, securely rooted tree.

I solemnly declare before the world and posterity that the false cunning with which little men would avoid danger is to me the worst consequence of fear and anxiety; that I would regard extreme despair as more justified if we were denied the possibility of confronting the danger with manly courage, calm determination, and a clear conscience.

That I do not forget the warnings of the past, the wisdom of centuries, and the noble example of great nations, in the giddy fear of our own day, nor do I exchange the history of the world for a page from a lying newspaper.

That I consider myself entirely free of self-interest; that I wish to confess my every thought and feeling openly to my fellow citizens; that I would consider myself lucky to die gloriously in a noble struggle for the freedom and dignity of the fatherland.

Will these beliefs win me and those who think as I do the contempt and derision of our fellow citizens?

Let posterity decide!

I lay these simple pages on the altar of the god of history, firmly believing that, once the present storm has passed, a venerable priest of that temple will take them up with care and bind them into the chronicle of our turbulent national life.

Then posterity will judge, exonerating those who fought bravely against the tide of corruption and remained true to their sense of duty as a sacred trust in their hearts.

Second Declaration

Because I have allowed myself to open my heart in the first part of this brief work, to say things in the language of passion that only the passions can and should say, I will do my best in the second part to speak only the language of calm reflection, in order to present a clear picture of our situation, and prove that passionate men are not incapable of thought just because their hearts do not close up like an octopus at every external shock.

1

A war of nine months, fought with little dedication and even less energy, with modest casualties,* appears to have shattered the innermost structure of the Prussian state and brought poverty, even abject misery, to the nation. But

* Note. The battle of Eylau, at which the Prussian state stood at the point of the sword, cost the Prussian forces no more than___dead and wounded. It was nevertheless the bloodiest battle of the Prussian campaign, as far as our troops were concerned. [Oscar von Lettow-Vorbeck, *Der Krieg von 1806 und 1807* (Berlin, 1892–96), 4: 110–11, estimates Prussian casualties at Eylau at 9.4 percent, considerably less than those suffered by their Russian ally. Prussian losses at Jena and Auerstädt were higher but included a high proportion of prisoners, so Clausewitz's assertion about "dead and wounded" may be correct. In contrast to the experience of other belligerents, Prussian casualties during the Napoleonic period were lower (as a proportion of forces engaged) than those sustained in the exceptionally hard-fought battles of the Frederician era.]

in fact it only seems so; for if one accepts the appearance as fact, where is the necessary connection between cause and effect?

It only arises from a lack of perspective and fear of a new war, which appearances are supposed to prove impossible.

The quartering of French troops; the barely tolerable indemnity imposed by the Peace of Tilsit and the Treaty of Paris,[3] which draws cash reserves out of the country; a misguided administration that focuses on appearances, and was already undermining the general welfare through exorbitant grain prices, excessive borrowing, a speculative craze among landowners, and changes in land tenure; these are additional reasons [for Prussia's misery], which make sense to the householder with troops to quarter, the financier, and the apprehensive administrator.

We do not intend to assess their exact weight and importance, though their significance must generally be overestimated, considering that most people believe the interruption of world trade is the least significant cause of our misery, that it is unknown to many and actually denied by a few paradoxical minds.

Yet nothing seems more obvious than the overwhelming weight and significance of this factor in human affairs.

Trade and commerce stream through every branch of society with the spirit of life and energy. How could trade, aided by improvements in shipping and our knowledge of geography, achieve its present scale, universality, security, and vigor without drawing virtually every element of human society into its circle of interests and penetrating into every sphere of life, becoming, over the centuries, the foundation of society itself?

This has actually happened. Millions of facts testify to it; hence the special necessity of controlling trade or destroying it, a task beyond any human power save that of a commander who has been victorious from the Ebro to the Niemen.

If this most universal, vital element of our social fabric is forcibly suppressed, what else can follow but an immediate collapse of all social relations or, more to the point, true *national bankruptcy*, in the sense of thousands upon thousands of individual bankruptcies, with which an ordinary state bankruptcy cannot even be compared?

This has been achieved by the destruction of the balance of power on the continent.

The emperor of France blocks trade, and the whole continent languishes in misery.

---

[3] The question of an indemnity for the war of 1806–1807 was postponed at Tilsit and resolved in the Treaty of Paris (September 1808). Prussia agreed to reduce its army to 42,000 men, to pay almost ten million francs to France, and to accept French garrisons in key fortresses until the indemnity was paid.

Along with this universal calamity has come another enemy of the common weal, domestic order, and economic revival: uncertainty.

It shakes the credit of the whole country and ruins the lives of hundreds of thousands of families. It cripples the activity of every inhabitant, and causes part of the nation's wealth to lie fallow, so a substantial share of the nation's production, and likewise the state's income, is lost.

The result of these evils can only be idleness, discontent, and corruption. It is impossible for a state to regain its health while it carries such poison in its veins.

But how can uncertainty be overcome?

As long as France's present relationship to the rest of Europe continues, all property and civil life will remain insecure. True salvation lies only in a struggle for independence.

But wouldn't an alliance with France also provide significant relief? Yes!— during the first moments, as the news was making its way down the line of financiers and speculators, but hardly in the long run. A French alliance offers no security, as Spain, Holland, Italy, and northern Germany prove. Of all the states that have dared to join with France since the Revolution— northern and central Italy, Spain, Portugal, Holland, Switzerland, southern Germany, and some north German princes—only tiny Switzerland and fragmented southern Germany still remain superficially independent. Perhaps five-sixths of these territories should be considered French property.

What outstanding security this alliance has brought! Everyone will say this to himself while forgetting about what happened to the public debt in Holland.[4] The subject of a state allied with France will possess just as little confidence in public order, law, and justice as the subject of any other.

Whether the serious spreading of resistance, a firm defense of the existence and honor of the state, and a courageous determination to sacrifice everything might not produce more confidence and security I leave to one side. The likelihood of such a worthwhile effect speaks for itself.

The integrity of our state and people cannot be restored in the face of this external pressure: they were equally foolish who hoped on the one hand that administrative means could achieve this renewal, and on the other that the administration would even have made the attempt. Such efforts would have been better spent preparing for war. Since the Peace of Tilsit, anyone wishing to restore the Prussian state should have thought of nothing except preparing to renew the struggle—about that and about nothing else. Soon we would have felt strong again, our relations with other states would have changed

---

[4] The collapse of Dutch trade with England following the imposition of the continental system forced the Dutch to pay interest on public debts in paper money, which rapidly lost its value. Clausewitz noted this at the time and considered it a warning of things to come. See Clausewitz to Gneisenau, October 20, 1810, in *Schriften*, 1: 634.

imperceptibly by themselves, and by and by the health of the nation would have recovered on its own.

If we cannot expect the state to heal and regenerate itself through adherence to France, then it is simply a question of whether the state, by temporarily sacrificing its dignity and security, can preserve its independence until the dangerous phase of the political storm has passed.

People hope the alliance with France will provide the means to do this.

This leads to a consideration of our international position and what we can hope to achieve by diplomacy.

2

If the Peace of Tilsit had really reconciled France with Prussia, an alliance should have followed at once. Through it France would have been able to involve Prussia as deeply in her interests, and lay equally heavy chains on her, as she had already done with Bavaria, Württemberg, Saxony, and so forth.

From then on Napoleon could have been sure of Prussia. Neither the king nor the nation would have had the courage to tear themselves free again. Once brought to this step, everyone would gradually have gotten used to the new chains, and if public opinion did not favor France, as it did in Saxony, Bavaria, and elsewhere, it would have made as little difference here as there. Even assuming that Prussia, because of her size and position, might not necessarily give in so completely, political tyranny offers a hundred means of hobbling a state's power: for instance, if half the Prussian army were sent to Spain; if men of energy and courage were excluded from office; if even more Prussian fortresses were occupied, and so on.

Napoleon knows his business too well to feel the least compunction about the methods he might have used against Prussia. An alliance presented a simple and natural means, ready at hand, and the results could not possibly have seemed insignificant.

Whether Prussia was amenable to such an alliance is no longer a question. Since the Peace of Tilsit she has never dared to oppose France, so it would have been even less likely at that moment. Besides, the men who negotiated the treaty on Prussia's side were still the king's main advisors, and since France had discovered through the treaty how devoted fear had made them to her interests, complete submission could be taken for granted. Prussia herself made overtures about an alliance, which were coldly rejected out of hand, and except for the few months of the Austrian war there was never a moment when firm language from France did not obtain whatever was wanted from Prussia.

Instead of making Prussia his instrument, to use against Spain, Austria, and Russia, Napoleon allows her to remain neutral.

This magnanimity was an obvious trap; for where else had France shown similar moderation, and how is moderation even possible for a state with vast resources, striving for vast goals? For France every breath is an act of force; *moderation would be just as irrational for her as slackness would be for anyone else.*

France allows Prussia to exist, but in a state of complete uncertainty about her future.

She seems to be unaware of internal developments in Prussia, nor to concern herself with them, except now and then when she lets Prussia feel her harshness, her pride, her enmity, her contempt. The vacillations of the cabinet, the factional struggles, the impatience of the people with the uncertain and oppressive conditions seem to matter little to France. War with Austria approaches. Prussia, teetering back and forth in hesitation, is perhaps at the point of siding with Austria. France thus acquires another not unimportant enemy, whose influence in northern Germany can have results that are by no means trivial. All these considerations, which France could clearly foresee at Tilsit, do not persuade the emperor to make Prussia his ally, to draw her into his service.

Are these observations exaggerated in any way? Certainly not! And what follows from them? That the emperor Napoleon already had Prussia's destruction in mind when he agreed to the Peace of Tilsit. The remaining power of this state was to be broken again, but above all the ruling house, on which his hatred had fastened, was to be expelled.

Prussia herself was supposed to speed the fulfillment of this plan by her conduct and mistakes; indeed, the appearance of guilt was supposed to fall entirely on her. This is why Napoleon placed the Prussian state in such a dangerous position, where an ordinary government could not possibly stand firm but where any false step could lead to immediate ruin. If it is only now, in 1812, that the moment is approaching when his plan can be put into effect, the explanation lies in intervening developments that Napoleon could not foresee.

The hatred that Napoleon bears toward the House of Hohenzollern is of course not obvious to everyone and not at all easy to explain. For some, however, it will be enough to know that at Tilsit a contemptuous coldness, indeed a suppressed hatred, could not be missed in the emperor's personal conduct toward Frederick William III and his family, while the royal family's conduct toward Napoleon (thanks to a sense of dignity undiminished by politics!) had a more worthy and dignified bearing, which can of course enrage a vain and passionate man even more. There are also specific facts whose significance cannot be mistaken. The basis of Napoleon's enmity probably lies above all in the liberality that characterizes the Prussian regime, which has attracted attention throughout Germany. Prussia, and particularly her ruling house, has public opinion on her side more than other states, and Napoleon is deeply hostile to this. The south German princes may be weary of French domination, but they have never been independent, they fear the vengeance of outsiders, and are without pride and self-esteem, half admirers and half flatterers of the French emperor. This is not the case with Frederick William III. This king, as everyone knows, is above all an upright man, incapable of hypocrisy: hatred of the French emperor is natural to him, and since he is sensitive and easily offended, his feelings are constantly inflamed by Napoleon's abuses and can never grow numb. If he has refrained from expressing those feelings for political reasons (great self-possession being natural to him in any case), if he has admirably sacrificed his own dignity and that of his people in this regard, his reticence could never deceive the French emperor, and nothing is more natural than that Napoleon should have seen more deeply into the king's heart than the king has into his.

Considering the position of the Prussian state, it is amazing that the government did not decide early on to free itself somewhat from this uncertainty, and at least agree internally on a consistent course of action, to create a system and remain unswervingly true to it. As things stood, and as was said at the time, there were two possibilities. The first was unconditional submission, the most loyal adherence to France. In that case we would have had to cooperate with France in everything, even force ourselves on her at times, and win her trust.

Whether this would have achieved the desired result (an alliance with France) is by no means certain, even unlikely, considering that nothing can be in the French interest that the emperor himself has not willed, and that he is not a man to be swayed by the interests of others. Whether an alliance with France would have led to independence for Prussia is even less certain. But be that as it may, it did not happen. Prussia, always ready to do France's bidding, nevertheless did not do enough to ingratiate herself, and had to find safety as best she could.

The other possibility was to create a military force Napoleon would fear; to introduce universal conscription, so that the burden was carried on all shoulders and so became lighter; to reorganize the army according to a new spirit; to exclude old, weak, and incompetent generals and staff officers; to stockpile weapons and munitions; to supply all the fortresses with ample provisions; to establish secure depots in fortified places and create a national militia; to severely punish incompetence and defeatism in the military and civil administrations; to replenish the ranks routinely after two to three years service, so that now, after four years, we would have had a force of at least 150,000 trained men, while reducing the military obligation of each subject.

All these measures were either not contrary to the treaty or easy to conceal, and France, moreover, was not always in a position to enforce Prussian obedience with swift and immediate reprisals, as she was immediately after Tilsit. If all dealings with France about these measures were conducted honestly and openly, if the king had decided, insofar as they affected only Prussia and France, to announce them in the press, he would have had public opinion entirely on his side, and would have become doubly dangerous to France.

It was perhaps only in this way that the false, seductive neutrality that was imposed on Prussia could have evolved unexpectedly into a true and strong neutrality, a neutrality a hundred times stronger than that observed before 1806. But these things belong to the past, and we bring them up only because the past leads to the present.

Prussia did not take this second approach either, because the necessary courage and determination, and political insight as well, were lacking. Without *courage and determination* great deeds are impossible, since danger is everywhere, and *politics* is not always a matter of cowardly trickery, although some consider them synonymous.

The king would have been capable of such resolution had he not been surrounded by two factions, one of which preached submission to France, because they feared a catastrophe that might require exceptional self-sacrifice, and because they lacked noble pride in their souls as well as historical knowledge. This faction hung like a lead weight on the best impulses of the king and thwarted or weakened all the measures he had courageously resolved upon despite his own apprehensions.

Turning now to the present, some questions arise:

1. *Is the present moment different from that of the Peace of Tilsit?*

Of course. Then Russia, having just left the war, was deeply entangled in France's interests; Austria was not to be feared; and Prussia herself lay disarmed, sick, powerless. Now Russia is again angry at France, and armed. Prussia, even if she has not done everything possible militarily, has at least not neglected the most essential measures, and is certainly not without means of resistance. Spain and England are tying down half of France's enormous power.

2. *Is an alliance with France possible now?*

Of course. But only because Prussia has done something for herself, because she has surpassed herself and shown a spark of life. It is only thanks to this that France has now offered her the benefit of an alliance.

3. *Is the recovery of the state, at least of its external independence, likely as a result of this alliance?*

Less so than ever. Precisely to the extent that circumstances have changed in Prussia's favor with respect to the first two questions, they have gotten worse with respect to this one.

Napoleon might or might not have allowed Prussia to succeed in attaching herself to France the way Bavaria did; there is no telling where the unfettered will of a successful general may lead.* But now that Napoleon has grown worried about the danger of a flank attack by Prussia; after he has realized that Prussia might not be crushed in an instant, but could remain a threat to him; that the last four years have bred more resentment than devotion to France there, and that the abuses she has suffered have been deeply felt and painfully oppressive—now this maniacal tyrant will not give up his plan to destroy Prussia. The alliance he offers is simply a means to this end. Things have turned out differently than he imagined: he realizes that in allowing Prussia to remain neutral he made a mistake he cannot reverse now, that he even needs Prussia; but he is determined not to make the same mistake twice. Having deprived himself of Prussia's power for four years, he does not wish to have made this sacrifice in vain. At the next suitable moment he means to seize the prize that he has held in reserve for so long.

Many will find that this argument is not strictly and absolutely necessary and will say: it might of course be true, but it is nevertheless possible for things to turn out differently. But they must pay attention to purely objective facts.

If we therefore take no account of Napoleon's intentions, his opinion of us, and his hatred, and stick strictly to the observable facts, the question arises: What advantages and assurances could flow from an alliance with France, and what disadvantages could be anticipated?

Advantages of an Alliance with France

1. Safe-guarding our existence—about half as likely as was true for Spain, Italy, Holland, and northern Germany.

2. Removing the war from our territory—entirely out of the question.

3. Delaying the war—equally unlikely, since the outbreak depends on a breach between France and Russia. Even an alliance with Russia, which is hardly necessary, and at any rate need not be made known, would not bring war closer by a single moment, since the main mischief has already occurred: Prussia's capacity to resist has reached a level where it is impossible to treat her like Hesse.[5] Further increases will not be a reason for Napoleon to break with Russia any sooner. Russia herself grows stronger every day, and the emperor does not act. Other reasons must therefore be decisive.

---

* Wallenstein. Schiller.

[5] When Hesse-Kassel was occupied by the French in October 1806, the elector was deposed, and the state was later incorporated into the Kingdom of Westphalia.

4. Lightening the burden of the war—this will not happen, since it makes *no difference* whether we fight with 20,000 men or 100,000, if we have to provide for 400,000 in any case. Prussia, however, will be the theater of operations between Russia and France no matter what, and all experience suggests the French are no better as *allies* than as enemies. It may be different with the Russians.

Disadvantages of an Alliance with France

1. We degrade ourselves and the nation if, out of fear, we fight for our worst enemy, a state that has robbed us of our greatness and abused us to the utmost. Our soldiers can only perform badly if we force them to shed their blood for a *cause* they loathe. A government that drives its people to do this drives them to depravity and despair.

2. We deliver ourselves with hands bound to the will of the French emperor. Any alliance with him must absolutely destroy our capacity to resist. He takes part of the army under his command; the rest is distributed so that it can do nothing against him. Some fortresses (particularly the harbors) are handed over to him, while the rest are so badly garrisoned and supplied that they cease to count for anything. Energetic men who are not beholden to France will be cashiered; the king will be surrounded by French officials and troops, constantly anxious about his freedom and honor, deprived of all capacity to resist the encroaching corruption. Even granting that this account may be exaggerated, that it may be possible to conclude an alliance with France on reasonable terms under which our existence should be secure, the question still arises, quite simply: Are the terms really genuine? Can they be? Aren't we supposed to be satisfied with mere appearances, which we use to deceive ourselves and justify our choice of the easier path?

The question answers itself, considering that any alliance will tie up part of the forces that we already find insufficient to resist the French, so we are sure to consider our partially bound, crippled forces even less adequate. Furthermore, there is nothing more natural than that a goal for which men have already made great sacrifices should call forth new sacrifices in the hope of redeeming the earlier ones.

In the final analysis, it is a matter of answering the following questions *frankly* and *honestly*:

Will the Prussian government, once it has taken the first great step and concluded an alliance with France—and granting also that its terms are entirely moderate and honorable—will it ever refuse a new demand if it is made with equal force?

Who among all those who now urge this alliance on the king and say they are thinking only of the king and the nation will urge resistance later on?

Are we not therefore absolutely certain to take one step after another toward our ruin and end up like Charles IV and his son?[6]

Oh, the reckless councilors, who give themselves credit for wisdom and foresight because they urge the king to take the easier path, while denouncing those who demand firmness and noble sacrifice as insane!

Will they dare show their faces when the king, overwhelmed by violence and disgrace, abandoned by his people, deserted by public opinion, stands alone, a poor prisoner? What will they see in their consciences then?

Such is the outlook for the king; and what for the people?

Woe to those who divide the king and the people, always setting the interest of the one against the other. This malicious sophistry is merely a fad to provide plausible grounds for avoiding a courageous decision.

The honor of the prince must give way to the interest of the nation, and the interest of the nation to the preservation of the ruling house. Thus we have gone around endlessly in circles, playing with words. The king is the representative of the nation. The nation has an automatic and perhaps unmerited part in whatever he does, whatever brings him honor in the eyes of the world and posterity. The king who perishes shamefully insults the nation and is the cause of its misfortune; the king who succumbs gloriously elevates the nation and his glorious name is balm on its wounds.

The nation whose king has lost his honor and freedom has lost both along with him, and will suffer internal decay and external repression. It will feel his misery, with no hope of escape, for it will blame itself for having given up too quickly and easily. It will despise itself more deeply every day, and raise the enemy higher, thus sinking further and further into cowardly fear and servility.

This will be the fate of a prince and a people that freely hand themselves over in chains to their natural, implacable, hereditary enemy, at a moment when a final, courageous resistance might still have been attempted, when resistance was their first duty to themselves and each other.

But what would be the fate of this king and his people if they should lose in a heroic struggle, fighting side by side for each other, so that the king is deposed and the people are subjugated?

Both would retain their honor, their mutual love and respect for each other! And would that be nothing in such misfortune? Precisely when one has lost everything, should this noble feeling be considered *worthless*? Would

---

[6] The king of Spain, Charles IV, and his son, Ferdinand VII, both tried to work with the French, but were forced to abdicate.

it hold *no* seed of future rebirth? Let each of us answer these questions according to his own heart and mind!

Since there is no external safety in the French alliance and no other remedy for our inner sickness than resistance to France, then resistance should be regarded as our ultimate salvation.

The idea of resistance should occupy the mind of everyone whose heart is not already full of horror at degradation like ours.

From it a firm determination must arise to cast off the yoke.

This determination on the part of the government and the people should lead to preparations for the great moment of struggle, without which the struggle will be impossible. Thus prepared, we should wait calmly for the right opportunity. *

If this is the only correct political attitude for a people in our position, we are nevertheless so far from it that there are a number of [psychological] stages to traverse before arriving at the decisive point.

We may well wish to be free of France's tyranny. We recognize the advantage of liberation, but not its *necessity*, which is something else entirely.

We would rather wait until *chance* contributes something to our cause— meaning the violent death of Napoleon. If this never happens, we will await his natural end. But the emperor can still live another thirty years, judging by his appearance, and if we have borne the yoke without a murmur for thirty years, who will dispute the right of Napoleon's successor to a secure and legitimate inheritance? Won't the same reservations arise? Is it certain that a weak ruler will succeed Napoleon on the throne? And if he were weak, what about the example of Rome, whose empire survived its great founder by four hundred years?

Besides, there is still the question of whether present conditions could last thirty years.

---

* At present, and until the outbreak of war between France and Russia, the issue before the Prussian cabinet is more a matter of making a decision than of acting.

No one proposes that Prussia undertake an offensive against France or suddenly refuse to fulfill her existing obligations; but we should not lay additional burdens on ourselves, nor give away the defensive strength that still exists, and coolly explain to France: that Prussia values its independence above all else, that she could never consent to see the means of preserving this independence taken away, and that she can admit no connection with France that does not fully guarantee her own security. All these explanations can only be delivered if we are *firmly resolved* to perish only with sword in hand. Everything depends on this resolve.

It is most unlikely that such language will hasten the end of peace, since Napoleon will hardly be so foolish as to consider the language more important than the facts, to allow Prussia to complete her rearmament, and then let himself be dragged into war by mere words. But if it does happen, we will simply have arrived a few months earlier at that virtually inevitable moment when all the folly of our frivolous policy is concentrated in a single instant.

Flatly, the answer is no. That is impossible. Sooner or later our misery must and will inspire unrest among the people, which will bring on all the troubles we now fear. It is therefore pointless to try to evade the issue in this way.

Indeed, the worst of it is that if all the superstitious hopes of weak hearts and minds were to come true, if the moment finally came when a child or a weakling became Napoleon's successor, rousing all of Europe to action, what would be the result except universal war, endless chaos, a bloody partisan struggle, an age of misery and destitution!

Is it not inconceivable folly for anyone to hope that when the time comes he will be left unmolested in peaceful possession of his property, free to remain uninvolved?

Must not everyone admit to himself that this future crisis will be more terrible than the present one—that such a war of isolated forces against multiple enemies will be more horrible than a war in which all forces are firmly united by duty, vengeance, hatred, and self-interest, against a *single, common* foe?

In truth it cannot be rational reflection that has shaped the mind and mood of the people, but fear of the most immediate evil and shortsighted self-interest.

People shrink before the danger, before the sacrifice it demands, above all before the improbability of success, of which they are firmly convinced. They therefore think it wise to avoid the danger.

It is true that the *probability* of success is against us. But under what political system would it not be against us? How could we expect the odds to be on our side after so many decades of folly heaped on folly, failure on failure, whose combined effects are now evident in our present misery? Indeed our misery consists precisely in the fact that we are surrounded by an abyss. How can anyone demand the probability of success! It is enough that success is not *impossible*; whoever asks for more contradicts himself.

It is futile, however, to try to justify inaction by pointing to the true [irrational] sources of public opinion, for in fact no one can take even the first step forward by means of the sort of rationalizing that likes to call itself *calm reflection* without getting caught in its contradictions.

People everywhere are crying: *reason alone must decide.* As if fear were not an emotion, as if they were capable of making a free and rational judgment. The only thing we can be sure of is that both political creeds, resistance and submission, are based on emotions; but the emotional basis of the first is courage, of the other fear. Fear cripples the intellect, courage inspires it.

These few general reflections can only lead to the conclusion that, whatever our condition, it is essential that we decide to fight to gain our independence. Let the enormous weight of recent events compel us to make this decision. It would be folly and weakness to evade the pressure, which would then only crush us more surely.

This truth requires no further proof. It does not matter at all whether we have more or less means with which to save ourselves; the decision should arise from the need for salvation, not from the ease of gaining it. There is no help for us but ourselves. There is no salvation except what is already in our power, in our minds and hearts.

TWELVE

On the German Federal Army (1818)

The following memorandum, on the organization of the German federal army, represents Clausewitz's most extended comment on the affairs of the German Federation. The original text is in French and undated. Its contents place its composition sometime in the first half of 1818, when the issues with which it deals were coming to a head.[1] The recipient, if there was one, is also unknown. The fact that Clausewitz wrote in French may mean the memorandum was intended for some diplomatic purpose, while the style and tone suggest a recipient he knew well enough to address frankly, perhaps Boyen or Ludwig von Wolzogen, with whom Clausewitz had served in Russia and who acted as Boyen's aide in the negotiations that were underway at the time Clausewitz must have written.

That the German Federation would dispose of some kind of military force had never been in doubt. Like the Holy Roman Empire, for which it was in some respects the replacement, the Federation was expected to be a bulwark against France and Russia and to maintain a minimum of constitutional order among the German states. Again like the empire, however, the Federation's second mission compromised the first, since the system of mixed or, more accurately, multiple sovereignties that it embodied undermined military efficiency. At the Vienna Congress it had been apparent that Germany's military possibilities were no less varied than the political ones, and action was deferred to the opening of the Federal Diet, which occurred in the fall of 1816.

By then only one of the alternatives bruited about eighteen months before had been put to rest: no German state was prepared to support a standing federal army garrisoned in free cities and federal fortresses, a proposal widely favored in patriotic circles and in the opposition press. The federal army, whatever its composition, would exist in peacetime only on paper. The issue was therefore how that force should be organized to insure that, when war came, it would assemble swiftly and fight well. Austria and Prussia both favored some type of divided force in which two main armies, with smaller auxiliary

---

[1] The manuscript can be dated from a small revision in the first paragraph, which originally referred to the idea that federal forces would comprise 2 percent of the population as "proposed." This was later changed to "agreed to," a correction that presumably occurred after the agreement was reached in April 1818. The change, though not its significance, is noted in the only published version of the memorandum, in *Schriften*, 2, part 2: 1141–51. The main points of Clausewitz's argument are also aired in a letter to Gneisenau, March 15, 1818 (ibid., 2, part 1: 330).

corps, would be mobilized under the leadership of the two German powers. The lesser German states, led by the influential representative from Württemberg, Karl von Wangenheim, also favored a divided force, but in three equal parts, the third comprising the forces of the "Third Germany," whose independence from Prussia and Austria would thus be symbolized and reinforced.

At the end of 1817 Prussia and Austria privately agreed to cooperate in promoting their common agenda in the Diet. Opposition from the other states proved intractable, however, and Austria soon reneged on its promises to Prussia, supporting instead a compromise that satisfied no one completely. Under it the Federation would deploy a single army, comprised of contingents proportional to the population of each member state and under a supreme commander appointed by the Diet—a position Austria expected would be filled in practice by an Austrian field marshal, as it had been in the campaigns of 1813–14. Nearly all military professionals regarded these arrangements, which became law in 1821, as less than ideal. Nevertheless, both Austria and Prussia finally preferred to adopt a plan that might not work rather than accept something that might work against their interests, as would have been true of any solution that increased the influence of the Federation's lesser members.

In its military dimensions, Clausewitz's analysis falls within the mainstream of expert opinion in Prussia. What is striking is the care he takes to justify his recommendations in political terms, and also his political point of view, which is by no means Prusso-centric. Clausewitz sees the Federation as a modest improvement on the "defective" constitution of the Holy Roman Empire, a characterization that suggests he might have preferred the federal bond to have been stronger. Given that it was not, however, it was wrong to create an army whose structure did not match the character of the polity it was supposed to defend. Above all, Clausewitz is anxious that questions of military organization and efficiency not be allowed to ride roughshod over the sovereignty of the small German princes—a superficially surprising conclusion, perhaps, but one fully in accord with his belief that military institutions should reflect as accurately as possible the political forces that animate and direct them.

Clausewitz does not think the Federation needs, or can properly employ, an army of its own. What it needed was military strength, which was not the same thing. Part of the price of compromise with the small states had been a reduction in the nominal size of the federal force, which, it was finally agreed, would equal 2 percent of the total population—a standard comparable to that of other powers but one Clausewitz considers inadequate to Germany's exposed geographical position. As always, he portrays his country's military predicament in overwhelmingly defensive terms, and he is convinced that the rest of

Europe will agree, if only the history of Germany's repeated victimization by France were honestly acknowledged.

Here his faith in historical arguments may have blinded him to other considerations to which he was normally sensitive—the effect, for instance, that a dramatic and, in the circumstances, wholly unexpected military buildup in Germany (including a dozen new fortresses) would have had on the balance of power in Europe. Clausewitz undoubtedly regarded the political fragmentation of the Federation as sufficient assurance against aggressive conduct: in its present form the Federation was just another coalition, the sort of arrangement he had regarded since his youth as best suited for defense against a single, powerful enemy. But whether Germany's neighbors would have seen things the same way is by no means certain.

It has always seemed to me that military affairs in Germany are being organized according to a false principle that has made them infinitely more complicated and difficult than they are by nature and deprived us of all hope of a good result. This principle is the formation of all German military forces into a single, great federal army, in which, even in peacetime, all the forces of the smaller German states, as well as the greater part of the Prussian army and a very considerable portion of Austria's, are supposed to play a part. Because this enormous army (450,000 men, based on 2 percent of the population, as has been agreed), exists as a united force in peacetime as a matter of law, and as a reality in time of war, it is natural that the smaller states feel themselves deprived of all power to dispose of their military forces and therefore of one of the most essential elements of their sovereignty. They have been forced to accede to this plan, but they have done so reluctantly and have accordingly lost all specific interest in the military organization of their own lands, the formation of their armies, etc. They have done their best to diminish considerably the general plan proposed by Austria and Prussia and to reduce as far as possible the sacrifices demanded of their armies and their subjects' resources. This is why we have been forced to settle for a military establishment based on 2 percent of the population rather than 3, as was proposed at the beginning.

What, then, are the advantages that result from constituting a federal army in this way, as a theoretically unified force even in peacetime? First of all, a collective organization that is better prepared and better proportioned; secondly, much greater confidence in its effective union in time of war. It is supposed that, if the princes of the Federation are given complete freedom to dispose of their armies in peacetime, and if the deployment they wish to make in time of war is dependent on nothing but specific treaties and conventions made at the moment of outbreak, their dispositions would be much less certain. One imagines they might get all sorts of plans and schemes in their heads that would be contrary to the general welfare of the Federation. I, however, am totally convinced that if, at the outbreak of war, the force of circumstances, the common danger, and the rational conduct of German states among themselves are not enough to impart a sound, healthy sense of direction to every German prince, old ordinances and institutions grown rusty in peace will be even less capable of doing so.

It is true that in war the employment of forces must be coordinated and that it is impossible to allow every great and small German prince to dispose of his own. Now, since the Federal Act requires all members to take part in any war of the Federation and forbids them from making a separate peace or truce, one might well say that at bottom they sacrifice nothing by giving up control of their armed forces once and for all in favor of a federal army, since they will never be in a position to use them any other way. But this argument is not precisely true for all parties. First of all, military operations in war can be directed in an orderly fashion without having all forces combined in a single army; this depends on immediate circumstances. Further, it may well be that one prince of the Federation has a particular interest in seeing his troops fight at one place rather than another, to see them combined with the troops of one power, or commanded by one particular general, rather than another. Thus there would appear to be a considerable difference between the political obligations imposed by the German Federal Act and the total abandonment by the Federation's members of the sovereignty that directs and maintains the armed forces of each state. And even if this difference should prove less great in reality than it appears to be, I still think one ought to take very seriously the penalty for offending even slightly the feelings of princes to whom one would seem to have accorded full and complete sovereignty. As far as the advantages that supposedly derive from a permanent federal army go, in the way of perfecting its organization, these will not be of great significance, since the organization will not exist except on paper, besides which that whole objective cannot be sufficiently important to compensate for the loss of a third of the total force.[2]

Up to now we have been considering whether the permanence of the federal army in peacetime might be highly useful. But one may also ask if it is wise to decide permanently in advance that Germany's armed forces should be united in wartime in a single army, that is, under a single commander in chief. It is impossible to foresee what will be the best relationships within the hierarchy of command that one is always forced to construct when there are large forces to be moved and employed in remote theaters. Having a commander in chief at the head of a huge army is clearly not enough to insure

---

[2] An oblique reference to the agreement by the lesser princes to accept a unified force in exchange for a reduction in its size from 3 to 2 percent of the population.

that one or another of its parts is able to serve the purpose for which it was created. The way forces are distributed; the commanders at every level and at the top; the kind of overall direction that should be established in the case where it is impossible to place all forces under a single commander; the choice of theaters of operation—these are no less dependent on immediate circumstances than every other aspect of military operations. To make major errors in these general arrangements is to render useless all the successes that could be achieved; it is to swim against the current.

I therefore believe it is absolutely necessary to abandon to the force of circumstances, the interests of the moment, the innumerable constellations of chance under whose influence every act of human history is made and accomplished—I say it is wise to abandon to these living and active forces the formulation of plans, the choice of means, and the assembly of the various parts that go into the great machine of war.

If, moreover, Germany's situation includes constant political and military relations that allow us to settle our plans in advance, these seem so totally contradictory to the idea of a single great army that they must be plainly stated. France's vulnerable points are at the extremities of her frontier with Germany. The center is where the most strength is, and consequently we would have to begin by dividing the army and separating its parts by 250 miles, that is to say, it will be necessary to change its organization.

It still remains to speak of Austria and Prussia in particular. It is natural that these two states, possessing provinces that are not part of the Federation, may have particular interests in time of war that may not conform perfectly to the interests of the Federation without entirely contradicting them. By wise arrangements adapted to circumstances, these diverging interests can be harmonized very well, as is seen in all of Germany's other alliances; but these possibilities will inevitably be constricted when all resources and means of action are combined, at great risk, in a single monstrous whole. This gigantic army, on which the whole security of Germany will depend, will necessarily be divided by the different interests of Austria, Prussia, and the states that lie between them. It will be a tool made from a brittle alloy, and those who serve in it will be occupied in holding it together instead of acting freely and boldly.

As far as Austria is concerned, the evil is less grave because she still possesses sufficient means to establish a separate theater of operations that she can direct with all her natural energy, according to her particular interests. Prussia, however, having furnished her contingent to the federal army, does not have sufficient forces left to do anything significant; she can no longer create a theater of operations for herself and play a role proportionate to the moral and military superiority that is rightly attributed to her. Thus, under the present system, Germany's best champion will decay as an individual, and her forces will be employed without the unique spirit that exalts them.

I am therefore utterly convinced that nothing would be better than to suspend all arrangements for the disposition and combination of Germany's armed forces until war begins, to make arrangements according to specific conventions and treaties at the moment of outbreak—as worked quite smoothly in practice in 1814 and 1815—and during peacetime and up to the conclusion of these conventions, to leave to Germany's princes the best disposition of their armies.

But then, people will say, Germany is disarmed at the moment of danger. This is the main point that remains to be explained. Germany should always be under arms, more than all the states that surround her, since she lies in the middle of them. Up to the present Germany has survived politically on the riches of Austria. A great part of the inheritance that this power, unique in modern history, accumulated over the years has been used in recent times to pay the cost of failed wars that inevitably followed from Germany's defective constitution. The Austrian state, which still today has territory and population equal to those of France and has always been sustained by the various monarchies over which its scepter ruled and still rules, should have been able to resist France on its own; and it is clear that if this has not been the case, if she has always been obliged to buy peace by the concession of a few provinces, this constant inferiority cannot be attributed to anything other than Germany's bad constitution. It is for this reason that Alsace and the bishoprics of Lorraine paid the price for the political upheavals of the first half of the seventeenth century; that the Belgian provinces were cut off in the second half; that the crowns of Spain and Sicily were sacrificed to the avarice of France in the first half of the eighteenth century, the rest of Belgium and Lorraine, and the left bank of the Rhine, traded for Lombardy and Tuscany in the second half.

It is therefore clear that Germany cannot rely on its historical memories to convince itself that it will always occupy a place among the independent nations of Europe and that it will not necessarily take a French Revolution and a Bonaparte to bring total ruin. The course of events over the last two centuries so clearly menaced all aspects of Germany's existence that one can say without exaggeration that it was the French Revolution that saved it.

With a glance at our history it would not seem to me difficult to convince the whole world that if Germany does not take very strong precautions, if she does not possess military institutions of great vigor, she will not survive. It is true that since the last war we have restored the balance somewhat with France, that our political constitution is somewhat improved, in view of the fact that the number of sovereign states is greatly diminished and the federal bond has been strengthened a bit. But all this does not disprove that a federal constitution is not inferior, as a political machine, to the constitutions of the unified monarchies that surround us. Furthermore, if France has recently been punished for its immoderate ambition, a spirit of vengeance has also been aroused there, which will not dissipate without having attempted to drive us back into submission.

Would it therefore be so difficult for Austria and Prussia to bring the German princes to the level of understanding and good will necessary to create a general basis for a military constitution proportionate to the dangers that surround us? It would seem to me that a single principle suffices for that—that of determining a constant proportion between a state's population and its armed forces, meaning troops ready to fight in the field, plus the fortresses it possesses. Prussia can begin a campaign with 300,000 men, and she has twenty-five fortresses for a population of ten million, which means 30,000 men and 2½ fortresses for every million inhabitants. I basically don't see why she would be embarrassed by what her institutions have achieved, and why she would not have the right to propose the same system to the other German states. But it is surely to be feared that she would be met by a unanimous cry of indignation, and it is certainly true that it would be very difficult for states that don't have fortresses to construct all at once a number proportionate to those that exist in Prussia thanks to the cares of many centuries past. But Prussia can always rely on the strength of her military institutions to show that she is not demanding the impossible when she proposes a military system for the rest of Germany far inferior to what she has done herself, which she is ready to maintain for the honor and security of Germany. I don't see what objection the small states could make if it were proposed that they maintain 20,000 men and one fortress for every million inhabitants. Germany would then dispose of 600,000 men and possess about ten or fifteen more fortified places. It is true that less onerous proposals have been rejected by the Federal Diet. But was it done for valid reasons? Wasn't it obviously the result of ill will on the part of the states of the second rank, who refused to support a large military establishment whose disposition would be snatched away from them, and for the creation of which they would still have to accept disagreeable legal burdens?

If Austria and Prussia were convinced of the urgent necessity of a force on this scale and made much greater efforts on their own, if they were united in supporting the necessity of these measures, and if they did not accompany their proposal with any onerous conditions, I cannot believe they could be forced to abandon it. Once agreement was reached on the fixed ratio of inhabitants to the number of troops and fortresses, it would only be a matter of constituting some kind of commission, under the authority of the Federal Diet, which would have the right to report from time to time on the condition of the armed forces of the various members. It could be that one or another small state might try to evade this agreement by overextending its *Landwehr* system,[3] which would make its armed forces ineffective and nothing but a sham; but such a deviation would easily be remedied by remonstrances, following a closer examination of the question on the floor of the Diet.

To state more clearly the results of my report, allow me to recapitulate the essential points. I conclude:

1. That it is contrary to the nature of things to recognize sovereign states and at the same time to wish to deprive them of the free disposition of their armed forces.

2. That it is contrary to the force of circumstances to deprive Prussia and Austria of an independent role in a war of the Federation, such as they have played up to now.

3. That it is contrary to all probability that, in the event of war, the formation of an army combining all German forces under a single commander would accord with other conditions.

4. That a supreme command that did not encompass the other forces of Prussia and Austria, nor those of Germany's other allies, would not be capable of giving overall strategic direction, and that as a consequence it will be an extra wheel in the machine of war, which will unnecessarily hamper its movements.

5. That it is contrary to Germany's interest and contrary to the success of her military efforts to minimize the play of particular interests among her members, because to do so saps the vigor from their forces and creates an inert mass.

6. That it is dangerous to rely on institutions created in peacetime, and perhaps long before the outbreak of war, because they necessarily decay and break down; and that it is better to make all arrangements that do not by nature require a great deal of time and preparation, at the moment when circumstances suggest and demand them.

7. That the only essential objective is therefore to be certain that the armed forces Germany may require really exist, and that the institutions that pertain to them do not fall asleep or degenerate.

[Addendum to point 4.] I need not observe that the sort of supreme command created by combining all the forces of the Federation in a single army is neither necessary for coordinated operations nor suited to exercise overall control. It is hardly credible that Prussia and Austria would submit the re-

[3] Meaning that small states would try to get by with just a militia, rather than support a standing army.

mainder of their forces to some general chosen by the Diet, and still less that Germany's other allies would do so. It will therefore always be necessary to constitute another, more extended command. There is, however, a truth that cannot escape us, which is that even today, when the forces and distances involved in war are so enormous, there is still only one sovereign, equally absolute in power and [political] character, capable of directing all aspects of a war among great nations. Any individual, that is, any man to whom power is delegated, will not suffice. There is, therefore, no better means available than the one employed in the last war, that is, an assembly of those monarchs who are the most powerful and have the greatest interests at stake, supported by the general staff of the main army, which directs operations as the group demands, while the generals in chief, at the heads of the various armies, are afforded very great power and responsibility, so that the great general staff has no need to involve itself in the details of the war.

It is prejudice to believe that military operations cannot be well conducted by a cabinet. The war of the Revolution shows clearly that it can; a cabinet that follows the armies closely is still more capable of doing so. Now and then, however, it must know enough not to wish to decide at a distance things that must be decided on the spot, and it is this lack of instinct, above all this lack of energy, that has often hindered the success of war plans made in the cabinets of presidents.

THIRTEEN

"Our Military Institutions" (1819)

In the years following the final defeat of France, a variety of economic, military, and political factors combined to threaten the achievements of Prussia's reformers. The indemnity imposed in 1808 and the war needed to regain independence had saddled the Prussian monarchy with a debt of unprecedented proportions. At the same time, the restraints on international trade that had marked the last years of Napoleon's regime, and whose evil effects Clausewitz had emphasized in the "Political Declaration," disappeared. Prussia was thus left open to a flood of low-priced goods and agricultural products from abroad, which had been building up for years behind the continental system and the English blockade and now led to a steep decline in grain prices, on which the revenues of the state depended. These miseries were further aggravated by the disastrous harvest of 1816 and near-famine that followed. Although the protectionist tariff enacted in 1818 offered some prospect of long-term relief, the pressure for greater austerity on the part of the government remained intense.

It was not unreasonable that this pressure should have been felt most acutely by the armed forces. Not only was the army the most expensive item in the state's budget, but the very decisiveness of its victory implied that a more modest establishment might be in order. These practical considerations were compounded by the social and political resentments that reform had inspired. Although it is difficult to disentangle all the motives for the criticism of the army after 1815, it cannot have been by chance that demands for retrenchment should have fallen most heavily on precisely those aspects of the new establishment—universal service and the Landwehr—that represented the gravest affront to traditional social and political arrangements.

The memorandum that follows is Clausewitz's most detailed defense of Prussia's military reforms. It begins with a brief statement of what contemporaries regarded as the most compelling argument in their favor: that they had succeeded. Clausewitz finds it puzzling that victory had failed to silence the critics, a fact that seemed to imply that other motives beyond a concern for military effectiveness were at work. But he does not dwell on the point and proceeds to consider the more pertinent question of whether the reformed army represented a good value to the state treasury.

Clausewitz's analysis begins with a complex comparison between the status quo (which he is defending), the army that met defeat in 1806, and the army of Frederick the Great. Clausewitz regards it as absurd that Frederick should *have become an idol of the reactionaries, and he seeks to reclaim the old king's heritage for its rightful heirs. Frederick, he argues, always had the largest and most efficient army the Prussian economy could support and would have been glad for one bigger and better still—a conclusion he thinks should have been obvious to anyone who remembered the extremity of Prussia's position at the end of the Seven Years' War. That the reformed army came closest to being such a force, moreover, was demonstrated by a comparison of the current military budget with budgets of the past, which showed that the present-day army was cheaper, man for man, than any of its predecessors, and better cared-for in human terms.* [1]

The first half of Clausewitz's memorandum is a demonstration of the usefulness of history for policy: it should serve as a compass, not an anchor. Frederick's achievements were not a timeless standard but provided a frame of reference by which contemporary institutions might be judged. Past glories could not be decisive in themselves—not Frederick's, and not the reformers' either. In another memorandum from this same period, addressed to Prince August, Clausewitz declared that the victories of 1813–15 were a vindication of the reforms "that should suffice for centuries," a remark that reveals less about his political judgment than about his emotional investment in the defense of Scharnhorst's work. [2] *In the present essay he passes lightly over the victories of the last war, in tacit recognition that those victories too would lose their saliency in time. The reforms that had made them possible should therefore be judged in light of their capacity to reconcile the needs of the state with the changing condition of Prussian society. It is in this respect that Clausewitz finds them superior to the practices of the past.*

The key to that superiority was the Landwehr, *whose defense dominates the remainder of the essay. The Prussian* Landwehr *was a sort of militia or national guard, raised by conscription, that was created in 1813 as part of the general mobilization against France. Its political resonances were exceptionally complex. Elsewhere in Germany popular forces of this kind had long been seen as alternatives or counterweights to standing armies and were associated*

---

[1] Clausewitz's discussion of the cost of the old and reformed military establishments, although accurate in comparative terms, is somewhat misleading. Clausewitz thought the decline in prices after 1816 was a favorable development, because it raised the value of taxes paid in cash relative to the goods purchased with them. This is true, but it should not obscure the larger economic contraction of which deflation was but one symptom. While serving as chief of staff of the Rhine army in 1817, Clausewitz wrote movingly to Gneisenau of the human suffering he witnessed in the Eifel Mountains (Clausewitz to Gneisenau, April 28, 1817, in *Schriften*, 2, part 1: 260–66); but he seems not to have related that experience to the fiscal difficulties facing the Prussian state. Clausewitz's incomplete understanding of Prussia's economic crisis does not affect his argument about the relative cheapness of the present-day army. But his belief that Prussia could well have afforded armed forces substantially larger than those it was currently supporting is unfounded.

[2] This memorandum is excerpted in *Politische Schriften und Briefe*, 242.

with the ancient rights of towns and estates, and also with caution in international affairs, militias being unsuited to aggression. These associations were seriously complicated by the French levée en masse, under which the nation in arms had become an explicitly democratic and exceptionally dynamic force. At the same time, however, compulsory universal service had been an implicit element of Prussian absolutism from the beginning, albeit one that had been set aside in practice because of its economic costs and because it contravened the personal, voluntary bonds that joined the crown and its noble officer corps.

Even during the Wars of Liberation, Frederick William III had been uneasy about the institutional autonomy of the Landwehr, which had been envisioned by the reformers who created it as a civilian force, trained and maintained separately from the line army. Such an arrangement inevitably left questions unanswered about the fighting quality of Landwehr formations, and it might have created technical problems during mobilization. The Landwehr was also a tempting target for those looking to reduce the state's expenses, and proposals to reduce its scope, typically by eliminating conscription in favor of a return to the furlough system employed before 1807, were a regular feature of budget discussions in Prussia after 1817. Beneath these issues, however, lay more fundamental fears about the Landwehr's political reliability and the potentially divisive influence of an institution conceived in conscious disregard of existing social distinctions. These fears were the real crux of the present debate, in Clausewitz's view, a fact he believed the Landwehr's critics sought to conceal behind an exaggerated concern with fiscal and operational details.

"Our Military Institutions" is one of Clausewitz's most uncompromising and polemical efforts, in which the dialectical style that characterizes most of his work is repeatedly overwhelmed by an impulse to bury his opponents in an avalanche of arguments, some incidental, some profound. His reasons for writing it are not known. Passing references to the king's mistrust of the reformers and to Hardenberg's irresponsible expansion of the civil administration suggest that he could not have intended it to circulate very widely. He may have prepared it simply to clarify his ideas, which received a more pointed formulation in a memorandum, "On the Political Advantages and Disadvantages on the Prussian Landwehr," written at the same time.[3] In 1821, however, Clausewitz submitted the present work for publication in a professional military journal. If anything, prevailing opinion had by then hardened even more firmly against the reformers, and the editors set the manuscript aside, evidently on grounds of prudence. It was finally published in 1858, at a time when the organization and political control of Prussia's armed forces were again becoming a major constitutional issue.[4]

[3] Reprinted immediately below.

[4] Zeitschrift für Kunst, Wissenschaft und Geschichte des Krieges 104 (1858): 42–67; reprinted

In 1808 and 1809 our military institutions were reorganized according to new principles. Scharnhorst was the chief architect of these great reforms. To push them through against the prejudices of the army and the landed interests—and the mistrust of the king—required exceptional intelligence, strength of character, and patience. The defeat from which we were just recovering, the ignominy and disgrace with which our forces had covered themselves, had nevertheless made such an effort and such reforms essential if a remedy for the present evils was to emerge. Most men felt that simply to rebuild the old order contradicted common sense, and this paved the way for the new work. What these new institutions achieved in the organization of the reduced army [after 1807], and finally in the wars of 1812 in Russia, 1813 in Germany, and 1814–15 in France, is obvious from events. Whoever finds no proof of the fitness and effectiveness of the reforms in these results and continues to take refuge in the claim that, under similar conditions, we would have achieved the same things with the old army, is either dishonest or incapable of thinking clearly about these matters.

We cannot pick out here the particular moments when our new institutions demonstrated their supreme importance and will simply observe that it would be nonsense to look for evidence against them in the brilliant outcome of the war. And yet the *skill* with which every obstacle was masterfully overcome; the dexterity with which all factions were united; the able men who supported the new institutions; the marvelous success we achieved on every battlefield; the brilliant peace, the new fame of our arms, the admiration of outsiders and other states for our military organization; the fear it inspired in *Paris*—all these are unable to guarantee it security, stability, loyalty, and confidence, nor to protect it against reaction, particularly from some men who lack experience and expertise, are incapable of great ideas, and belabor the pettiest details in order to undermine the great structures that men of genius created in.

Nothing in the world, particularly in politics, is more dangerous than to confuse the small with the great, to be led by the former, and so neglect to put our trust in greatness. It is for this reason that the spirit of reaction has acquired more weight than it would deserve on rational grounds. The arguments presented for and against our new military institutions grasp at so many details, left and right, back and forth, without a firm starting point or a clear conclusion, that no one can reach a final decision. This suits the purpose of the opposition, however, because this way the details they pick out acquire

(with omissions) in *Politische Schriften und Briefe*, 142–53, and (complete) in *Verstreute kleine Schriften*, 277–99.

much greater weight and force, besides which they are better able to conceal the real grounds for their aversion. In examining these matters we shall begin by asking: What are the decisive points here, which provide a basis for a general conclusion? Let us consider first of all the following three issues:

1. The strength of the army, particularly its fighting power.
2. The cost of maintaining the army relative to the income of the state.
3. The cost of the old army relative to that of the present one.

1

The *first* question cannot be answered definitively. Minister of War von Boyen has tried to provide a definitive answer in a brief pamphlet on the subject; but one can easily see that his arguments, although correct in their own terms, nevertheless cannot be sustained.

The Prussian state, with eleven million inhabitants, stands at the same level as the great powers of Europe, which rule thirty or forty million. It lies among them in the middle of the European state system, it is envied by great and small alike because of its rapid development, and it cannot possibly maintain its position without exertions that are uncommon in other states. Indeed, there are many otherwise honest and intelligent men in the government who declare, as always, that Prussia ought to sink to the second rank of states where it belongs. We make only two points in reply to this cut-rate wisdom: that no one could make such a proposal to a prince without being considered a *simpleton*; and that Prussia has now maintained her position for eighty years, while making outstanding progress domestically, so in reality the question has already been decided. Since Prussia does not want to give up her position, it is clear that her military power cannot be too great, that is, it must be as great as the total resources of the state, freely expressing all its natural qualities, will allow.

Here the difference between attack and defense must be kept in mind from the start. The former may be of the utmost importance to the state, useful and desirable as far as its preeminence and fame among other states is concerned; the latter, however, absolutely requires the greatest effort. Self-defense is not a matter of more or less honor and fame, but of existence or nonexistence. It follows from this that nothing distinguishes a statesman more than the creation, alongside an effective military establishment, of a martial spirit and institutions among the people; for everyone knows that an effective defense against a stronger enemy depends not just on a good army, but on the collaboration of the whole population, by which we mean not insurrection and guerrilla warfare, but the greater overall effort that results from a lively sense of popular participation, a warlike spirit, and efficient national institutions. The question [of the army's strength] thus turns on another: How strong *could* the army and the fighting power of the people be?

Whatever other economic factors might be brought to bear on this question, it must be conceded that nowadays the answer depends primarily on money. Today money can compensate for everything, and for this reason it is the measure, or rather the multiplier, of all active forces. As far as the second question goes—how great the size and fighting power of the army can be in relation to its cost—we intend to address it later on. Here we shall only remark that Frederick the Great maintained a force of 200,000 men, which he found appropriate to a population of six million, so that now, with a population of eleven million, we ought to have a force of almost 400,000 if we wish to hold to his standard; for it is obvious that Frederick made his army as strong as his means allowed, and during the Seven Years' War he found himself in such a grave predicament that he might well have wished for an army twice as large, had it been available. I hope people will now cease objecting that Prussia has no need for such a large army. Frederick had the largest possible army. If we too make ours as large as we can, we shall only be following his example, and it would be silly to argue that the results would overshoot the mark. If, moreover, we give this large army an additional measure of strength, by means of martial institutions that knit together the whole population, we would only be doing what the changed times demand. The element of war, free now from its various chains, operates with all its raw natural power, so that it always becomes a matter of life and death. Sooner or later we shall really have to defend our skins.

2

The second point pertains to the cost of the peacetime army in relation to the income of the state. This is a simple matter. In the best years of his reign Frederick the Great had an income of almost twenty million taler; his army cost about thirteen million, two-thirds of his income. In the last years before our defeat the state's income was about thirty-two million, of which the military consumed half. Since the last war our income has reached fifty-five million, of which ten million are consumed by interest on the state debt, so forty-five million remain for operating expenses. Our armed forces cost about twenty-two million annually, which is still not half the total allotted for the whole administration. If we subtract payments in kind formerly exacted from the population, which are now treated as cash in the accounts of the Ministry of War, the cost of the military establishment scarcely exceeds nineteen million taler.

A simple comparison of these figures shows that we now devote relatively less money to the military than Frederick and his successors did up to 1806. What, then, has caused the expenses of the rest of the government to rise so quickly, having increased by five million since 1806, while its income has grown by not even one million? By what right is it demanded that the five million taler deficit be made up by the military budget, when it is notorious that the civil administration consumes this five million, without accomplishing any more than before? If the army presently costs a few million more than it did before 1806, there are very good reasons for this, as we shall show in the next section. The increased cost of the civil administration, however, is almost solely the result of the rather irresponsible liberality of Prince Hardenberg, who for personal reasons has established an extremely costly administrative system, and in particular has rapidly increased the salaries of most of its members by 30 to 40 percent. He did this at a time when the cost of living was admittedly still high, in other words when the value of money was lower. Today, however, the value of money is not in fact lower than in 1806; rather, the perquisites and privileges of the bureaucracy have become more luxurious. In the last five or six years the value of money has increased by 40 percent. As a result the subject's taxes are worth 40 percent more to the state, he is therefore crushed by an excessive burden, and the administration, already too costly when money was worth less, exceeds any reasonable standard now that money is worth more. It has become fashionable among writers to heap scorn on the fact that the military consumes half of a state's income. They seem to regard the army as a kind of incidental expense. On the other hand, one could certainly argue that the money the people provide to maintain a unified state ought to be used above all to defend it against other similar states—in short, that the main justification for the state's existence is defense against an outside enemy. Accordingly, the sums spent on the military would appear to be the most essential, being intended directly for this purpose, while the rest would seem incidental. We do not put any great stock in this argument; but let it serve to illustrate how far the correct point of view has been distorted. We consider the few historical comparisons we have offered to be the most important evidence, but believe in any case that if Prussia's military establishment accounts for half her expenses she should not be ashamed of it, nor be considered a barbarous garrison state, but instead should be proud of it.

3

The third issue is the cost of our old army compared to that of the present. Frederick the Great had an army of 190,000 men. But of these only 92,000 were with the colors, while the remainder were on leave and in reserve. Thus his standing army can be reckoned at 92,000 men; this cost nearly thirteen million taler. In 1806 our army totaled 240,000 men, of which only 108,000 were with the colors; this cost about eighteen million.

To increase the actual standing army by some 10,000 men thus cost an extra five million taler. This was due to a number of factors, but the two most important were that in the interim prices had risen substantially, and that it was necessary to support officers for the 50,000 men who would reinforce the army in wartime—officers are always the most expensive part of a military budget. In 1817 our standing army amounted to 114,000 men, only 6,000 more than in 1806, and cost twenty-two million taler, four million more. But to that must be added the fighting power of the part of the *Landwehr* that could be mobilized at once, which would bring the total to 300,000 men, 60,000 more than in 1806. If we also add the second echelon of the *Landwehr*, which would certainly count in a defensive war, the number of fighting men would increase by 180,000 more. Indeed, one would have to say that if this extra four million taler had really been put to the test in war, it would have borne better fruit than the extra five million did in 1806. For however little one may think of the second echelon of reserves, it must be admitted that in a defensive war good use could be made of them in the fortresses.

The increased cost of the new army, moreover, derives entirely from factors unrelated to its size, so that the growth of the state's military power should be seen purely as a product of improved organization. For instance:

1. Consider the hunger and deprivation that prevailed in the Prussian army under Frederick the Great, and almost up to 1806. Only a man who served in the line as a junior officer has any real notion of it. It is no exaggeration to say that a beggar was better off than a serving soldier. In the last years before the lost war the soldier's bread ration was increased to $1\frac{1}{5}$ pounds per day, and his condition was so improved that we can say his nutrition had effectively been doubled. Today noncommissioned officers are paid better, the artillery has been given a raise, and in more expensive garrison towns soldiers are granted an extra twelve groschen worth of vegetables per month. The great mass of soldiers are in fact no better paid than in 1806; but now they live mainly in barracks, where their upkeep is much easier, though the expense to the army is somewhat higher.

We cannot claim that junior officers to the level of company commander and higher officers to the level of regimental commander are now paid better and more in line with their circumstances than before, since company commanders have simultaneously lost such a substantial portion of their income;[5] but officers were less desperately in need of better living conditions than those in the ranks from sergeant on down, in any case.

[5] See *Observations on Prussia*, note 2, above.

2. Just as bad as the soldier's food was his clothing. It had grown steadily worse since the Seven Years' War, thanks to the stagnation of the state's income and the general rise in prices, and in the end it was but a semblance of clothing. It often happened that when a soldier pulled on his trousers for the first time, and found them a bit tight, they would come apart like a fish net. The long nap of the fabric concealed the broken threads, so as long as it was new it might have been taken for sound material. On close inspection, however, or after it was worn a little while, it seemed more like women's lace than real cloth. When a soldier wore out his uniform the buttons were cut off, because these, according to the administration, were "iron"; so soldiers were found on street corners everywhere without buttons, with hungry faces and pleading eyes. That the so-called small parts of the uniform were handled no better is obvious, since they certainly could not come out of the state's money, and the responsible company commander had to pay for them out of his reserve funds. There was no question of a coat, still less of forage caps or gloves; all equipment, even weapons, was the worst in Europe. Today the soldier is clothed without conspicuous neglect; his weapon and equipment are among the best in Europe; he has acquired a neat, even impressive appearance. This could not have been done without considerable extra expense. The main parts of a musketeer's uniform used to cost 3½ taler and now cost over 4. A dragoon's uniform, which cost 4½ taler before, now costs 18 taler 15 groschen, and the total extra expense for this category alone comes to half a million taler. We must say, however, that the extra expense would by no means have achieved its goal had it not been combined with better organization, a two-year exchange period for uniforms, a commissary to manage the budget for the small uniform parts, and so forth.

3. Invalids are better cared for now. In the past there was no other care than what was provided by invalid companies and homes, or the so-called mercy money. Now a considerable number of those disabled in war are retired on a full pension.

4. The price of horses has risen appreciably, so remounts for the cavalry cost more, despite the smaller number kept with the standing army. A cuirassier's horse, for which no more than 80 taler would have been paid in the past, now commonly costs 100–120.

5. In the past the cavalry would have been sent to graze for ten weeks per year, which is no longer done, and naturally creates substantial extra expense for the army. This practice was given up because it was found to be harmful to the cavalry and the country and did not fit in with the rest of the new organization.

6. All impressing of civilian carriages has ended, so the military must pay extra for postage and transportation.

7. The number of fortresses has increased considerably, and since we do not want them to fall into ruins, as in 1806, they are an additional expense.

8. Substantially more is being spent on education, particularly for officers, which again is not necessarily required by the new system.

9. Finally, the requisitioning (at very low prices) of grain for bread and forage [to be stockpiled] in so-called magazines has ceased, and both are bought at market prices and paid for in cash by the Ministry of War. This by itself may amount to 1½ to 2 million taler, depending on prices. It is of course self-evident that the abolition of requisitioning has nothing to do with the military reforms but was done solely for the good of the country and its economy.

Anyone who takes all this into account will agree that the military budget has grown not because of the army's increased size, nor its essentially new structure, but only because of the burdens the rural population is now spared, and because of essential improvements in the conditions of the soldier's existence. Minister von Boyen claims in his pamphlet—and it would certainly not be difficult to prove—that an army with the strength and organization of that of 1806, under the conditions described above, would cost twenty-three million taler today, a million more than the present army actually costs.

Having set aside objections about the excessive size of the army, let us consider the chief points of difference between our former military institutions and those of today. In our army there is always a question whether those who cannot be kept in the line, that is, with the colors, should be supported on furlough or in a *Landwehr*. The main issue is thus which system, for a given sum, yields the greatest increase in the strength of the standing army in wartime. Clearly it is the *Landwehr*, since the furlough system requires the support of 5–6,000 more officers, which would cost several million taler. This is clear if we consider that an army the strength of that in 1806 would now cost twenty-three million, while the new army, which in 1817 was stronger by 8,000 men plus several fortresses (which account for another million), would have cost twenty-four million under the old system. Under the new system, however, it cost only twenty-two million even in 1817, before the decline of grain prices. The new system thus costs two million less, and at the same time provides 60,000 more men for war. These 60,000 are one-fifth of the entire force, and the two million are one-tenth of the entire budget. The total savings of the new system would amount to three-tenths of the entire budget [under the old system], almost a third, even if we take no account whatever of the second echelon of the *Landwehr*.

As to the wartime strength of the army, moreover, the *Landwehr* also has another side. The concept of the *Landwehr* encompasses and touches the entire people; the official limitations imposed on it are basically artificial and could easily be set aside in case of a major emergency. The concept of a standing army with a furlough system is inherently limited, and the emergency measures allowed by law seem to violate the concept itself, by an act of force. Do not suppose that we are merely playing tricks with ideas. Fully half our lives, and the structure of our society, depend on shared ideas working in the accustomed way, and it would be totally irrational to laugh at the law because it seeks to channel those ideas in one direction or another. But the moral power of the *Landwehr* also affects the way people live. When all state institutions are organized around an armed *Landwehr*, when all the state's energies are directed toward it, when all officials, high and low, are instructed to treat this institution, which in principle knows no bounds, as an expression of the absolute power of the nation, then any direction imparted to it from above will produce entirely different results than if everything remained confined within an institution divorced from the people themselves.

The *Landwehr* is a regional institution, to which the state lends as much support as it can; the rest comes from the provincial governments, whose officials are instructed and organized to serve it. The standing army with its furlough system is an institution of state. Everything that affects it must be determined directly by the state's senior officials, and even initiated by them. The provincial estates, which exert a positive influence over a *Landwehr*, are passive [in relation to a standing army], that is, more or less resistant. In 1806, when we found ourselves in a life-or-death struggle, we had a standing army and not one man more. Of this standing army, 240,000 strong on paper, not even 170,000 were present at Jena and Auerstädt. This shows how the theoretical size of a military force melts away the moment it is used. Such an erosion of fighting power always occurs and cannot be avoided; but of course the weakness of our army in Saxony was also made much worse by understrength battalions produced by foreign recruitment and the old system of internal levies. In 1806 we actually intended to increase the army by 40,000 men; but how much time and preparation would have been needed to do this!

Compare this with what happened in 1813. East Prussia began to raise its *Landwehr* before the peace with Russia was concluded, while the province was still partly in the hands of the enemy, partly under the authority of General Yorck. Silesia and the Mark organized theirs in the middle of the storm of war, with armies moving back and forth across their territory. The central government contributed virtually nothing except the weapons and ammunition pouches. The overall result of arming the *Landwehr* was a force of 120,000 men, of which perhaps 60,000 could have been used at the start of 1813, when the standing army amounted to only 30,000 men. Clearly such accomplishments must be given due weight in considering this issue.

The ability to produce a greater—indeed a much greater—force in time of war for the same cost, with no fixed limit; to infuse the entire people with a warlike spirit; to bind the army and the people together, drawing upon the strength of the whole nation in a defensive struggle—these are the main advantages of the *Landwehr* system, which are of such significance because in our time the *Landwehr* alone is capable of harnessing the raw, elemental power of war, to the point where its other advantages scarcely come into account, although they are still of greater significance than the disadvantages of which the system is accused. Let us now briefly consider these secondary benefits.

1. Universal military service is only possible under the *Landwehr* system. Every man can certainly be called upon to give up three years from his civilian life while he is young; but to spend four to six weeks with the colors every year for twenty years is an obligation from which a good third of the male population must be excused. Quite apart from the idea of justice that universal service expresses, it is impossible to create an equally strong military force any other way.

2. The short, three-year term of service is possible only with a *Landwehr*. This is a great boon to people of every class, because everyone prefers to fulfill his personal obligation as quickly as possible and would rather give up three years of his youth, when he has not yet begun a career, than be bound to serve through twenty years of his life.

3. Only the *Landwehr* makes it possible to have an army made up entirely of young men aged twenty to twenty-five. Youth is essential to the art of war. An old soldier, grown old in war and covered with wounds, is obviously worth a great deal, but not an old, worn-out peasant, taken from his village to the barracks for the twenty-fourth time and then sent home again, a man annoyed at having to leave his wife and child without support who heartily wishes the whole army would go to the devil. It is particularly advantageous in peacetime for the army to consist of young men between twenty-one and thirty-three. Youth is more educable and more inclined and better suited to war games.

4. Only the *Landwehr* allows the term of service to be compressed from twenty or twenty-four years under the old system to three years; but there is also no doubt that it is easier to impart a martial character to the soldier's mind, habits, and values if he is subject to the same discipline for three years running, rather than being put through it for a month every year for twenty-four years. The whole idea that we now have raw recruits where once we had old, experienced soldiers is an illusion. In the old days a soldier who served twenty or twenty-four years would only have spent about two of them with the colors. Such a man would indeed be old, but not on that account an old soldier. The so-called recruit already exceeds this man's term of service by a good third.

5. Large bases and regular maneuvers by the standing army are only possible under the *Landwehr* system. The furlough system encourages small staffs and their division among small garrisons, where they can remain close to the men on furlough who are constantly coming and going. Yet nothing is more necessary to the development of the army—to its physical and moral health, so to speak—than large bases and regular maneuvers. The latter, however, depend on the former. It is obvious that maneuvers can be more relevant, realistic, comprehensive, and diverse, and can make better use of the three-year service period, if they are conducted by substantial bodies of troops over wide areas rather than by an isolated battalion grown stale and rusty in some small town. The troops' discipline, spirit, and sense of duty are all transformed if the senior commander—that is, the man personally responsible to the king—always has his men under his eye, rather than leaving these matters primarily to the battalion commanders. The intense feeling of duty and the energy with which that duty is performed will be increased no end, and only this will prevent the corrupting laziness that became a positive sickness among the officers and men in our old army, a poison that sapped its power.

If large bases make continuous maneuvers possible, they are also the indirect means of improving the soldier's food and clothing. Large garrisons must have barracks, and it is only there, given the soldier's modest pay, that he can be protected from hunger, and then only when the business is handled with a certain industry, with strict supervision, care, and diligence—all of which can come only from officers, and then only when their own advancement is at stake, that is, when everything takes place under the eyes of their superiors. Roughly the same is true for those elements of the uniform handled by commissaries attached to individual units. Only in this way could we have controlled the miserable hunger and shabbiness, the revolting beggary that hampered our army and made it a mockery in the eyes of Europe.

6. The useless waste of energy by men constantly coming and going on furlough will be avoided. Today the soldier goes off to the colors only once to satisfy his three-year service and returns once, where before he had to do it every year, twenty to twenty-four times in his life. The need to report for *Landwehr* maneuvers, which happens only every two years and is much less of a burden, does not contradict this, since it is still true that no energy is wasted in transit during the soldier's thirty-six months of service with the line.

7. The furlough system is linked to the overall system of regimental replacement districts. When war comes, this naturally creates a certain *esprit de corps* among men from the same area, which is agreeable and useful. But it cannot be denied that the system does not work in wartime, since it is unavoidable that this or that unit suffers more than another and requires more replacements, which must still be drawn from a general pool of re-

serves. The corps replacement districts introduced by the military reforms are a very serviceable compromise, which still preserves feelings of regional camaraderie.

This is all we have to say on behalf of the *Landwehr* as part of our present system. We now wish to consider the three main grounds for opposition to it, so that all the other arguments made against it can be recognized merely as clever disguises for these real reasons.

The *first* reason for opposition is universal military service. Our nobleman finds it an unbearable thought to serve in the ranks with his peasants. To be sure, the distinction between the estates is still enormously greater in northern Germany than in southern Europe. The feudal system, under which the peasant is not really a citizen but virtually a subject of the nobleman, has remained more or less intact here until recent times, and it is understandable that it should seem more natural that the noble is the officer by virtue of his status, and the peasant the common soldier, rather than the reverse, which if necessary could sometimes happen under our new system. If our feudal system were truly intact and still possessed its original power, it would indeed be foolish to overthrow such a natural order merely because of a philosophical principle. But the feudal system has waned, here as elsewhere. Having lost the last of its power in the second half of the eighteenth century, it is now being legally overturned by new state institutions. Unless we wish to cut these back and return to where we were, we must concede that the nobleman's prerogative of command in the army is no longer fixed in the nature of things.

Given our general cultural level, universal military service, which clearly seems attractive and entirely fair in itself, will of course create many practical difficulties. The French have tried to avoid these by allowing the use of substitutes. In Prussia the same thing is supposed to have been achieved by allowing one year of voluntary service [as an alternative to conscription]. Without some such compromise the system would be unmanageable. We prefer to pass over the question of which approach is better, for we cannot find in the use of substitutes the abuse and impropriety for which some despise it, and overall it seems to us a matter of indifference which compromise is chosen. But considering that in France and southern Germany universal service already exists, that it is undeniably associated with ideas about the rights and obligations of citizens that are already well established in our culture, and that it is in any case the sort of principle that ought not to be recanted once it has been acknowledged, we do not believe it is still feasible today to give in to the nobility on this issue. At the same time, however, we must observe that the principle of universal service is not fundamentally connected to our new military institutions, and specifically that it is not an essential element of the *Landwehr* system. People may well prefer to restore the old furlough system as a way of smuggling in the old exemption from military service, because one old practice somehow seems related to the other.

Finally, let us put the nobleman at ease by noting how seldom, in practice, the *specific* case will arise which is supposed to reveal the incongruity of the whole system: namely, that of the nobleman carrying a musket alongside his peasant. The greater part of the nobility either serve as officers in the standing army or will do so in the *Landwehr,* or hold high offices in the civil administration, most of whose members will be exempt from service in the *Landwehr.* Cases in which the nobleman actually serves with the peasant would therefore exist only as rare exceptions, and indeed only among very young noblemen.

The *second* reason for opposing the *Landwehr* is the poor quality of its officer corps. Since the *Landwehr* constitutes two-thirds of our forces in wartime this is considered a matter of the greatest importance. People think that the kind of officer we could now have in the *Landwehr,* for instance a nobleman who left the service some time ago, perhaps after serving only a few years, or an official who only knows how to work a pen, or a merchant, grocer, innkeeper, manufacturer, or artisan—someone [in other words] who has never thought of anything but how to improve his business—cannot be compared to the young nobleman or officer's son who has seen guard- and garrison service since his fifteenth year. But basically opposition is caused not so much by patriotic concern for the technical inadequacy of *Landwehr* officers as by the disagreeable feeling of seeing the former character of the officer corps changed by so many alien additions, to see the son of a nobleman serve with the son of a grocer, or even under him. This feeling—a response to an unfamiliar way of doing things—deserves no special consideration. But if the point is that *esprit de corps,* the manners of good society, even a certain military uniformity of behavior must be lost in an officer corps constituted in this way—then we reply that people who think these things are necessary, that their loss will cause the officer corps to fall into disrepute, clearly exaggerate and overestimate the value of these qualities. What such an officer corps loses in professional polish will be made up in part by the opportunity to draw capable and energetic individuals from the entire population. Consider how many outstanding military leaders came forward during the insurrections in Poland, Spain, and France. We too saw a number of *Landwehr* officers, who had never been soldiers before, serve with distinction in the last war. This is well known and would have been even more apparent if the war had lasted longer.

The *third* source of opposition to the *Landwehr* is fear of revolution. It is said that the *Landwehr* system arms the people and thus lends every revolution far greater strength, total superiority over the standing army.

Here people are being misled by vague conceptions, and we have the following to say in opposition:

1. All recent revolutions were made in conjunction with the standing army; but the mother of them all, the most important of all, the French Revolution, took place without a national guard. Though the standing army did not play a major role in the Revolution, neither did it provide a bulwark against it. The Guards gave way at once and helped overthrow the Bastille; and lest anyone believe this was an isolated case, let us add that on October 5–6 the Flanders regiment made common cause with the people, that the Queen's Regiment in Nancy rebelled out of the blue, and that in 1792 the entire line army of France fought under the flag of the republic. True the French army occupied a position far more isolated from the nation than ours ever would, and indeed than ours ever did even under the old system.

2. The brute force of the people, employed as a revolutionary tool, centers on the capital; but here the *Landwehr* has little or no impact. If we follow the course of most revolutions, whatever takes place between the central government and the inhabitants of the capital generally sets the tone for the provinces. A few large cities may be exceptions and play an independent role, but ordinarily not for long.

3. It cannot be denied that in a true civil war the *Landwehr* would make it easier for rebellious segments of the population to arm themselves. But such wars, which are caused by recklessness and factionalism and should not be confused with revolutions, are extremely rare in history. Whenever they do occur they have profound motives that would have caused the break even without the *Landwehr*. Resistance to foreign domination, religious fanaticism, or, as in England and France, the desire for complete social transformation, are such causes, and we have no fear of these things, not even a thought. To believe in the possibility of such a disruption of our present circumstances would be to believe in ghosts; and to ignore external danger because of this illusory evil would be to embrace death for fear of dying.

Prussia has the need to arm her entire people so that she can withstand the two giants who will always threaten her from east and west. Should she fear her own people more than these two giants?

FOURTEEN

"On the Political Advantages and Disavantages of the Prussian *Landwehr*" (1819)

On December 6, 1819, the campaign against the Landwehr *reached an important milestone, in the form of a royal order reorganizing it along lines that would insure its subordination to the line army. Conscription districts were redrawn to conform to those of the regular forces, a number of armories were closed or relocated to more secure locations, the independent* Landwehr *inspectorate was abolished, and the* Landwehr *as a whole was recast into regiments matching those of the line. Eleven days later, Clausewitz, presumably unaware of the steps that had already been ordered, sent the following memorandum to Gneisenau with the suggestion that he pass it along to Hardenberg, who might wish to make use of its arguments against those who sought the* Landwehr's *destruction.* [1]

The presentation could hardly have been more forthright or more idiosyncratic. At a time when German governments felt safer than at any point in the last twenty-five years, Clausewitz's stark portrayal of Prussia's vulnerability, already familiar from the essay on "Military Institutions" reprinted above, would have struck most contemporaries as more than a little exaggerated. Strictly speaking, Hardenberg could have found nothing to object to in Clausewitz's demand that state institutions answer first of all to the needs of external security, a point of view that was deeply rooted in the Prussian past. Clausewitz, however, was not content simply to affirm the military advantages of the Landwehr *while discounting the political risk. He believed the anxiety the* Landwehr *had inspired was a sign of political danger whose source he locates not simply in the social resentments of the elite but, even more tellingly, in "the government's sense that it is isolated" from society. And here Clausewitz speaks with a voice well outside the mainstream of political debate in Prussia: the "political advantage" of the* Landwehr *turns out to be that it represented*

---

[1] Clausewitz to Gneisenau, December 17, 1819, in *Schriften*, 2, part 1: 367. The royal order of December 6 was made public two weeks later, and its contents were probably not widely known before then. But that some sort of crisis was at hand was suggested by the proliferation of rumors to which Clausewitz alludes in his letter, and by the resignation of Boyen's main collaborator on the general staff, Karl Wilhelm von Grolman, which also occurred on the 17th. The central role that the Landwehr issue played in Clausewitz's political views during these years is shown in Paret, *Clausewitz and the State*, 286–298.

a natural step toward a parliamentary regime, a step for which Prussia's chancellor had scant inclination.

Hardenberg seems not to have received Clausewitz's memorandum, though Gneisenau may have apprised him of its contents. Even so, Clausewitz would have reason to feel that his concerns had not been entirely overlooked. On December 22, the day the Landwehr's reorganization was made public, Hardenberg wrote to Gneisenau to reassure him that, all rumors to the contrary, the Landwehr's existence was not in doubt.[2] This was true, though the campaign against it would persist for some years yet; and Clausewitz took some comfort from the news.[3] At the same time, though, the Landwehr had ceased to count politically. The subordination of the Landwehr to the line may have improved its military efficiency, but it deprived it of most connection to local society and provincial government, and also of any chance to fill the quasi-constitutional role Clausewitz attributed to it. On December 25 Boyen, the Landwehr's chief patron, resigned as minister of war. He was followed a month later by Wilhelm von Humboldt, the leader of the constitutional movement in the Prussian ministry. Thereafter there was no one in authority who shared Clausewitz's belief that the Landwehr's qualities as a fighting force were in any way linked to its political role, which he understood to be not the expansion of state power over the people, but the harnessing of popular energy on behalf of the Prussian state.

Like the memorandum on "Military Institutions," the present work remained unpublished during Clausewitz's lifetime; it first appeared in Schwartz's biography. The text printed here follows the original manuscript as published by Werner Hahlweg, which varies slightly from Schwartz's version: like the first generation of Clausewitz's editors, Schwartz, working in the 1870s, was unable to resist the temptation to soften some of his subject's rough edges.[4] Hahlweg's edition also reproduces Gneisenau's marginal comments, which reveal a certain skepticism about some aspects of Clausewitz's presentation. When Clausewitz declares that the Tirolean rebels who rose against the French in 1809 had remained loyal to Austria, Gneisenau noted dryly that "the Tirolese have always been troublesome subjects for Austria." To Clausewitz's rhetorical question, "Were the people of France armed in 1789?"

---

[2] Hardenberg to Gneisenau, December 22, 1819, in Pertz-Delbrück, *Gneisenau*, 5: 401.

[3] Clausewitz to Carl von der Groeben, December 26, 1819, in Eberhard Kessel, "Zu Boyens Entlassung," *Historische Zeitschrift* 175 (1953): 52.

[4] "Ueber die politischen Vortheile und Nachtheile der Preußischen Landwehr-Einrichtung," in *Schriften*, 2, part 1: 367–72; cf. Schwartz, *Leben*, 2: 288–93. Schwartz's changes are stylistic rather than substantive and therefore less serious than those of Ranke or of the anonymous editor of *The Campaign of 1812*. Nevertheless, it is hard to see why, for instance, a sentence that actually begins "We wish to continue speaking" should have been changed to read "We are able to continue the discussion," unless the object was to make Clausewitz a shade more polite than he meant to be.

Gneisenau responded that "the French people were indeed better armed than other nations, and then became [more] so through the creation of the national guard." A few lines later, finally, he questions whether the French army had really been such a "prime" example of a professional, regular force and goes on to observe that, while Clausewitz sees that army "melt[ing] down . . . under the rays of the revolutionary spirit," it was in fact specifically undermined by the national guard.

These, needless to say, are observations of the highest relevance to the political struggle in which Clausewitz and Gneisenau were both engaged. They offer further evidence that Clausewitz's ideas, and the emphatic way he presented them, could seem extreme even to those who shared his point of view.

By organizing a significant part of the population, about one-third of all able-bodied men, into regular regiments, by giving them officers out of their own ranks, and by depositing arms in open armories in their midst, the institution of the *Landwehr obviously places weapons in the hands of the people.*

The Prussian people, like any people, can hardly be entirely content. We can even say that logically total contentment would be quite impossible. But we live in an age that is characterized by vague aspirations and a spirit of disaffection with government; *thus it is now doubly dangerous to place weapons in the hands of the people.*

In times of internal disquiet and disaffection among the lower classes, any government must regard the sword as the ultimate support of law and sovereignty after all means of persuasion and wisdom have proved to no avail. But the sword no longer gives any protection if it is not exclusively in the hands of the government, if the rebellious part of the population is armed equally well.

We do not mean to challenge the inner logic of this sequence of propositions and conclusions; we merely wish to look at them from another angle. On the scale of truth and wisdom they are outweighed by other considerations, and in effect eliminated.

To arm the people—that is, to adopt the institution of the *Landwehr*—raises the defensive potential of the state to a point that cannot be equaled by regular forces. With the same financial support and the same sacrifice on the part of the population, a standing army will never achieve the overall fighting strength that is made possible by the *Landwehr* system, whatever the details of its organization. If this is denied we would have to resort to different arguments than we intend here. We wish to continue speaking only to those who provisionally acknowledge the truth of our statement, a truth that, apart from *a priori* evidence, is strongly supported by a comparison of our experiences in 1806 and 1813.

The *Landwehr* increases the danger of revolution; disarming the *Landwehr* increases the danger of invasion and enslavement. On the historical evidence, which is the greater danger? Where in the German past do we find the revolutionary uprisings that are so prominent in the histories of Italy, France, and England? In what century, in what German state? I think people who mistrust the *Landwehr* should be embarrassed by this question. Was it perhaps in Prussia that our calm, peaceful Germany showed its violent side most openly? Was Germany especially agitated during the eighteenth century?

We know nothing of any revolution, of any genuine rebellion. Do we know nothing of invasion?

If in some sense it may be risky to rule a people in arms, isn't it far more dangerous to rule an unarmed people?

We entreat those who are strongly affected by present difficulties to answer this question conscientiously. The second point that we hope to clarify somewhat is the relationship between a disarmed population on the one hand and the internal order and security of a government on the other, so that we can determine the benefits of disarmament and compare them with its disadvantages.

Is it solely or primarily the availability of weapons that matters?

Have the Tirolese been less obedient and loyal because they were armed?

Were the people of France armed in 1789? Furthermore, are *Landwehr* and a standing army true political opposites, as is often claimed? When popular attitudes begin to be corrupted, is it so easy to keep them from penetrating the standing army? Wasn't the army under Louis XVI a prime example of a regular, professional force, and did it not melt down and disappear under the rays of the revolutionary spirit, like snow in springtime?

In short, can we regard the abolition of the *Landwehr* and the enlargement of the standing army as a talisman against revolutionary flames once the sparks are already flying?

Nothing could be as harmful as this belief. In the final analysis, the sword on which a government must rely when it is attacked by a deceived, intoxicated population is the warlike character of the ruler and his dynasty, his righteousness and determination. These qualities will always inspire men with a sense of justice to close ranks around the throne.

We mention this extreme possibility merely to indicate that we do not suggest that the sole or the only valid means to restore calm is always to give way, show endless meekness, suffer a martyrdom of patience. But it seems not very useful to talk about extremes when a conflict has not even arisen. The term *standing army* could not exorcise the calamity if it were approaching; and it is not the *Landwehr* that forms the core of the threat. Honest and intelligent treatment—this alone can maintain and strengthen loyalty and devotion in the army, the *Landwehr*, and the people. There can be no security without these feelings, which in turn are stronger than any threat a *Landwehr* may pose.

The third point we must mention concerns the origin of all this concern. What else is its source except the government's sense that it is isolated? The government sees that a spirit of dissatisfaction and open opposition is stirring. It fears that sooner or later this force will explode. How can it resist? The strength of its army is negated by a *Landwehr* that is much larger. Consequently we are advised to abolish the *Landwehr* so we can depend on the army.

We believe we have shown that this is no true solution. [Instead] let the government gather around it representatives of the people, elected from those who share the true interests of government and are known to the people. Let this be the government's main support, friend, and ally, as Parliament has been for a century the support of the king of England. With this institution let the government mobilize the energies of a valiant people against its external enemies and rivals; with this institution let the government enchain reckless forces if they turn against their own community in frenzy and ferment. From our standpoint we see no other way, and the goal can hardly be achieved more easily and cheaply. Whoever promises to cure the problem with palliatives should be regarded as a charlatan who only makes the sickness worse.

And wouldn't disarming the people make an impression on the public that would itself be a first sign that things were getting worse? If tension already existed, wouldn't this increase it, and wouldn't the remaining trust in the government be destroyed?

This consideration is admittedly of minor significance from the point of view of political philosophy, but its practical relevance is great. To disarm the people will scarcely allay the danger of internal unrest; on the contrary, we may be more than justified in thinking that such a policy would intensify it. And by how much would it add to the dangers that threaten from outside!

We don't want to refer to the present international situation and offer no opinion on whether or not it is favorable. We only wish to consider the general condition of Prussia since she became a major power, her relations with other states, and the particular conditions that define and characterize her existence.

Prussia is surrounded by powerful antagonists. Her territorial gains as well as her internal development have aroused the envy and hatred of others. In particular, the glory of her arms has inspired hidden resentment among the large and small German states, and the spiteful intention to damage her.

It is said that Prussia has an overstrained military system, which simply means that the Prussian system is stretched more tautly than that of other states. In this way Prussia has overcome her limited resources and remained level with other major powers. What would happen if Prussia were to loosen this so-called excessive tautness? The state's position and importance would significantly suffer, and once in decline others would not find it difficult to overcome her completely. To other powers this prospect must be too enticing for them to refrain from coaxing us in all sorts of ways to take a first voluntary step downward. Haunted by fear of the [popular] sword, we relinquish it and let ourselves be led away in chains.

Only great institutions, holding and channeling genuine forces and infused by a living spirit can maintain us on our present level—not empty forms of the sort we had before 1806, echoes of glory, growing fainter every year. Our recent history conveys this truth too clearly, word for word, for us to ignore it if we have the least intention to recognize the facts.

And so let the men of 1806, who seek salvation in the decrepit forms of that period, search their consciences and honestly face the questions we have raised here. Let them feel the enormous responsibility they assume when their hands, which perhaps have never done serious work, begin to destroy the edifice on which our magnificent fate rested in 1813, 1814, and 1815, like the goddess of victory on her chariot.

FIFTEEN

"Agitation" (early 1820s)

With the exception of On War, *none of Clausewitz's writings present greater interpretive problems than the following essay, entitled, with lapidary simplicity, "Agitation."*[1] *Much of the difficulty stems from our ignorance of the author's purpose and of the exact context in which it was written. Internal references to the Carlsbad Decrees of September 1819 and to Joseph Görres's book,* Germany and the Revolution, *which appeared at the same time, allow the manuscript to be dated from the early 1820s;*[2] *but the inconsistent style and dramatic shifts of focus that mark it suggest a work written in isolated stages, perhaps over a period of years, and never subjected to comprehensive revision. Clausewitz's correspondence is of little help: his surviving letters from this period contain few references to political matters.*

The essay's intended audience is also mysterious. The first quarter of the text, an extended analysis of the decline of the European nobility and the origins of the French Revolution, has the dispassionate tone of a work destined for publication as a short book or in a learned journal. As the focus shifts to contemporary conditions, however, the organization becomes more haphazard, the content more impressionistic, the language scathing in its sarcasm. The last few pages, in which Clausewitz recalls his experiences as a staff officer in the Rhineland in 1817, are more personal, while at the same time introducing a variety of technical military details that seem out of place.

These formal incongruities are partly a reflection of Clausewitz's ambiguous personal position during the years when this essay was written. For a while in the spring of 1819 Clausewitz was the leading candidate to fill Prussia's vacant ambassadorship to Great Britain. The king, however, was finally unable to overcome his doubts about Clausewitz's political reliability. At several crucial junctures in the recent past—in 1812, when he abandoned Prussia with-

---

[1] "Umtriebe," first published in Schwartz, *Leben*, 2: 200–44; reprinted (with one minor excision) in Rothfels, *Politische Schriften und Briefe*, 153–95. The only comprehensive analysis is in Paret, *Clausewitz and the State*, 298–306. The political meaning of the word "Umtriebe," as well as the significance of the movement to which it referred, were both becoming widely recognized at the time Clausewitz wrote. A special entry under this heading, in which "Umtriebe" is defined as synonymous with "demagoguery," was published as an appendix to the final volume of the fifth edition of the Brockhaus *Conversations-Lexicon* (Leipzig, 1819–20), 10: 978–92.

[2] One sheet of notes for the essay also includes a separate reference to Hardenberg's death, which occurred on November 26, 1822.

out permission rather than serve the French; in December of 1812, when he negotiated the agreement neutralizing the Prussian contingent of the Grande Armée; and, during the weeks that followed, when he helped organize the East Prussian Landwehr without the king's consent—Clausewitz had shown himself willing to place his own judgment above that of the government. Whether such a man would have been suited to a diplomatic assignment would have been a fair question under any circumstances, and in the atmosphere of general crisis then enveloping Germany it was the only question that mattered. Even after the appointment as ambassador to Great Britain had fallen through, however, Clausewitz continued to put himself forward for similar positions until the end of 1823, and it is possible that some of the harshness with which he judges the "agitators" derived from a wish to reassure the king that he was not one of them.

To have imagined that someone of Clausewitz's character and experience could have felt much sympathy for the visionary proposals that had been circulating among German students and political activists since the Congress of Vienna might seem absurd. Nevertheless, it was not entirely unreasonable that he should have felt obliged to answer for the consequences of political passions he and his fellow reformers had helped call into existence. The experience out of which the present unrest had crystallized, after all, had been the Wars of Liberation. Karl Sand, the student who murdered August von Kotzebue in March of 1819, thus providing the final pretext for the resurgence of reaction that would ruin Clausewitz's ambassadorial prospects, had been a volunteer against France five years before, the kind of man whom the author of the "Political Declaration" would have embraced as an ally.[3] If some of the venom in the present essay may have been an expedient pose, in other words, it also expressed genuine frustration on the part of someone who had assisted in letting the genie of popular politics out of the bottle, and now despaired of getting it back inside.

Most historians have been inclined to discount the seriousness of the political unrest that occurred in Germany after 1815. So was Clausewitz. Part of the incongruity of the middle part of the essay stems from his failure to reconcile his desire to grapple with the ideas of the agitators and his scorn at their obvious impracticality. The violence of events like the Wartburg Festival, which Clausewitz mentions, was entirely symbolic: it featured a bonfire in

---

[3] See also the notebook entry from 1809 (pp. 277–78, above) in which Clausewitz's longing for a national rising against France led him to express the private hope that "the feeling of leaving a narrow, prosaic life behind—not painlessly, not playfully, but driven by an all-powerful destiny—of taking up a truly poetic existence, full of idealism and dignity, would take hold of our educated youth." The numerous apologia that Sand wrote following Kotzebue's murder (see, for instance, a letter from Sand to his family, published in the *Allgemeine Zeitung* of Augsburg, April 16–17, 1819) contained many similar statements.

which some military paraphernalia was burned, along with sheets of paper bearing the titles of books deemed offensive to the national cause. The confusion of political values among its organizers—who wished to commemorate both the three-hundredth anniversary of the Reformation and the fourth anniversary of the battle of Leipzig—was equally obvious. All of this would seem to argue for patience or indifference on the part of those who knew better what real politics was.

But real politics was precisely what was at stake in Clausewitz's eyes, though his interest in mending his fences with the Prussian establishment may have led him to obscure the issue to some extent. Agitation did not threaten the government or the civil peace of Prussia. What it threatened was the future of reform, which had always answered to the dictates of reason, never to public opinion. The reformers had viewed the latter chiefly as a weapon for use in the extremity of war. The demands of peace were different. When the Prussian government had declared, in the wake of Jena and Auerstädt, that "the first duty of the citizen is to remain calm," it could hardly have been more wrong from Clausewitz's point of view. It was not defeat, but victory, that should have brought tranquility, and it is the failure of the agitators to recognize this that fuels Clausewitz's anger.

As always, Clausewitz sought to base his discussion of contemporary conditions on an analysis of their historical genesis. It is to this problem that he devotes the first part of the essay, a remarkable survey of the social transformation of Europe brought about by the rise of the centralized state, the growing power of the middle classes, and the increasingly tenuous position of the nobility. These pages stand out among Clausewitz's political works for their historical insight and breadth of vision. But the connections that would have made them the real foundation for what follows are never constructed, and to that extent their promise remained unfulfilled.

What those connections might have looked like is hard to say, though Clausewitz's repeated references to the agitators' dubious social base—"academic and nonacademic youth" is only slightly unfair as a description—may be an important clue. For Clausewitz, political ideas acquire weight and legitimacy from their congruence with concrete interests, and to this extent the agitators of the 1820s would seem to suffer from the same sort of irrelevance as the self-absorbed aristocrats of the past. Yet it is hard to believe Clausewitz would have been more sympathetic to the agitators if their ideas had achieved greater resonance among the Prussian middle class, whose rightful claim to political significance he would already seem obliged, on the historical evidence, to concede. In the broadest terms, however, this failure to connect may be as significant as any other aspect of this generally remarkable work: in its alternating moments of brilliance and exasperation, "Agitation" reveals, more clearly than anything else Clausewitz wrote, both the depth of the reforming vision

that had saved the Prussian state, and its equally profound limitations as a
source of inspiration for a more democratic public life in the future.

After nearly all European states had developed into absolute monarchies during the seventeenth and eighteenth centuries, the nobility retained its privileges only in relation to the rest of society, not in relation to the prince. The noble dominated the peasant and enjoyed advantages over the bourgeois, but he no longer held a share of sovereign power and had become a subject like the others. This gave his relationship to bourgeois and peasant the appearance of privilege pure and simple, a kind of unwarranted favor.

At the same time a new estate, or rather, as a brilliant French writer observed, *un nouveau peuple*, was everywhere on the rise; the middle class, that is, all those who were neither nobles nor their vassals, gradually gained self-consciousness as it acquired greater wealth and energy.

This estate, which developed in the towns and had earlier been very small, had by and by grown far larger than the nobility.

This middle class, that is, the townsmen, had earlier enjoyed the same kind of inequality in relation to the noble's subject, the peasant, as the noble enjoyed in relation to them. The gap separating the estate of free men from that of serfs or peasants was as great as that between the noble and the bourgeois. Thus the middle class felt raised up in its turn. It had its own dignity, and in times and places where towns flourished most vigorously its members developed a sense of self-esteem that compared well with that of the partly impoverished, decayed, and parasitic nobility, and could even exceed it; in addition, the cities had their own small share of sovereignty, which was sufficient to their limited spheres, and they often found themselves at war with the noble and thus felt themselves to be his equal. This rivalry between the towns and the nobility was entirely different from that later on between the nobility and the middle classes. It was an open conflict, which the relative weakness of states at that time made possible, a mutual struggle for advantages that the other side already possessed.

Society was thus divided into three distinct estates: the nobility, the middle class, and the subjects of the nobility. This division could be considered entirely natural, for it arose because of the way the European social order was disrupted by the barbarian invasions. Only the nobility could be considered the true people; the gradually developing middle class was but a poor relation; the great mass, the subjects of the nobility, did not count. They were destined to farm the land and perform other personal service, and in so doing could feel more or less enslaved and oppressed, or more or less comfortable. Those who find this form of human society so degrading forget that it has been the structure of all peoples in a more or less natural state, specifically the much-heralded ancient republics. Thus social relationships at that time were free of tension, and when interests happened to collide the issue was quickly settled in open struggle. By and by these conditions changed, as all things must in this world. Social relationships changed because the different estates progressed along different paths, and they did so because they embodied different principles.

The noble possessed his property through the sword, either as a true conquest or by expropriation from those who were unarmed. His natural element was war—the preservation of wealth through war, and the acquisition of more. Once direct conquest became impossible, because there was nothing left to conquer, the noble sought employment in military service to the state, which was the basis of the entire feudal system. This form of employment has continued into modern times and has come to involve a class of abuses and privileges that we will consider further, and which we mention here only to indicate their historical origin.

This way of life finally had to come to an end, once the states of Europe established themselves one after another and everywhere claimed possession of the land. The crusades were supposed to be a new, inexhaustible source of riches, but they led only to the impoverishment and ruin of the noble in his homeland.

Since the noble knew no other means of supporting himself except by the sword, the moment when there was nothing more to be gained by it was the true culminating point of his existence.

Like any population the nobility's numbers increased according to natural laws. Thus its wealth was repeatedly divided; sporadic adherence to rules of primogeniture could only slow the process somewhat, not prevent it. Ill-conceived efforts to obtain new wealth, meaning those that produced no result and failed to cover their costs, like the crusades and similar ventures, and above all war among themselves, further depleted the nobility's resources. That it should take a long time for an entire class of people to recognize such a change in their situation, or rather that they should only come to recognize it long after the change has occurred, is easily understandable. The immediate press of circumstances is usually all that matters, and through it customs and habits are gradually transformed; but this always comes too late. Each specific difficulty or predicament will be seen as the result of unique conditions, temporary hard times, declining standards. Thus the noble continued in his old extravagant ways, his wealth dissipated and encumbered with debt, and only later did he realize, through the fog of debts and unmet obligations, that his financial circumstances were entirely different than he had imagined.

To be sure, a new source of income had presented itself to the noble, since he held the most important positions in the increasingly elaborate state bureaucracies as well as at court. But this easy wealth, divorced from principles of thrift, only led to new extravagance, contributed little to the accumulation of capital, and eventually disappeared, to the extent that princes proceeded to rationalize their states' finances.

The noble's intellectual horizons completely excluded any thought of industrial activity; thus there was nothing to offset this loss.

It is true, of course, that by and by the noble's habits and way of life became more subdued—from lord to subject, from feudal vassal to private man, but always a little too late, always a step behind and under pressure of adversity.

Thus the noble has survived to our own day. We still remember from our youth the troop of servants, the ostentatious show of livery, clothing, and arms, without which a noble house was thought unable to survive. Only in recent times do we see noblemen managing their property according to commercial principles and turning, when necessary, to manufacturing and trade in agricultural products.

If we now consider that the princes initially did more than their part in depriving the noble of his original importance by curtailing and finally eliminating his share of sovereign power, nothing is more reasonable and natural than the way this estate declined from its zenith over the centuries, drew closer to the other two estates and increasingly came to resemble them, so that eventually the nobility took on the character of a decayed ruin, undermined by time.

In contrast, it is entirely characteristic of the middle class that it has never been able to contemplate any activity apart from increasing its wealth through diligence and hard work. It is the nature of things that the poor and laboring classes always contribute somewhat more to the economy than they consume. This small surplus gradually accumulates like a residue and constitutes the nation's capital. The collective wealth of the middle class thus could not fail to increase substantially over the centuries, and this, together with its growing numbers, inevitably made this estate more significant. All the wealth squandered by the nobility through poor management flowed in the natural course of trade to the commercial and industrial classes.

This same acquisitive principle also applies to the peasantry, because the peasant is also a *worker*. For a long time, and in most places, his circumstances have prevented him from increasing his wealth to the extent he might have, but they have not made it totally impossible. The conditions of serfdom have changed in various ways, and in many places the peasant has gained freedom; in many others, where serfdom survives, he has gradually achieved much greater prosperity. Above all, peasants on the crown lands of most states have been able to work their way up. Thus the peasantry, the vast majority of every nation, also has its property, and with it some rights of its own. Its numbers have also increased dramatically, and as a result of all these things so has its importance to the state. It has drawn closer to the middle class, and the gap between them has narrowed.

If we now consider how the concept of the state has only evolved in recent centuries, how power has grown stronger at the top as fragmented lands combined into a unified whole, it becomes clear how—precisely because the estates grew closer to each other and were bound together in the unity of the state—the differences in their rights and duties became more evident and led to tension.

To this must be added the stimulating effect of the new learning. Earlier, through the mediation of the church, the sciences had more or less belonged to the nobility, that is, the landowning class; now they became the property of the middle class. Scholars and philosophers became the spokesmen not merely for the bourgeoisie, but also for the peasantry. The philosophical analysis of the basic principles of social organization was based primarily on the concept of humanity, to which, however, the concept of the people— that is, the majority—was closely related. It was entirely in the interest of these ideas to discard completely the distinction between free citizens and the nobility's subjects, so that these two estates could be conceived as a single, much greater whole, comprising the peasantry with its numbers and the middle class with its industry and education. They likewise deliberately neglected the great distinctions that already existed within the peasantry, and, because in some regions true serfdom or slavery still existed, they preferred to describe the whole class of those who worked the land as a class of slaves.

Under the new conditions created by strong, unified states, and in light of the views of the philosophers, the rights of the noble now seemed to be unwarranted favoritism, and his place in the state pure usurpation.

Just the same, his position and rights had an entirely natural historical origin; they were the remnant of what they had once been.

To some extent the noble controlled the property of the peasant, who was his subject and in many places his serf. He was the peasant's natural-born lord, in the sense that his authority was not delegated to him by the state; he paid no taxes on his own land; he was exempt from many other levies; he was not required to perform personal service at the behest of the state; he possessed an exclusive right to certain official positions. All these privileges and rights were a natural result of his earlier condition, when he alone had been a citizen, and indeed the citizen of a free state in whose government he had shared. Then the mass of the people counted for nothing and the middle class for very little; now the masses had entered the ranks of those who counted, and the middle class had joined forces with it. *Le nouveau peuple* had become four or five hundred times larger than *l'ancien peuple*, and in the eyes of philosophy, as of ordinary common sense, the enormity of its majority was the essential basis for its claims.

341

Two factors made matters even worse, as became evident in the eighteenth century.

The first was that the noble had ceased to be the principal defender of the country. In the Middle Ages, when the knight in armor was the chief weapon and feudal obligation the sole form of military organization, an army could only be small, and only those who were not poor and propertyless could take part in war. Of course, the noble might have equipped and armed his subjects, but he preferred to perform this honorable service personally, and nothing was more natural or beneficial to his political standing. To be sure, the noble brought his vassals to the battlefield with him as foot soldiers, but they always made up an inconsequential part of the army. Thus the conduct of war, the defense of the country, became the true personal occupation of the noble within the weakly constituted state. Through it he also sought to support himself outside the bonds of feudal obligation; and as his skill and power gradually ceased to be fully consumed by domestic wars, he carried them over to external wars, as the condottiere of foreign armies. One sees in this an effort by the landless part of the nobility to make something of themselves and acquire a distinct profession that could stand alongside the industrial activity of the middle classes.

The army of knights gradually disappeared, in part because the introduction of gunpowder displaced it, but also because the resistance of the towns and the Swiss had shown that a large and skillful force of foot soldiers could defeat it. The increasing unity of the state also came into play; princes, rather than rely on feudal service, preferred to pay mercenaries, which made their armies more numerous and more dependent on them. From now on the noble lost the status conferred by personal service that he had claimed at the start of the state's development. Of course he continued to display a great affinity for the profession of arms; he became a condottiere; he became an officer commanding other mercenaries. But all this could not fully make up the loss of his earlier role, in part because these occupations also attracted many commoners, in part, and this was the main thing, because war became less frequent—or more precisely because war, which had earlier been broken up into a thousand small skirmishes, was now fused into a few great acts of violence, which were fought with much larger armies but were also separated by much longer periods of peace.

How could the noble's service as an officer in a standing army bolster his pride in his estate now that he could no longer defend the state in the moment of danger without the help of the middle class, at the same time that long periods of peacetime service continually undermined the mercenary's importance and reputation? In peacetime an officer's post was considered a half-sinecure, and even in war it was still a form of privilege to serve as an officer rather than as a common soldier. It is easy to see that the noble's preferential identification with the profession of arms would no longer be considered an honorable *corporate duty*, but rather a corporate prerogative, and that in any case it could not be considered truly equivalent to other forms of productive personal activity in which the noble did not participate.

The noble also sought such activity in the civil administration, which expanded and developed along with the centralized state; but this too was seen not as a sacrifice but as a privilege.

Basically it was very natural that, in the transition from feudalism to absolute monarchy, the noble took the best positions in the army and civil administration for himself. He had in fact been lord and master, and that could not wear off so quickly that, under new conditions, he would not still have been the natural authority and intermediary between the prince and his subjects, nor that the peasant soldiers who were his subjects would not have followed him as an officer in the field. This state of affairs was certainly *natural*, otherwise it could not have lasted for several centuries. But this was only a transitional period, and it was inevitable that things that seemed entirely natural at the beginning no longer seemed so at the end. Thus the noble lost the personal calling that distinguished his estate and likewise the respect that followed from the fine, honorable obligation to defend the country. What he received in return was considered by others to be usurpation and privilege at their expense.

The second great liability of the noble, which made the tension between him and the other estates that much greater, is the large part he played in the scandalous conduct of state administration and the ignoble profits he sought to derive from it.

We need only consider the host of sinecures and court offices that were the order of the day in France before the Revolution, and the unbelievable income that derived from them; that these offices were bestowed as pure patronage, generally not on individuals but on families, often in perpetuity on the children as well; and that one person often held many such posts, which merely allowed a noble house to survive in its old, opulent style long after its original capital had dwindled away. The gift of these offices clearly bore the traces of old feudal practice. Since there was no more land with which great men could be rewarded, it became a matter of offices, pensions, revenues. That this was an abuse in the eyes of reason was as plain as day; but an abuse that springs from commonly accepted ideas is also strongly supported by them, and it is no surprise that the princes and the nobility did not immediately wish to follow the philosophers in this matter. It did not seem at all unreasonable to them that the state should exist for their sake, and not they for it.

Thus the totally changed condition of the nobility—the unhealthy place it was given in the new framework of the state on the one hand and the cultural advance of the bourgeoisie on the other—created such tension that a resolution in one form or another became necessary, either gradually through voluntary changes or suddenly by force.

This tension we consider to be the most significant cause of the French Revolution.

The other is the abuse of administrative power.

In the Middle Ages the power of the princes, whether great or small, was extremely limited. With the advance of culture, national wealth and working capital increased, and so did the power of the princes. Money can be thought of as acting like oil, which reduces natural friction and permits all forces to operate with much greater independence and flexibility. It was money that made it possible for the supreme authority in the state to pull together the forces it needed to strengthen itself, like the core of a crystallizing mass.

As money gradually spread and established itself throughout society, providing the princes with the means to purchase personal services and to obtain them where they were cheapest, many sources of friction fell away. A mass of inertia that otherwise opposed the power of the state no longer needed to be overcome. Now the first great step toward sovereignty was taken. It consisted in this: that the princes acted alone, even if they might not yet decide alone. The estates had lost their function, but not yet their rights. Instead of the service they had contributed in the past, they now contributed money. With the instruments the princes acquired in this way they proceeded to subjugate the estates even further, and limit their rights, which was all the more easily done because the old feudal constitution contained little that was orderly, firm, and serviceable, so that in the chaos of existing relationships there was always a faction within the estates that proved more inclined to extend the power of the prince than to obstruct it.

Thus supreme power in the state progressed toward absolute monarchy as we knew it in the eighteenth century. With the simplification of the state's constitution, however, came an increasingly complex state administration. In fact, it grew in step with the culture of the nation, and it was no wonder that the princes were not immediately equal to these conditions and only gradually learned effective administrative principles through their own difficulties and mistakes. In this matter, too, the princes could not yield to purely philosophical considerations. They had deprived the estates of their share of sovereignty or were in the process of doing so, and they could accomplish this only by taking most of the rewards at their disposal and bestowing them on those who were prepared to serve them. The theoretical rights and claims of the lower classes, which gradually emerged from the mists, could not yet weigh as heavily with the princes as the claims of the nobility and the towns, which wanted to be compensated with favors and privileges for what they had been forced to give up. Thus the administrative excesses, confusion, and extravagance of governments in the sixteenth, seventeenth, and early eighteenth centuries developed in a seemingly natural way. The errors, weaknesses, enthusiasms, and vices of individual princes also came into play and set the crown of corruption on the whole enterprise in the eyes of the philosophers.

These philosophers were neither accustomed nor inclined to view social conditions as a product of historical forces; they proceeded from the abstract concept of a social contract and therefore found only unspeakable injustice and corruption everywhere. Thus they inflamed people's passions, and [the resulting] political fanaticism had the same effect as the religious fanaticism of an earlier age: it became the fermenting agent that would bring the whole mass to a boil.

In our opinion, then, the French Revolution came about for two main reasons. The first is the strained relationship between the classes, the great favoritism shown the nobility, the great dependence, and, it must be said, in part the great oppression of the peasants. The second is the disorganized, biased, and wasteful administration.

Not a few scholars will shrug their shoulders at this glance at history and come forward with a hundred objections. How many might not be cited from Möser alone![4] Yet it is the author's opinion that an individual must form his own ideas about such things; thus he does not mean to impose his views on his reader like a doctrine. Rather, he has stated his own way of thinking in order to stimulate reflection on the part of others, some of whom may well find they agree with him.

We have deemed this commonsense review of the history of our social conditions necessary so that we can see clearly in what political conditions we really find ourselves.

When the enormous majority challenged the minority in France, the nobility had to give way. It was no longer strong enough to resist this force. The Old Regime collapsed—and collapsed forever, because once an organic whole has been broken it may be glued together again, but its original unity can never be restored. The masses, furthermore, broke the scepter that had ruled them so despotically, and set up a mixed government. This shattering of all social relationships, which were already under great strain, was much easier than the creation of a new regime, and it could be foreseen that after a violent upheaval there would be much groping around and that some decades would be needed to explore new ideas before a new form of government could put down firm roots.

[4] An allusion to Justus Möser's last essays in the *Berliner Monatsschrift* (1794), in which he portrays the Revolution as an artificial disruption of the natural flow of history and of the organic society of the Old Regime.

The philosophers wanted to base everything on the rights of man. They saw these as a force opposed to the absolute monarch and as setting necessary limits on his power. In this regard, however, the Revolution actually demanded only an end to outrageous administrative abuses and a guarantee that they would not recur.

Once the colossal breach occurred in France, it was inevitable that the rest of Europe would be affected by it.

In Germany conditions had been somewhat different than in France. The history of the German lands and their estates is the same. But the higher nobles had raised themselves to the level of territorial lords, and so entered another class; they were neither objects of jealousy nor agents of abuses. The structure of the German empire was extremely weak, and had changed little since the Middle Ages. The small states that existed within it did not possess true sovereignty and still had to acknowledge a lord higher than themselves. On the whole, administrative abuses could not become as serious in the small lands. If there was an occasional spendthrift among the German princes, surrounded by court favorites and mistresses, he was nevertheless an exception and hardly mattered alongside the injustice, two or three times as great, that resulted from mere ignorance or lack of supervision on the part of the princes. In general, however, most German states were administered very prudently and paternalistically in comparison to what one saw elsewhere.

This was particularly true of Prussia. Among all her Hohenzollern rulers, there had been only two spendthrifts, Frederick I and Frederick William II. All the rest were not only good stewards, but in many cases the most financially adept rulers of their time.

Although the principles of state finance were less advanced in Austria than in Prussia, the line of economically capable rulers there is even longer. It is a striking fact that, since the founding of that monarchy by Frederick III, not a single profligate prince has ascended the throne.

All these conditions meant that, although Germany's international position had declined and decayed and her cultural development had been forcibly retarded by the many wars fought on her territory, the sense of internal well-being was nevertheless greater there than in France, Spain, and many other lands. The tension in the inner life of the state was therefore less pronounced, and the impulse to revolution basically did not exist.

Nevertheless, the French example inspired people in Germany. Even the most peaceful men, who were otherwise scarcely able to rise above received opinion, felt that by and by relations among the estates ought to be adjusted, that the peasantry deserved more property, and commerce more freedom. Of course these changes could occur without revolution, but the desire for them meant that people approved *this goal* of the French Revolution even if they rejected its means.

It was different with the scholars and philosophers.

The scholars, who in Germany worry themselves over a few Greek and Latin authors, their heads full of antique freedom and classical constitutions they do not understand, and which have not existed for two or three thousand years; the philosophers, who settle everything according to universal concepts, whose minds are too distinguished to bother about local conditions and historical experience—these people were strongly taken with the philosophy and politics of Paris, and the majority threw themselves into the maelstrom of revolutionary ideas in a wholly different way than the average citizen.

To them the French Revolution seemed to offer a political paradise, a golden age, and it was therefore taken for granted that this new dawn would not be confined to a single country but must extend to all civilized nations; that lawyers, doctors, and professors should govern according to philosophical ideas and academic principles. And for the names and forms of ancient times to be reborn—that was more than their minds could bear. A spirit of restless engagement, secret hopes and desires, began to stir in them and sought to influence the other classes, among whom, if only one inflammable point could be found, the fire would blaze forth.

It was unfortunate that the French Revolution coincided with two German regimes that, each in its own way, tended to increase sympathy for it. The first is that of the emperor Joseph II. Without question this virtuous prince, who was devoted to the welfare of his people, lacked practical judgment and a firm, sure hand in the application of his liberal ideas. He had to abandon many of them because he had not implemented them in the right way. To this was added his early death, with the result that his reign awakened more hopes and desires than it satisfied and set minds to thinking along lines that closely resembled those of the French revolutionaries.

The second government is that of Frederick William II in Prussia. His wastefulness, his mistresses, his immoral officials, his absurd visions, his religious edicts were all things that recalled the worst epochs of other lands, cost the government the respect of the people, and made the benefits of revolution more understandable to many.

Without this unfortunate coincidence the French Revolution, despite the scholars and philosophers, would have had far less impact in Germany than it did.

As it was, its impact on public sentiments was essentially that of an external influence rather than an inner inspiration, and as grave as matters appeared—when the inhabitants of Mainz betrayed their city and established a Jacobin Club of German intellectuals, or when the Order of Illuminati spread throughout the south—the complete domestic peace that prevailed in Germany during the revolutionary wars is ample proof that attitudes here were far from those in France.

347

If the majority of Germany's intellectuals shared the views of those in France, their power nevertheless was not great, since the Parisian intellectuals had not made the Revolution alone.

The turn the French Revolution took toward the most extreme democracy, the cruelty that filled the years 1792–94, naturally tended to reduce sympathy for it in Germany. When more moderate principles, a more peaceful attitude, and a more reasonable constitution emerged during the years 1795–99, this sympathy revived to some extent, but now the public's attention was diverted by the French campaign of conquest, by fear of war, invasion, contributions, quartering of troops, expropriation, etc. Thus the danger posed by the electrified atmosphere of the Revolution always passed quickly in Germany, if it ever actually existed. The consulate, the empire, and the first strides toward universal monarchy finally brought an end to the tension that had developed in the 1790s, and now there were at most a few friends of the Legion of Honor who still concerned themselves with French institutions. At this point there could no longer be any question of upheaval or revolution, since there was a man in France who had learned very well how to keep his foot on the neck of Mother Revolution herself. French intellectuals were now on their guard lest they appear to display republican tendencies, and the whole arsenal of philosophical arguments was shut down.

Germany's intellectuals, for whom this turn of events was something of a slap in the face, gradually changed their tune as well and either fell silent or joined the voices of the new generation, which had eyes for nothing except the external threat to Germany's independence.

Since this danger was truly present to a high degree, and since the mass of people, insofar as they reflected on such matters, could not delude themselves about it, a great and natural national feeling was now forged out of the need to see France defeated and Germany independent once more. At bottom, this feeling was common to the whole German people, and if there were two political points of view, one of which favored resistance to France while the other considered resistance futile, the latter was based on nothing except despondency and fear of immediate hardships and had no effect on the general desire for security and independence. Those few clever types who believed *France's ascendancy* and domination could actually lead to a better social organization for Germany were an inconsequential minority.

The shocking blows suffered by Austria, the collapse of Prussia, the events in Spain, and the advance to Moscow were the stages by which feelings of French invincibility and our own helplessness increased; but at the same time, so did hatred of France. When French power, now severely overextended, finally broke during the retreat from Moscow, excitement was in the air everywhere, and the nation had but one purpose, one idea: victory over the French and the restoration of the old borders. This wish was completely fulfilled. The struggle lasted until 1815, but ended with France confined to her old borders, Germany reestablished in hers, and the tyrant firmly chained to his island prison.

It was at this point that the so-called agitation of the German people began, whose origin and nature we will now consider.

The strain created by the French Revolution was past. The wish to be free of the French yoke was satisfied, thus true peace and order, necessary for the nation's recovery after its long exertion, should have been restored, and so it undoubtedly was and still is as far as the mass of people are concerned.

It was not merely that the French Revolution had lost its hold on German opinion of its own account, but rather that the great changes in social conditions that preceded Germany's liberation had resolved a mass of incongruities and gently guided the nation in the same direction in which the Revolution was supposed to have led.

Consider the changes that occurred in Prussia and the south German states after 1805. The way was opened for the great majority of the people, the peasantry, to own land; the noble was deprived of his exemption from taxes and personal service; monopolies and guild restrictions were abolished; the middle class was given access to all offices in the state; taxes paid in kind, which had been carried on the shoulders of particular groups, were lifted, and the burden was divided among the population as a whole. All these had been objectives of the French Revolution; all were now achieved in Germany without violence.

The second main cause of the French Revolution, terrible administrative abuses, did not exist in any German state. Prudent princes were on every throne. Nowhere was the wealth of the people drained off into dubious channels.

But in recent years, when agitated feelings could find expression in ambition and action, a part of educated society had set itself two new goals: one was the unity of the German people; the other, constitutions.

A glance at Germany's history and circumstances shows that it is totally laughable to think that Germany could suddenly achieve true unity in 1815. Nevertheless, it is easy to see how this idea and desire could arise among Germany's youth at a time when they were fighting for Germany against France; but this idea should obviously have remained confined to these academic and nonacademic youths, or rather they should have given it up when they reached maturity. This did not happen. The idea of establishing a German empire that would improve on the Holy Roman Empire of old captivated the academic community. The Vienna Congress, which created not a German empire but only a German Federation, was denounced; a longing for national unity arose everywhere; the people's efforts in the war with

France were extolled; the conduct of their princes in the crisis was condemned; and so, compounded of truth and falsehood, reasonable ideas and absurd ones, some to the point, others pointless, a fermentation began that would have to find release somehow.

Germany can reach political unity in *one* way only—through the sword, when one state subdues all the others. The time has not arrived for such subjugation, and if it should ever come it is impossible to predict at present which of the German states will become master of the rest.

But Germany's free-thinking youth thought least of all of this sort of transformation. They had another illusion in mind from the start, from which they soon moved on to others that were even more illusory.

The first illusion was that the German princes would give up their sovereignty in favor of an Areopagus or, as some wished, a German emperor; but the princes were supposed to concede even more to this new sovereign than the old imperial constitution had required. These princes, however, were still relishing their recent advance to true sovereignty, and it was hardly to be expected that they would take two steps backward to satisfy Germany's youth. Their desire was thus truly childish, and the dismay with which they greeted the concessions made to Germany's princes by the great powers during the war and the Vienna Congress deserves no better name. Once these people saw that their initial hopes had been completely illusory, the secret aspirations at the bottom of their hearts grew even bolder. They imagined it might be possible for a powerful national movement one day to make Germany into a free and united republic. Liberal constitutions in the individual states and a close-knit union of students throughout Germany seemed to offer a way forward toward this still rather foggy and ambiguous goal.

Among German youth it was mainly their participation in the Wars of Liberation that awakened their sense of power; among their teachers it was the idea that the doors Bonaparte had closed were now open to them again. In their opinion the German people had helped themselves far more than they had been helped by their princes. In Spain the people had clearly stood entirely alone, and a radically liberal constitution had been the result. A movement back in that direction had also been necessary in France, and who knew how many others might follow. Thus they concluded that freedom had not yet lost the game with servitude, and that the moment might still be approaching when learning would triumph over money and status, when the spiritual world would rule the material. But that could occur most readily if Germany were to become a great republic, that is, if there were no more princes taking up the places rightfully due the royalty of intellect. It was in line with these broad visions and obscure longings that they tried, as far as they could and were permitted, to educate the young.

Our young people thus became more and more agitated and increasingly drawn toward the formation of a national union, while occasionally seeking to influence others through their writings, speeches, and deeds.

Aside from this first goal, born of misguided enthusiasm, there was another closer at hand: the promotion of constitutions in the individual German states. In part they saw these as a way to begin creating a free and united Germany; in part they considered constitutions the most immediate and pressing need of the day.

The wish to limit pure or, if one likes, absolute monarchy through participation of the estates is an idea that is particularly natural when great abuses, incompetence, and partiality bring about the desire to restore order and justice through an increase in the political dialogue.

Although the German governments cannot be accused of major abuses, nevertheless at a time that demanded so much effort on the part of the subject it was natural to wish that a number of responsible men of different classes assist the government, prevent error and injustice, and give everyone a greater sense of security.

But improvement of the administration was not the main reason why men were so eager for a constitution. In their opinion, the main fault of which the German governments stood accused was their weak and shameful foreign policy. Without their slipshod, shortsighted policies, which operated only from one day to the next, French domination of Europe would have been completely impossible. In Spain the people had freed themselves from the bondage their unworthy princes had imposed upon them, and England, the only free state in Europe, had also been the only one that always conducted itself honorably. Even the monstrous politics of ancient Rome were brought into it; but while the reproach was certainly well founded, it is still doubtful that the proposed remedy would have been effective.

The role played by a state toward other powers is only *indirectly* and by no means *significantly* linked to its constitution; and although one might believe that a certain steadiness, consequentiality, and security in foreign policy should naturally result from a constitution, history—unless we are very much mistaken—does not bear this out.

The English played their international role most effectively under Elizabeth and Cromwell, when they enjoyed the least internal freedom; the Swiss, on the other hand, have long since accepted their political insignificance; the Dutch lost their independence earlier than their neighbors; the Americans have not always shown themselves worthy of the great continent they represent; and there is nothing whatever to say about a free state like Poland.

The deliberations of a parliament can reinforce a government's policy, but they can also cripple it, and the one is as likely as the other. The geographic position of the state makes a great difference. If geography guarantees a state a certain independence, as in the case of England, America, and Holland, its domestic politics and international conduct take on a different character. If, however, it is surrounded on all sides by dangers, like the German states, and if, like them, it is also of small or moderate size, it can survive the dangers it faces only by means of secrecy, resolution, and diplomatic dexterity, and these are not the natural attributes of parliamentary bodies.

We are well aware that deliberative assemblies play no direct part in the foreign policy of their governments. This does not happen even in England. But their *indirect* influence over policy will nevertheless stamp it with something of the assembly's character.

If any institution can contribute to the wisdom, firmness, and consistency of a state's foreign policy, it is in our opinion a ministry and state council.

If there is no state council nor even a unified ministry, but only individual ministers, as in Prussia before 1806, if the royal cabinet settles everything,[5] then the personality of the prince must be decisive. But if a council of experienced men and a unified ministry exist, they constitute a body that never dies or undergoes any drastic change, so certain principles can be established and preserved through it. Because such a body exists under the authority of the prince, it can never be an obstacle to his power and independence, and it will only do good, strengthening the weak ruler and opening the eyes of the shortsighted.

If the state council is not too small, a basic standard for membership in it and the ministry will emerge, and these will certainly become the mainstay of the executive, stronger and more independent than one might at first suppose, and one that will also contribute to domestic administration.

This was not the view of those who wanted to use the weakness of Germany's princes to prove the need to have a national assembly at their side. They did not focus on the heart of the matter, but on the surface. They were concerned not with the real actions and policies of governments, but with the fine speeches of parliaments.

But there were naturally hundreds of other reasons for these people to desire a constitution, apart from improving administration and foreign policy. A constitution calls innumerable petty interests into play in public life, and that in itself was a great impetus. The great interests of the state become the basis for a kind of currency that circulates through certain parts of society and vitalizes its political commerce. If we look closely at the history of the French Revolution under the National Assembly, we get an idea of the *reality* of this effect. All the hustle and bustle, energy and friction, fear and hope, anxiety and joy, the solidarity of friends and the persecution of enemies, the enthusiasm, the domination of others, and finally the deft use of force by one side or the other—all this makes for a rich, vital political life, reminiscent of the

[5] See "Observations on Prussia," note 1, above.

352

public squares of Athens and the Forum of ancient Rome. The quiet business of private existence seems like stagnation in comparison to this sort of public life, and in this sense it is in constant opposition to the rottenness and torpor of the times.

Of course a mere constitution, a pair of chambers that busy themselves advising the government, were not sufficient to create this ideal public life. Its proponents therefore tried from the start to turn the idea of a constitution in the direction of more democratic, provocative forms of popular representation. The existence of two chambers was a particular horror to them, its aristocratic aspect a reactionary evil.

We have often heard calm, reasonable men speak most unreasonably about the value of such a turbulent public life, in which everyone is constantly thinking about what the state did yesterday, is doing today, will do tomorrow, to the point where the citizen can scarcely close his eyes at night in peace.

As if an individual could only share in the life of the state by taking the business of government directly to heart; as if this feverish desire to manage everything were not in fact a kind of sickness; as if, even when such active participation is guaranteed, it did not finally come down to a few restless souls in the capital and the commercial centers, with the mass of people remaining spectators in the streets. But the masses will also be aroused, of course, and their passions will swing back and forth; yet this back and forth is precisely the problem.

If the subject is to be linked properly with the state, he must understand its main interests. These must be great and permanent, and the citizen's support of this permanent direction must constitute his participation. The government must be so organized that it deserves his confidence. This confidence need not be blind or absolute. He can evaluate the government's actions, and his heart can give them greater or lesser approval. In this judgment and greater or lesser approval on the part of the subject, the government can recognize the stars that guide it and enable it to travel more easily and quickly.

This sort of public life accords with the orderly pursuit of one's private affairs, which must surely occupy the greater if not the noblest part of the citizen's energies. In this regard, too, the citizen is a part of the state. The honesty, diligence, orderliness, energy, and effort with which he goes about his own affairs all contribute significantly to it.

We therefore believe the goal of our political institutions must be: competence and uprightness in private life, and a warm sympathy for the country's great interests. It is not our intention to show what institutions lead to these goals; rather, we will simply say that this absurd unrest, this disorderly, one-sided concern with politics, by which the keenest minds are kept running around in circles, is a true abnormality, based on the example of small, highly unstable republics. But as we have said, there were eminently reasonable men who could imagine no other relationship between the citizen and state, because they had allowed themselves to be persuaded that things have to be this way and failed to achieve a clear understanding on their own. They were preoccupied by the contrasting example of the Prussian state before 1806, whose faculties had become numb, like those of an old man who has suffered a stroke.

If there were reasonable, well-meaning, honest men who felt this way, the number who desired such conditions out of ambition, vanity, and self-interest was even greater, and so the longing of young people for an era of rejuvenation found ample guidance and encouragement among their elders. It was precisely in these youth that older men placed their trust. From them a race would be born that would bring about a rebirth of public life through its profound sense of freedom, its zeal and energy, and so supplant the old order and build up the new one with ease.

Whatever extravagant ideas may have shot up here and there among our youth, whatever forms these may have taken, however many individual associations may have existed, none of them are worth pursuing even if that were truly possible. That such tendencies existed is proven by many writings and deeds and by the results of the official investigations these inspired. Those who still deny the evidence, who explain it away as a figment of the imagination, are not being honest or have allowed themselves to be duped by the dishonest.

Two sensational events above all caused an uproar in Germany and Europe: the Wartburg Festival in 1817, and Kotzebue's murder in 1819. Both expressed the same feeling—passionate hatred of those who think differently: the *Evil-Minded*, as Cromwell's Puritans called them, the *Philistines* today. In the present case the violence and lust for power came a little too soon. The Puritans and Jacobins did not reveal their plans openly at the start, but only gradually, after they had the sword in their hands; German youth, however, did not fully understand these matters and immediately let the cat out of the bag.

Now the governments grew hostile toward them, and inquisitorial investigations were begun that stumbled on a broad web of fraternities and secret societies.

The south German governments hurried to get on with their constitutional work, but they had no intention of moving as quickly or in the direction the students wanted. In Württemberg the constitutional movement seemed completely shattered. Hesse, Hanover, and the other northern states seemed not yet to have given the matter any thought. All eyes therefore turned to Prussia. When there were still no signs of movement in 1815 and 1816 a sense of astonishment began to grow; it was clear that the king was unwilling and

Prince Hardenberg reluctant to fulfill the [king's] promise [of a constitution, given in 1813]. This was entirely natural in both cases, but our students and their leaders in the academic community nevertheless found it outrageous and saw it as a betrayal of the people, to whom they expressed their feelings without reserve. Thus the number of those dissatisfied with Prussia grew in Germany and in Prussia. Particularly in Prussia the secret societies, vaguely dedicated to the improvement of political conditions, grew stronger. The *size* of the state, the *liberality* of its administration, its openness to outsiders, the presence of many scholars and philosophers—these made Prussia the chief playground for political agitation in Germany.

Let us inquire, then: apart from these remote, illusory ideas about German unity and a German republic, what was there about the German states themselves that was so damnable or burdensome as to inspire these reformers and drive them together? Was there a single German state at the time that was marked by administrative abuse? Had any injustice occurred that cried out to heaven for redress? Do the princes revel in luxury, do their hunting parties trample their subjects' fields? Do they go to war out of pride or ambition? Are art and scholarship retarded and left to starve everywhere? Are the people anywhere being tyrannized, guillotined, gunned down, shot, banished, or imprisoned? No, by all accounts, in newspapers and learned journals alike. It is extraordinarily difficult to say what exactly is supposed to be so hateful about the present regime, what exactly is the cause of this fury.

Tendencies, Principles, Ideas, Objectives, Desires, Rights, Duties, Despotism, Repression—the essence of the whole business turns on these disembodied abstractions. Two other concepts, widely misused in practice, are also involved—the *Age* and the *People*—which form the core around which the others accumulate like interlocking crystals, so that a pretentious gobbledygook of accusations gets concocted which is no less nonsensical for all its fancy signs and symbols.

Anyone who wants to become familiar with these ideas in their most representative form must read a book that was banned when it first appeared, *Germany and the Revolution* by [Joseph] Görres, a brilliant man, but consumed by a passionate democratic lust for power.

The book is supposed to be a major indictment of the German governments; but it constantly floats along among general pronouncements, images, allegories and illusions, fabrications and mere rhetoric. Only two issues are clearly identified: the first is the failure of Germany to unite in a new empire; the second, standing armies. Neither gives any particular indication of the author's sound common sense.

This Görres would be well suited to play a role in a revolution. He would be a Vergniaud or a Danton, driving men to extremes with a stentorian voice and volcanic eloquence until he himself is finally carried away by the flood and hurled into the abyss. He is fierce, passionate, cutting, domineering, bold, and resolute, and withall energetic.

Born in Coblenz, he was in his youth a passionate admirer of the French Revolution, and much of his writing from that period is worthy of the most scurrilous sans-culotte. In 1797 he went to Paris to promote the creation of a Cisrhénan Republic with the aid of General Hoche, who had won the Rhinelanders' special affection.[6] But Hoche died suddenly, and Görres returned to his constituents in Coblenz, because—as he told the author himself—he saw that the members of the Directory were already wearing silk stockings again and that nothing could be accomplished with such people.

During Bonaparte's reign Görres kept quite still, like all the others who later became so noisy. Once the power of France was broken, however, he came out enthusiastically for the German cause in his *Merkur*.[7]

But of course, as later became clear, the German cause was to him something other than the mere fame of German arms and the independence of the country. He already had an image of Germany's regeneration in mind, and when this did not occur as he imagined he began to turn into such a wrathful prophet that the Prussian government, which had previously flattered him with pensions and kind words, finally gave him up and expelled him from its territory.

From his writings it is hard to know for sure what Görres really wants. Despite all the philosophy, history, and science that dominate his works, there is still a lack of clear common sense and straight, simple truth. He habitually adopts such an elevated standpoint that he gets carried away by generalities and touches on concrete cases only, as it were, with his toes and fingertips. Heaven knows whether we Germans will ever be cured of this unfortunate longing for the realm of abstractions, whether we will ever learn from the French to think clearly and distinctly about political and social questions; but the present moment is not encouraging, and thanks to the vogue of natural philosophy we are now stuck in this vice more deeply than ever.[8]

What possible good can it do in the real world to spin an idea out into a fine thread that only a tenth part of your readers can even see and follow with

---

[6] Louis-Lazare Hoche, commander in chief of the Army of the Moselle, was famous for the thoroughness with which he despoiled the Rhineland.

[7] Görres's *Rheinischer Merkur* was the most important newspaper inspired by the Wars of Liberation. It was initially supported by the Prussian government but was suppressed in 1816 after its promotion of German unity became an embarrassment.

[8] *Naturphilosophie*, a strain of post-Kantian idealism associated above all with Friedrich Schelling, who asserted the absolute identity of reason and nature; and in somewhat different form with Hegel, who sought to explain the natural world and the sociopolitical order in terms of the self-realization of Absolute Spirit. Objective phenomena were understood as imperfect expressions of abstract forces, which represented a higher, more complete reality.

their own eyes, and of which the rest of society will remain eternally ignorant; [and then] to hang from this thread, which cannot even bear its own weight, generalities no more substantial than soap bubbles, on which the multicolored lights of rhetorical eloquence are then allowed to play?

In all practical matters it is essential to stay close to concrete facts, in order to be comprehensible to ourselves and others, and not merely comprehensible, but convincing; and convincing not merely because of our conclusions, but because of the nature of things, because of our point of view. Evil that really exists should be called by its real name; the most direct remedy should be sought, and once found, identified.

Most of the errors and inadequacies of government in our time stem not from the ill will of the rulers, but from the natural difficulty of existing conditions; to criticize such failures would thus inspire a just and natural defense. But our academics do precisely the opposite, and so does this Görres. They remain at the level of general accusations, which would evaporate at once if only they were *named*; but rather than do so they make up for the feebleness of their generalities by the energy of their insults and curses, which is no different from the basest rabble-rousing, however elevated the words and concepts may be.

It remains uncertain whether Görres might not in fact have a better idea of what he wants than he finds it prudent to reveal, since he is not entirely incapable of cunning, and his early career as well as his whole demeanor suggest that only a rigidly democratic form of government and society can be to his taste. Of course he takes great care not to associate himself completely with the levelers of our time; now and then he takes the side of the nobility, the clergy, feudalism, or Catholicism, against their opposites. But he does it mainly by taking up one side in order to browbeat the other—he stands up for something when he can use it to oppose something else. He does the same thing with revolution. He calls out to one side: beware of revolution, it achieves nothing; and then he turns to the other and says: but things have gone so far that revolution is unavoidable. Finally he gives a general sketch of *his* constitution: there we find a king, a standing army, nobility and clergy; the democratic element, however, is not set alongside these, but rather inoculated against them, and his chamber of deputies is like a vat of seething chemicals.

In private life Görres is upright, honorable, and unselfish; his life has a simplicity bordering on sans-culottism. But these virtues count for little once a man enters the maelstrom of revolution. We have seen this among the French Girondins, even among the Jacobins. The majority were distinguished by talent and virtue in private life, and yet once the tide of revolution had burst forth they became in almost equal measure fools and villains. How

357

well Görres's sense of morality would hold up if it came into conflict with his political passion is evident in his judgment of Sand's deed.[9]

We have thought it useful to consider this man here because, more than any other, he has been the leader of the chorus, and the appearance of judiciousness that he affects should be taken simply as a sign that he stands much higher than the troops he leads.

Thus in 1818 we find Germany's academic youth excited and agitating for a *political rebirth*. They do not know themselves what this is or should mean; neither do the professors who gave them the idea—or one thinks it means one thing, another something else. Above all, it was to be demonstrated and established that the German governments (notwithstanding the poor quality of the others in Europe) are utterly rotten, collectively villainous (to focus on the princes personally would have been much too tasteless and would have collapsed at once), that they want only evil, to block progress, that they do not understand the times, do not love the people.

Furthermore, it is to be taken for granted that our times—the last years of the war, and particularly the deeds of Lützow's unruly volunteers[10] perhaps excepted—are a putrid morass, a slough of corruption; and further still, that Germany in the Middle Ages had been a magnificent entity, full of brilliance, glory, strength, and virtue. In short, the world must change again. Youth must be taught to grasp the idea of the state; a sturdy citizen of medieval Augsburg or Nuremberg is to be the ideal type. For the time being one can make a start with some nuances of dress, or hairstyle, of demeanor, and of speech. Germany must regain her unity, if not with an emperor, then as a republic. In order to bring about this rebirth, youth everywhere must unite in associations great and small, for which the fraternities and regional clubs at the universities will provide the vehicles. This affiliation is to be a lifelong bond, so adults in their official posts and private occupations will follow the course to which they committed themselves in their youth. Since a new ring is added to the tree of the German nation with each three-year cycle of university study, the trunk will eventually be permeated by such men, and then the rest of the people, who fall into their hands in the primary and secondary schools, can easily be made to go along.

This is where things stood in 1818. At the Carlsbad Conference [the following year] these matters were given careful consideration by the German

[9] In a pamphlet entitled "Kotzebue and What Killed Him," printed a week or so after the assassination, Görres argued that Sand and his victim were instruments of larger forces—liberalism in the one case, despotism in the other—so that questions of individual moral responsibility had to take second place.

[10] One of several volunteer detachments created in 1813 as a way of attracting men of property and education into the *Landwehr*. Many student radicals of the postwar period had served in these units.

governments, and it was decided that this tendency should be curbed by every available means.

Let us now ask, what did Germany, and especially Prussia, have to fear from all this, and what did it have to do?

Germany and Prussia had no need to fear a major upheaval, which never results from minor causes, and the major causes, as we have said, had either never existed or had been drained off into channels that had been deliberately created for them. Specifically, an enormous amount had been done in Prussia under Prince Hardenberg's administration to correct the imbalance in the rights and duties of the different classes in society.

The main goal of this agitation, the political unification of Germany, was so illusory, indeed so childish, that no significant effect on the general population could possibly be feared.

To be sure, grounds for discontent were not lacking in Prussia, and more substantial ones than those that were agitating the students; but they were not at all concerned with these, or only slightly.

The first cause for discontent involved the nobility. Since 1807 they had lost a significant part of their property,[11] while the state's institutions had increasingly tended toward the equalization of rights and duties, for which the best methods were not always chosen. And so, when a democratizing point of view became more and more evident in the academic community, a seemingly natural reaction developed among the nobility, who sought, as always at such moments, not just to maintain present conditions, but to turn back the clock wherever possible. The many strains of the war years had severely damaged the landowner's position. His new relationship to the peasantry made the management of his estate much more costly, and he therefore felt himself in a terrible bind, from which discontent quite naturally arose. But that this discontent did not support the plans of the demagogues, but rather contradicted them, is clear.

The other cause for dissatisfaction was more general, affecting all those who owned property—namely, extremely high taxes.

The war years had resulted in a debt of two hundred million taler, which required annual interest payments of ten million taler; the state's income would thus have to be raised by as much as 20 percent. Prince Hardenberg, however, was not a good financial manager. He had markedly raised the pay of all officials without a qualm—one might well say irresponsibly—and instead of simplifying the administration he made it more complex and expensive. The military establishment also required some millions more, because

---

[11] Between 1807 and 1816 serfdom was (with some exceptions) abolished in Prussia, a step that those who opposed it saw as a violation of property rights. In the aftermath, landowners who lacked cash to pay free peasant laborers—as might be true, for instance, of small estates whose produce was consumed locally—sometimes lost their land as well.

a number of levies paid in kind were eliminated, and some small pay raises took place. Thus the state now took fifty million taler in taxes, where it once had taken only thirty-six million. Its population had grown by almost a million, to be sure, but its territory had shrunk considerably.

Thus an unaccustomed pressure was felt from this quarter too, which naturally led to complaints. But no reasonable man would consider looking for a remedy to this specific problem in the illusory schemes of the demagogues.

A third cause of discontent was the disruption of trade. Such things always accompany major territorial changes. A state's tariff system closes the border with its former province, and until new channels of trade open up this creates shortages, difficulties, and obstacles of every kind, and inspires great lamentation, since no group complains as easily and as much as merchants and manufacturers.

In Prussia this was particularly true in the Rhine provinces, which could no longer trade freely with France and the Netherlands, nor find any real substitute in the distant Prussian mother state. Far more substantial and troubling, however, was the simultaneous interruption of the Silesian linen trade, the cause of which has still not been fully understood. As a result Silesia lost trade worth ten million taler per year, and all its manufacturing districts fell into poverty and distress. It is evident that the plans of Germany's youth could not be of much help against this evil either; and while these problems were partly connected to the idea of free trade in Germany, this was nevertheless such a distant prospect, and offered so little immediate relief, that the existing pressure could hardly seek release in that way. Yet there is no denying that in the Rhineland commercial interests and political agitation could intersect from time to time, just as there is no denying that in that area those interests were highly significant to the population as a whole and were generally understood by them.

Let us consider, then, the grievances that were attributed to the Rhineland. The inhabitants of the area around Mainz, Coblenz, Trier, and Aachen (those from Cologne and the lower Rhine are of a different character) are, rather like the Belgians, lively and fickle. Vivacious by nature, energetic, intelligent, they gladly participate in public life, possess considerable imagination, and are rarely satisfied with things as they are. Yet the people generally, and particularly in the countryside, are quite friendly, while those in the towns are somewhat arrogant.

When the French Revolution broke out, they were for the most part subjects of ecclesiastical princes. They immediately pricked up their ears, and when the Revolution reached full flower, if one may use such an expression, and German arms no longer proved to be its equal, they gave themselves to it wholeheartedly. They were torn from Germany, the ecclesiastical princes disappeared from the scene, and most of the imperial nobility departed to receive compensation elsewhere. Now French revolutionary principles flowed over the Rhineland with all their disintegrative force and brought changes in the social fabric that were almost greater than those in France itself. Relatively speaking, the number of cloisters and ecclesiastical estates sold off was much greater; and there was the land of the departed nobility as well, which was all parceled out very quickly, so that a numerous, prosperous, free middle class soon sprang up. Thus the place was by no means ill-prepared to become a democratic republic, and it seemed that on the border of a great and powerful republic a small one might well live quite comfortably under its protection. That the Rhinelanders were Germans, that they still belonged to the German empire and ought to regard the French as natural enemies, *was a point of view that was not yet in vogue.*

More than anything, in fact, the Rhinelanders wanted the establishment of a Cisrhénan Republic, and a few of their ringleaders, including Görres, as we mentioned, wanted to take steps in that direction in Paris in 1797. Although this idea was less illusory than present-day notions of a German empire or a German republic, they still had to learn that in the real world things move as directed by dominant interests. The French Directory, which already possessed the Rhenish lands by conquest, was not going to give them up for a mere idea; in the Treaty of Lunéville the Rhineland was incorporated into the greater French empire.

Two discontented parties now naturally came into existence: one that favored the old princes, one that favored a republic. Their numbers grew the more France reverted toward absolute monarchy, and also because the French occupation, conscription, and tariffs were more oppressive here than elsewhere.

In any event, the Rhinelanders were not good Frenchmen by the time German arms returned to the Rhine. All at once it became the fashion to be enthusiastically German; no one thought clearly about the political arrangements this implied. In the meantime, the Middle Ages had become all the rage among the writers and they liked to dream about something resembling a German margraviate. This dream too did not come true; most of the Rhineland became Prussian, some Bavarian, Hessian, even Oldenburgian, Koburgian, and Homburgian, because the last three princes received small territories in the old Palatinate as compensation. People were upset about this fragmentation, although under the old empire the territory had been even more divided. The number of discontented grew larger still, thanks to a new party, namely the Bonapartists, who were fairly numerous among the former employees of the French administration.

Prussia thus found her Rhine provinces divided among clearly dissatisfied parties. This should not, however, be taken too seriously. All these factions had objections to becoming Prussian; each believed that the regime they cherished in their hearts would offer great advantages over that of Prussia, insofar as the latter was known, and it was not known here from its best side. Right from the start, however, there were no grounds for complaint, so the criticism of these factions was mere froth. The Prussian government arrived on the scene with the most respectful reassurances, showered the people with flattery, and went to work with a tact and delicacy bordering almost on fear. It guaranteed them their legal system, in which they put great store, and allowed four years to elapse before imposing new indirect taxes in place of the abrogated *droits réunis*, so that from 1814 to 1817 the Rhinelanders were notorious for paying not even two-thirds of the taxes they paid in the past, or would have had to pay now, measured by the standard of the other Prussian provinces. To this must be added the considerable income brought in by the construction of fortresses at Coblenz, Ehrenbreitstein, Cologne, and Jülich, and the substantial restitution that the Second Treaty of Paris forced France to make for the loans it owed to its former subjects, money that now flowed into the coffers of communities and individuals. All this meant that, during the first years of Prussian rule, the Rhinelanders felt uncommonly comfortable and prosperous.

Only one significant cause of discontent actually existed: the unreasonable, highly burdensome way Prussia managed the quartering of its troops. During the wars and between the campaigns of 1814 and 1815, this region had to feed and house numerous troops. It is a known fact how heavily this weighed on individuals. Immediately after the peace, we kept 30,000 men in the Rhine provinces and equally many with the army in France. For lack of barracks the first 30,000 stayed among the townspeople and peasantry, and since they were regarded almost as a peacetime garrison, most were housed close together in individual towns. The pay of a Prussian soldier is such that, in the absence of organized barracks, he can only starve unless he is fed by his landlord; the burden on the inhabitants was thus much greater than their subsidy. Under our new military organization, moreover, almost a third of the entire 60,000-man force was sent home every year, and another third arrived to replace them. There was thus a steady back and forth movement by very considerable bodies of troops on a few stage roads that ran mainly through very poor areas. The compensation the state provided for troops in transit came to 2 groschen per head, which may have been scarcely a third of the cash expense incurred by the landlord for each man, since when quarters had to be purchased they usually cost 1½ francs.

When General Boyen, who was minister of war, came to the Rhine provinces in 1817, the author, who as chief of staff [of the Rhine army] was closely concerned with these matters, proposed a major reform. He suggested that these arrangements might be the only real grounds for discontent among the Rhinelanders, and that they might be enough to make our army hated among them. General Boyen asked *how* reform could be accomplished; the author replied, "Through adequate cash compensation." "The state is not rich enough for that," was the answer. The *state*, that is to say, the funds the Ministry of War had at its disposal, for otherwise this would be nonsense. What is possible for the small strip of land on which the burden of quartering troops unfortunately fell must obviously be even more possible for the whole country, and when all shoulders bear the burden the weight is felt the least. The old provinces had achieved and suffered so much that if the Rhine provinces were now pressed especially hard there was no injustice in it; but the charge that was laid on them could still have been shared by everyone there. But of course a minister of war did not have the power to levy a tax over the whole region, and if he were to embark on a policy of providing full cash compensation he could never prevent it from being charged against his office, something of which all ministers have a horror. In short, things stayed as they were.

Another related circumstance had to do with the maintenance of troops.

In the years of peace [after 1795] each Prussian soldier was allowed 12 groschen per month for his quarters. These 12 groschen went to the landlord or were used to support the barracks and its facilities when troops were housed there. In addition, an officer received a monthly stipend for his quarters. Because this stipend was spent locally, in the town were the troops stayed, the state provided no subsidy for quartering officers, since they brought considerable sums into the community every year, which were deemed sufficient compensation. At that time, when the soldier received nothing to speak of from the citizen except shelter, a miserable bed, a place by the fire, and an obligatory ration of salt; when the officer received a very modest, fixed sum for quarters; and when the number of men to be quartered was relatively very small, this approach might work. This system was now introduced in a most unreasonable way in the Rhine provinces. Common soldiers were mostly housed and fed by the inhabitants, and since we have already described this burden, we will pass over it here. For officers, however, the direct requisition of quarters was now gradually replaced by cash payment. In 1810 a new regulation was enacted that determined an officer's right [to quarters of a particular quality] according to his rank. These standards were modest enough, indeed Spartan in character, but it was also stated that, if the regular allowance should prove insufficient to secure appropriate quarters, the officer would be entitled to obtain them by direct requisition. Since the allowance was notoriously inadequate for its purpose, the result was that communities were forced to pay contributions if they wanted to protect themselves from requisitioning. On the Rhine these contributions must have risen so high that they often amounted to three times the original allowance, so that for cities like Coblenz and Trier, which housed 6–8,000 men, the result was a very considerable expense that had somewhat the appearance of arbitrary oppression. These matters were closely connected to the overall policy on quartering troops and increased the general discontent with it.

On the other hand, another of our most important military institutions, universal service and the *Landwehr,* was not unappealing to the Rhinelanders. They had already gotten to know the former to some extent from the French under worse conditions, that is, when their conscripted youth were regularly dragged off to whatever theater of war was opening up. In part, they believed these institutions had a somewhat popular character, which appealed to their nature. These measures therefore found incomparably better acceptance in this region than in the old provinces.

The officials that the government sent to the Rhineland could not really win the full confidence of the inhabitants, who would have preferred to have only Rhinelanders in these posts, and also perhaps because they feared the traditional Prussian arrogance, which was not entirely lacking. Nevertheless, as far as the real and important qualities of the men went, the choices were made with great care, not at all as before in Warsaw, so accusations of the kind of which Görres too is guilty are truly slanderous. All the senior officials whom the author met on the Rhine up to 1818 were men of outstanding probity and unblemished reputations, and most were highly competent in precisely the same degree. The author also knows of no instance, during the four years he spent on the Rhine, in which a junior administrator proved notably incompetent.

Thus up to 1818 the Rhinelanders had so little reason to complain that they ought rather to have thanked the Prussian government for five years of the most accommodating and mild administration. In his many trips through the region the author also observed a general attitude of satisfaction and contentment among the people. Such dissatisfaction as existed in the province or appeared in the newspapers was mainly the carping of factions in the towns, former officials, academics and pseudo-academics, manufacturers, merchants, etc., who were motivated partly by their own interests, but primarily by sophistry and restless vanity.

Among these groups the excessive flattery, bordering on insincerity and obsequiousness, displayed by many officials for lack of tact, and out of weakness even by Prince Hardenberg, had adverse consequences: it made their spokesmen all the more brazen, it led even some old-Prussian officials into false ideas, and it made the masses, despite their contentment, into spectators at a little war involving the government, which they observed with some satisfaction. It showed that the government had no firm plan or definite course and deprived it to some extent of the respect it needed. Another, more important cause also contributed to this.

In 1816, as is well known, there was a massive crop failure throughout southern and western Germany, which led to a true famine in 1817, insofar as this is still possible at our present level of development. The Rhineland, which is heavily populated, was particularly hard hit. The government now showed itself entirely sympathetic and eager to help. The king established an emergency relief fund of two million taler, and in the spring of 1817 he sent [Finance] Minister Klewitz to the region to investigate firsthand the best use for this money. But the ministry in Berlin behaved so incredibly irresponsibly and inconsistently that not one of these good decisions was actually implemented, and the Rhinelanders had to manage their food shortage themselves. There is virtually no doubt that cargos of grain purchased in North Sea ports were sold off at higher prices to the government of Württemberg, among others, by agents in Holland. Neither Prince Hardenberg nor the Prussian Ministry of Trade, headed by Count Bülow, has as yet cleared up this matter, the first because of weakness and consideration for his nephew, Count Bülow himself out of a desire to conceal his mistakes, or whatever else.

The relief the Rhinelanders received was thus totally insignificant and because, unlike most neighboring states, local officials had ordered no ban on food exports—partly out of faith in the promised relief, partly out of respect for a theoretical principle [free trade]—the shortage was felt more keenly in Prussia's provinces than elsewhere.

The author, who traveled on horseback through the Eifel Mountains in the spring of 1817 and spent most nights in villages and small towns, often had a heart-rending view of this misery, since this area was among the poorest in the region. He saw wasted figures, scarcely human in appearance, creeping around the fields trying to glean some nourishment from unharvested, immature, and already half-rotten potatoes.

The experience convinced the author that the exceptional effort a government makes in such cases is not as disproportionate as it might seem at first glance, and that modest sums, if they are used effectively, can achieve a great deal, indeed everything, as far as relieving suffering goes in areas where it would lead to complete ruin. Specifically, a food shortage in a culture like ours is always felt in extreme form only by the *lowest* class, those with no property whatever, who live by a meager daily wage. All the rest help themselves one way or another. Thus it simply comes down to providing individual communities with enough assistance for them to supply bread to the poorest class at or below the usual price. To do this, purchases must be made far away, but ready cash will also be necessary, since relief can often be had more quickly and even more cheaply nearby. Provincial governments and other local authorities, above all the communal leaders, must have immediate power to control distribution and take other emergency measures; but the central government must also send a few capable men to the province as commissaries, with sufficient authority to give orders on the spot in order to reduce the ruinous time lost by paperwork, counteract fear, and prevent abuses.

Anyone who has looked such misery in the face will forever be filled with a sense of obligation, which the government, too, should possess and act on in such calamities. It is for that reason that the author has never been able to recall without bitterness and an outraged heart the lack of scruple that led the Prussian government to drop the matter.

After this digression, let us return once more to our theme.

If this great blunder by the Prussian government gave the Rhinelanders the idea that it might be weak or lacking in nerve and strength, its great eagerness and good intentions must still have convinced them of its good will; and since an evil is soon forgotten once it is overcome, however much one has suffered, the situation as a whole did not really damage the government in the eyes of the Rhinelanders.

Thus the reasons for discontent that existed in Prussia when political agitation was reaching its culminating point had no natural connection to that agitation, nor could those reasons give it any practical weight. And having already shown that the forces set in motion by the French Revolution could not be aroused in Germany and Prussia, we come to the question: What should the Prussian government have done about the unrest?

With respect to one particular group the drive for new conditions had a serious side, namely this: that if it ran its course undisturbed, the entire educational establishment would be contaminated; a distorted, unhealthy point of view would take hold of the rising generation and gain an enduring foothold among a significant part of the population, until it finally brought about conditions fatal to itself and so produced its own cure. In the process, as we have said, much time could pass, during which much foolishness could occur that would be detrimental, even dangerous, to the life of the state. If we consider that all officials and the majority of urban businessmen receive a formal education, and that for much of their lives the instruction they received in school has more influence than the instruction afforded by life itself and the free development of the intellect, it is clear that, especially in Prussia, where the number of students and public officials is so large, the corruption of education must affect and pervert a substantial part of the population. Even in the primary schools, a dumb ox of a schoolmaster with a few political slogans learned in the gymnasium or the seminary can twist people's minds; and even if this sort of thing will not strike deep roots, at least among the critical, reflective north Germans, it can still send momentary ripples through the masses, which in combination with other circumstances can lead to a crisis. We know from history that other nations have gone through such paroxysms.

Thus, to guard against these detrimental consequences of political unrest was necessarily a very serious, primary concern of the government. We will have more to say about this below.

Under present conditions, on the other hand, if the government obtained the necessary advice and thought the matter through clearly, all the factors mentioned so far should have given it a great sense of security. But of course the illegal, destructive ideas and plans of our young people and those who egged them on were so obvious that it was a perfectly shrewd and natural precaution to cut off this minor evil at the roots.

Early repression was one way to keep these ideas from harming the next generation. At present the evil was small and insignificant; if one let it alone it would grow. Although it could never lead to the goal these people set for themselves, it could nevertheless become damaging, and the more scope it acquired the more difficult it would be to defeat. Besides, it was contrary to the dignity of the government, and damaging to the public respect it required, for it to allow these views to flaunt themselves so openly. The government owed it to itself and to its effectiveness in the future to step in, and would have been held accountable by the people had it not done so.

That, to be sure, was not the judgment of the academics, who regarded this youthful striving merely as the expression of noble sentiments. Even if the ideas were essentially silly and wrong, they thought it beneficial for the common good that they were expressed, and they considered it truly obscurantist not to allow the young people to play with their ideas. Such nonsense seduced even the most reasonable and fair-minded individuals into wrong ideas and untimely anger against the government. Almost the only supporters of the government's measures were passionate reactionaries; those who on reasonable grounds recognized clearly not only the duties of government, but also how much a government can reasonably tolerate in such cases, were few indeed.

The matter came up for discussion among the governments at the Carlsbad Conference. Austria, which since Joseph's day would have gladly become the jailer of the human spirit and which in Prince Metternich now possessed a spokesman who, lacking great gifts, sought to overcome this problem merely by means of a dogmatically aristocratic stance, presented the issue as if all existing governments were already at risk and accused Prussia especially of being the very seat of revolutionary agitation, and in some of her recent reforms of actually being its shield.

The first part of this was not entirely unjust, since it is true that at that time the unrest had gone further here than elsewhere; the latter charge referred to our military institutions, which were too democratic for the Austrians. They believed a dangerous spirit of independence prevailed in our army, and that in time of revolution our *Landwehr* might prove exceptionally dangerous.

This view of our army's spirit was caused mainly by the opposition of old Blücher and his staff to the ruinous plans that prevailed at allied headquarters and among the diplomats in 1814. At that time Blücher had often spoken out strongly against the foolishness of a certain faction, which can fairly be called Austrian, since Prince Metternich was its leader and a half-dozen members of the Austrian General Staff served as its principal minions. It was the general policy of this party not to cease negotiating with Bonaparte until the last instant, to keep the army inactive, to take to their heels at the slightest provocation, and above all to exploit dissension in Austria's favor. When old Blücher scolded the Austrians about their military competence; when he and his army sought their own theater of operations, so as not to share in the inactivity and disgrace of the main army; when, on February 23, 1814, he insisted on marching for Paris on his own, at a time when Prince Schwarzenberg was being persuaded by Metternich to order a general retreat—in all this the Austrians believed they saw not just the old hussar, but the Prussian General Staff, which, having broken the habit of strict obedience, had adopted an independent attitude. This too was not entirely wrong, except that what was considered a tendency toward disobedience and dangerous independence was nothing more than a feeling for the nation's honor and welfare. Had the king of Prussia been with *his* army, the situation would have looked different. As it was it appeared that the king shared the Austrian view, which, however, was by no means the case, as soon became clear. On February 26 the king prevented the further retreat of the main army, and four weeks later he decided, along with the czar, that the army would march not toward Langres and the Rhine, but toward Paris, all of which was contrary to the ideas, viewpoint, and wishes of Prince Metternich. But of course the latter did not give up the idea that the Prussian army was a power in itself, a state within a state.

Another episode significantly strengthened this impression in Vienna.

During the congress, as conflict developed over whether Prussia should receive Saxony or not and as Prince Metternich was devising the petty policies that would give Austria the upper hand, he received a note one day from a Prussian general, who was indignant over this politicking and the obstacles being put in the way of Prussia's expansion. He complained bitterly to Metternich and warned him that the Prussian army would not just let the matter drop, should someone wish to deprive the state of its richly deserved reward.

SIXTEEN

"Europe since the Polish Partitions"
(1831)

Early in December 1830, Clausewitz was appointed chief of staff to an observation corps being assembled on Prussia's eastern frontier, an appointment arranged by Gneisenau, who had been recalled from retirement to command the new formation. The corps had been made necessary by the collapse of Russia's protectorate in Poland following a popular rebellion in Warsaw on November 29—one of many similar episodes inspired by the overthrow of Charles X in France four months earlier, but one that confronted Prussia with some especially disagreeable problems. On the whole, informed opinion in Berlin was wary of intervening in Poland. More vital interests were at stake in the west, notably in the question whether Belgium's independence from France would continue, and any diversion of resources from that theater was given grudgingly. Nevertheless, a wave of municipal riots and rural jacqueries had swept through Prussia's Rhine provinces early in the fall, and the prospect that the Warsaw rising would incite rebellion among Prussia's Polish-speaking inhabitants in the east could not be ignored. More remote, but also more disturbing, was the possibility that the Polish rebellion would succeed and present a resurgent France with a natural ally in eastern Europe.

By the end of 1830 these issues had come to dominate Prussian policy, and they also dominate the following essay, which Clausewitz wrote in Berlin early in 1831 while preparing to take up his new assignment. For years, Clausewitz had chafed at the complaisant view of international relations that had prevailed since the Congress of Vienna, where the realities of international power had been largely papered over by talk of monarchical legitimacy and solidarity. Even in 1819 he had been convinced that "sooner or later" Prussia "would really have to defend [its] skin."[1] With the reappearance of the tricolor on the spires of Notre Dame, there was every reason to believe the time had come, not because the revolution might take root in Germany—a possibility he never considers—but because it threatened to arouse once more the power of the French state.

As a contribution to the literature of counterrevolution, the present essay makes peculiar reading. Strictly speaking it does not matter to Clausewitz

---

[1] "Our Military Institutions," above.

who rules in France, or in Poland. His argument derives its weight from the historical persistence of the fundamental interests of both countries, despite intervening constitutional changes. Whatever their political complexion, they were bound to share a common desire to enrich themselves at the expense of the German states between them. Nor is Clausewitz proposing that Prussia launch its armies in a counterrevolutionary crusade—certainly not toward Paris, a step he judged both impolitic and militarily infeasible;[2] and, barring serious failure on the part of the Russians, not toward Warsaw, either. On the contrary, to have done so would have contradicted the spirit of the entire essay, which is above all an argument for a foreign policy based on concrete interests and an exact appreciation of power relationships.

As events progressed, Clausewitz would find no reason to quarrel with Prussia's benevolent neutrality toward the Russian police action in Poland. It is his impatience with public rather than official opinion that gives this essay its bite. In the 1790s German writers who favored the Revolution had often pointed to the partitions of Poland as exemplifying the cynicism of the Old Regime, in contrast to the contemporary flourishing of "Sister Republics" under French auspices. The Polish question flared up again at the Congress of Vienna, where the national aspirations of the Poles—like those of the Germans, this time—were once more sacrificed on the altar of the balance of power, a common fate that deepened the sympathy of German liberals for their eastern neighbors.

For Clausewitz, on the other hand, the balance of power was no vain superstition. It was, if not true religion, at least the bedrock on which the peace of Europe rested. That the Poles should have had to pay the forfeit was undoubtedly an accident of history. But so too was the inordinate attention their cause attracted in Germany. Pursued to its logical limits, the principle of national self-determination led to absurdity. That being so, sympathy for Poland could only be a fad, based on a selective reading of the past.

Clausewitz seems to have written this essay simply to clarify his thinking about the most pressing issue of the day. Although it may have circulated privately among his friends, it was first published in Schwartz's biography.[3] It may be compared, however, to a more limited defense of Prussian conduct that Clausewitz published as a letter to the Zeitung des Grossherzogtums Posen in July 1831. In it, as Peter Paret, who rediscovered the letter, has observed, Clausewitz applies his conception of the state as an amoral agent, whose

---

[2] Peter Paret (*Clausewitz and the State*, 396–405) has pointed out that the notion that Clausewitz favored preventive war following the July Revolution, first advanced by Heinrich von Treitschke (*Deutsche Geschichte im neunzehnten Jahrhundert* [Leipzig, 1879–94], 4: 45, 202), is not supported by his personal diary and correspondence, nor by his contemporary memoranda on military subjects, all of which portray Prussia's position in defensive terms.

[3] Schwartz, *Leben*, 2: 401–7; reprinted in *Politische Schriften und Briefe*, 222–29.

safety is of paramount concern, to a specific issue.[4] *Despite Prussia's official neutrality, Russian forces operating in Poland obtained significant support from Prussia, in the form of supplies purchased and stored in Prussian territory. These practices brought a public protest from the leader of the Polish forces, Jan Skrzynecki, and a sharp if somewhat disingenuous rebuttal from Clausewitz.*

Here is the letter, the last of Clausewitz's writings to appear while he was alive.

> *This letter [by Skryznecki] is apparently a device to renew certain ridiculous and wholly imaginary assertions, and serve them up to a credulous public. Nothing is true in these statements except that the Russians bought foodstuff and supplies for cash from private dealers in the Prussian provinces—mainly grain, hay, and straw—that they shipped their purchases on rented barges and wagons to the points where they needed them, that in addition they wanted to use the barges to transport troops across the Vistula, and now have in fact done so. Everything else is a deliberate lie. One must be very ignorant in the history of international law to find a breach of neutrality in such actions, if, indeed, it is possible to apply the concept of neutrality to an insurgent power that is not recognized by a single government in the world. When the French army crossed the Rhine during the Seven Years' War, it employed vessels of the neutral Dutch republic and subsisted on Dutch wheat. When, in turn, Duke Ferdinand of Brunswick crossed the Rhine in 1758, he did exactly the same. It is probably asking too much that a Warsaw journalist should be aware of such matters. But the Poles must know little of their own history, or be deeply ashamed of certain pages in it, if they can't recall the depots which Russia established on the territory of their magnificent, neutral republic during the Seven Years' War. At that time, after all, Poland was still a populous nation; the partitions had not yet occurred. Indeed, the partitions were made necessary by the disorderly, almost Tartar-like administration of the vast areas the Poles possessed. The commercial dealings with Prussian subjects to which reference is made in no way involve the Prussian government. If such traffic were to be in the nature of an intervention, how would one have to categorize the active help by means of money, arms, and volunteers that other countries have tolerated in order to give a boost to the Belgian and Polish rebellions?*

The tone is combative to a fault: a few weeks after the letter appeared, Clausewitz received a cabinet order, signed by Frederick William III, praising

---

[4] Peter Paret, "An Anonymous Letter by Clausewitz on the Polish Insurrection of 1830–1831," *Journal of Modern History* 42 (1970): 184–90.

the "form and content" of his defense of Prussian policy. The underlying conception of international relations on which the letter is based, however, is far more austere than the king seems to have realized—an unideological, even anti-ideological realism that had no more in common with the Holy Alliance than it did with the Polish revolution.

The condition of Europe has been completely transformed since the partitions of Poland—not by the partitions themselves, however, despite what people usually say, but by the simultaneous expansion of French power. Since John Sobiesky's death, Poland was such a nullity in the European balance of power that her disappearance in itself could have no effect whatever on it;[5] it was only important indirectly, insofar as it led to speculation that revolutionary France would have received the support of this northern power. The essential question now is whether it is in Europe's interest [for France] to have such a weight [on her side].

In the time of Louis XIV, when the natural superiority of France first emerged and began to weigh upon her neighbors, Germany was not yet threatened to the extent she is today. The anti-French system included Spain, all of Italy, the Netherlands, and England, while Poland was powerless and unfit to play a European role. The existence of Poland thus did not pose the same danger to us Germans as her restoration would today. After Louis XIV, France was in the hands of weak and peace-loving governments for almost eighty years and seemed to have given up her plan to dominate the continent. In that period the connection between Poland and France, although not insignificant, was nevertheless directed toward matters of secondary importance. At the same time, people were already constantly saying that Poland was France's natural ally. For the time being, however, this natural relationship made no difference.

If there are many people today, even in Germany, who wish on purely moral grounds to see Poland restored, and who take comfort politically in the idea that Poland existed in the past without endangering or harassing Germany, this is because they are not keeping the condition of Europe as a whole in mind. A glance at this should be sufficient to disabuse them.

And what, moreover, are the moral grounds that make the restoration of Poland so desirable?

No one, however wise and erudite, will persuade us that he is able to survey the whole, endlessly complex, centuries-long history of nations, as the hand of providence leads them toward some unknown, dimly imagined goal,

---

[5] John III Sobiesky was electoral king of Poland from 1674 to 1696. His death led to the dynastic union of Poland and Saxony, during which Polish independence came to an end.

nor to pronounce the ultimate moral law by which they are guided. What we see of the history and development of nations is but a brief span, and it is only [the limitations of our knowledge] that can reassure us about the fate of mankind, since we so often see nations and states achieve unity and independence, only to disappear once again.

If the political philosophers of our day wish to reform the process of national development and demand an explanation why so many once-independent peoples should have disappeared and been absorbed by others, they will have to call providence herself to stand trial. And, if this is an absurdity, why should they begin with the Kingdom of Poland? That is, why should they consider the partition of this country, and its disappearance as a state, from a moral, as opposed to historical-political, standpoint? We can only say flatly: this moralistic attitude toward the question of Poland's restoration is unjustified. This tendency of public opinion is nothing more than a fad, which is based more on an aesthetic than on a moral principle. People enjoy this sort of enthusiasm, like the sentimental suffering of a melodrama, and they give in to the diversion because they think it costs them nothing; because they only see two players, Russia and Poland, separated from them by the proscenium; and because they do not suspect that they are part of the play, indeed that they will have to pay for the entire performance.

Although the role of public opinion in Germany is nothing compared to what it is in France, no reasonable person can deny that under present circumstances it is foolish to give in to a fad, rather than to think for ourselves, to play around with ideas involving the supreme interests of the fatherland, and end up caught in a false enthusiasm that makes us incapable of grasping the truth.

The restoration of Poland affects Germany above all because Germany lies between Poland and France, two countries whose national characteristics are altogether foreign to her; but it also affects Europe as a whole. Poland can only be restored at the expense of Austria and Prussia, and once restored she would put constant pressure on these two powers. What is the significance of this dual relationship?

Austria's population would decline by four million; but she is also in danger of losing six million more in Italy—at least those who favor Poland would say so, and for the same reasons. And, what is more, the same conditions that could drive Austria to the first step would also drive her to the second, so the causal relationship between them is undeniable. But if the Austrian monarchy were weakened by the loss of ten million subjects, Hungary's position within it would gradually change, and it is by no means an exaggeration to say that the principle of national restoration would shake the Austrian monarchy to its foundations.

With Prussia things are even worse. She would scarcely have parted with the million inhabitants of the Grand Duchy of Posen[6] when claims would be made against the west Prussian provinces and Danzig, and for exactly the same reasons that applied to the grand duchy. East Prussia would then be separated from the rest of the country, and since it was once a Polish fief and a great part of its population is linguistically Polish and Lithuanian, we can see how insecure Prussia's hold on this territory would be.

These would be the direct consequences of the restoration of Poland; there are also indirect consequences to consider. Any war Austria and Prussia might fight with France would be accompanied by war with Poland, which would inevitably be drawn in by French money and intrigue (intrigue being the only element of French policy to have survived the Revolution). Even if we imagine this new Poland as relatively weak and constantly threatened by Russia, it would still exert sufficient pressure on both Austria and Prussia to divert a portion of their forces away from France, and hamper a free flexing of their muscles. The Poles, in Austria's rear, would influence Hungary, which is always somewhat unstable; Prussia would not be able to hold her own between the Oder and the Vistula, but would have to base her defense behind the Oder, fifty miles from her capital. For the land between the Oder and the Vistula is on the one hand entirely lacking in natural barriers and Prussian fortresses (with the minor exception of Colberg), and on the other without substantial towns (except for Posen and Danzig, both of which are fortified). As a result a successful offensive blow, which would be essential to the region's defense, could never be driven home. Deprived of a quarter of its population and a third of its territory, this crippled warrior would have to hold the shield close above his head with the left arm, while the right arm wields the sword against France, four hundred miles away.

Can any reasonable man believe this to be in the interest of Europe? In particular can England, whose public opinion now favors Poland so strongly, believe it? Which European state is England's natural opposite? France, without question; it would at least be difficult to name another. Or do the philosophers believe such opposition is unnecessary? That would be very un-philosophical, since the whole physical and spiritual order of nature is maintained by the equilibrium of opposites. Or do they seek an equilibrium of political principles—do they propose to balance the so-called liberalism of the west against the so-called despotism of the east? But this is a matter of belief, and like matters of belief during the Reformation it has to be considered separately from those factors that affect the external security of states. Although political and religious principles and beliefs usually go hand in hand with material interests and external security, they can never be a substitute for them. Suppose so-called despotism were to disappear completely,

[6] A strip of formerly Polish territory linking East Prussia and Silesia that had been ceded to Prussia in 1815.

so that all peoples were as free and happy as those of Paris are now, and those of Dresden were until a few months ago.[7] Would an idyllic peace then prevail among the nations, would the clash of interests and passions that has always threatened their security disappear? Obviously not. The source of conflict among nations is not to be sought in slogans but in the sum total of their spiritual and material relationships, and for this purpose it is surely advisable to consult history. This teaches that, except for a few years that were not the most glorious in her history, England has always found France to be the most determined opponent of her greatness and expansion and has struggled against her. This conflict has been fought out directly only on the sea; but on the continent it has been done through the support England gave to other powers whenever they were threatened by the overweening might and arrogance of France. In recent years, however, these powers have been mainly Austria and Prussia, and after them Russia. How can England suppose that its interest is served by weakening one of these powers, still less by weakening all three?

We have focused on England among the states of Europe because it is just too absurd to see public opinion developing there in a way that indirectly favors the glory of France.

But if we ask how far the rest of Europe is concerned with the restoration of Poland, our answer must naturally take into account only the external security and independence of states, and not the interests and ambitions of those parties within them who, with the help of French bayonets, would completely overturn the social order. As to the former, we can only ask which of the two parties that have faced each other on the continent since 1789 have been most able and inclined to dominate and limit the independence of others—France on the one side, or Austria, Prussia, and Russia on the other? The public record of those years is a sufficient answer. France has predominated since the treaties with Prussia and Spain in 1795, as those very treaties, and all that followed, amply demonstrate. Under Bonaparte this predominance was gradually transformed into despotism, and Europe lay for fourteen years with its neck under the boot of France. In 1814 and 1815 this relationship was abruptly reversed, but how? Only as a reaction to fourteen years of servitude that had offended all sense of decency and as a consequence of the overextension of French power, which led to the unprecedented defeat of 1812, and only with the help of a universal crusade by all the nations of Europe against a common foe.

Thus while France required nothing more than her own power, her cen-

---

[7] In September 1830 a mob of peasants and weavers, waving the tricolor and cheering the French, broke into the Dresden town hall and burned the records of the police. The army was unable to restore order, and the king of Saxony was driven from the capital, to which he had been unable to return at the time Clausewitz's essay was written. The rebellion was finally put down in April 1831.

tral position on the continent, her easily defended frontiers, her unity, her martial spirit, and an outstanding leader to subjugate Europe, Europe required a trial of fourteen years and the most exceptional conditions and circumstances to throw off this yoke and dominate France.

And yet how fleeting the results of this mutual conquest have been! France has not shown the least timidity in aggressively demanding new territories with every new treaty, in tearing apart the most ancient bonds of states and peoples, in promoting the most arbitrary and ephemeral political structures, in combining the most shocking treachery with force. The allies, on the other hand, have taken nothing from a defeated France except the spoils she stole from other lands since the Revolution. They took back what belonged to them; but they did not feel strong enough to reduce France herself, by taking away the provinces she acquired in the seventeenth century as the first step along her path of conquest. At the time they might certainly have done so. But the allies were afraid to inspire too strong a spirit of revenge in a country of great inherent strength; they preferred, by means of a policy of unprecedented moderation, to reconcile the French with their king, themselves, and the rest of Europe. This is the real reason for the leniency shown toward France. The words of the Treaty [of Paris], "*il faut que la France soit forte*,"[8] make sense only as a mere phrase, which was supposed to be a *Captatio* to the French and a mask for the true motive of the allied cabinets.

What follows, then, from the allies' real motive for moderation? That even a disarmed and defeated France, as a homogeneous, unified, well-situated, well-protected, wealthy, warlike, and spirited nation, contains within herself the means of securing her long-term integrity and independence; that she may lose these for a time if they lead her into reckless adventures; but that they will always revive by themselves.

This conclusion derives not just from the history of the last forty years, but from the whole history of France since it became a unified monarchy. Neither the earlier alliances and efforts by Spain, Germany, England, and the Netherlands, nor those later on by Austria, Prussia, England, and Russia, have been able to halt the French advance. The cause unquestionably lies in the inherent advantages France enjoys, which have already been mentioned and which contrast in many respects with the conflicting interests of her opponents: diverse lands with diverse interests, which unite only when the danger has reached its height and it is already too late; [among them] the German states, so exceptionally weak in their political structure, so divided in their sense of direction, and always with another enemy at their back, be it Turkey, or Poland, or Sweden, by which their power is divided.

---

[8] "It is necessary that France should be strong."

SEVENTEEN

"On the Basic Question of Germany's Existence" (1831)

This essay, like that on "Europe since the Polish Partitions," was written in Berlin early in 1831. Although broader in scope and more polished in presentation, it makes the same general argument: that the exigencies of Prussia's international position should prevail over considerations of ideology or moral sympathy.

Apart from the great economy of its argument, which brings together many of the themes that had run through Clausewitz's writings on international relations from the start, the most striking feature of this piece, as was mentioned earlier,[1] is probably his desire that it should receive the widest possible circulation. No documents or correspondence touching Clausewitz's efforts to publish the article survive, and the reasons for its rejection by the paper to which he sent it, the Allgemeine Zeitung *of Augsburg, are also unknown. Hans Rothfels speculated that Clausewitz's tough-minded devotion to raison d'état might not have been congenial to the AZ's publisher, Johann Cotta, whose liberal sympathies were well known.[2] In fact, however, Cotta's personal reaction to the revolutions of 1830 was one of profound alarm and not so different from Clausewitz's as Rothfels might have imagined.[3]*

More to the point, the Allgemeine Zeitung *was distinguished among German newspapers by its respect for diversity and authoritative opinion. Although Clausewitz's identity apparently remained unknown, Cotta was also approached about the article by Clausewitz's friend, Johann Eichhorn, an official in the Prussian foreign ministry who knew Cotta and whose seniority*

---

[1] P. 234, above.

[2] *Politische Schriften und Briefe*, xxxii–iii.

[3] Cotta, who had done as much as anyone then living to advance the cause of the German press, was troubled by the way journalists seemed to be sowing political dissension. "Even if all the complaints of the opposition press are true," he wondered in one of several articles on the confused state of German public opinion, "is it *national*, is it *patriotic*, in a time of pressing danger, and under the threat of powerful enemies, . . . to sow mistrust between the rulers and the ruled, to spread mistrust and disorder?" "Ueber den Geist der deutschen Opposition und ihrer Organe," *Allgemeine Zeitung*, November 11, 1831. See also Daniel Moran, *Toward the Century of Words: Johann Cotta and the Politics of the Public Realm in Germany, 1795–1832* (Berkeley and Los Angeles, 1990), 269–70.

and position would ordinarily have been decisive with the AZ's editors. It is possible, however, that the decision was taken out of their hands by the government in Munich, which was determined to avoid any commitments in Poland—not, it need hardly be said, from any sympathy for the revolution, but because it feared the loss of independence that might result from becoming entangled in Prussia's interests. Whether the Bavarian authorities intervened in this case is unknown. But the overall level of manipulation and intrigue surrounding the Allgemeine Zeitung and other Bavarian periodicals at this time was high.[4]

At the very least, it is worth noting that the barriers in the way of the nation's political education were by no means entirely of its own making. Germany's rulers readily tolerated the political sentimentality Clausewitz found so dangerous, and had generally shown little interest in cultivating public opinion in their own behalf. This would soon begin to change, at least in Prussia, though Clausewitz, who died in the fall of 1831, would not live to see it. Less than two years later Ranke's Historisch-politische Zeitschrift would be founded in Berlin—the first serious political periodical to appear there since Heinrich von Kleist's short-lived Berliner Abendblätter twenty years before, and one in which the primacy of foreign policy, the requirements of national power, and the uniqueness of each nation's history would be controlling concerns.[5] Ranke published the first of Clausewitz's posthumous works, the essay on Scharnhorst reprinted above. Had he known of the present work he might have found it equally timely. In the event, it remained unknown for almost fifty years.[6]

It is absolutely essential that we Germans reduce the many political questions preoccupying us today to one fundamental question, that of *our existence.*

People at every level of society are talking about the revolt in Belgium. To one it is not unwelcome, because it seems natural to him; others are saddened by its treachery, or its constitutional deficiencies, or the ferocity with which human passion bursts forth and destroys the common weal. To still others the whole business is, if not irrelevant, at least without particular sig-

[4] Moran, *Toward the Century of Words*, 264.

[5] In contrast to Kleist's *Abendblätter*, which was forced out of existence by Hardenberg, the *Historisch-politische Zeitschrift* enjoyed the support of Prussia's foreign minister, Bernstorff, and his subordinate, Clausewitz's friend Eichhorn, whose desire to see a political journal established in Berlin may have been heightened by the *Allgemeine Zeitung's* rejection of Clausewitz's article. See Carl Varrentrap, "Rankes *Historisch-politische Zeitschrift* und das Berliner *Politische Wochenblatt*," *Historische Zeitschrift* 99 (1907): 47n.

[6] "Zurückführung der vielen politischen Fragen, welche Deutschland beschäftigen, auf die unserer Gesamtexistenz," in Schwartz, *Leben*, 2: 408–17; reprinted in *Politische Schriften und Briefe*, 229–38.

nificance for Germany. They think only in terms of normal relations among the courts of Europe and have picked up enough history to suppose that an episode of this kind is not worth serious consideration.

We do not intend to debate whether the revolt of the Belgians is justifiable from their standpoint, or whether it is worthwhile for them. Now that it has happened their point of view, although by no means irrelevant, is less important for the future and for our ideas, feelings, and desires than the relationship of this revolt and the future position of Belgium to our, that is to Germany's, interests.

Since the disappearance of Burgundy as a buffer between Germany and France, the former has struggled ceaselessly against the ambition and political domination of the latter, and has kept French power at bay with difficulty.

The bishoprics of Lorraine were already lost under Charles V; the Thirty Years' War cost us Alsace and Strasbourg.

The Belgian provinces had by then fallen to the Spanish line of the House of Austria. Louis XIV's wars of conquest were directed mainly at these. He swallowed up Burgundy and nibbled at the frontiers of Flanders. But throughout the half-century ending with the Peace of Utrecht, Germany was protected by the not-yet-extinguished power of Spain and the newly created power of the United Netherlands, and Belgium was considered the bulwark behind which Germany found safety. Most of the fighting took place in Belgium, and with the exception of the War of the Spanish Succession, when the alliance between France and Bavaria brought a French army into Germany, the French never succeeded in penetrating Germany and establishing themselves there.

Thanks to this relentless and demanding struggle, possession of Belgium remained with the House of Austria, passing into the hands of its German line at the Peace of Utrecht.

Up to the French Revolution there were no more major wars between Germany and France. But even in the Wars of the Austrian Succession in 1740–48, when Germany's internal fragmentation initially allowed a French army to get as far as Bohemia, Belgium eventually became the main theater of operations, where French power exhausted itself.

Even in the revolutionary wars up to 1795, the main battles always occurred in Belgium, and there was no question of any lasting conquest in Germany until Austria had given up these lands (probably too quickly). From then on the left bank of the Rhine was lost, and the fields of the south German states were trodden underfoot by French armies. That northern Germany remained undisturbed for ten more years was due to the palliative effect of Prussian neutrality, for which a high price would be paid in 1806.

Having surveyed the history of wars in Europe since the sixteenth century, let us consider whether Belgium's condition can be a matter of indifference for Germany today.

Belgium was not just a bulwark for Germany and Europe; it was also a *pied à terre* for the English when they wished to assist the troubled continent, which, as the military history of the last 150 years clearly shows, they have often done to outstanding effect.

General Richmond called Belgium *le camp retranché de l'ennemi,*[7] which it is in fact, but with the difference that for centuries this *camp retranché* has never led to aggression against France, but has instead been used only to defend Europe against a restless and ambitious France.

Everything the French say about natural borders, by which they now mean the Scheldt, the Maas, and the Rhine, and perhaps in future the Weser and then the Elbe, has nothing to do with the security of their state, but only with the security of their dominance in Europe. This has still not been threatened in any way. France still has the borders Louis XIV won for her, and the fact that none of her natural opponents by itself is a match for her constitutes a substantial guarantee of her security. On the other hand, it is undeniable that, if France wants to rule Europe, as she did in the first thirteen years of this century, she must have the Rhine again. This is the only question that remains to be settled.

Whatever we may think about the revolt in Belgium, then, and however we may imagine that state's political future, we must never let this supremely important point out of our minds, *nor out of our hearts.*

Italy is another matter of interest to our politicians. Here too people are increasingly inclined to adopt a supposedly cosmopolitan viewpoint, rather than one based on our own interests.

Whether that country will ever become an independent state, whether it can ever achieve unity, is a question stretching far into the future, which no one who is not satisfied with illusions can answer now. One thing, however, is already quite clear: the emancipation of Italy must not be sought at the expense of our own independence. We ask the German cosmopolitan whether he would rather see Italy divided and partly subject to foreign powers, and Germany *independent*; or conversely, Germany subjugated, driven from the ranks of independent nations, and Italy free? This is the way the question has to be put if we are not afraid to face the truth.

Suppose there is a general rebellion of all the people of Italy against their governments—can this have any other *political tendency* than to bind Italy to the homogeneous French nation that first inspired and supported the rebellion?

---

[7] "The entrenched camp of the enemy"; Charles Lennox, First Duke of Richmond, was an English Catholic who served as a general in the armies of Louis XIV.

We are by no means convinced that such a reaction, such an eruption by the Italian masses, will lead to an independent and honorable position for Italy. What it will undoubtedly lead to, however, is the greatest difficulty for Germany in its own struggle for dignity and independence.

When Italy was conquered in 1796–97, partly because of internal unrest, partly because of Austrian mistakes during the war, Bonaparte's flags were soon waving almost under the walls of Vienna, and the Peace of Campo Formio had to be concluded, which brought the French victor 180 miles closer to Germany's borders.

Yet at that time (1796) the struggle for Italy was in some respects very hard-fought. Although the Austrians quickly lost their territory west of the Mincio, the battle for Mantua was more determined and more honorable in its duration. The audacious Bonaparte had to spend eight months on this outpost before he could set out on his proud march to the Austrian capital. Without Mantua, Jourdan would not have been defeated at Würzburg and Vienna would have fallen into French hands in the summer of 1796, nine years earlier than it did.

Thus Italy must also be reckoned a bulwark of Germany, and we cannot remain indifferent if temporary political confusion on the part of the reckless and disunited Italians gives France the upper hand in her struggle against the power at the center of Europe's resistance to her—namely, against Germany.

Finally, and most especially at present, there is the question of Poland. A very able people, but one that for centuries has remained half-Tartar in the midst of civilized European states, now wishes to reassert its Tartar nature and persuade us that in doing so it would create a useful buffer against Russia. But this requires conditions that do not exist. First the Poles would have to have the means to raise themselves quickly to the level of a European state. This is completely impossible. Granted, as an independent state they might actually succeed in filling this role some day, but only some day, perhaps in a hundred years. Second, a useful buffer against Russia would require a friendly attitude toward the Germans among the Poles themselves. But there is no people toward whom the Poles have displayed more contempt than the Germans, mainly because there is none that offers a stronger contrast to their national character. Furthermore, there is no nation with which Poland would have a more enduring conflict of interests than Germany, particularly Prussia. The Polish lands once stretched to the Baltic; their language is still spoken there to some extent; they find a natural outlet for their raw materials there. Even the Germans of East Prussia were once Polish vassals. But now, as everyone knows, the Poles are a vain and, particularly toward us, a proud people. They would therefore desire nothing so much as to use their newly independent position to satisfy their material and moral interests at our expense, and if they succeed nothing will be more natural than the urge gradually to reclaim all the territory through which the river of Slavic peoples once flowed—a course that clearly reached the Elbe, and whose historical existence is evident in the survival of such fragmentary tribes as the Wends. We wonder whether there is any more natural enemy for us than these Poles, and whether it would not be utterly absurd for us to imagine Russia playing the same part, a Russia half-oriented toward Asia, whose rulers have been closely bound to our own for two generations. In any case, there is nothing to fear from Russia as long as *everything* must be feared from France. Poland and France, in contrast, have long been regarded as natural allies; every newspaper reader knows this even if he knows no history at all.

But what is the object of this natural alliance? Clearly, what lies between them: the German powers.

Under these conditions, and given the present state of affairs in the east and west, could we really delude ourselves enough to wish for the so-called liberation of the Poles in the interest of humanity? Is humanity better served by the resurrection of the Sarmatians than by the preservation of the Germani?

Woe to us if Russia should reach the point of giving up the Polish crown and withdrawing from her Polish provinces—Lithuania, Volhynia, and Podolia—which some German philosophers imagine would be a golden age in the east. Russia, once forced or seduced into this act, would turn completely away from Western Europe, from which she would have nothing to hope for, nor to fear. Germany would be left to her fate, and the Poles and the French, who disdain us even more than they hate us, would reach out their hands to the Elbe. It is for this reason that the Polish question, like those of Belgium and Italy, touches our most fundamental and sacred interest, and involves the question of our collective existence.

We cannot doubt for a moment that this is how European affairs are viewed by the radical party in Paris, and in turn by all the vain and reckless elements of an essentially vain and reckless people. Their most recent revolution *derived its greatest power from this idea*. Inconsolable at having lost the scepter of Europe in 1813, they hope to regain it by means of a new international order and a pervasive spirit of popular discontent. The *only reason* the French hate the Bourbons so much is that they are a major obstacle to this plan. Give them a new Bonaparte and they will abandon the Charter and share the utopia of philosophers and doctrinaires with him.

The French, particularly insofar as they are represented by the Parisian radicals and their newspapers, want to put their foot on the neck of Europe once more. To do this they must overcome the German powers, since all the other European states can only rally in opposition behind them. Germany constitutes the true center of resistance, and once it is removed from the balance of power all the rest collapses along with it. That this view is not a fantasy, nor based on any arbitrary assumptions, is proven by the language of the French liberal press and the speakers in their assembly. If we do not intend to recognize and acknowledge this danger, we really should be ashamed of ourselves and admit that we are totally incapable of sound political judgment.

From first to last the cabinets of Europe do not doubt French intentions for a moment; it is only the opinion of the educated classes that is in doubt, in part because they do not grasp the issues comprehensively. They view the questions raised here in isolation, and also do not know how to evaluate them.

There is simply no other way to explain why so many people, when considering the question of war and peace, assume the initiative always lies with one or another of France's opponents. Russia, Austria, Prussia, England— each is brought before the bar of public opinion, so that people can praise their love of peace, on the one hand, and express alarm about their armaments and warlike outlook, on the other.

The fact that people attribute such divergent attitudes to these states should be sufficient proof that they are caught in a completely false system. How can anyone imagine, at such a perilous moment, when the peace and security of Europe as a whole and of every state individually is at stake, that any of them would pursue an independent policy, adopt an independent point of view, in order to prepare for an attack on France or anything of the kind? France's absolute security against attack rests on this moral impossibility. For such an attack to succeed it would have to be *agreed upon, prepared, and carried out* by a majority of these powers, not to say by all of them, something that could never go unnoticed and would be unmistakable to the cabinets of Europe as well as to the educated public long before the outbreak of hostilities. But nothing of this kind has ever happened before. On the contrary, from the first moment of the July Revolution up to the present hour, England, Prussia, and Austria have shown themselves determined to preserve the peace, that is, to remain on the defensive and wait to see whether the demon that threatens to arise in France, and is still struggling to be born, will burst forth and hurl itself against Germany.

This defensive attitude is by no means a sign of indifference, since it is essential that the powers [opposing France] have the sympathy of all sound heads and pure hearts on their side and against the enemy. A war of the kind to be expected here must not be fought as a cabinet war, but with the hearts of the people. To secure this great advantage the powers will never give up their defensive posture.

If it is therefore a question of the possibility or probability or inevitability of war, we can only look to Paris and judge carefully whether the passion and arrogance of the radicals will carry the government along, or even turn directly to the masses, in order to bring about a second golden age of Bonapartism.

What is the overall result of our reflections? That it is time to think of ourselves and not to play around with remote and useless questions that corrupt pure patriotic feelings. If France forces us to do battle *it will be, more than ever, a struggle for existence.* Not that we think our cause is so weak that the French could easily crush us, as their reckless extremists may suppose, but because a struggle for such comprehensive interests, born of such great passion, can have no other character. If we Germans do not arm ourselves with a spirit and a passion like that of 1813, Germany will not be equal to its demanding circumstances, and it can then be dislodged from the position where the Treaties of Paris placed it.

We have suggested the other world-historical consequences that might flow from this. The powers are arming for this struggle because they have been expecting it. We, their subjects, should not let ourselves be taken by surprise in our own hearts. Let us arm ourselves with ideals and feelings worthy of this great moment, and likewise infuse our arms with this spirit, without which they will not withstand an enemy that does everything with passion.

If we step onto the field of battle armed with this spiritual and physical strength, then we may hope for a good outcome from this new crisis.

The French are a reckless people. They throw themselves into this struggle out of mere vanity and imagine that they possess such moral superiority over the Germans that, unless they are defeated by overwhelming force, decisive success is certain.

They believe they are now safe from overwhelming force because popular insurrections are supposed to have put all the other European powers in chains, so they see almost no danger in the approaching conflict.

They conceive of the whole war as if it were a single battle like Austerlitz or Jena. They forget the long, uncertain fight they had to carry on alone against the power of Austria. They forget that in 1799, when the war suddenly shifted back to the borders of Dauphiné, no more than an auxiliary force of 20,000 Russians was responsible; that they must now face German forces with an entirely new organization, structure, and vigor; and, finally, that they themselves are not of one mind, not of one spirit. Nothing is more common today than to conceive of a capital's radical party as representing the entire people, and yet this is always more or less illusory, and this more or less serious misconception will always have consequences in real life.

Let them give in to their illusions and their exalted vanity. If we Germans do our duty they will see that their arrogant plans lead to nothing, and that those who tread the path of war will be brought down by the misery of their own people. We Germans, however, all of us, must be determined to resist this demon, and for that we need the power of a noble pride —loyalty to our princes and our fatherland, and also loyalty to ourselves.

384

INDEX

NOTE: The index combines proper names, military and political events, and topical entries in a single list. Battles are listed under the wars or campaigns in which they occurred.

absolutism, 32–36, 238, 244, 247–49, 273, 338–44, 346, 361

Alexander I, Czar of Russia (1777–1825), 66–67, 69, 83, 98, 266–68; in the campaign of 1812, 112–18, 120, 122–33, 137, 139–40, 168, 170–71, 174, 181, 189, 198–99

Alexander III, the Great, King of Macedonia (356–323 B.C.), 262

Allgemeine Zeitung (Augsburg), 234, 336n, 377–78

Allgemeines Landrecht (Prussian law code, 1794), 33

Alvensleben, Philipp Karl von, Count (Prussian statesman, 1745–1802), 58

Amiens, Peace of (25 March 1802), 70

Ancillon, Johann Peter Friedrich von (Prussian statesman and historian, 1767–1837), 9

Anhalt-Dessau. See Leopold I, Prince of

Anne, Queen of Great Britain (1665–1714), 241

antiquity, 241, 261–62, 264, 279, 281, 283, 338–39, 347. *See also* Roman Empire

Arakcheev, Alexi Andreivich, Count (Russian general, 1769–1834), 117, 129–30

aristocracy. *See* nobility

Armfeld [Armfel't], Gustav Maurits von, Count (Swedish and Russian general, 1757–1814), 118, 124

art, 241, 265–66

Augerau, Pierre-François-Charles, Duke of Castiglione (French marshal, 1757–1816), 281

August, Prince of Prussia (second cousin of Frederick William III, 1779–1843), 51, 237, 263n, 314

Austria: before 1789, 16, 75–76, 243, 246, 309, 346, 379; during the French Revolution, 55, 64–65, 309, 347; during the War of the Third Coalition, 50, 65–67, 74; during the campaigns of 1806–1807, 69–70, 72, 77; during the campaign of 1809, 73, 94, 201, 263, 275, 276; during the campaign of 1812, 97, 120, 196, 204; during the Wars of Liberation, 98, 206; after 1815, 304–12, 367–68, 373. *See also* Austrian Succession, Wars of; Holy Roman Empire

Austrian Succession, Wars of [First and Second Silesian Wars] (1740–1742, 1744–1745), 19–29, 37, 104, 379; Mollwitz, battle of (10 April 1741), 21, 23; Czaslau, battle of (17 May 1742), 23, 24; Hohenfriedberg, battle of (4 June 1745), 23, 25; Soor, battle of (30 September 1745), 22–23, 25; Katholisch-Hennersdorf, engagement at (23 November 1745), 26; Kesselsdorf, battle of (15 December 1745), 26. *See also* Breslau, Peace of; Dresden, Peace of

Auvray, Friedrich d' (Russian general), 174, 192, 194, 197

Bachelu, Gilbert-Désiré-Joseph de, Baron (French general, 1777–1849), 195

Bagavout, Karl Feodorovich (Russian general, 1761–1812), 146, 154, 156

Bagration, Peter Ivanovich, Prince (Russian general, 1765–1812), 115, 120, 122, 131–32, 137, 148–52, 156, 161

balance of power. *See* international relations, and balance of power

Barclay de Tolly, Mikhail, Prince (Russian field marshal and statesman, 1761–1818), 114, 115, 118, 124, 127–42, 144, 155, 161, 169

Barrère de Vieuzac, Bertrand (French lawyer and revolutionary, 1755–1841), 255

Basel, Peace of (5 April 1795), 42, 50, 54, 58, 64, 73–74, 237, 375

Bassano, Duke of. *See* Maret, Hughes-Bernard

Bavaria, 66, 276, 294, 298, 377–78, 379

Beauharnais, Eugène de, Viceroy of Italy (Napoleon's stepson, 1781–1824), 148–53, 156, 179

Behrens, C.B.A., 227

Belgium, 369, 371, 378–80, 382

Belle-Isle, Charles-Louis-Auguste Fouquet, Duke of (French marshal, 1684–1761), 28

Bennigsen, Levin August Theophil von, Count (Russian general, 1745–1826), 118, 124, 142, 155, 171

Berengar I, King of Italy (888–924), 248

Berg, Grand Duke of. *See* Murat, Joachim

Berlin, Convention of (3 November 1805), 59, 67

Berliner Abendblätter, 378n

Bernadotte, Jean-Baptiste-Jules, Prince of Ponte Corvo, King of Sweden (1763–1844), 67

Bernstorff, Christian Günther von, Count (Prussian statesman, 1769–1835), 87, 378n

Berwick, James Fitzjames, Duke of (French marshal, 1670–1734), 16, 17, 18

Beyme, Karl Friedrich (Prussian statesman, 1765–1838), 32, 50, 61, 66

Blücher, Gebhard Lebrecht von, Prince Blücher von Wahlstatt (Prussian field marshal, 1742–1819), 91–92, 98, 108, 109, 205, 207–18, 368

Bologna, Congress of (October 1529–February 1530), 243

Bose, Ernst Ludwig Hans von, Baron (Saxon and Russian officer), 172

Boufflers, Louis-François, Duke of (French marshal, 1644–1711), 17

bourgeoisie, 7, 36, 228, 234, 327, 337–38, 340–41

Boyen, Ludwig Leopold Gottlieb Hermann von (Prussian general and statesman, 1771–1848), 62, 114, 285, 304, 317, 322, 329n, 330, 362–63

Breslau, Peace of (11 June 1742), 24

Brunswick-Lüneburg, Karl Wilhelm Ferdinand, Duke of (Prussian field marshal, 1735–1806), 38, 42–44, 53, 54, 55, 57, 64, 66, 83, 90–91

Brunswick-Wolfenbüttel, Ferdinand, Duke

of (Prussian field marshal, 1721–1792), 108, 371

Bückeburg, Wilhelm von. *See* Schaumburg-Lippe-Bückeburg, Friedrich Wilhelm Ernst zu, Count

Bülow, Dietrich Adam Heinrich von (military author, 1760–1807), 103

Bülow, Ludwig Friedrich Viktor Hans von, Count (Prussian statesman, 1774–1825), 365

Bülow von Dennewitz, Friedrich Wilhelm, Count (Prussian general, 1755–1816), 98, 213, 214

Burgundy, Duke of. *See* Louis, Duke of Burgundy

Buturlin, Dmitrii Petrovich (Russian officer and military author, 1790–1849), 143, 147, 166, 200

Cambrai: League of (1508–1510), 242–43; Treaty of (2 August 1529), 243

campaign of 1787. *See* Holland, revolt of 1787

Campaign of 1796 in Italy, 5, 13

campaign of 1806, 44, 120, 251, 291; Saalfeld, engagement at (10 October 1806), 49n; Auerstädt, battle of (14 October 1806), 44, 51, 82, 91, 92, 115, 238, 323; Jena, battle of (14 October 1806), 47, 57, 82, 91, 323, 384; capitulation of Prussian fortresses, 47, 55–56, 92, 260. *See also* Königsberg, Convention of

campaign of 1807, 92–93, 118, 266–67, 291; Eylau, battle of (8 February 1807), 93, 109, 281, 291n; Friedland, battle of (14 June 1807), 30, 118n, 279. *See also* Tilsit, Peace of

campaign of 1809, 136n, 201, 233, 263, 275, 294–95; Aspern-Essling, battle of (21–22 May 1809), 275n; Wagram, battle of (5–6 July 1809), 275; Znaim, engagement at (10–11 July 1809), 275; Tirolean uprising, 275, 276–77, 330, 332. *See also* Schönbrunn, Peace of

campaign of 1812, 57, 110–204; Drissa, encampment at (summer 1812), 112, 120, 123–28; Kliastichi, battle of (31 July 1812), 170; Smolensk, battle of (17 August 1812), 137, 139, 143, 161, 167; Polotsk, first battle of (18 August 1812), 170;

Borodino, battle of (7 September 1812), 111, 140–42, 143, 144–59, 171; Moscow, occupation and destruction of (14 September–19 October 1812), 163–69, 201, 202; Maloyaroslavetz, battle of (24–25 October 1812), 173; Smoliantsy, battle of (14 November 1812), 175, 176; Krasnoï, battle of (17 November 1812), 176, 179, 180, 181; Berezina, battle of the (26–28 November 1812), 176–79, 181; Taurog-gen, Convention of (29 December 1812), 112, 185–200. See also Paris, Treaty of (24 February 1812)

campaign of 1813, 77, 93, 323; Gross-görschen [Lützen], battle of (2 May 1813), 88, 94, 98–99, 109; Bautzen, battle of (20–21 May 1813), 98; Dresden, battle of (26–27 August 1813), 218; Leipzig, battle of (16–18 October 1813), 337. See also Liberation, German Wars of: as a political event

campaign of 1814, 20, 93, 205–19, 309, 362, 368; Bar-sur-Aube, battle of (24 January 1814), 208, 218; Brienne, battle of (29 January 1814), 209, 215; La Rothière, battle of (1 February 1814), 208, 209, 212–13, 215–16; Laon, battle of (9–10 March 1814), 208, 209, 215, 218; Arcis-sur-Aube, battle of (20–21 March 1814), 208, 209, 214, 215, 218; Paris, battle of (29–31 March 1814), 208, 218–19. See also Liberation, German Wars of: as a political event

campaign of 1815, 309, 362; Waterloo, battle of (18 June 1815), 6. See also Paris, Second Peace of

Campo Formio, Peace of (17 October 1797), 65, 381

Carlsbad Conference (6–31 August 1819), 358–59, 367–68; Decrees (20 September 1819), 335

Catherine Pavlovna, Grand Duchess of Russia, Queen of Württemberg (1788–1819), 127, 172

censorship, 6, 30–31, 85, 87, 93n, 233, 378

Charlemagne, King of the Franks, Holy Roman Emperor (c. 742–814), 248

Charles IV, King of Spain (1748–1819), 300

Charles V, Holy Roman Emperor (1500–1558), 242–43, 379

Charles VI, Holy Roman Emperor (1685–1740), 20

Charles VII, King of France (1403–1461), 241, 261

Charles VIII, King of France (1470–1497), 261

Charles X, King of France (1757–1836), 369

Charles Alexander, Prince [Duke] of Lorraine and Bar (Austrian field marshal, 1712–1780), 22–26

Charles Frederick Albert, Margrave of Brandenburg-Schwedt (Prussian commander, 1705–1762), 29

Chasot, Ludwig August Friedrich von, Count (Prussian officer, 1763–1813), 114, 172

Cisrhénan Republic. See Rhineland

Clausewitz, Karl von: early life and education, 4, 9, 40–41, 225, 229, 237; during the War of the First Coalition, 6, 19, 40; during the campaigns of 1806–1807, 30, 238–39, 250, 252; during the reform era, 30, 85–86, 225, 227, 263n, 264; decision to enter Russian service, 114, 226, 285–91; during the campaign of 1812, 85, 111–12, 115, 117, 123, 125–32, 135–40, 147–55, 160n, 161–65, 170–74, 178, 181, 190–96; during the Wars of Liberation, 85, 336; career after 1815, 30, 225–27, 362–66; candidacy for ambassadorship to Great Britain, 6, 226, 335–36; during the revolutions of 1830, 369, 378. See also radicalism, Clausewitz's; Scharnhorst, Gerhard Johann David von, influence on Clausewitz

Clausewitz family: Friedrich Gabriel von (father, 1740–1802), 40; Friedrich Vollmar Karl Heinrich von (brother, 1771–1854), 184; Marie von, née von Brühl (wife, 1779–1836), 87, 110, 112, 160n, 251n, 264n; Wilhelm Benedikt von (brother, 1773–1849), 184

coalitions, 241–43, 245–46, 263, 306, 376

Coigny, Jean-Antoine-François de Franquetot, Count de (French general, 1702–1748), 22 command, 245–46, 307–308, 311–12; in the eighteenth century, 16–17, 26; in the Napoleonic era, 39, 44, 48, 118, 131–33, 140–42, 165, 212–13

Confederation of the Rhine, 70–71, 72, 293, 296, 349

conscription: under the canton system, 37, 39, 40, 81, 322, 325; after the reform of the Prussian army, 229, 296, 313, 324, 326, 364. See also mercenaries

Constantine Caesarevich Pavlovich, Grand Duke of Russia (brother of Alexander I, 1779–1831), 133, 137

Cotta, Johann Friedrich, Baron von Cottendorf (German publisher, 1764–1832), 377–78

Cromwell, Oliver (English soldier and statesman, 1599–1658), 351, 354

Danton, Georges-Jacques (French revolutionary, 1759–1794), 355

Daun, Leopold Josef von, Count, Prince of Thiano (Austrian field marshal, 1705–1766), 49

Davout, Louis-Nicolas, Duke of Auerstädt, Prince of Eckmühl (French marshal, 1770–1823), 97, 148, 156

Delbrück, Hans, 5

democracy, 36, 235, 338, 355, 357

Diebitsch-Zabalkansky, Hans Karl Friedrich Anton von, Count (Russian field marshal, 1785–1831), 175, 177, 184–86, 188–92, 194–97

Doctorov, Dmitrii Sergeivich (Russian general, 1756–1816), 156

Dohna-Schlobitten, Friedrich Karl Emil von, Count (Prussian and Russian officer, 1784–1859), 191, 195

Doumerc, Jean-Pierre, Baron (French general, 1767–1847), 174

Dresden, Peace of (25 December 1745), 20, 26

Dumas, Mathieu, Count (French general and military author, 1753–1837), 103

economics, 248–49, 339–40; after 1815, 359–60, 362–66; and the Prussian reforms, 292–93, 313, 314n, 315, 318–22; and war, under the old regime, 16, 27–28, 63

Eichhorn, Johann Albrecht Friedrich (Prussian statesman, 1779–1856), 377, 378n

Elizabeth I, Queen of England (1533–1603), 351

England. See Great Britain

Essen, Magnus Gustav von, Baron (Russian general and military governor of Riga, 1760–1813), 125, 133, 171, 174, 188

Eugène François, Prince of Savoy-Carignan, Margrave of Saluzzo (Austrian general, 1663–1736), 15

Eugene. See Beauharnais, Eugène de, Viceroy of Italy

Fabius Maximus Cunctator (Roman commander, d. 203 B.C.), 281

Ferdinand, Prince of Prussia (brother of Frederick the Great, 1730–1813), 51

Ferdinand II, the Catholic, King of Aragon and (as Ferdinand V) Castile (1452–1516), 248

Ferdinand VII, King of Spain (1784–1833), 300

feudalism, 36, 261, 326, 342–44

Fichte, Johann Gottlieb (German philosopher, 1762–1814), 279–84

Finkenstein, Karl Wilhelm, Count Fink von (Prussian statesman, 1714–1800), 58

First Coalition, War of (1792–1797), 37, 41, 43, 52, 64; Valmy, battle of (20 September 1792), 57; Menin, siege of (30 April 1794), 89–90, 106, 109; Würzburg, battle of (3 September 1796), 381; Mantua, siege(s) of (4 June–31 July 1796, 24 August 1796–2 February 1797), 381. See also Basel, Peace of; Campo Formio, Peace of; Amiens, Peace of

Fleury, André-Hercule de, Cardinal (French statesman, 1653–1743), 28

Fouqué, Heinrich August, Baron de la Motte (Prussian general, 1698–1774), 23

Fox, Charles James (British statesman, 1749–1806), 70, 72

France, 268, 308, 332; foreign affairs under the old regime, 22, 24, 28, 241, 242, 243, 309, 372, 375, 379; geography and natural resources, 240, 252, 256, 376; language, 252, 253, 255–56; in the Middle Ages, 244, 248, 261; politics and society under the old regime, 254, 261, 343,

346; politics and society after 1815, 310, 374–76, 380; and the revolutions of 1830, 369, 381–84. *See also* French Revolution; Napoleon I, Emperor of the French; Spanish Succession, War of

Francis I, King of France (1494–1547), 261

Francis II (I), Holy Roman Emperor, Emperor of Austria (1768–1835), 58

Frederick I, Elector of Brandenburg, King in Prussia (1657–1713), 346

Frederick II, the Great, King of Prussia (1712–1786): as architect of the Prussian army, 37, 90, 314, 318–20; as architect of the Prussian state, 31, 32, 34, 63, 75–76; during the Wars of the Austrian Succession, 19–29; during the Seven Years' War, 243; political ideas of, 269, 287; posthumous reputation and influence, 9, 12, 45–46, 115, 288, 313–14; mentioned, 43, 49, 51, 59, 91, 234. *See also* strategy and tactics, Frederician

Frederick III, German king, Holy Roman Emperor (1415–1493), 346

Frederick William, Elector of Brandenburg, called the Great Elector (1620–1688), 36, 63

Frederick William I, King of Prussia (1688–1740), 32–33

Frederick William II, King of Prussia (1744–1797), 33–34, 38, 57–59, 63–64, 346–47

Frederick William III, King of Prussia (1770–1840): before 1806, 42–44, 50, 66, 71; in the reform era, 93–95, 96, 97, 103–104, 106, 226, 267, 297, 315–16; during the campaigns of 1812–1815, 114, 188, 195, 198–99, 213, 315, 336, 368; after 1815, 354–55, 371–72; personality of, 32n, 34–36, 38, 39, 62, 66, 189, 295–96; mentioned, 33, 59, 90, 92, 289

French Revolution: causes, 6–7, 8, 228–29, 343–44; and German opinion, 346–49, 356, 360–61; international consequences of, 73–74, 76, 229, 230, 234, 238–41, 249–50, 252, 309, 361, 370, 372, 375–76; political character of, 223–24, 228, 254–55, 277, 328, 330–32, 347–48, 357–58; and war, 7–8, 11, 27, 37, 46, 76, 88, 90, 102, 282, 312, 315, 327, 379. *See also* First Coalition, War of

Gentz, Friedrich von (German political writer, 1764–1832), 9

George III, King of Great Britain (1738–1820), 69

German Federation, 241, 304–12, 349–51, 376

Germany: geography and natural resources, 244, 258, 260, 305, 328, 352, 373; language, 257; in the Middle Ages, 244, 248–49, 259, 261, 346, 358. *See also* Confederation of the Rhine; German Federation; Holy Roman Empire

Germany and the Revolution, 335, 355

Geusau, Levin von (Prussian general, 1734–1808), 51

Gneisenau, August Wilhelm Anton, Count Neidhardt von (Prussian field marshal, 1760–1831): correspondence with Clausewitz, 13n, 86n, 304n; as a reformer, 85–86, 98, 285, 329–31; as a soldier, 114–15, 205, 369

Görres, Johann Joseph von (German political writer, 1776–1848), 335, 355–58, 361

Gouvion Saint-Cyr, Laurent, Marquis de (French marshal, 1764–1830), 174

Grandjean, Charles-Louis-Dieudonné (French general, 1768–1828), 182, 185, 186, 195–96

Grawert, Julius August Reinhold von (Prussian general, 1756–1821), 57–58, 97, 187

Great Britain: before 1789, 243, 351, 372, 375; in the Napoleonic era, 64–66, 69–72, 81–82, 114–15, 206, 276, 297, 351; politics and society, 240–41, 244, 332, 333, 374–75; mentioned, 16, 17, 22, 24, 77, 91, 248. *See also* Hanover

Grey, Charles, Lord Howick (British statesmen, 1764–1845), 72

Grolman, Karl Wilhelm Georg von (Prussian general, 1777–1843), 329n

Gustav I Vasa, King of Sweden (1496–1560), 244

Gustav II Adolf (Gustavus Adolphus), King of Sweden (1594–1632), 12

Gustav IV Adolf, King of Sweden (1778–1837), 69–70

Hammerstein, Rudolf Georg Wilhelm von, Baron (Hanoverian general, 1755–1811), 89–90, 108, 109

Hannibal (Carthaginian general, 247–183 B.C.), 281n

Hanover, 22, 67, 68–71, 89–90, 354

Hardenberg, Karl August von, Prince (Prussian statesman, 1750–1822): before 1806, 43, 59, 62, 65–67, 69, 71; in the reform era, 86, 96–97, 189, 199, 319, 359, 378n; after 1815, 329–30, 335n, 355, 359, 364–65

Hatzfeldt, Franz Ludwig von, Prince (Prussian general and diplomat, 1756–1827), 199

Haugwitz, Christian August Heinrich Kurt von, Count (Prussian statesman, 1752–1831), 50, 58–59, 60, 61, 65–71, 73, 83, 189

Hegel, Georg Wilhelm Friedrich (German philosopher, 1770–1831), 4, 356n

Heinrich, Prince of Prussia (brother of Frederick William III, 1781–1846), 50

Henckel von Donnersmarck, Wilhelm Ludwig Viktor, Count (Prussian officer, 1775–1849), 195

Henry IV, King of France (1553–1610), 261

Herzberg, Ewald Friedrich von, Count (Prussian statesman, 1725–1975), 58

Hesse-Homburg, Ludwig Wilhelm Friedrich, Prince [Landgraf] of (Prussian general, 1770–1839), 218

Hesse-Kassel. See William II, Elector of

Hesse-Philippsthal-Barchfeld, Ernst Konstantin, Margrave of (Russian general, 1771–1849), 149, 152

Heudelet de Bierre, Etienne de, Count (French general, 1770–1857), 196, 199

Historisch-politische Zeitschrift (Berlin), 87, 378

history: as a discipline, 7, 9, 12–14, 20; and the idea of progress, 7, 9, 13, 225; individuals in, 8, 32, 88, 112–13, 199–200, 223–24, 247; and objectivity, 5, 12, 31; and politics, 6–8, 12, 60, 223–25, 228–29, 231, 237–38, 265, 314, 345; and theory, 3–5, 9–11, 13, 88, 100, 103–104, 129, 206–208

Hoche, Louis-Lazare (French general, 1768–1797), 356

Hohenlohe-Ingelfingen, Friedrich Ludwig, Prince of (Prussian general, 1746–1818), 44, 47, 51, 54, 55, 57, 91

Holland: revolt of 1787, 41, 54, 63–64; in the Napoleonic era, 277, 293, 298; mentioned, 16, 17, 22, 242, 351, 372, 379

Holy League (1510), 242–43

Holy Roman Empire, 16, 223, 238, 244, 304–305, 309, 349, 379

Howard, George, Lord Morpeth, Earl of Carlisle (British statesman, 1773–1848), 82

Humboldt, Karl Wilhelm von, Baron (Prussian statesman, 1767–1835), 62, 330

international relations, 5, 24, 29, 41, 229–34, 237–49, 266–69, 286, 369–84; and balance of power, 76, 229, 238–39, 243–44, 247–49, 276, 292, 306, 370, 372, 374, 382

Italy: in the Middle Ages and the Renaissance, 240–44, 248–49, 269, 279; in the Revolutionary and Napoleonic eras, 169n, 241, 293, 381; during the revolutions of 1830, 373–74, 380–81, 382; mentioned, 17, 22, 58, 61, 332, 372

Italy, Viceroy of. See Beauharnais, Eugène de

Jacobinism. See radicalism

John III Sobiesky, King of Poland (1624–1696), 372

Jomini, Antoine-Henri, Baron (military author, 1779–1869), 8, 103, 134

Joseph I, Holy Roman Emperor (1678–1711), 241

Joseph II, Holy Roman Emperor (1741–1790), 347, 367

Jourdan, Jean-Baptiste (French marshal, 1762–1833), 381

Julius II [Giuliano della Rovere], Pope (1443–1513), 242–43

July Revolution. See revolutions of 1830

Junot, Jean-Andoche, Duke of Abrantès (1771–1813), 148–49, 156

Kalckreuth, Friedrich Adolf von, Count (Prussian field marshal, 1737–1818), 70, 91

Kankrin, Egon Frantzevich (Russian officer and statesman, 1774–1845), 119

Kant, Immanuel (German philosopher, 1724–1804), 231

Karl August, Duke of Saxe-Weimar-Eisen-ach (1775–1828), 83, 92

Kaunitz-Rietberg, Wenzel Anton von, Prince (Austrian chancellor, 1711–1794), 234

Kleist, Franz Kasimir von (Prussian general, 1736–1808), 55–56

Kleist, Heinrich von (German writer, 1777–1811), 378n

Kleist von Nollendorf, Friedrich Heinrich Ferdinand Emil, Count (Prussian officer, later field marshal, 1762–1823), 46–47, 182, 184–86, 199, 212, 216

Klewiz, Wilhelm Anton von (Prussian statesman, 1760–1838), 365

Knobelsdorff, Friedrich Wilhelm Ernst von, Baron (Prussian general and diplomat, 1752–1820), 81, 82, 83–84

Köckritz, Karl Leopold von (Prussian general, 1753–1829), 59

Königsberg, Convention of (November 1806–January 1807), 72, 81

Konownitzin, Peter Petrovich (Russian general), 149

Kotzebue, Johann August von (German dramatist and political writer, 1761–1819), 336, 354, 358

Krusemark, Friedrich Wilhelm Ludwig von (Prussian general and diplomat, 1767–1822), 72, 82, 182, 188

Kutusov (Russian general), 182, 185–86, 197

Kutusov, Mikhail Hilarionovich, Prince of Smolensk (Russian field marshal, 1745–1813), 135n, 137, 140–42, 144–45, 149, 152, 155–60, 166–69, 173, 177–80, 198

Labanov-Rostorski, Dmitrii Ivanovich (Russian general, 1758–1838), 118, 133

Lacy, Franz Moritz von, Count (Austrian field marshal, 1725–1801), 49, 57

Landwehr, 311; Austrian, 94; Prussian, 94n, 98, 313–15, 320–28, 329–34, 336, 364, 367

Langeron, Alexander, Count (Russian general, 1763–1831), 212

Lannes, Jean, Duke of Montebello (French marshal, 1769–1809), 275n

Le Coq, Karl Ludwig Edler von (Prussian general, 1753–1829), 81

League of Virtue, 95–96, 289

Lehwald, Johann von (Prussian field marshal, 1685–1768), 26

Leo X [Giovanni de' Medici], Pope (1475–1521), 243

Leopold I, Holy Roman Emperor (1640–1705), 241

Leopold I, Prince of Anhalt-Dessau (Prussian field marshal, 1676–1747), 26

L'Estocq, Anton Wilhelm von (Prussian general, 1738–1815), 92

Levis [Löwis] of Menar, Friedrich (Russian general), 191, 196

liberalism: attributed to the Prussian state, 36, 41, 355; Clausewitz's relationship to, 227–28, 231–33, 235, 329–30, 333; in Germany, 10, 87, 231–33, 349–55, 370; and representative institutions, 227, 231–33, 273–74, 329–30, 333, 351–55

Liberation, German Wars of (1813–1815): as a political event, 98, 226, 232, 314–15, 327, 331, 334, 336–37, 349–50, 358, 384. See also campaign of 1813; campaign of 1814; campaign of 1815

Lichtenau, Wilhelmine Enke, Countess (mistress of Frederick William II, 1752?–1820), 59, 60

Lieven, Christoph Andreivich, Prince (Russian diplomat, 1774–1838), 128, 135

logistics and supplies: during the Wars of the Austrian Succession, 20, 23, 25, 27; during the campaign of 1812, 143, 160–63, 165, 202–203; in the Prussian army, 37, 39–40, 320–22, 325, 362–64

Lombard, Johann Wilhelm (Prussian statesman, 1767–1812), 32, 50, 59–61, 66, 71, 73, 75

Lorraine, Prince of. See Charles Alexander, Prince [Duke] of Lorraine and Bar

Louis XI, King of France (1423–1483), 261

Louis XII, King of France (1462–1515), 261

Louis XIV, King of France (1638–1715), 15–16, 18, 241, 254, 261, 372, 380

Louis XVI, King of France (1754–1793), 255, 332

Louis, Duke of Burgundy (French commander, 1682–1712), 16

Louis Ferdinand, Prince of Prussia (second cousin of Frederick William III, Prussian general, 1772–1806), 31, 47–51

Louvois, François-Michel Le Tellier, Marquis de (French statesman, 1641–1691), 18n

Lucchesini, Girolamo de, Marquis (Prussian diplomat, 1751–1825), 71, 82, 83

Luden, Heinrich (German historian, 1780–1847), 10

Lunéville, Peace of (8 February 1801), 65, 74, 361

Lützow, Adolf Ludwig von (Prussian officer and *Freikorps* leader, 1782–1819), 136n, 358

Lützow, Leopold Wichard Heinrich von (Prussian officer, 1786–1844), 135, 136n

Lycurgus (Spartan lawgiver, 9th century B.C.), 264

Macdonald, Etienne-Jacques-Joseph-Alexandre, Duke of Tarentum (French marshal, 1765–1840), 181–88, 190–98, 200, 213, 215

Machiavelli, Niccolò (Florentine statesman and political philosopher, 1469–1527), 9, 237, 244, 268–69, 279–82, 284

Madrid, Treaty of (14 January 1526), 242–43

Maintenon, Françoise d'Aubigné, Marquise de, called Madame de Maintenon (French noblewoman, consort of Louis XIV, 1635–1719), 15–16, 18

maneuvers and drill, 40, 55, 324, 325

Maret, Hughes-Bernard, Duke of Bassano (French statesman, 1763–1839), 188, 193–94

Maria Theresa, Empress of Austria (1717–1780), 28

Marlborough, John Churchill, First Duke of (British general, 1650–1722), 15

Marmont, Auguste-Frederic-Louis Viesse de, Duke of Ragusa (French marshal, 1774–1852), 209, 215

Masséna, André, Duke of Rivoli, Prince of Essling (1758–1817), 128n

Massenbach, Christian Karl August Ludwig von, Baron (Prussian staff officer and military author, 1758–1827), 44, 47, 51–55, 91

Massenbach, Friedrich Eberhard Fabian von (Prussian general, 1753–1819), 182, 184, 190, 194, 195

Méhée de la Touche, Jean-Claude-Hippolyte (French author and spy, 1760?–1826), 65

Mencken, Anastasius Ludwig (Prussian statesman, 1752–1801), 61

mercenaries, 20, 37, 39, 241. *See also* conscription

Metternich, Klemens Lothar Wenzel, Prince of Metternich-Winneburg (Austrian statesman, 1773–1859), 209n, 367–68

Michaud-Beaurejour, Alexander Franzevich, Count (Sardinian and Russian officer, 1774–1841), 131, 171

Middle Ages, 10, 37, 240–41, 244, 247–49, 281–82, 339, 346. *See also* feudalism

middle class. *See* bourgeoisie

Milan, Duke of. *See* Sforza, Francesco Maria

militia. See *Landwehr*

Miloradovitch, Mikhail Andreivich, Count (Russian general, 1770–1835), 159–60, 163–65, 171, 181

Möllendorff, Wichard Joachim Heinrich von (Prussian field marshal, 1724–1816), 38, 41, 44–45, 82, 116, 117

Montesquieu, Charles-Louis de Secondat, Baron de La Brède et de (French lawyer and political philosopher, 1689–1755), 9, 237, 244

Moreau, Jean-Victor (French general, 1763–1813), 255

Morpeth, Lord. *See* Howard, George

Mortier, Adolphe-Edouard-Casimir-Joseph, Duke of Treviso (French marshal, 1768–1835), 209, 215

Möser, Justus (German historian and statesman, 1720–1794), 9, 345

Muchin, Semjon Alexandrovich (Russian general), 118, 134

Müller, Johannes von (Swiss historian, 1752–1809), 9, 10, 12, 50, 282

Murat, Joachim, Grand Duke of Berg, King of Naples (1767–1815), 71, 84, 159, 163, 164, 181

Naples, King of. *See* Murat, Joachim

Napoleon I, Emperor of the French (1769–1821): attitude and policy toward Prussia, 57, 67–68, 70–71, 276–77, 286, 294–98; during the campaign of 1812, 141, 148,

157–58, 160, 162, 166, 169, 173, 176–79, 181, 201–202; during the campaign of 1814, 208–19; and French politics and government, 84, 252, 254–55, 272; personality and reputation, 140, 157, 179–80, 204, 216; as a soldier, 113, 201–204, 251, 281, 348, 381; as a statesman, 201–204, 245, 263, 375; mentioned, 6, 13, 47, 54, 81, 91, 98, 119, 128, 144, 200, 275, 301, 356, 368. See also strategy and tactics, Napoleonic

national character, 41, 75, 373; French, 239, 250–61; German, 229, 244, 250–52, 255, 256–61

national guard, French, 277n, 328, 331

Natzmer, Leopold Anton Oldwig von (Prussian officer, 1782–1861), 199

Neipperg, Wilhelm Reinhard von, Count (Austrian field marshal, 1684–1774), 21

Ney, Michel, Duke of Elchingen, Prince of the Moskva (French marshal, 1769–1815), 148, 156, 179

Niebuhr, Barthold Georg (German historian, 1776–1831), 13

Noailles, Adrien-Maurice, Count d'Ayen (French marshal, 1678–1766), 22

nobility, 12, 75, 337; opposition to reform among, 234, 315, 326–27, 359; traditional role and decline of, 36–37, 228, 261, 338–45

Oldenburg, Duke of. See Peter Friedrich Ludwig, Duke of Oldenburg-Holstein

Oldenburg, Georg Peter Ludwig, Prince of (brother-in-law of Alexander I, 1784–1812), 127, 172

On War, 3, 4, 5, 10n, 11–12n, 19, 76n, 88, 111, 169n

Orange, Wilhelm Friedrich Georg Ludwig, Prince of (brother-in-law of Frederick William III, 1772–1843), 51, 71

Orléans, Philippe, Duke of, regent of France (French commander, 1674–1723), 17

Orlov, Count (Russian officer), 129–30

Osarovski, Adam Petrovich, Count (Russian officer, 1776–1855), 118, 154

Osten-Sacken, Fabien Gottlieb, Count (Russian general, 1752–1837), 171, 212

Ostermann-Tolstoi, Alexander Ivanovich, Count (Russian general, 1772–1857), 146, 154, 156

Oubril, Pierre d', Baron (Russian diplomat), 72

Oudinot, Nicolas-Charles, Duke of Reggio (French marshal, 1767–1847), 174–75, 213

Pahlen, Peter von der, Count (Russian general, 1777–1864), 136, 137, 176

papacy, 241, 249. See also Julius II; Leo X

Paret, Peter, 226–27, 370

Paris, Convention of [pursuant to the Peace of Pressburg] (15 February 1806), 68–69; [Second] Peace of (20 November 1815), 362, 376, 384; Treaty of [pursuant to the Peace of Tilsit] (8 September 1808), 292, 313; Treaty of [preparatory to the campaign of 1812] (24 February 1812), 97, 113, 226

parties and factions, political, 228, 232, 259, 273–74; and opposition to France in Prussia, 74–75, 87, 95, 113, 287–91, 297. See also liberalism

Paulucci, Philipp Ossipovich, Marquis (Russian general, military governor of Riga, 1779–1849), 133, 173–74, 188

Peace of Utrecht [Treaties of Utrecht, Rastatt, and Baden] (April 1713–September 1714), 379

peasantry, 228, 326–27, 338–41

Peninsular War (1807–1814), 120, 136n, 201, 276–77, 294, 297, 348; Bussaco, battle of (27 September 1810), 128; Torres Vedras, lines of (October 1810–March 1811), 123, 128

Pepin III, the Short, King of the Franks (714–768), 248

Perrin, Claude-Victor, Duke of Bellune (French marshal, 1764–1841), 174–75, 178, 213

Peter III, Czar of Russia (1728–1762), 243

Peter Friedrich Ludwig, Duke of Oldenburg-Holstein (1755–1829), 174

Péthion de Villeneuve, Jérôme (Mayor of Paris, 1756–1794), 255

Philip V, King of Spain, Duke of Anjou (1683–1746), 18

philosophers, 42, 252, 257, 259, 270–71, 284, 373–74, 381. *See also* rationalism; theory

Phull, Karl Ludwig August Friedrich von (Prussian staff officer and Russian general, 1757–1826), 44, 51–53; during the campaign of 1812, 112, 115–19, 120, 122–33

Pitt, William, the Younger (British statesman, 1759–1806), 70

Platov, Matvei Ivanovich, Count (Cossack leader, 1761–1818), 149, 154–55, 181

Poland, 244, 327, 351; insurrection in (November 1830–September 1831), 223n, 227, 233–34, 369–76, 381–82; partitions of (1772–1795), 54, 370, 372

Poniatowski, Joseph Anton, Prince (French marshal, 1763–1813), 148–49, 156, 158, 173

press, 73–74, 233–34, 254, 259, 269–70, 277, 382–83

Pressburg, Peace of (26 December 1805), 65, 68, 70

Prussia, army of: under Frederick the Great, 20, 37, 45, 75–76, 318–20; on the eve of reform, 36–41, 49–53, 65, 77–78, 318–22, 363; during the campaign of 1806, 78–81, 91, 251, 281, 320, 323; in the reform era, 93–99, 102–104, 229, 296–97, 316–28; after 1815, 304–12, 313–28, 329–34, 362–64. See also *Landwehr*, Prussian

Prussia, foreign policy of: from the Peace of Basel to 1805, 58–60, 63–65, 238, 288; in 1805–1807, 65–73, 81–84; in the reform era, 94–95, 96–97, 263, 294–95; in 1812, 189, 196, 226, 287–303; after 1815, 304–12, 329, 333–34, 369

Prussia, politics and government in: under the old regime, 32–36, 38, 346–47; on the eve of reform, 41–42, 60, 61, 74–75, 84, 354; in the reform era, 62, 91, 94–97, 99, 224–25, 264, 276–78, 349; in 1812, 188–89, 229, 285–303; from 1813 to 1819, 316–28, 329–34, 335–38, 354–55, 356n, 361–66; after 1819, 86–87, 366–67. *See also* Frederick II, the Great; Frederick William III; Scharnhorst, Gerhard David von

Prussia, public opinion in: to 1807, 41–42, 53, 60, 73–75; in the reform era, 87, 94–

96, 188, 264, 277–78, 288–91, 297, 302. *See also* radicalism

public opinion, 202, 234–35, 300, 352–53, 375, 378; in France, 254–55, 259–60, 373, 382–83; in Germany, 232–33, 240, 258, 259–60, 296, 373–74, 378–84. *See also* press; radicalism

radicalism; in Germany, 96, 227, 232–33, 274, 328, 330–34, 336–38, 347–68; Clausewitz's, 6, 226, 227, 329–31, 335–36

Raevski, Nikolai Nikolaivich (Russian general, 1771–1829), 156, 171

Ranke, Leopold von (German historian, 1795–1886), 9, 13, 87, 89n, 90n, 93n, 378

rationalism: and German national character, 257–59; in military theory, 4, 52, 55, 103–104, 115, 124, 126–27, 208, 282, 284; in politics, 224, 253, 326, 345–47, 355–57. *See also* philosophers; theory

Raumer, Friedrich von (German historian, 1781–1873), 10

Reformation, Protestant, 248, 337, 374

religion, 241, 264–65, 374. *See also* papacy

republicanism, 229, 231, 248–49, 250–51, 254, 258–89, 352–54

revolutions of 1830, 233–34, 369–70, 377–84

Rheinischer Merkur (Coblenz), 356

Rhineland, 62, 356, 359–66, 369

Richmond, Charles Lennox, First Duke of (French general, 1672–1723), 380

Ritter, Karl (German geographer and historian, 1779–1859), 13

Robertson, William (Scottish historian, 1721–1793), 9, 261n

Roeder, Friedrich Erhard Leopold von (Prussian officer, 1786–1834), 194, 195

Roman Empire, 239, 245, 248, 250, 262, 268, 281, 351

Rostopchin, Feodor Vasilievich, Count (Russian general, 1763–1826), 167–68

Rothfels, Hans, 226–27, 237, 238, 377

Rüchel, Ernst Friedrich Wilhelm Philipp von (Prussian general, 1754–1823), 32, 41, 44, 45–46, 51

Russia: before 1789, 243, 244; during the War of the Third Coalition, 55, 59, 64–67; during the campaigns of 1806–1807,

69, 70, 72, 77, 79, 81, 82, 109; after the Peace of Tilsit, 85, 263, 266–68, 297; after 1812, 97–98, 206, 241, 370–71, 381–82. *See also* campaign of 1812

Russo-German Legion, 172, 174, 191

Rutowski, Friedrich August von, Count (Saxon general), 26

Sacken. *See* Osten-Sacken, Fabien Gottlieb

Saint-Cyr. *See* Gouvion Saint-Cyr, Laurent

Saint Priest, Guillaume-Emmanuel de, Count (Russian general, 1776–1814), 213, 214

Saldern, Friedrich Christoph von (Prussian general, 1719–1785), 55

Sand, Karl Ludwig (political activist, 1795–1819), 336, 358

Savigny, Friedrich Karl von (German jurist, 1779–1861), 13

Saxony: during the campaign of 1806, 72, 77, 79–80, 83, 92, 97–98; as a French client state, 276, 294; mentioned, 20, 24, 26, 368, 375

Scharnhorst, Gerhard Johann David von (Prussian general, 1755–1813): early career, 51–53, 85, 89–90; during the campaign of 1806, 90–93; in the reform era, 58, 85, 93–99, 102, 106–107, 113–16, 128, 187, 189, 225, 316; influence on Clausewitz, 10–12, 85, 88, 237, 314; personality of, 95, 99–102, 105–109, 224; mentioned, 45, 289n

Schaumburg-Lippe-Bückeburg, Friedrich Wilhelm Ernst zu, Count (English-Hanovarian soldier and military educator, 1724–1777), 89

Schelling, Friedrich Wilhelm Joseph (German philospher, 1775–1854), 356n

Scheppelov (Russian general), 182, 185, 192, 197–98

Schill, Ferdinand Baptista von (Prussian officer, 1776–1809), 275

Schiller, Johann Christoph Friedrich von (German writer, 1759–1805), 9, 12, 112, 298n

Schlegel, August Wilhelm (German writer, 1767–1845), 250n

Schlegel, Friedrich (German writer, 1772–1829), 250n

Schlosser, Friedrich Christoph (German historian, 1776–1861), 10

Schmettau, Friedrich Wilhelm Karl von, Count (Prussian general, 1742–1806), 51

Schönbrunn, Convention of (15 December 1805), 68–69, 189; Peace of (14 October 1809), 276

Schuckmann, Friedrich von, Baron (Prussian statesman, 1755–1834), 62

Schulenburg-Kehnert, Friedrich Wilhelm von der, Count (Prussian statesman, 1742–1815), 33, 58n, 61

Schuvalov, Paul Andreivich, Count (Russian officer, 1776–1825), 118

Schwarzenberg, Karl Philipp von, Prince (Austrian field marshal, 1771–1820), 208–18, 368

Scipio Africanus Major (Roman commander, 236–184? B.C.), 281

Sebastiani de la Porta, Horace-François-Bastien, Count (French general, 1772–1851), 163–64

Seckendorf, Friedrich Heinrich von, Count (Austrian field marshal, 1673–1763), 22

Second Coalition, War of (1798–1802), 58, 64, 384. *See also* Lunéville, Peace of

Ségur, Philippe-Paul de, Count (French general and military author, 1780–1873), 24

Seven Years' War (1756–1763), 42, 45, 55, 242–43, 314, 318, 371; Rossbach, battle of (5 November 1757), 147; Leuthen, battle of (5 December 1757), 147; Bunzelwitz, encampment at (20 August–25 September 1761), 123

Seydlitz-Kurzbach, Anton Friedrich Florian von (Prussian officer, 1777–1832), 188, 191, 195, 196–97

Sforza, Francesco Maria, Duke of Milan (1495–1535), 243

Skrzynecki, Jan Zygmunt (Polish general and revolutionary leader, 1787–1860), 371

Sobiesky. *See* John III Sobiesky, King of Poland

Spain, 295, 298; foreign affairs, 242, 243, 246, 372; politics and society, 240–41, 244, 327, 346, 350–51; treaty with France (22 July 1795), 375. *See also* Spanish Succession, War of; Peninsular War

Spanish Succession, War of (1701–1713), 15–18, 379; Oudenaarde, battle of (11 July 1708), 16; Malplaquet, battle of (11 September 1709), 17

Stein, Heinrich Friedrich Karl vom, Baron (Prussian statesman, 1757–1831), 51, 62, 94–95, 170

Steinheil, Fabian Gotthard von, Baron (Russian general, 1762–1831), 170–71, 175

strategy and tactics, 57, 80, 245–46, 281–83; in the campaign of 1812, 122–26, 142–48, 165, 169, 170–71, 179–80; Frederician, 8, 20–29, 45–46, 147; Napoleonic, 8, 90, 92, 103–104, 157–58, 173, 201–204, 281. See also campaign of 1814; theory, military

Suvorov-Rimnisky, Alexander Vasilievich, Prince of Italia (Russian field marshal, 1729–1800), 137, 140

Sweden: before 1789, 244, 247; during the campaigns of 1805–1806, 69–70, 72

Swiss Confederation, 259, 281–82, 293, 342, 351

Talleyrand-Périgord, Charles Maurice de, Bishop of Autun, Prince of Benavente (French statesman, 1754–1838), 67–68, 70, 84, 97

Tempelhoff, Georg Friedrich Ludwig von (Prussian general and military author, 1737–1807), 103

theory: military, 8, 10, 52–53, 55, 102–105, 134–35, 207–208, 213n, 280–81; political, 7, 41, 229, 231, 341. See also history, and theory; rationalism

Thile, Adolf Eduard von (Prussian officer, 1784–1861), 195

Third Coalition, War of (1805), 50, 66–68, 74; Austerlitz, battle of (2 December 1805), 68, 140, 384. See also Berlin, Convention of; Paris, Convention of; Pressburg, Peace of; Schönbrunn, Convention of

Tiedemann, Karl Ludwig Heinrich von (Prussian officer, 1777–1812), 171

Tilsit, Peace [Treaties] of (7–9 July 1807), 62, 93, 94, 226, 263, 266–68, 292–97

Tocqueville, Alexis de, 235

Toll, Karl Friedrich, Count (Russian officer,

1777–1842), 129–30, 134, 135–36, 139, 140, 142, 144, 147–52, 154, 161, 165, 167

Tolstoy, Leo, 113

Tormassov, Alexander Petrovich, Count (Russian general, 1752–1819), 115, 120, 180

Treitschke, Heinrich von, 370n

Tshitsagov, Pavel Vasilievich (Russian admiral, 1767–1849), 122, 171, 176–79, 180–81, 198, 200

Tugendbund. See League of Virtue

Turenne, Henri de Latour d'Auvergne de, Viscount (French marshal, 1611–1675), 18n

Tutschkov, Nikolai Alexandrovich (Russian general, 1761–1812), 146, 147, 148–49, 155, 156, 159

Ursins, Marie-Anne de la Trémoille, Princess des (lady-in-waiting to the queen of Spain, 1642–1722), 16, 18

Uvarov, Feodor Petrovich (Russian general, 1773–1824), 137, 152–55, 159

Vendôme, Louis-Joseph de, Duke (French general, 1654–1712), 16, 17, 18

Vergniaud, Pierre-Victurnien (French revolutionary, 1753–1793), 355

Victor. See Perrin, Claude-Victor

Vienna, Congress of (November 1814–June 1815), 304, 349–50, 369, 370; treaty of. See Schönbrunn, Convention of

Villars, Claude-Louis-Hector de, Duke (French marshal, 1653–1734), 16–17, 18

Vlastov, M. G. (Cossack leader, 1767–1848), 185

Volkonsky, Peter Mikhailovich, Prince (Russian statesman and general, 1776–1852), 117, 118, 129–30

Voltaire [François Marie Arouet] (French writer, 1694–1778), 61n, 269

Wallenstein, Albrecht Wenzel Eusebius von, Duke of Friedland (Imperial general, 1583–1634), 194

Wallmoden-Gimborn, Ludwig von, Count (Hanoverian general, 1736–1811), 89–90

Wangenheim, Karl August von, Baron (Württemberg statesman, 1773–1850), 305 war: "friction" in, 11–12n, 165–66, 180, 194, 225, 282; and international relations, 19, 22–27, 169, 201–204, 206, 209n, 230; limited and unlimited, 5, 15–16, 18, 20, 207; and politics, 16–18, 141, 274–76, 299, 304–12, 330, 378–84; popular or guerrilla, 17, 201, 203–204, 275; psychological factors in, 140–41, 153, 201–202, 206–207, 209, 212–18, 280–84, 324; and society, 20, 247–49, 282–84, 286, 317–18, 323–27, 339, 342. *See also* coalitions; command; French Revolution, and war; logistics and supply; maneuvers and drill; strategy and tactics

Wartburg Festival (18–19 October 1817), 336–37, 354

Wartensleben, Leopold Alexander von, Count (Prussian general, 1745–1822), 56

Weimar, Duke of. *See* Karl August, Duke of Saxe-Weimar-Eisenach

Wellington, Arthur Wellesley, First Duke of (British general, 1769–1852), 120, 128n

Westphalia, Peace of [Treaties of Münster and Osnabrück] (30 January and 24 October 1648), 246–47

Wilhelm, Prince of Prussia (brother of Frederick William III, 1783–1851), 51

William II, Elector of Hesse-Kassel (1777–1847), 83, 298n

William III, Prince of Orange, King of Great Britain (1650–1702), 241

Winzingerode, Ferdinand von, Baron (Russian general, 1770–1818), 66, 213, 214, 216

Wittgenstein, Ludwig Adolf Peter, Prince of Sayn-Wittgenstein-Ludwigsburg (Russian field marshal, 1769–1843), 98, 142, 161, 170–71, 174–79, 180, 181, 182–86, 192, 196–200

Wolzogen, Ludwig Julius Adolf Friedrich von, Baron (Prussian and Russian officer, 1773–1845), 123–25, 128–29, 134–36, 139, 304

Wrede, Karl Philipp von, Prince (Bavarian field marshal, 1767–1838), 175

Württemberg, 354, 365

Württemberg, Alexander, Prince [Duke] of (Russian general, d. 1833), 132–33

Yermalov, Alexi Petrovich (Russian general, 1772–1861), 133–34, 135, 139, 142

Yorck von Wartenburg, Hans David Ludwig, Count (Prussian field marshal, 1759–1830), 58, 97, 112, 182, 212, 216, 323; and the Convention of Tauroggen, 185–200

Zastrow, Friedrich Wilhelm Christian von (Prussian general and diplomat, 1752–1830), 44, 46

Ziethen, Hans Joachim von (Prussian general, 1699–1786), 29